W9-BDI-988

GIANNIS

GIANNIS

THE IMPROBABLE RISE
OF AN NBA MVP

MIRIN FADER

hachette
BOOKS

New York

Copyright © 2021 by Mirin Fader

Cover design by Amanda Kain
Cover photograph © Mark Blinch/Getty Images
Cover copyright © 2021 by Hachette Book Group, Inc.

Hachette Book Group supports the right to free expression and the value of copyright. The purpose of copyright is to encourage writers and artists to produce the creative works that enrich our culture.

The scanning, uploading, and distribution of this book without permission is a theft of the author's intellectual property. If you would like permission to use material from the book (other than for review purposes), please contact permissions@hbgusa.com. Thank you for your support of the author's rights.

Hachette Books
Hachette Book Group
1290 Avenue of the Americas
New York, NY 10104
HachetteBooks.com
Twitter.com/HachetteBooks
Instagram.com/HachetteBooks

First Edition: August 2021

Published by Hachette Books, an imprint of Perseus Books, LLC, a subsidiary of Hachette Book Group, Inc. The Hachette Books name and logo is a trademark of the Hachette Book Group.

The Hachette Speakers Bureau provides a wide range of authors for speaking events. To find out more, go to www.hachettespeakersbureau.com or call (866) 376-6591.

The publisher is not responsible for websites (or their content) that are not owned by the publisher.

Library of Congress Control Number: 2021939362

ISBNs: 978-0-306-92412-5 (hardcover); 978-0-306-92410-1 (ebook)

Printed in the United States of America

LSC-C

Printing 1, 2021

CONTENTS

For my family

However far the stream flows, it never forgets its source.
—NIGERIAN PROVERB

One minute of patience, ten years of peace.
—GREEK PROVERB

PROLOGUE

Giannis Antetokounmpo and his family didn't have much time. They had until sundown to get out of their apartment. They had fallen short on the rent. Again. They were being evicted. Again.

The landlord, in Sepolia, Athens, where Giannis and his family lived, had been barging into their apartment, telling them they had maybe a day, maybe two, to leave. But this time, the family wasn't so lucky.

Veronica, Giannis's mother, told him and his brothers to pack their things. Thanasis, the oldest of the four; Giannis; Kostas; and Alex, the youngest, didn't ask any questions. They didn't want to add to the burden. So they nodded, kept quiet, gathered their clothes.

But after packing all their belongings, Giannis and his brothers looked at each other, staring at their massive fridge in the kitchen, each thinking, *What are we going to do with this?* Charles, their father, looked around, trying to find something to leverage the fridge with.

Then Kostas, nine years old at the time, spotted a small skateboard. "Let's put it on the skateboard!" he squealed. Giannis, twelve, and his father stared blankly at each other. What other option did they have? "Let's give it a try," Charles said. The three of them managed to hoist the fridge on top of the skateboard.

It seemed impossible, this giant fridge on a puny skateboard.

It looked ridiculous.

But Giannis held up one side, while Kostas and Charles held up the others, and they wheeled the fridge out the front door.

As a twelve-year-old, Giannis was already used to moving. Not knowing what would happen next. All he knew was that he couldn't show fear. Couldn't cry. His younger brothers depended on him, looked up to him. "He'd come up to us and explain to us why we were leaving," Kostas recalls. Giannis was calm but stern when he spoke, even though he himself was just a kid. When he told his brothers everything would be OK, they believed him.

As they began wheeling the fridge down the road, Giannis reassured them that it would not break. They had about a mile to go, as they'd be staying at a friend's house until they figured out where to live next.

They kept holding on to the fridge, praying it wouldn't tip over. They didn't care who was looking at them. Judging them. They wheeled and wheeled, pushed and pushed, as the hot sun beat down their backs. The fridge kept wobbling, threatening to topple over on the narrow sidewalk, especially when the skateboard grazed over loose stones on the uneven pavement.

They breathed a sigh of relief upon making it to the friend's house. Their arms were sore, their hands stiff. The sky was dark. Standing in the elevator, fridge beside them, they couldn't believe that little skateboard didn't break.

* * *

Veronica remembers those nights in Greece. Remembers the uncertainty she felt, the strength she had to project. Her boys couldn't know that she was worried. Scared. She never acted that way. Sometimes she'd leave the house at 11:00 p.m. to travel to places beyond Athens to sell trinkets on the street to make money to feed her children. She knew she had to provide for her boys.

"You do what you need to do to survive. If you have children, you have to *survive*," says Veronica, known to her friends as Vera. She and Charles had emigrated from Lagos, Nigeria, to Greece in 1991 in search of a better life.

She's clutching a white wristband she wears every day that reads "God is here." "God is good," she says. "You have to be strong and never lose hope." It is by the grace of God, she thinks, that she is sitting with Giannis in the nearly ten-thousand-square-foot mansion she now shares with him; Alex; and Giannis's girlfriend, Mariah Riddlesprigger, in River Hills, an affluent community near Milwaukee.

Her son, now a six-foot-eleven NBA star and one of the best basketball players in the world, is making millions of dollars. Something that seemed unfathomable in Sepolia back when Veronica, Charles, Giannis, and his brothers would dress up in their Sunday best, wearing polished-up hand-me-down clothes, and flash wide smiles when meeting with prospective landlords, trying to fool them into believing that they were well off. *Worthy.*

Veronica won't forget what that feels like. "You don't change, because you know that some people still do not have. You do not take a step higher," Veronica says. "We are still who we are."

Rain settles on the slender trees surrounding the family's brick Milwaukee home. Tall branches form a canopy over a narrow lane leading to the front door. The area is quiet. Tranquil. An elderly couple holds hands while walking their shih tzu in the middle of the road.

Mariah opens the door on this muggy June day in 2019. Mila, the family's goldendoodle, jumps up and down, almost leaping outside onto the gold doormat stamped with a giant black *A* in the center. "Mila just wants to say hi," Mariah says. Inside, there is a sign that says "Family" in cursive, as well as a print that reads "Turn your worries into prayer."

Alex is downstairs in the basement, sitting on a couch in front of four flat-screen TVs. There's a pool table, air hockey, foosball, table tennis. A popcorn machine and scattered basketballs and trophies. There are boxes still to unpack, as the family moved here just a few months back. They used to live downtown, near Fiserv Forum, where the Bucks play. They've moved five times since coming to the US in 2013, when Giannis was drafted fifteenth overall by the Bucks.

A lot has changed. Giannis preserves each change through black-framed photos. There's a 2013 piece titled "American Dream" from a Greek magazine. "You see this in the seats every time you fly in and out of Greece," Alex says, beaming. There's his *Esquire* cover, his *Sports*

Illustrated cover. There's also a portrait of the outdoor court in Greece where the brothers used to play. "It's a reminder: that's where we started from," Alex says.

Back then, when they barely had food to eat, Charles would go without eating a day or two when needed for the family to get by. "We've got to make the most of today," Charles would often tell his boys. "Tomorrow is not promised."

Giannis saw the way his father would sacrifice, so he began sacrificing too. Giannis would scramble to find one or two euros for a yogurt or croissant, pretend that he had eaten, and give the food to his younger brothers. He'd go to sleep with his stomach rumbling, trying to forget that he was hungry but satisfied that he was helping the family.

They were evicted more times than they can remember. "A lot," Alex says, trying to recall a number, then repeats himself: "A *lot*." Kostas remembers three times clearly, then "a couple times before that" less clearly. The years blend, fold into each other, fracture into memories where only *feeling* remains.

Alex remembers the feeling of panic, of time shrinking, when the landlord would rush into their place, shouting at them to leave. He remembers arguments, the back-and-forth about payments, with his parents pleading, "We just need more time. Please. Just a little bit more time."

* * *

Giannis often thinks of those days now that he will never have to worry about finding shelter, finding food.

And neither will Alex.

Giannis is keenly conscious of the fact that Alex, living in America and attending private school, came of age in a very different environment from the one he experienced at the same age. "It's hard to be motivated when you have everything. When your life is good," Giannis says. "I didn't have a choice. I *had* to be motivated."

It is still in the back of Giannis's mind: *Not having*. Moving. Sacrificing. Maybe it always will be.

"What drives Giannis so much is that he's afraid that at any moment somebody could take it all away," says Josh Oppenheimer, Bucks assistant coach and close friend. "And I think that's why he works so hard."

That's apparent as Giannis stands on the court in Milwaukee's downtown practice facility on this June afternoon. His eyes narrow. He's not smiling. He rarely is when he's here. He approaches basketball as if he is still the child in Sepolia, waving sunglasses in the air on the street, hoping someone will buy from him.

So he doesn't take off possessions. Doesn't rest much. Has to be told to take breaks, has to be removed from the gym. He operates like he is one poor outing away from being cut.

"Our work ethic comes from what we've been through," Giannis says.

Which is why he can't tolerate the lackadaisical manner in which then-seventeen-year-old Alex, one of the top prospects in the area, is practicing one afternoon. Alex is wearing a "God is here" wristband, identical to his mother's; he considers it sacred because she blessed it with holy water and prayed over it. He is jogging, not sprinting, as he knows Giannis would have preferred.

Alex starts dribbling. His legs turn into scissors as he slices a basketball between them, showing off his seven-foot, two-inch wingspan. He is six feet seven and crafty. Building speed. Probably because he knows Giannis is watching.

He yearns to impress Giannis, and Giannis in turn sees in him a younger version of himself. A slimmer version of himself. Alex starts toward the hoop from the three-point line and softly lays the ball in. *Too* softly. Giannis's shoulders stiffen. There's a sense of urgency. There always is when he watches Alex, the one he nurtures, protects, and mentors, almost like a father would. "I get more nervous going to watch Alex play in a high school game than playing in the Eastern Conference Finals," Giannis says, his head tilting, tracking the flight of Alex's next jumper.

When the two are together, the court is a cocoon. A place just for them. A place where they do not have to think about grief or pressure or money or failure.

We just need more time.

When Giannis speaks to Alex, most often in Greek, he is blunt but empathetic. Intense but warm. Sure of the plan he's created for his brothers since they lived in Sepolia. Giannis assures Alex that if he works hard, if he gives everything, he can get to the NBA, just as Thanasis (Bucks) and Kostas (Lakers) did. And not just get there but star there. "I definitely think Alex can be better than me," Giannis says.

Having all his brothers make the NBA is Giannis's biggest motivation, besides winning an NBA championship for Milwaukee and a gold medal for the Greek national team. "It's crazy. It seems like a dream," Kostas says, given that a decade ago, he says, "we didn't even play basketball."

Giannis is trying to teach all his brothers, but particularly Alex, discipline and focus—to not get distracted by anyone or anything outside the cocoon. "It's just *me*," Giannis says, pointing to his chest, "and *you*." He points to Alex's chest. "Nobody else. Just *me* and *you*."

He often reminds Alex where they've been. Those dark nights. Those uncertain nights. Giannis tells Alex what it feels like to play in front of twenty thousand people screaming insults, trying to get in his head: he knows his brother might soon face the same.

"Lock that shit out!" Giannis says. "It's just *me* and *you*."

Alex nods. He knows his brother has pure intentions. Nobody pushes Alex harder than Giannis. Nobody cheers louder for Alex than Giannis. "Just trust me," Giannis often tells him. "I've been in your shoes. You *got this*."

The time together is for Giannis's sake too. After the two work out, the sharp parts of Giannis soften. He and Alex laugh and laugh. Share the same hearty, cheesy laugh too—the kind that starts in the belly and ends in tears.

Sometimes Giannis looks at Alex and glows. Full of pride, full of love. And fear. He wants to protect Alex from the things he's been through. It's a long list. He wants Alex to understand that he will fail at times, but he must always keep moving ahead. He wants to teach him to not care what people think. To choose friends wisely. To avoid social media. To take care of his body. To drink more water, less lemon-lime Gatorade. To be fundamentally sound. To cry when he needs to. To respect the game. To respect himself. To uplift their mother—always.

CHAPTER 1

HUNGER

Giannis was six years old when he started selling items on the street to help his family. He'd go with Thanasis and his mother. They'd find items for cheap, maybe one or two euros, in poorer neighborhoods and then sell them for more, maybe three or four euros, in better, more suburban neighborhoods.

They'd travel to beaches, especially upscale ones such as Alimos Beach, to pitch their goods, hoping the wealthy visitors would buy something. Giannis would hold Veronica's hand, dangling an item in the air, hoping someone would find his adorable puffy cheeks endearing, his big sweet smile inviting.

Giannis didn't understand what they were doing at first. What was really happening. How deeply they were suffering. But he knew things weren't good. He knew he was hungry. He'd see their pantry, their fridge, bare. Some days they didn't sell enough to have a meal until late into the night. He saw that being *here*, convincing someone to buy something from them, was a matter of eating or not eating. Surviving or not surviving.

And he saw the way his mother never slumped her shoulders, never lowered her chin. She kept faith even when she didn't feel like she could keep going. Even when it didn't seem possible that she would be able to feed her boys, her husband. "God is good," she'd remind them. She sold whatever she could find: sunglasses, DVDs, knockoff purses, watches, toys, clothes, beauty products. "Anything," Veronica says.

Once little Alex was born, she'd take him on trips closer to home, waking up early for the Laikh Market in Sepolia on Wednesdays. The Laikh was an open-air market in the center of town with a bunch of stands. It had everything: produce, herbs, tea, yogurt. Migrants would sell trinkets off to the side, oftentimes not having legal permits to sell goods there.

In later years, Veronica traveled farther and farther to hawk her wares. She didn't want to leave Alex for extended periods of time, so he became her close companion. "I traveled out of Athens, traveled for three days," Veronica says. "I couldn't be by myself. That is my baby."

Veronica didn't want this life, to stand on the street corner for hours on end. But her options were limited. As a Black migrant, she struggled to find other steady work, especially in the years following the financial crisis of 2008. It was the worst economic downturn since the 1930s. Banks failed. Stocks cratered. Europe fell into a steep recession.

Jobs, especially the ones Charles and Veronica and other migrants were searching for, were scarce. Even Greek citizens couldn't find work. About 21.5 million citizens of the European Union were out of work, and as many as two-fifths of Greek youths were unemployed. Many lost their homes, lost family members to sickness, and were unable to afford medical expenses, let alone rent in the already-crowded housing districts.

It was hard enough for white Greek citizens to survive, but for a migrant woman from Nigeria? Difficult beyond measure. Though she raised her kids in Greece, walked the sidewalks in Greece, and went to church in Greece, she was not considered Greek. To many Greeks, she simply was a Black woman raising Black children. They didn't respect her employment history, her accomplishments from back home in Nigeria.

"When I was in Nigeria, I've been a secretary, I've worked in offices. I walked in very big places, but when you go to Greece, they don't recognize," Veronica says. "They don't want that."

*　　*　　*

Back in early 1991, Charles and Veronica were living in Lagos, Nigeria, with their eldest son, Francis, who was born in 1988. They were trying to figure out where to go. What to do. The country was growing more unstable by the day. Nigeria had endured six coups and three presidential assassinations since its independence in 1960, as well as the 1967–1970 Nigerian Civil War, also known as the Biafra war, which had claimed the lives of an estimated one to three million people.

The Nigerian economy had plummeted by the late 1980s. The country prided itself on its oil, with oil accounting for 95 percent of Nigeria's exports. But when energy prices and oil revenues crashed, the country found itself with $21 billion in foreign debt. And by the time General Ibrahim Babangida had taken power in a coup in 1985, Nigeria was, as a Ministry of Finance report at the time put it, "on the verge of external bankruptcy."

Charles, from the Yoruba tribe, and Veronica, from the Igbo tribe, felt more and more uncertain about a future there. It seemed impossible to find work. Veronica always loved to sing and was even a background singer for an album recorded in Nigeria, singing traditional songs with a few in English. She loved Whitney Houston, Celine Dion, and reggae too, but there didn't seem to be much opportunity in Nigeria. Charles was a talented soccer player who played professionally in Nigeria. He had natural speed, athleticism, and mental toughness, but opportunities were dwindling in sports as well.

It was difficult, staring down the unknown. Contemplating leaving for someplace where neither knew anyone. Neither knew what to expect. Nigeria was home. But in the summer of '91, they took a leap of faith, setting off for Germany. Francis remained in Nigeria, in the care of his grandparents.

Charles had the opportunity to play professional soccer in Germany, and that's where the two thought they'd stay. Greece wasn't originally part of the plan. But when the family arrived in Germany, Charles suffered a career-ending injury. They didn't think there would be an opportunity to stay, as two Black migrants, so they were on the move.

Again.

They decided to go to Greece, a destination that many migrants either passed through for more prosperous destinations in Europe or stayed to see if they might be granted asylum. It was there in Greece, in Sepolia, a city north of the center of Athens, where Veronica gave birth to Thanasis, whose full name is Athanasios, in 1992. Thanasis's name was inspired by Charles's love of the Greek word for *immortality*: Athanasia (αθανασία). Giannis was born in '94, Kostas (Konstantinos) in '97, and Alex (Alexandros) in '01. Four Black children in a predominantly white country.

"We've always been outsiders," Alex says.

Veronica and Charles gave them Greek first names to help them assimilate into their adopted country, given that they, as well as their parents, were considered illegal immigrants. Unlike in America, there is no birthright citizenship; being born in Greece does not automatically confer citizenship.

But the meaning of their African name is something they continued to hold dear: Adetokunbo means "crown that came from faraway seas" in Charles's Yoruba tongue (*ade* means "king"). Giannis's middle name, Ugo, means "the crown of God" in Veronica's Igbo tongue.

Sepolia was a crowded, bustling place, predominantly occupied by immigrants. Not just African immigrants but Albanians, Pakistanis, Afghans, Bangladeshis—all trying to find shelter, find work. Like Charles and Veronica, many had emigrated in hopes of starting over. They soon found there was little opportunity to do so.

"They were staying there because the rents are low," says Notis A. Mitarachi, Greece's minister of migration and asylum, "and because they can exercise their occupation—most of them are street merchants—in the same area and the neighboring streets."

The dense neighborhood was full of midrise apartment buildings, some stacked five or six stories high, with open balconies on each floor. The Metro Line 1 train (the "electric train" or *ilektriko*) ran in a stone-clad open cut in the street, a level below the adjacent sidewalk.

There were many small cafés and coffee shops but fewer green spaces and sports facilities than in other areas of the capital. Parking was tight, especially for bigger cars, because the area was so dense. Housing was difficult to secure without citizenship papers because one needed a tax number, which is provided only to those with legal status or asylum applicants. But everything was in walking distance, Alex remembers. "Everybody knows each other," he says. "Everybody was just close."

Veronica mostly babysat and cleaned homes. At one point, she worked as a cleaner at the train station in Sepolia. She'd get home aching, tired. But she remained upbeat. She kept working. "It's on me. I'm the mom," Veronica says. "I will give my kids everything. I have to work."

Charles became a handyman of sorts, an electrician at one point. Alex remembers him working as a valet at another point, constantly battling periods of unemployment.

Giannis saw how his parents would stiffen after a long day's work, try to mask their pain. "We saw them work every day to provide for us," Giannis says. He'd watch his dad sit at the table, not eating. Trying to smile through it. Charles would always tell the kids, "Don't worry about it. I'm not eating. I have to make sure my kids eat."

And then they'd be told they had to leave. They'd gather their things again. On to the next place, a place that was just as cramped. They typically had just enough money to keep the lights on, but sometimes the family was forced to make difficult choices.

"Giannis told me that his mother had to sell her wedding ring just to have them have food," says Michael Carter-Williams, close friend and former Bucks teammate from 2015 to 2016. "He really came from nothing."

* * *

Giannis learned to be a persuasive street vendor. He knew how to turn on his charm—how to get people to like him, to buy something from him. He learned that from his mom. She didn't want him to go with her at first, but he would insist: "No, I'm coming with you."

He was stubborn, convincing people that they needed items they hadn't considered essential. He'd keep asking question after question. He felt he was the best salesman in the family, besides his mom, of course. He wouldn't give up, peppering prospective buyers with questions.

"You want this glass," he'd say.

"No."

"Oh, they're really nice; they're going to help you do *this*."

"Ah, no. We good."

"But why?"

He was persistent, refusing to take no for an answer. He didn't have a choice. His family needed him. Sometimes Giannis would be sitting on a bench by himself. He looked lonely, introspective. Sometimes people would leave food items, clothes, even money, for him to buy something. But most of the time, he was with his family. At first they worked close to their neighborhood. Later they would travel together for extended periods, sometimes seven days in a row, maybe two weeks in a row, to other areas, mainly suburban areas, all over Greece.

They'd drive for five hours, ten hours, during summers. Giannis would look out the window, see areas he had never heard of. Then they'd spot a beach. For an afternoon, they'd sit on the sand under the sun. Just get to relax for a few hours. Not worry about money for a few hours. Feel their toes in the sand, jump into the cool blue water. They swam and laughed, and the water glittered a deep blue green. They were able to have *fun*. Let go.

Then they'd go to the next village, sell, sleep. Travel, sell, sleep. Miles and miles away. Travel, sell, sleep. But even through these struggles, they found joy.

They always found joy in each other.

*　*　*

Giannis wanted to be a professional soccer player at age eleven, just like one of his idols, Thierry Henry, the legendary French striker. Giannis also wanted to emulate his dad. Dribble like him. Score like him. Move like him. Giannis was as focused, as intense, as his dad was, approaching pickup games as if they were real matches.

That's how Charles operated. He would teach the kids about maximizing time, maximizing every minute. "Make sure what you give your time to is worth it," Charles would tell them. "You shouldn't wait one more day than what's necessary. If you could accomplish something today, why wait until tomorrow? Go get it today!"

Charles pushed the brothers into sports not just because of his own career but because he wanted them to avoid drugs and other negative influences. Charles had his own soccer career cut short by injury, but Giannis was determined to have a different outcome. Charles had hoped so too. "I'm pretty sure he was hoping we'd all become soccer players," Alex says.

He'd tell them physical injuries were part of competing. Part of giving your everything on the field. "Take care of your body," he would tell them. One day, Thanasis bruised his finger on the field and didn't know what to do. Charles came with a hot towel, massaged the spot over and over, the finger, the hand, until the swelling went down. He used juju medicine, a traditional West African spiritual practice that involves amulets and spells. "Don't worry," Charles told Thanasis. "It's happened to me too."

But the boys were kicked off their first soccer team because the coaches said they were too skinny and didn't have enough muscles—or skills—to play. But they kept playing on their own, challenging each other.

The only time they weren't playing soccer was when they were playing Ping-Pong. Games were intense. Each brother out for blood. Or they'd be running relay races at a nearby track, timing each other to see who would win.

But Giannis still loved soccer. He started dreaming. Hoping he could make it big. He found the sport to be exciting. Fast paced. After school, he and his brothers would head to a small field close to home and play. On the weekends, sometimes Charles would come along. Charles was in his forties at the time, but he was still tall and athletic. Fast. The family would spot some eighteen-year-olds playing and ask them to play pickup. "They'd be like, 'Man, these kids are scoring on us!'" Kostas says. "We'd kill them."

Sometimes even Veronica would play, filling in at goalie. Giannis and Thanasis were strikers. Kostas played defense and midfield. Alex was too young to take it seriously enough to have a position, but he'd come with them to the field, trailing behind. "We were all really good," Kostas says.

The men and women in the earlier generations of the family were all tall, long, and athletic, as was Veronica. Track was her sport. She loved running. Loved competing. Her favorite events were the high jump, the long jump, and the two-hundred-meter sprint. She and Kostas used to play-fight when they'd get mad at each other, and he could see why she was so competitive in sports back then. "She's strong as hell," Kostas says, laughing.

Charles and Veronica wanted their kids to exhibit good sportsmanship. But also to be competitive. They'd have competitions to see which boy could clean up his room or complete chores the best, and Giannis would often win—he *always* took it seriously. They taught their boys to show respect to others. Especially to their elders and to family, referencing the common Nigerian proverb "If you love your father, if you love your mother, you'll live long."

Giannis remembered his dad teaching him about Nelson Mandela and the things that he could learn from such a selfless person who'd sacrificed his own well-being for the good of other people. That left a lasting impression on Giannis. He saw that his own dad modeled those characteristics too. Saw how, if Charles made a big bowl of spaghetti for the family that was to last the whole day, he barely ate any, instead waiting for his boys to eat.

Charles was Giannis's role model. He seemed to always have a smile on his face despite enormous pressures at home. He always said "Hello" and "How are you?" to strangers. You would never know he was suffering. On the brink of not making it. "He was a kind soul," Veronica says. "Very kind. Very kind husband, very kind daddy. Very kind human being."

Veronica smiles, thinking of the biggest lesson he taught the kids: "He teach them how to love," she says.

The boys knew they were loved. But they also kept praying, believing that God was watching them. Looking out for them. They prayed for some kind of relief. For the day when Veronica did not have to come home from a long day of selling, back aching, mind racing, figuring out how to find the next meal.

* * *

They found refuge in Agios Meletios Church, a beautiful Greek Orthodox church in Sepolia. The church, built in 1872, was a simple structure with narrow roundheaded windows trimmed in a burnt-sienna tone. Inside was a tall space with arched openings and elaborate chandeliers, with ecclesiastical icons high on the archway piers. The place was dim, smelling of beeswax candles and incense.

The Antetokounmpos were one of the few Black families, standing out among the congregation, but they would go to services often, with the boys attending Sunday school. They developed a close relationship with Father Evangelos Ganas. All the boys would be baptized there, Giannis and Alex in 2012 on a special day in Greece: October 28, which is Oxi Day, commemorating October 28, 1940, when former Greek prime minister Ioannis Metaxas denied Italian dictator Benito Mussolini's request to allow Italian troops to cross the border into Greece.

Sometimes church leaders gave the family food and other items, helping out when they could. Ganas accepted the boys as they were: Greek children who were also Black. He remembers Giannis's eyes: always looking around, always curious. A little bit shy but always polite. His spirit just seemed buoyed—and Ganas knew Giannis had every reason to feel defeated. He saw innocence and hope in all the brothers, and in Veronica a kindhearted person trying her best.

Within the walls of the church, the Antetokounmpos were insulated, at least for a few hours, from the burdens of life on the outside. They made friends, too, with neighbors. Neighbors who saw how well mannered the boys were, how humble.

Ganas remembers these moments fondly, but he doesn't ask for any credit for helping Giannis. Giving him food. Lending an ear. It was not nearly enough to feed four boys, he insists, but it helped. Over the years, local Greek journalists have posited him as the "Greek Priest Who Saved Giannis." That label bothers Ganas. He rejects it. "I have not saved anyone. Only Christ saves," Ganas says. "I love Giannis and his family, and the fact that he was raised in our neighborhood and was baptized in our parish and has pleasant memories from Sepolia makes me happy."

Ganas still thinks about Giannis often. "I still pray for him," he says.

His mind returns to Giannis's eyes. Those innocent eyes. Praying, never expecting. Asking, never taking. Just trying to survive.

* * *

Spiros Velliniatis swears he heard God talking to him. Moving him. *Steering* him toward three young Black boys running around. He didn't yet know their names, Giannis, Kostas, and Alex (Thanasis wasn't there that day), or that they were future basketball stars. They were just kids playing tag. But Velliniatis, a local coach in Athens, looked closer at thirteen-year-old Giannis, and he felt something, he recalls. Something divine.

This is not possible, he thought to himself. *God is talking to me.*

What he saw was Giannis's long limbs, his Gumby-like arms. What he noticed was that Giannis never seemed to tire, running, running, running. He was just having fun, but there seemed to be a seriousness about him, a focus to him.

All my life, I am trying to find this.

Velliniatis likened seeing a young Giannis to stumbling on a young Mozart, even though that sounds absurd. It *was* absurd. Giannis hadn't yet grown into his body, let alone morphed into a basketball prodigy or genius. When Velliniatis speaks, he tends to embellish, as if he were reliving the story rather than merely presenting it. He is a storyteller at heart, and this is a great one: failed coach discovers impoverished kid who transcends poverty to become a global basketball icon.

Velliniatis walked over to the boys. "Where are you from?" he asked Giannis, who seemed quiet, shy.

"Nigeria," Velliniatis remembers Giannis telling him.

"Do you do any sports?"

"No."

"What jobs do your parents do?"

"My mom takes care of people. My dad is working in a garage."

Velliniatis sensed that the boys' parents did not have stable work. He knew there was little opportunity for Black people in Sepolia. "If I find work for your parents—it would be five hundred euros a month—will you play basketball for me?"

Giannis paused. Looked at his brothers. They fell silent, confused by what they were hearing. *Who is this man? What does he want from us?* After a few minutes, though, and with some hesitation, Giannis half-heartedly agreed, and Velliniatis told him to bring his parents to the playground so they could have a conversation.

"In this moment," Velliniatis says, "Giannis made the decision of his lifetime."

Velliniatis thought this moment *was* some kind of cosmic miracle. Some kind of sign from above after years of his own tumult, of failure. His own hoop dreams had fallen apart. He wanted to play in the NBA but didn't make it. As he recalls, he felt unloved after a woman he loved broke his heart and left him in his youth. He felt aimless, just floating. No dreams, no plans. Nowhere to go.

OK, life is like this. You tried your best. You didn't make it.

But finding Giannis felt like a new beginning to him. He saw something special in Giannis.

God is talking to me.

Velliniatis's story sounds amazing. It *is* amazing. But few genuinely thought Giannis was amazing back then. Giannis was scrawny, thin as a rail, and helpless on the court: he committed travel violation after travel violation with the ball.

And the way Velliniatis has framed his relationship with Giannis in recent years has caused a rift with the family, a rift that continues to widen. They do not speak nowadays. Velliniatis professes to be hurt, feels like he is owed something, some compensation—"seven percent," he mentions specifically—since he gave the family money, food, opportunity, hope. Something when they had nothing.

And he *did* "discover" Giannis, after all. Handed Giannis an orange leather ball and said, "Why don't you try it? See if you like it?"

* * *

Velliniatis was drawn to Giannis in some way because he himself felt like an outsider all his life. Velliniatis was from a "mixed background," as he puts it, half Greek and half German, growing up in Greece. "It was a difficult way to grow up, not fitting in to either society," he says.

He felt a certain connection to the immigrant community. Connected to their plight, somehow, even though he was white and they were Black—and he never faced, and would never know what it felt like to face, the kind of discrimination and inequities they did. Still, in hopes of helping them gain access to Greek clubs, he continued to find talented Black migrants, including Michalis Afolanio, who would go on to become the first African Greek to ever speak before the Hellenic parliament, as well as Greek rapper MC Yinka, whose real name is Emmanuel Olayinka Afolayan.

"We were the first generation, the children of immigrants. The first Afro-Greeks," says Afolayan, who was born in 1981 in Greece to Nigerian parents who had migrated in the '70s. He lived most of his life without papers. Afolayan loved basketball but didn't have many opportunities to play. He made friends, including Thanasis (Thanasis would come over to his home in Attika Square to hang out with Afolayan's younger sister, Victoria), and felt accepted, especially since he quickly learned Greek. But classmates lobbed racist slurs at him as well.

"The way they treated immigrants was a bit fucked up," Afolayan says. "Being Afro-Greek in the eighties, I was like an alien."

Velliniatis mentored him and helped him play for his team, Pegasus United, in Kato Patisia. "Spiros saw that the African community has talented people, and maybe he admired them," Afolayan says. "He wanted to help because there was a lot of wasted talent, people that didn't have access to certain rights." Meaning they could not get citizenship and therefore, in some cases, could not join sports teams. Greek law at the time prohibited undocumented immigrants over the age of fifteen from playing organized sports without a sponsor, according to Velliniatis. "We were not people, in this society," Afolayan says.

Velliniatis became a respected coach in Athens, known for bringing in top-tier talent from poor neighborhoods. "He was trying to find diamonds in the rough," says Harris Stavrou, a Greek sports journalist. Diamonds that wanted to be coached. "His main job was to find playground talents," says Stefanos Dedas, a Greek coach who now coaches Hapoel Holon in Israel. "Not skilled guys, not talented guys, not shooters. Physical guys. Maybe taller, maybe longer."

Velliniatis joined Filathlitikos B.C., a club in the city of Zografou, becoming coach Takis Zivas's assistant. Zivas needed talent—quickly. Filathlitikos wasn't exactly a small club or a big club. It was, however, a mediocre club. In need of something unexpected.

So when Velliniatis found Giannis and his brothers on the playground in Sepolia, he thought, *I'm going to help them.* He was excited, thinking how the brothers could potentially bring Filathlitikos out of mediocrity.

Problem was, Giannis didn't want anything to do with basketball. He hated it.

* * *

Giannis's heart was still in soccer, given that his dad was such a fantastic player. The thirteen-year-old still wanted to somehow turn pro in soccer. He had zero interest in basketball. Though basketball seemed like it could help pay the bills—given Velliniatis and the club's offer—he couldn't see dedicating himself fully to the sport, focusing on the more immediate task of street-corner salesmanship.

Velliniatis pleaded. He wouldn't give up. "Give it a chance," Velliniatis remembers telling Giannis. "For your family."

Family was the only reason Giannis was open to listening to this strange man who wouldn't leave him and his brothers alone. Giannis wanted to be just like Thanasis, so when basketball meant hanging out with Thanasis more, Giannis decided to give it a try. Velliniatis made a deal: try it out for fun, play for one month, and the team, Filathlitikos, would help out financially.

Thanasis loved basketball, but Giannis kept pleading with his older brother to play soccer with him. Still, Giannis couldn't pass up the money. They needed to eat.

There were a couple of problems, though.

First, the club was farther away, in a completely different neighborhood. Zografou, where the gym is located, was ten miles away. They'd have to leave school, walk twenty minutes to the train station, hop on a train, then hop on another train, the Metro Line 2 (the Red Line), then walk twenty minutes, then hop on bus 230, just to get to their team's gym for practice. It was about a fifty-minute trip.

Second, Giannis and Thanasis would need a sponsor, quickly, because of the Greek law that prohibited undocumented immigrants over the age of fifteen from playing without one. Thanasis was about to turn fifteen, so

Velliniatis had to lobby on the boys' behalf to allow them to play. Vellini-atis found a way and drove them to Zografou for their first Filathlitikos practice.

Filathlitikos practiced in a small gym. Or, as Kostas describes it, "a little-ass gym." It *was* tiny. Run down. It was so hot—the air-conditioning rarely worked—that humidity created precipitation that slid down the walls. There was no hot water. The showers were old, leaky; the tiles were faded. There were only about five hundred seats.

"It's not like a USA court," says Coach Zivas, whose friend Lefteris Zarmakoupis is translating for him. The gym had two standard baskets. A couple of basketballs. "It's not a great gym, but it had the basics," says Giorgos Kordas, former Filathlitikos teammate.

Zivas wasn't sure what to expect when thirteen-year-old Giannis walked in with two of his brothers, Kostas and Thanasis. Zivas kept an open mind but tempered his expectations. Giannis was young. He would need time to develop. Nobody knew who the kid was. Who any of his brothers were. "We had to see if they were good for basketball," Zivas says.

Giannis and his brothers looked around excitedly at the empty court, the leather basketballs. "Obviously they hadn't entered a closed basketball court in their lives until then," says Grigoris Melas, a Filathlitikos assis-tant coach, who now coaches at Giannis's AntetokounBros Academy in Athens.

The coaches watched young Giannis run up and down the floor. He was so thin, so lanky, so *skinny*, that it looked like he might fall over if someone tapped him on the shoulder. Zivas thought one word to himself: *shadow*. He kept saying the word, over and over, in his mind. *Shadow . . . shadow . . . shadow . . .*

"He really was like a shadow," Zivas says, in that Giannis was quiet and unassuming. He was one of those tall players who would slouch just a bit to blend in. He was polite and friendly but didn't say much to anyone. He still didn't really want to be there.

He wanted to be outside on the pitch. Kicking a soccer ball. Plus, he wasn't very good at basketball at first. He had limited resources: the first time he ever shot a ball, he shot bank shots with a soccer ball at a broken rim. "Giannis is getting five hundred euros a month, and he doesn't even know how to dribble the ball," Velliniatis recalls. "He doesn't know *nothing*."

It was true! Giannis couldn't dribble. Didn't understand basketball. His hands seemed to be ahead of his feet. He'd trip over himself. The ball would trickle off his knee. He'd carry the ball. "I feel like he was confused, like all of us," Kostas says, laughing. "His first game he had a whole lot of travel violations."

His biggest weakness? "Pretty much everything," Kordas says. "He wasn't that good at first. He was passionate, though."

Giannis instinctively ran hard, but he just didn't know where to run. The older players would post him up, have their way with him. He was behind, as starting to learn basketball at thirteen was, and still is, considered late. And so the more Zivas watched, the more he was convinced: "Giannis is not ready for this," Zivas says. "He wasn't ready to play basketball."

And Zivas had a hunch about why, just looking at Giannis's body. "He wasn't eating the portions that he needed to," Zivas says. "That's why he was very slim."

Some parents complained at first that the club was giving money to a kid with so little skill, so little potential. Velliniatis told parents to give Giannis time to improve, to not be so harsh to a kid in need. "The Greeks do not understand what those kids and this family was going through," he says.

Once, Thanasis wasn't playing well in a game, and Velliniatis took him to a Greek restaurant afterward, and he remembers Thanasis eating eight souvlaki with double bread—a *very* large amount of food. Velliniatis had a friend eat with them. "I told my friend after," Velliniatis says, "now you understand—it's not that the kid is not talented. It's that these kids are starving."

Zivas remained patient. Making sure Giannis continued to show up to play was a priority for him. Giannis clearly had a ways to go, filling into his body, learning the rules of the game. He was raw, but he showed some promise. Zivas watched the way Giannis would never be the last one on sprints. The way he'd sprint back after a turnover no matter what. The way he wouldn't give up after getting scored on three times; he would come back more angry, more stubborn, for the fourth.

"It was very obvious from the start, his determination," Zivas says. "I think he was born with this."

Giannis would often play one-on-one with Tselios Konstantinos, another teammate. Konstantinos was the better shooter, but Giannis never stopped hustling. "He was fighting for every point," Konstantinos says. "He's strong willed."

One day, Velliniatis had the players line up against the wall and sit for wall squats for as long as possible. Thighs burned, calves shook. Every player dipped over, couldn't handle it anymore, at five minutes. Giannis's legs wobbled, but he wouldn't collapse. He lasted for seven minutes.

* * *

Still, even with the help of the club, the Antetokounmpos continued to struggle financially. They were not an anomaly in Athens, though. This particular stretch of time was difficult for many Greeks, not just migrants, because of the financial crisis.

As more and more Black and brown migrants came to Greece, fleeing authoritarian regimes and political unrest, tensions rose even higher. Greek citizens blamed the newly arrived migrants for their economic troubles. And there seemed to be no relief in sight. A second wave of hardship would later hit: by early 2012, one in three Greeks lived below the poverty line. The minimum wage was reduced by 22 percent. More than twenty thousand were homeless.

Without papers, Charles and Veronica were forced to take under-the-table work wherever they could, but it was never enough. Velliniatis recalls growing more concerned for the family. He started subsidizing the Antetokoumpos out of his own pocket, he says, even when he himself didn't have much. He became close with the boys, spending time training them, teaching them the fundamentals of the game.

"He loved us too much. I cannot say where the love comes from," Giannis later told OnMilwaukee. "I didn't even know him so well. He helped us so much." He was, Giannis said, "like a second father for me."

One morning, Velliniatis took him to a national training camp in the area that lasted a few days. Giorgos Pantelakis, Velliniatis's friend, was coaching the camp. Pantelakis, who now coaches the women's team for the Greek powerhouse Olympiacos, picked up Giannis in his Toyota, handing him a sandwich in the back seat. Giannis was surprised. Grateful. He was reserved but started opening up about his brothers, his surroundings.

"He was very mature for his age," Pantelakis says. "He was a thirteen-year-old kid, but he spoke like a twenty-year-old guy."

But once they arrived at the gym, Pantelakis realized Giannis had a long way to go in terms of maturing on the court. "He was very weak," Pantelakis says. "You couldn't imagine that this guy will be an NBA superstar."

What was clear was that there was an edge to him. A hardness to him. He ripped down rebounds fiercely. He'd practice moves he couldn't master over and over rather than drink water during breaks. And in games, kids knocked him around, but he never stayed down on the floor for more than a second or two before popping back up. "He wasn't as strong as the other kids at the camp, but he tried two hundred percent more than every kid," Pantelakis says.

The camp would start at 8:00 a.m. each day. After the first day, Giannis asked the coaches politely, "Can I come to practice early?" He showed up forty minutes early every day after that. He never left the gym for the duration of the day. The other kids rested or went swimming in between, but Giannis kept working. "He sees something he is not good at, he tries ten times more," Pantelakis says. "He doesn't let it go."

He was improving because of the hours he put in. And the hours Velliniatis and other coaches spent teaching him. "There was no miracle, no recipe," Velliniatis says. "You cannot learn mathematics by yourself. Somebody has to teach you."

Pantelakis told his fiancée about Giannis, told her he was not very good at basketball but that she had to come to the gym to see how hard he played. And that is what she saw: Giannis missed every shot, to the point that players backed off him and just *let* him shoot.

Clank!

Clank!

Clank!

But then, after the game, she saw Giannis head to the side of the court and practice dunking. Yes, *dunking*, even though he could barely make a layup.

Something burned in him to fly. Rise higher and higher to the basket. He'd start at the free throw line and practice his steps, trying to get his rhythm down. He failed and failed, struggled to even grip the ball. For the next five days, he leaped and failed, leaped and failed. Wouldn't leave until he dunked.

On the last day of the camp, he finally dunked the ball. Well, sort of. He laid the ball in *aggressively*, dunking it in with his fingertips. It was not *really* a dunk. But Giannis smiled, so proud of himself.

The excitement dissolved, though, as soon as he left the gym. His worries were never far behind.

*   *   *

Giannis and his brothers weren't consistently coming to Filathlitikos's practices. Maybe two or three times a week. They had to work. Provide for their family, especially on the weekends, taking those long trips outside the city to peddle their wares.

Sometimes they'd be in and out to the point that the coaches couldn't predict *when* they would show: they'd be gone for a month, back for a month, missing for two months, back for a month. Especially Giannis, who worked the longest hours.

And when Giannis *was* at practice, he wasn't really focused on basketball. He was there, but he wasn't *there*. His mind was on selling. Scrambling. Surviving.

Club officials felt they needed to speak with the family. It was hard to pin Charles and Veronica down because they were working so much.

"The children played with Filathlitikos for six years," Zivas says. "We see Charles and Veronica less than ten times."

The club tried to help the family in a variety of ways. The general manager of Filathlitikos, Giannis Smyrlis, was also the owner of a cleaning service, and he offered Charles and Veronica work cleaning buildings. They didn't take the job, but Zivas kept pushing. He offered food in his fridge, allowed the boys to stay over. He would ask them, before every practice, "Did you eat today?" He would save them a yogurt, a croissant. Anything he could to keep the boys somewhat nourished, at least enough to make it through a practice.

Their teammates began to catch on to what they were going through. Christos Saloustros, Giannis's close friend on the team, started noticing that Giannis wasn't eating. He'd ask Giannis, "Are you OK? Are you hungry? Do you want something to eat?"

Giannis would shake his head. "No, I'm OK."

"But then you were seeing them [the brothers] lie," Saloustros says. "In their eyes, you can see that they are hungry."

Saloustros, who now plays for the Greek club Peristeri and remains a close friend, would bring Giannis food no matter how many times Giannis declined. He was worried about his friend. The entire team was. Nikos Gkikas, another close friend on the team who remains close to Giannis, remembers how intently little Alex would look at him as he ate a snack before practice. That's when Gkikas fully realized the extent of their hardship. "From the first moment, we knew," says Gkikas, who now plays for AEK Athens. "We saw four Black guys that were skinny as shit."

Once, Konstantinos, Giannis's teammate, had his mother make Giannis a bowl of rice and chicken. A month later, Konstantinos remembers Giannis telling him, "Oh man, I remember this dish. It was *amazing*." Konstantinos laughs at this memory. "In my opinion it was the simplest meal," he says. "So I said, 'What the fuck? What is he eating on a daily basis?' I didn't know."

No one did, because Giannis never talked about it. He didn't want people to know. To feel sorry for him. He just wanted to compete. Compete *hard*. "He never asked from me or the other players for any sort of money," says Melas, the assistant coach.

Melas didn't understand the extent of Giannis's family's troubles until, one afternoon, he noticed Giannis looked really exhausted from training. Bent over, gasping for air, exhausted. He just could not go anymore. And that was really unlike him. "I realized how starving and weak he was," Melas says.

And then Giannis fainted, collapsed on the floor. He hadn't had breakfast, hadn't eaten anything all day. Everyone rushed over to him, and Zivas sent a few to get food. From then on, everyone started asking Giannis if he needed food—especially Melas, who tried to make sure he always had a snack with him to give to Giannis. He'd often give him some change for a croissant. "This is something I put the blame on me for not having supported him earlier," Melas says.

Giannis would sprint and hustle and sprint and hustle. Basketball wasn't necessarily his refuge yet. But it was a convenient distraction. When his hands were dribbling, he didn't have to think about hunger. When his legs were sprinting, he didn't have to think about hunger.

Hunger was something he learned to downplay. Hunger was something he learned to compartmentalize. Until practice ended and he could not keep sprinting, keep distracting himself. He'd go back home, stiffen his lip, and act like the leader his brothers needed. Act like he had already eaten so that he could give to his brothers. Act like his stomach was not growling.

CHAPTER 2

DREAMING

Giannis wanted to be just like Thanasis. They were extremely close, being the two oldest brothers, aside from Francis, who had remained in Nigeria. Wherever Thanasis was, Giannis was. Whatever Thanasis said, Giannis repeated.

"Nobody is untouchable," Thanasis would tell Giannis. "The tallest towers in the world can still get torn down."

Thirteen-year-old Giannis internalized those phrases, would repeat them over and over. Then he'd put them into practice, guarding Thanasis, who was much stronger, much more physical. Thanasis dominated him then, but the lesson was clear: never back down from anyone.

Thanasis would foul Giannis, put an elbow in his back in the post. Rough him up. Thanasis learned toughness from their father. Once, Charles argued with Thanasis when he saw him playing casually in the neighborhood, taking it way too easy on his opponents. "What you are doing is not right," Charles said. "Do not let the other guy breathe! If you want to be great, it all starts with the way you think."

Both brothers were mentally tough, but they had different demeanors: Thanasis was gregarious, Giannis quiet. Thanasis acted on instinct; Giannis was more thoughtful about his choices. But each always seemed to know what the other was thinking. How the other was feeling. "I think of both of them like a fist—one fist together," says Michalis Kamperidis, Giannis's former Filathlitikos and U-20 national-team teammate and close friend to this day. "They inspired each other."

Most knew *Thanasis* as the talented basketball player in the family; Giannis was still known as *Thanasis's brother*. The tagalong kid brother in Thanasis's shadow. Which was perfectly OK with Giannis because he idolized his big brother.

Thanasis saw potential in Giannis, though he knew Giannis had a ways to go. "It wasn't like I watched him and I was like, 'Oh, I knew that Giannis was going to be good.' No," Thanasis says. "But we believed in each other."

Thanasis would never let his younger brother believe that he *could* beat him, though. Besides, Giannis was still too slight to shove back, to compete; he was still learning to get used to contact, muscling his way to the basket. He shied away every time, almost afraid of anyone touching him.

Oftentimes, though, the two couldn't play at the same time because they had to share sneakers. The family only had enough money for one pair. Giannis would have to wear two pairs of socks to fit snugly into Thanasis's size 15 shoes for his own game, then hand them off for Thanasis's game right after, as he was playing in the older division. Their games were often on Tuesday nights, back-to-back.

After a while, the shoes would be worn down, the soles peeling, but it didn't matter to either of them. If the shoes laced up, it could work. They made anything work.

* * *

The brothers shared everything, from T-shirts to shorts to pants to socks. "Whatever didn't fit me, Alex would take," Kostas says. "Whatever didn't fit Giannis, I would take."

They also slept in the same room: two on a bunk bed, two on an adjacent couch. Thanasis would force Alex and Kostas to sleep on the creaky bunk bed because they were younger. Alex and Kostas didn't want to sleep there, but whatever their older brothers told them to do, they did.

"Our household never had something that was individual to somebody," Alex says. "Everything that we had was for everybody. That's why there wasn't that many arguments between us, because when you don't have stuff that's individual to you, and you share everything, it's like, what is there to fight about?"

They'd split food, often one souvlaki between them, each taking a bite before handing it to the next, cracking jokes about whatever happened that day. They managed to always find something to smile about, Kostas recalls, because they learned the difference between *want* and *need*. Stopped thinking about what they wanted. Stopped thinking about what they didn't have—they focused on gratitude for what they *did* have. "You might think you have it bad; then somebody right next to you has it worse," Kostas says.

Their parents taught them to value what they had. Never made them feel less than. "My parents gave me everything while having nothing at the same time," Alex says. "If you would have asked me what I wanted, I would have said this and this and that. But if you would have asked me what I *need*? I don't need anything but my family."

They all knew if they had each other, they would somehow be OK. Someone was always there to listen, to offer advice. To laugh with. Alongside so much pain, so much uncertainty, was joy.

Sometimes, after playing together for hours, the boys would head to Filathlitikos's court in Zografou for practice. They often didn't have money for bus tickets, so they walked the ten miles, round trip. It would take at least two hours. That was even more difficult to do after having played—oftentimes on an empty stomach. But they'd walk and joke, making a game out of each step. Thankful for the legs that allowed them to walk, to jump, they kept moving.

"Whenever we were together, we always had *fun*," Kostas says.

Especially when Veronica cooked. She put her soul into every dish, any kind of rice, but especially *fufu*, a traditional African dish that she'd serve with a stew or soup. The boys loved it. Loved eating together. Just *being* together.

And Veronica wasn't the only one who could cook in the house. "My dad used to cook better than my mom. He'd be killing it," Kostas says, laughing. "He used to make meat pies."

In those rare moments when Veronica wasn't working, or cooking, or strategizing the family's next move, she played basketball with her boys outside. They'd challenge her to shoot three-pointers. The only thing she couldn't do was dunk.

Watching her smile, even just for an hour, was a joy no one could take away from the boys.

* * *

Giannis, around thirteen, and Thanasis, around fifteen, began street-vending on their own, sans parents. The first time they went alone, they had fun walking in the sun for five hours straight, joking around, fighting, getting mad at each other, making up, joking again. They made nearly $150, an astounding amount, on one of those days. Charles and Veronica were so happy. So proud.

Then they'd go do it again the next day. It was a grind. Sometimes they'd make just ten dollars, selling a toy, a watch, but it was enough to not starve that day. And that was considered a good day.

After a long day's work, sometimes Thanasis would look at Giannis and say, "Let's do something with our lives so we never have to do this again."

Thanasis was starting to find his own friends, often leaving Giannis with Kostas and Alex. So even though Giannis was still quite young, he became the leader of his brothers. Giannis seemed older than he was. Wherever Giannis said they were going, Kostas and Alex went. No lip, no question. They were in awe of Giannis.

Giannis didn't tell Kostas and Alex how badly they were struggling as a family. He wouldn't tell them, *We don't have food. We can't pay the rent tomorrow. You can't hang out with your friend because we gotta work.* Those things would cross his mind, but he didn't want his brothers to feel afraid. To feel pain.

Giannis would convey what was happening with his eyes. He would give Alex and Kostas this *look.* This disappointed look that explained what words couldn't when Alex used to ask for frivolous things, like a PlayStation 2. Giannis's face would tighten. His eyes, deep and brown and piercing, would deliver: *You know we can't get that.*

So Alex and Kostas learned to stop asking. To hide *wanting.* Giannis did too. He wanted a TV more than anything but hid his desires. His father often told him, "Always want more, but never be greedy."

"We were so close as a family it doesn't sound real: 'Your family don't argue? You don't go through issues?' We really didn't go through no major issues," Alex says. "Our main problems were financial. Just being able to stand on our feet and keep up with our surroundings."

They didn't have the option of *not* making it. They had to make it. Somehow. And Giannis would make sure of it. Do whatever he had to do to make sure of it. To make sure he did not have to see Alex's crestfallen look one more time.

You know we can't get that.

* * *

The boys were coming to Filathlitikos practice a bit more, but the real fun happened on the outside court, Tritonas court in Sepolia. Nestled among some stores, just a few minutes away from the family's home, the court became their refuge. Sometimes their friends would come too, and they'd play late into the evening in the summers, if they weren't preoccupied with a long selling trip for the next day.

There, they didn't have to think about money. They could just *play*. Make fun of each other for shooting air balls. "They loved it," Veronica says. "They *loved* playing basketball." She always knew her sons would accomplish something. She didn't know if they'd stick with basketball or pursue soccer, but she could see a bright future when she looked at them. She never pressured them to do anything, but she wanted to help them in whatever they chose.

And they loved when their dad would join them. Charles was about forty-three, able to dunk the ball—and he had never played basketball in his life. He didn't *really* know how to play—he'd travel all over the place, commit all sorts of dribbling violations—but somehow, he'd rise up to the rim and hammer the ball home, leaving his boys in awe.

When Charles wasn't playing with them, he was encouraging them. When they'd have a bad game, he'd soothe them by telling them, "Tomorrow is another day. Let go of the past. Just keep working."

The boys thought Charles was the most successful man in the world, even though some days he didn't have a euro in his pocket.

* * *

Giannis was far from a leader on his Filathlitikos team. He didn't really fit in. He towered over everyone. His arms were so lanky he could gather two, three, teammates under his wingspan. He was still learning the basics. Even his classmates at school wouldn't pick him for half-court games; that motivated him to one day be so good that he could choose not to play with *them*.

Giannis did show potential, though: he was naturally athletic and innovative in the open floor, which was not as common at the time. Greek basketball tended to be more possession oriented in the half-court set—pass, pass, pass for the best shot.

Then there were more obvious differences between him and his peers. "People didn't even know what his name was. It was something like 'You have to see that tall Black guy from Filathlitikos,'" says Alexandros Trigas, former assistant coach for Panathinaikos's U-18 team, which played against Giannis and Filathlitikos. He's now a journalist for Sport24.gr. "We didn't have anything like him."

Giannis had a chance to flourish under Zivas's system because Zivas's team didn't play traditional Greek basketball. Zivas wanted his teams to run a fast break, play fast in transition. Generate as many possessions as possible. "He gives his players a lot of freedom," says Dedas, the Greek coach now at the helm of Hapoel Holon. "It's up-tempo, and Greek basketball is not a high-tempo game. In Greece, what we like to play is the big man coming to set the pick and roll."

Instead of molding players into his system, Zivas molded his system *around* the kind of players he had. At the same time, Zivas was strict and instilled discipline. He taught fundamentals—how to finish around the rim, how to correctly pivot. But during games, he let his players be more creative. "He's different from other coaches because he trusts the players," says Konstantinos, Giannis's former Filathlitikos teammate. "He lets the players do what they want to do."

Giannis's length and speed were perfect for Zivas's improvisational system. He started to grab rebounds and take off downcourt. He didn't have to pass the ball to the point guard; he *was* the point guard. And then sometimes he was the small forward. Or the power forward. Zivas never made him choose.

Zivas didn't just let Giannis have free rein, though. The kid needed guidance. Zivas was happy to play that role. Almost like a father figure would. He'd try to help him come out of his shell. Be more talkative. "He treats me like his own child," Giannis later told Sport24.gr. "He made me love basketball."

He didn't love basketball just yet, though. And Zivas couldn't control Giannis's whereabouts. He was patient when Giannis would leave, then return. Leave, then return. He understood what Giannis and his family were going through. But then Giannis started leaving for longer periods of time. At one point, Velliniatis, who was still an assistant coach with the team, couldn't find Giannis for four weeks. "Giannis stopped coming," Velliniatis says.

Velliniatis was sure Giannis was a lost cause. *The boy quit for good*, he thought. Zivas urged Velliniatis to not give up. To do *something*. Velliniatis agreed. He went to Giannis's family's apartment for one last plea. He bought Giannis a book: a biography of soccer legend Diego Maradona. He knew Giannis still wished he could become a pro soccer player, and when he saw the book at a local bazaar, he had to snag it for him.

Giannis opened the door, and Velliniatis walked in, sat down. He handed Giannis the book. "This is *you*," Velliniatis said, pointing to Maradona on the cover. "You are the Maradona of basketball."

Giannis was quiet. Didn't say anything at first. Maradona seemed worlds apart, but Velliniatis kept talking. Kept trying to convince him to come back to basketball. "It will give you a better quality of life," Velliniatis told him. "You should not be afraid of any consequences for abandoning the team again. Just come back."

Giannis did come back. Velliniatis wasn't sure if Giannis had read the book, but that didn't matter; he was back. Zivas saw Giannis's determination come back too. "He was all the time focused," Zivas says. "He was passionate."

So passionate that he kept trying to dunk. It wasn't enough that he had "dunked" at that national training camp. This time, he wanted to *dunk* dunk. Stuff it down with authority. He spent hours after every practice clutching the ball at the free throw line, trying to get his footwork down to accelerate to the rim. Again, he kept coming up short. Messing up his steps. Or softly tapping the ball in. But he kept trying, and eventually, he threw down a real dunk.

He was proud of himself. But he still struggled physically in terms of holding his ground. More often than not, opponents clobbered him. "He was really weak," says Gkikas, his Filathlitikos teammate and close friend. "That was his main problem. He was there to fight. But it was like a hundred kilos versus sixty kilos. So from the beginning, it was a very difficult fight for him. But he never gave up."

Once, Filathlitikos was playing against Panathinaikos's U-18 team, a rivalry game for the two clubs, especially since Panathinaikos had a player named Vasilis Charalampopoulos, who was considered one of the most talented at his age and who now plays for Olympiacos. Giannis would often guard him, as well as another standout, Georgios Diamantakos, who stood almost seven feet tall.

One of those games, Diamantakos kept posting Giannis up, again and again. "Giannis was not so strong," says Diamantakos, who now plays for Apollon Patras. But offensively, Giannis was grabbing the rebound, even doing Eurosteps, which would come to be his signature move years later. "We couldn't reach him. It was like he was dancing," Diamantakos says.

Still, Diamantakos had his way with him. That made Giannis more determined, and he started fighting back. Started blocking shots. "That was his talent," Diamantakos says. "That's what we were afraid of: his long arms. When he jumped? That was it."

Giannis had a passion for defense. Genuinely enjoyed it, while other players groaned at having to bend low, having to sprint back. But defense was something Giannis could always control; he could always control how hard he played. How much he cared.

And he started to care a whole lot more than he had when he first started playing. Back when he didn't want to be caught anywhere *near* a basketball court. After the team would finish a 9:00 a.m. practice, everyone would go home, rest, eat, and return at 5:00 p.m. for a second training session. They'd come back to the court and see the same thing every time: "Giannis haven't left the court," says Saloustros, the Filathlitikos teammate and close friend.

That rubbed off on other players. "He was working so hard—and made me work hard," says Kamperidis, Giannis's other Filathlitikos teammate and close friend, who now plays for the Greek club Larisa.

Giannis started to get closer to his teammates. They realized he was loyal, smart. Kind, hardworking. Really funny. Goofy. "Sometimes he would make really bad jokes," Saloustros says, laughing. "We love him because his soul is a little kid." Meaning he was genuine. Didn't care about looking cool. "He makes you laugh because he's adorable," Saloustros says. "You cannot say anything to him back, like 'Come on, Giannis—stop it,' but he will make you laugh again some other way."

They were surprised by how polite Giannis was. When addressing his teammates or speaking of them in conversation, Giannis would preface their names with "Mister"—Mr. Christos, Mr. Nikos. They'd tell him to stop since they were all the same age. There was no need for such formalities. But Giannis insisted. It was a sign of respect. Which is why he also spoke in the plural to them, another Greek sign of respect usually reserved for elders.

Giannis often did things he wasn't asked to, like mopping the court after practice. He saw that the court was dirty, dusty, and he'd find the mop and push it across the surface of the entire floor, up and back, up and back. He didn't do it in front of his teammates. Didn't do it in front of his coaches. They accidentally found him mopping one day and were stunned.

Giannis didn't want credit. He just wanted to show his team that he cared for them. Because they were looking out for not just him but his entire family.

It took him time to open up to his teammates. To trust them. Giannis didn't ordinarily trust people outside his family. He was a Black migrant in a majority-white country. Police often patrolled, stopping immigrants. So he learned from a young age to keep things to himself. Keep quiet. Just in case. "He trusts maybe five to ten people, even now," Gkikas says. "Some things build your character that you cannot get rid of as time goes by." But "Giannis is not shy," Veronica says, smiling. It takes her son time to figure out who is worthy of confiding in.

Gkikas sensed that Giannis began to really trust him about a year into their friendship, when he'd give Kostas and Alex money, maybe five euros, to go to the Sepolia market to buy a yogurt, souvlaki, or a piece of fruit. Whatever they wanted. Gkikas would ask the younger two brothers to get him a Gatorade even though he didn't need one. He just wanted to use the Gatorade as an excuse to get them to the market so that they could buy food for themselves.

But Kostas and Alex took the trip to the market very seriously. They insisted on bringing back the change to Gkikas each time. They also made sure to bring him back the receipt, though Gkikas never asked for one. Kostas and Alex didn't want Gkikas to think that they were taking advantage of him. "I just gave them money and said, 'It's yours,'" Gkikas says. "They were proud guys. They'd never accept this."

Gkikas didn't care about their pride. He kept giving them whatever he had. He just didn't want to see them go home from practice hungry. Especially little Alex. It tugged at Gkikas, seeing the look in Alex's eyes when Alex would watch him eat.

And Gkikas himself was not loaded with money. None of the teammates were. "We weren't any rich guys," Gkikas says. But he, along with Saloustros, Kamperidis, and other teammates and their families, would try to help as much as possible. They'd give the brothers their old Nike shoes or shirts or jerseys. "We understood their situation. We saw the brothers had the potential to become something great, but they were lacking the money to do it, so we were providing them with whatever we could so they could have a more decent lifestyle," Gkikas says.

Saloustros's mother would sneak Giannis an extra banana or Gatorade before practice. "We were sharing everything that we have," Saloustros says. "There was so much people looking out for him, not because everybody expected that he will become this that he is now, but because of his character and of him just being *Giannis*."

Kamperidis's mother would make Giannis rice, which he loved, and pasta, with small cookies for dessert. Another favorite was *soutzoukakia*, a Greek baked-meatball dish. He and Kamperidis grew closer because they had similar personalities: both quiet, both grinders. Giannis began to confide in him about his family, about his fears. "We love each other," Kamperidis says.

The team didn't help Giannis because they wanted something in return. "We are family," Gkikas says. "He's a human being; he needs something, and we're going to give it to him. We did it from the bottom of our hearts. Nothing but love.

"I speak for my teammates and I," Gkikas continues. "Even if Giannis hadn't made it to the NBA, we'd do it again."

When the team won games, they'd all go out to eat at a souvlaki tavern in Zografou and have souvlaki and gyros. Giannis loved the pita gyros koble with tzatziki, tomato, onions, and pork. He usually had two of them with Coke.

But as much as his teammates and their families tried to help, it was never enough. Giannis would almost always give the food or money to his parents, his brothers. They were all still barely scraping by.

* * *

One afternoon, a kid named Rahman Rana walked into the Zografou gym. Velliniatis had found Rana, whose family is from Pakistan, on the street in a way similar to how he'd found Giannis. Velliniatis thought Rana had potential, given that he was six feet tall, and asked him if he'd be interested in playing for Filathlitikos. Rana thought he might as well give it a try.

For some reason, though, Giannis and Rana *hated* each other that first practice. And the next couple of weeks of practice after that. They'd go at each other on the court, trash-talk each other. Rana knew Giannis was way better than him, which irritated him even more. But once they started talking, getting to know each other, along with another teammate, Andrian Nkwònia, who was Black, the trio became inseparable. They called themselves brothers.

Rana and Giannis began to bond over shared experiences of racism.

Rana remembers Giannis being called "Blackie." And that some told him, "Go back to your country."

Rana was called "Paki." Some told him, "You smell like garlic. You smell like shit." "Go back to your country." "Go eat some curry."

Rana would hear about schoolmates making fun of Giannis for selling with his mom in the streets. "People really treated him badly," Rana says.

"We were treated as second-class citizens. We were outsiders in society, so we bonded."

Rana was poor too. Like Giannis, he oftentimes came to practice hungry. Rana's father had had a stroke at forty and couldn't get a pension. His family was making about ten dollars a day. They had to portion out a small amount of food, just as Giannis's family did, to last the duration of the day. Maybe a plate of rice. Sometimes his family sacrificed food to pay for electricity. Once Giannis saw that Rana's situation was just like his, he felt like he could trust Rana. Open up to him.

It would be a full year before Giannis told Rana about Francis, his brother still living in Nigeria. One day, it just came out. "You know, Thanasis isn't the oldest," Giannis told him. "We have a brother named Francis. He's in Nigeria still." Giannis wouldn't talk about him much, wouldn't explain further. Rana surmised that Francis was staying with Giannis's grandparents for financial reasons but could never be sure.

As they became closer, Rana invited Giannis over to his home, and Rana's mom would share some spaghetti with salsa. But when Rana visited Giannis's family's apartment, he was shocked. He thought his own situation was difficult, but Giannis's was worse. Rana saw two old, broken sofas, provided by the church as charity.

"Let me show you my room," Giannis told him. It was an empty room: just a sheet, a blanket, a bed, and his basketball medals. Giannis looked around at the bare walls, the empty space. Told Rana his dream was to have a TV one day and a chair to put on one side of the room. He'd buy a bunch of books too.

And yet Veronica always found a way to fix a plate for Rana. Even if that meant she wouldn't have any for herself. That was the way Giannis was with Rana too.

"Are you hungry?" Giannis would ask him before practice, splitting the croissant he'd scrounged around for. "Eat—we have practice soon."

"He was such a nice person," Rana says. "It was too much sacrificing. He was always making sure we were all OK and not starving like him."

When the two weren't at practice, they'd take long walks around Sepolia. They'd talk about their dreams, if they could run away and live different lives. Giannis often said he wanted to play in Greek's highest division, A1, or play for another team in EuroLeague. He wanted to emulate his favorite player, Greek legend Dimitris Diamantidis, who was a crafty, left-handed, pass-first playmaker and who is now the general manager of Panathinaikos.

"Basketball was the only way Giannis could forget about everything happening in his life," Rana says. "He told me when he plays, the problems are gone. And he's happy.

"Basketball gave him a reason for living," Rana says.

During their downtime, Giannis, Rana, and Nkwònia would explore the city, trying to take their minds off things. They hung out near the Acropolis. They once climbed Mount Lycabettus, the highest point in Athens, at about nine hundred feet above sea level. It was beautiful, peering out over the pine trees. The trio felt a sense of teamwork, having made it to the top. There, they caught a glimpse of another life, a richer life: the nineteenth-century Chapel of Saint George, a large amphitheater where famous musicians played, including Ray Charles, Bob Dylan, and B.B. King.

The trio took a photo together: baby-faced Giannis in a light blue polo throwing up a peace sign; Rana mean-mug smirking in a navy shirt; Nkwònia in a gray tee giving a serious look, eyes wide, pointing at the camera. They were trying to look cool, but deep down, "we were so happy," Rana says.

When Giannis was outside, with his friends, or on the court, he didn't have to pretend that things were OK like he did at home. Smile when his parents asked him how he was. Tell the landlords who came knocking, "We'll pay you later! We're just waiting to get paid! We promise!" For a moment, he could forget about everything they were going through. Forget that oftentimes he wouldn't eat his first meal of the day until 11:00 p.m.

So he kept distracting himself, making sure he was always on the move. Another place they went after morning practices was Public, a technology store in Syntagma Square, the central square of Athens. The place was upscale, beautifully designed, with tables outside shielded by orange awnings. When Giannis and Rana walked in, they felt rich. *Nice.* Like they belonged somewhere that fancy. Nobody questioned them, asked why they were there.

The store had an Xbox that they could play for free, for two, three hours. They'd play FIFA, their favorite, wishing they had an Xbox at home. But for those few hours, Public *was* home.

They'd go anywhere to avoid being home.

"He couldn't stay in the house because he was really depressed," Rana says. So Giannis and Rana would stay out late after practice and find a place to sit. Rana could tell that his friend was hurting, though he kept a lot of it inside. Until he couldn't anymore. Giannis would finally allow his guard to come down and burst into tears.

"I look at my mother," Giannis would tell Rana in between sobs. "I see how she is. I see how hard she's trying to get things for us, and I'm helpless. I cannot do anything. I feel destroyed."

Sometimes Thanasis would show up, finding the two on a bench, making sure they were OK. Safe. Thanasis would rub Giannis's back, try to soothe him. "Don't cry. Don't shed tears for anyone," Thanasis would say. "We will make it."

* * *

Unnoticed, Giannis had started to sprout, to become a little taller, a little more coordinated. He had developed excellent court vision, watching EuroLeague games, soaking in the technical part of the game. He was still skinny, but he knew how to outsmart opponents. Plus, his arms were so long, his hands so big, he could always snatch the ball and *go*. He was so fluid dribbling the ball up court.

He showed enough potential to be allowed to practice with the men's team while still competing with the junior team. Tselios Konstantinos, who had left the team for a period of time, came back to find a completely different Giannis. Giannis was now playing thirty minutes a game.

"Giannis? Giannis, this small guy?" Konstantinos said to Zivas, walking into the gym on his first day back.

"Yeah, Giannis," Zivas said, smiling. "He's *something*."

Konstantinos couldn't believe it. "I went to practice, and I saw him, and he was really, really tall. I said, 'What the fuck? What happened?'"

Some possessions, Giannis would do something spectacular: block a shot with his left hand, leap up court quicker than guards half his size. "He was really, really tall, and I think that moment, we all knew he would play," Kordas says.

Giannis would try to guard the best player in practice. And this time, *he* was having his way with guys. *He* was dictating the tempo. *He* was driving the ball to the basket strong. "Everybody was surprised," Saloustros says.

Giannis had worked and worked. And he was becoming more and more versatile. One day he'd be guarding the point guard; the next day he'd be guarding the center. He became a matchup problem. Teams tried to put peskier, smaller guards on him to disrupt him on the break or bigger bodies on him in the post to knock him around. But he held his ground more than he had in the past.

"We didn't even pay attention to him in the beginning," says Trigas, the Panathinaikos U-18 assistant coach, "but then everything in the scouting report had to do with him."

Giannis started to gain some confidence. One day, Saloustros remembers Giannis telling him, "I'm going to get better. I'm going to be the best." He meant it not in an arrogant way but in a determined, focused way. "He never stopped working," Saloustros says.

At one point, Giannis, Rana, and Nkwònia were supposed to attend a party. They were excited to meet some girls. The plan was to go after practice, but after practice ended, Giannis wanted to keep shooting. Rana asked why he wasn't coming to the party as he'd agreed to.

"When I play basketball, when I'm here," Giannis told him, "practicing these moves, dunking, shooting, this is my girlfriend. I forget about girls. I forget about everything. I just don't want to go."

"We thought he was weird," Rana says. "But Giannis stayed for the next men's practice even after his own workout."

Alex started to notice the shift in the way people talked about his big brother. "Giannis is amazing," strangers would say to him as he'd be shooting around on the outside courts. Alex would laugh to himself. He has known that since he was little. To him, Giannis was practically a Greek *god.* "Me and Giannis were best friends," Alex says. "It doesn't get much closer than us."

Strangers began to compliment Alex on his own game. But Alex didn't feel any more validated. Giannis had already told him that he was worthy since he had picked up a ball. Giannis was always encouraging his brothers, always teaching them. "We never really waited for somebody to tell us that we really have potential," Alex says. "We all knew what each other could do because we compete with each other every day."

They didn't know much about how good anyone else was, though, outside Greece. Giannis didn't know much about American players at first. The NBA was some distant, abstract concept they had no way of knowing about. "We didn't have internet," Kostas says. "We couldn't watch NBA games."

They didn't know the names of any teams or players until people began to come up to them on the courts, telling them they reminded them of certain NBA players. Even legends. "You're long like Julius Erving, Dr. J," they'd say to Giannis. The brothers would nod, smile, say thank you, but then they'd look at each other, confused, no one wanting to say out loud what they were all thinking: *Who's Dr. J?*

After everyone left, they'd go find an internet café, somehow scramble together three euros to connect to the wireless internet for two hours, and search Dr. J. They'd watch highlights of him on YouTube. Soon, they started to find highlights of other players too, especially Allen Iverson.

Giannis fell in love with Iverson. His crossovers, his passion. His intensity. The way he'd weave his smaller frame in and out of the paint. The way he'd dance with a defender, crossing the ball back and forth. "Kostas!" Giannis would say. "Look at AI! Look at what he's doing! Man, nobody can guard this guy!"

Kostas became obsessed with Iverson too. "We would go and just watch AI highlights every day," Kostas says, laughing. "*Every* day. He was so small, and that's what made us be like, 'Yo, this guy is so small, and he still gets buckets? Nobody can stop him.'"

But they didn't want to just *play* like Iverson. They wanted to *look* like him too. One day, they came home and asked Veronica, "Mom, can you

braid our hair like Allen Iverson? He plays for the Philadelphia 76ers."
Veronica laughed. Giannis and Kostas didn't flinch. They were absolutely
serious. And so, after a long day's work, she braided their hair into cornrows.

The more two-hour slots they could afford at the internet cafés, the
more players they discovered. And they were mesmerized, finding LeBron
James, watching him blend different positions, his athleticism allowing
him to muscle through defenders to the basket.

Finding Kobe Bryant and Kevin Durant changed everything for
Giannis, though. He wanted to be as creative as Kobe, as hardworking
as Kobe; as versatile as Durant, as long as Durant. He began to idolize
Durant especially, who was just budding into a star for the Oklahoma City
Thunder. Giannis would study him every day after attending classes at
53rd High School in Sepolia.

He'd practice Durant's moves, especially dribble crossover pull-ups.
"He'd do it at practice and call out [Durant's] name," says Kamperidis,
who would often watch highlights with him.

Then Giannis had a chance to see his hero in person. Durant visited
Athens for a Nike event at the Mall Athens in August 2010. Two basketball courts were set up. A DJ blasted 50 Cent and Ne-Yo's "Baby by Me"
and Jim Jones's "We Fly High" as Greek kids huddled around the courts,
awed by Durant shooting threes. Giannis and his Filathlitikos teammates
were in the crowd watching. Giannis was thrilled seeing Durant up close
as Durant went around the court to high-five fans.

Then, a few hours later, Giannis went to Zografou for practice. Right
before training began, Giannis walked up to Coach Melas, looking excited.
Almost giddy. Like he was about to burst. "Coach!" Giannis told Melas.
"I'm going to become a new Durant. An NBA player. I will have my own
signature shoe."

But he knew he had a ways to go. He wasn't strong enough yet. He
wasn't talented enough yet. He believed he *could* be good one day. That's
why after the team had traveled to Crete for a road game and finished
practicing, everyone left the court except Giannis.

The team bus was pulling away when they noticed Giannis wasn't there.
Then they realized: he was still on the court, trying to master a move.

He returned to the bus covered in sweat. They made him go shower, but Giannis didn't care about showering. He just needed to get back on that court to master that move.

* * *

Giannis began to notice the way Rana hesitated during practice. He'd pass up a shot, play timidly. "I see potential in you. I see talent in you," Giannis told him one day. "But you're afraid to show it."

The coaches weren't as impressed with Rana. They thought he was a nice kid but didn't have much of a future in basketball. Rana always seemed to be afraid of everything. "I didn't believe in myself," Rana says. Yet Giannis continued to ask the coaches to put Rana in the game more. He really believed in his friend.

"You're a great player, but you don't enjoy the game," Giannis told Rana. "If you don't enjoy it, you can't be successful. Play it because you love it."

Rana was surprised. *Why does Giannis sound so much older than he is?* he thought. That's when Rana wanted to be like Giannis. He saw the ease with which Giannis talked to girls. Rana was the opposite: shy and anxious. His legs would even wobble. He felt like he was the ugliest boy in Athens. Giannis could read his friend's moods, knowing when he was spiraling into self-loathing.

"Have you looked at yourself!" Giannis told him one day. "Bro, you're more attractive than me!"

Rana shook his head. "No, I'm not, bro."

"Look at you! You have good hair. Let's go. Let's go and talk to this girl. You will see: no one thinks you're ugly."

So Giannis went up to a couple of girls, with Rana by his side, and said to them, "Isn't this guy attractive?"

Giannis even helped Rana get over his fear of swimming. "You won't drown. I'm here for you," Giannis told him, taking his friend's hand and slowly bringing him into the water at Kavouri, a tranquil beach in Vouliagmeni, a prestigious seaside suburb south of Athens. Giannis wanted to show his friend that if he tried something new, he wouldn't fail. He might even have fun. "He was just always there for me," Rana says.

That's what Giannis did. Giannis recognized Rana was going hungry, as he often was. One day, Giannis took Rana to his church because they'd often have free meals downstairs for kids who couldn't afford them, plus games for kids to play. Rana protested at first. He wasn't sure if he would be allowed inside, since he's Muslim.

"Why? Just come!" Giannis said. "We won't go pray; we will just go get some food. I'll tell the priest you're a Christian, and you can get free souvlaki."

"OK. Fine," Rana said.

The two were downstairs in the church, playing Ping-Pong, when the priest walked up to them and said to Rana, "Hello. Where are you from, sir?"

Rana started to panic; his legs started to shake. He was trying to find the words but couldn't. Giannis jumped in. "Oh, he's from here! He's poor too! He's humble! He's a Christian! A *really* good Christian!"

Rana contemplated whether he should come clean and tell the priest the truth, but the priest kept nodding.

"OK," the priest said. "I'll go bring some souvlaki."

Giannis smiled, and the two boys waited until the priest was gone before they burst out laughing. "See, bro?" Giannis told Rana. "You gotta trust me."

* * *

Giannis and his family moved into a semibasement apartment in a non-descript tan stucco building at the intersection of 46 Christomanou and Dodonis, in the heart of Sepolia. The apartment had shuttered windows high on the wall near the apartment ceiling, peeking out above grade, with a perfect view of the sidewalk.

The landlord, Dimitrios Katifelis, mostly rented to Greek college students and immigrants who primarily came from African countries, as well as from Bulgaria and Albania.

Katifelis signed a lease with Charles and Veronica on July 29, 2009. The rent was €250 a month. A few months later, an Athens-based lawyer named Panos Prokos received a call from Katifelis saying that Charles was late in his rent payments.

Prokos recalls he sent Charles a letter in a strict lawyerly tone that he needed to honor his contractual obligations. In response, Veronica called Prokos and asked if she and Charles could stop by his office.

Veronica impressed Prokos with her composure. "Not that Charles was not serious—it's just that it was obvious that she was the family's matriarch," Prokos says.

Charles was friendly, polite—smiling, even—very much the backbone of the family, but it seemed clear to Prokos that Charles was grounded by Veronica. They asked Prokos to communicate to Katifelis that he needed to be patient, that they worked the street markets and, at the time, were not having much luck selling and therefore didn't have much income. Veronica told Prokos she had four boys to support, something Prokos and Katifelis hadn't known.

Prokos relayed the information back to Katifelis, and Katifelis agreed to wait until the family could gain some income that would enable them to pay the rent. But the wait was long—and painful—for everyone involved: they struggled to pay rent or paid late until September 2010, when Katifelis had no choice but to call the family again. They owed part of June's rent, as well as July's, August's, and September's. Katifelis had unsuccessfully called several times, but the Antetokounmpos didn't pick up.

Prokos now issued a legal demand calling for Charles to fulfill his financial obligations. A couple of days later, Charles and Veronica came to see Prokos again. They again told him about their struggles to make ends meet. Prokos was empathetic—Charles and Veronica seemed like they were trying their hardest and wanted badly to get back on track with payments.

Veronica was working harder than ever. Sometimes she'd come home from working so tired, feeling so weak, but she would still wash her boys' socks that were soaked from practice because none of them had a spare pair. But she tried not to show them her fatigue; she wanted to be happy—or rather, she wanted her boys to remember her that way. She wanted them to develop happy memories, conscious of the way kids will remember hardships.

Months passed, and the family got back on track making their rent, albeit with great difficulty. Until another drought: September 2011, when they were three months past due in rent. Katifelis asked Prokos to send a second demand, and this time, Veronica brought Thanasis, nineteen, and Giannis, sixteen. Charles couldn't make it because he was working.

Prokos could tell the boys were athletes, but what impressed him was their positive attitude. How well they spoke Greek. How polite they were. "They were serious, disciplined, respectful kids," Prokos says. "They knew exactly what they wanted from life." Thanasis and Giannis told Prokos that they wanted to receive Greek citizenship; they went to a Greek school, and their friends were Greek. They felt Greek in every way. And they loved basketball.

They told Prokos how they helped the family sell. Thanasis told Prokos that he was fit enough to be able to run away from cops should they raid their permitless outdoor market on the sidewalks of Athens, because at times they sold in illegal outdoor markets. Giannis told Prokos the one thing he couldn't stand was having trouble falling asleep because of the constant rumbling of his empty stomach at night.

"I was really moved," Prokos says. "I saw two young men, obviously blessed by nature, mature, respectable, who deserved an opportunity."

Prokos allowed the family more time to make their payments. Allowed the family grace when few would extend that to them. But Prokos maintains his role was minimal. "I do not wish to make a big deal out of it," he says. "It was my very small gift to Giannis, who had moved me. It was so that his stomach stopped aching from hunger."

Katifelis was compelled to help for similar reasons. "We did what we could for them," Katifelis says. "We weren't rich; we didn't have lots of money. But they were good people," he says.

Katifelis and Prokos were not the only strangers who looked out for Giannis and his brothers. A Greek woman named Marietta Sgourdeou, a respected actress who often performed at Stathmos Theater in Athens, was someone the boys affectionately referred to as their "godmom."

She'd allow the boys to come to her home in Glyfada, a suburb of Athens by the sea, and she'd sometimes cook for them. Giannis's friends and teammates aren't sure how the boys met Sgourdeou but remember them going to her home often. She became close to the family. She introduced the boys to a world of music and literature, taking them to a concert by the famous composer Mikis Theodorakis, where they met Maria Hors. Hors was a legendary choreographer for the Olympic lighting ceremony. She performed at the very first televised Olympics in 1936.

Thanasis and Giannis were introduced to Greek culture, ancient drama. Books like *The Brothers Karamazov*, the 1880 novel by Russian Fyodor Dostoevsky. But Sgourdeou's kindness extended beyond the boys. When Giannis brought Rana to her house one time, she cooked a hot meal for him too, realizing that he was also in need. Neither boy had eaten all day.

"She was the nicest woman I've ever seen," Rana says. "She gave Giannis a lot of love. I was like, how is a white Greek woman a godmother of Giannis? How is that possible? Who would do this for us, especially people in the Black community? I couldn't believe it."

* * *

Giannis Tzikas, an older gray-haired man with black-rimmed glasses, used to see Giannis and his brothers walk down Dirrachiou Street, where Tzikas's café, Kivotos Café, was (and still is) located. It's a narrow street with midrise buildings, cafés, and shops, including clothing stores, electronics stores, hair salons, and bakeries. Kivotos sits at the sharp tree-clad corner where Dirrachiou and Dramas come together.

Tzikas noticed how the boys never traveled alone. They were always together. They were always cracking jokes, play-fighting in the street.

Tzikas could tell by their clothes they didn't have much. He became curious about them, especially after the brothers started saying "hello" and "good morning" and nodding to him as they passed by.

One day, Giannis took his brothers inside Kivotos, which means "ark" in Greek. It's a beautiful place, with a brown picket fence enclosing outdoor tables that sit under a white canopy, shielded from the Greek sun. Large picture windows surround the café, opening up to a dark-wood bar inside.

The walls inside are adorned with Greek national-team photos—so many that the white paint of the walls can hardly be seen. Four basketballs sit above a cabinet. Tzikas is a huge basketball fan.

"Do you guys play basketball?" Tzikas asked the boys that day.

They nodded. Alex was a giveaway, though: he was carrying a basketball at his hip. "The basketball was always bigger than him," says Tzikas, now sixty-six, as his daughter, Maria Drimpa, translates for him inside the café he has now owned for more than twenty years.

Now there are framed pictures of Giannis's NBA jerseys. His number 13 Greek national-team jersey. His 2018 NBA All-Star jersey. A black-and-white bust of Giannis's face sits above a row of liquor bottles. Nearby are more photos: Veronica smiling, sitting in a red car in 2015. Giannis wearing his white-and-blue "Hellas" Greek national-team shooting shirt and putting his arm around Tzikas in 2014. Giannis reaching to grab Tzikas's hand after a national-team game from 2018.

They are family now. But back then, Tzikas just saw four boys in need. As Tzikas got to know the boys better, he saw how polite they were. How they always said thank you. Tzikas gave the boys sandwiches, bananas, apples, and water. Sometimes he'd fix them fresh fruit juice or their favorite: a strawberry milkshake.

He was drawn to them because his own father came from a poor family. "I know how it is to be hungry," Tzikas says.

White Greeks began to notice how much Tzikas was helping the family. And they weren't happy about it. "Some people said to me, 'Why are you feeding the Black kids?'" Tzikas says.

He would hear people on the street say, as the boys walked by, "Look at these Black boys." Giannis would keep walking. Wouldn't talk about it. What was there to say? He was just trying to survive. He put a smile on his face as if he didn't hear it.

"There is a lot of racists," Tzikas says. "Racism made things difficult here." But Tzikas was different. "I didn't care about their color."

One day, the boys asked Tzikas if they could work at his café. They needed money. Things at home were getting worse. "We were at a *really* low point," Alex says. "As a family, our thing is, you gotta work for your stuff. And you gotta explore every option before you ask somebody. So if you ever see me or any of my family go ask somebody for something, that means we've done everything we possibly could to get that thing, but we just can't. We're *truly* in need. We don't just want that thing; we *need* it."

Tzikas told them no, they could not work there, but he'd help out with food if they went to practice more regularly. He told Giannis to practice hard. He saw a future in him. "You're going to be a basketball player," Tzikas told him.

Tzikas knew there wasn't much of an alternative. "If Giannis worked here, he would quit basketball," Tzikas says. "And I didn't want this."

They were thankful that Tzikas cared. He had no reason to, other than the goodness of his heart. "We were blessed to be around someone like that," Alex says. "To this day, he says to us, 'Man, I wish I could have helped out more.'"

One memory makes Tzikas smile.

One day, Tzikas's wife, Katerina Drimpa, told Giannis to come and take a picture inside the café. "When you grow up," she said, "you will be a big basketball player, and you will forget us."

Giannis just stared at her, blankly, almost hurt at the possibility.

"No," he said. "Wherever I go, I will never forget you."

* * *

Giannis continued to frequent internet cafés, watching videos of NBA highlights with voice-overs of motivational speeches about not making excuses, about working hard, such as "Inch by Inch." Highlights of NBA superstars flashed across the screen, and Giannis was in awe.

Dwyane Wade driving to the hoop.

"Inch by inch, play by play, till we're finished," the voice of Tony D'Amato, Al Pacino's character in *Any Given Sunday*, said. "We're in hell right now, gentlemen. Believe me. We can stay here, get the shit kicked out of us, or we can fight our way back."

Kobe Bryant closing his eyes before a game . . . Kevin Garnett pounding his chest.

"Life's this game of inches; the margin of error is so small that you won't quite make it."

Then he'd watch another video, called "Don't Stop Until You Succeed." There were Durant and LeBron, running on treadmills while carrying medicine balls.

"When you want to succeed as bad as you want to breathe, then you'll be successful."

Giannis started to let himself dream. Really *dream*. He *had* to transform himself into the players on that screen. He didn't know much about who they were, but he knew he wanted to be them. Run faster than them. Out-play them. Be *there*. In America.

The NBA was no longer some abstract concept. It became everything to him. All he thought about, besides helping his family. Once, Saloustros remembers, while Giannis was watching NBA highlights, Giannis pointed to a Chicago Bulls uniform and told his friend, "You see that jersey?"

"Yeah," Saloustros said.

"One day, I'm going to be wearing one of those jerseys in the NBA."

On another occasion, Giannis pointed to the Greek national-team uniform, telling Saloustros, "You see that jersey? I will wear it. This jersey will read 'Antetokounmpo' on the back of it."

Saloustros laughs remembering this. This confidence brewing in his friend. It wasn't loud; it wasn't cocky. It was a quiet assuredness. And it often came out during practice, when Giannis would compliment the shoes of his teammates, especially when the new Kobes came out. "Nice shoes," Giannis would tell his teammates. Then Giannis would whisper to Saloustros, "I'm going to have many of these one day. Don't worry. Trust me."

Around this time, NBA player Josh Smith came to Greece, and Giannis saw him and asked for an autograph. He saw how huge Smith was up close. He knew he couldn't compete with him. Not yet, at least.

Then Kobe came to Greece. There was so much buzz around his arrival. Giannis was with Velliniatis at the time, looking through Kobe's highlights. His up-fakes. His baseline jumpers. His turnaround fadeaways.

"How much money does Kobe make?" Giannis asked Velliniatis.

"Maybe around twenty-five million a year," Velliniatis said.

Giannis thought of how much he and his family were struggling. *I gotta make it to the NBA. I gotta try to make as much money as Kobe made.* But deep down, he didn't know if he would make it.

*   *   *

When Giannis started dreaming, his brothers started dreaming. It was like Giannis coming up with the vision gave them permission to let their minds wander. Let wishes, *wants*, come in. Alex and Kostas began to demand more out of each other. They saw how disappointed Giannis would be in himself when he lost games. How Giannis would ask Melas, the assistant coach, for his statistics after the game and ask how he could perform better. The next day, they'd watch the game and discuss how he could improve his defense, his shot blocking.

"Giannis was always defending the best player of the opponent," Melas says. "He didn't like sitting on the bench. He was always asking for more playing time. He would get vocal, almost coaching sometimes."

That competitiveness rubbed off on his brothers. They became hungry as well. They all started waking up early and watching the NBA games. Giannis told them it was *their* dream—not just his dream. It would be Thanasis's dream. Kostas's dream. Alex's dream.

If he could make it, they all would make it. Charles told Giannis and Thanasis that often: "Take care of your brothers. Whatever you do, take care of your brothers." The boys took in every word Charles said. Would feel pride on the occasions he wasn't working and could come to their games. He'd cheer them on so enthusiastically, especially little Alex, when he'd yell, "Go, Alex, go!"

Charles was surprised Alex started taking basketball as seriously as his older brothers. He was so young, and his body looked nothing like his brothers'. But when Alex told his father he was really trying to be good at basketball, he gave him a nod of approval. "Give it all you've got!" Charles told him.

The boys would look at other kids funny when they told them that they just played for fun. "We'd be like, 'Oh, OK, that's cool. We play basketball for fun too, but we play basketball for much, much bigger reasons,'" Alex says.

We just need more time—his mother's words always in his head.

Watching Giannis evolve, garner more attention, Alex saw potential and pain in that orange leather ball. That ball could be the difference between a good day and a bad day, between having and not having. Some nights, everything they dreamed of doing with that ball seemed just out of reach.

Giannis wouldn't accept that conclusion. He pushed all of them in drills—especially Alex. That was when he started telling Alex that one day he could be better than him. Alex didn't dare question his brother. But Alex just looked at Giannis's body, then back at his own, and thought, *How?*

At the same time, Alex's head swelled as his skills improved. Alex started thinking he was really good just because he was bigger than the other kids. Giannis wouldn't tolerate that. Though just a teenager, Giannis had a determination to lift his family from one continent to another—that could not be shaken. So he would not allow his youngest brother to become complacent.

One day, Giannis told Alex that there are a lot more players in the world, in other countries, in America, who are good at basketball. Who are *great* at basketball. Better than him. Better than any of them.

"There's so much more out there," Giannis said. "You have to keep working."

Sometimes, in the summer, Giannis would stay in the gym all day. "He could stay ten hours," Gkikas says. Everyone else would leave. Giannis might not have had anything to eat. He might not have had bus money. Sometimes it was just too late at night. But he'd complete his team's practice, then the men's team practice, then work out in the gym by himself. Shoot, shoot, shoot.

He'd stay past dinner, partially because his home was several bus rides away. He would rather stay. Stay with the nets, the cones. The leather ball. *Keep working, keep working*, he could hear his father urging.

When his arms were numb, too tired to keep shooting, he'd find his customary spot on a beat-up blue mattress, where players would stretch, just behind the basket, and curl up. No blanket, no pillow. He didn't need anything. Shutting his eyes, he'd doze off, fall asleep, dreaming of something better.

* * *

The day before Christmas, migrant children and teens often participated in *kalanta*, where they'd travel to upscale areas in Athens and sing Christmas carols in shops, in people's houses, wherever anyone would give them money.

Giannis told Rana, "I'm going to buy my family a TV and a PlayStation," two things he had wanted. He went with his brothers Kostas and Alex, while Rana and Nkwònia went together. The two groups wanted to see who could bring home the most money.

But Giannis's group got a head start because Giannis insisted on singing at 6:00 a.m. He went all day until 5:00 p.m. He didn't eat anything the entire time. Didn't stop and rest for a second. He would not be deterred.

Giannis managed to pocket €800 and buy the TV and PlayStation. Veronica was so proud of her son. Charles was too. Every time Charles clicked on the TV, he felt a burst of pride that they owned this device. They could watch whatever they wanted, whenever they wanted. Then he'd beam at his son. His son who understood the true meaning of hard work.

CHAPTER 3

STATELESS

"Go home, monkeys!" Filathlitikos had traveled to Crete, about 245 miles away from Athens, for a road game when Giannis was about sixteen. Local fans were hostile to all Filathlitikos players, but especially to Giannis and Thanasis.

It was painful. Unrelenting. Fans threw soda cans, bottles of water, and even coins onto the court. After the game, Giannis and Thanasis cried. "They were just shattered," Rana says. "It was the saddest day, just seeing how racist people are. We were working hard to be accepted in this society, and people were just rejecting us."

Rana saw the way Giannis ignored it, pretended as if he didn't hear it. But often Giannis couldn't do that, like the day he sang Christmas carols to buy his family a TV. Giannis went into a coffee shop to sing, and the owner shooed him out with a broom, as if Giannis's mere presence in the shop was toxic. And if that wasn't humiliating enough, the owner said, "We don't want your kind here. You shouldn't be singing Greek Christmas carols."

People often assumed Giannis was older than he was because he was so tall and lanky. Sometimes that allowed him entry to dance clubs with Thanasis. Rana remembers Giannis telling him about one such night when Giannis and Thanasis were hanging out, talking to a few girls, when a white man approached Giannis and said, "Look at this Black kid!"

They exchanged a few words, and within minutes, the man and Giannis ended up outside tussling. The man shouted, "I hope you go back to your country with your monkey people!"

Thanasis rushed outside, spotting Giannis on the ground, the man practically choking him. Thanasis flew over, tore the man off his brother, and then punched him out.

He would do anything for his brother.

*   *   *

Though these incidents took a toll, the brothers *were* embraced by many neighbors, friends, and schoolmates. Though they were the only Black kids at their school, 53rd High School in Sepolia, they'd gather with kids and parents from the school every Sunday, and Veronica remembered feeling that her family felt loved.

Giannis's teammates treated him well also. "We treat him like he was one of us," Gkikas says. And he was. They spoke the same language. Went to the same church. Jogged on the same sidewalks. Rode the same buses—the Red Line metro, third stop at the end for Sepolia. "Giannis is more Greek than the Greeks," says veteran player Nikos Zisis, Giannis's former Greek national-team teammate whose nickname is "The Lord of the Rings." He currently plays for AEK Athens. "Giannis loves this country."

But not everyone treated them so well.

"We were treated like every other immigrant," Alex says, "which is: not very great." Alex began to notice the way some people said hi to them and some didn't. Didn't even *look* at them. Recognize them. "The way they just looked at us as if we were lesser," Alex says. "Our neighborhood did a great job to not make us feel like racism is a problem," says Alex, given that their neighborhood was filled with migrants, "but that doesn't mean that every neighborhood did."

The brothers knew they couldn't walk alone in certain areas at night. Even together, they were still a target. Still a threat to the white vigilantes who sometimes roamed the streets looking for migrants to terrorize. Black and brown kids, especially. Kids who looked like the brothers.

The Golden Dawn, a racist, violent Neo-Nazi Greek party, would chase, rob, and even murder migrants, especially those from South Asia, Africa, and the Middle East. They'd target diverse neighborhoods like Sepolia, nearby Kypseli, and Agios Panteleimonas.

Golden Dawn's goal was intimidation, sometimes by throwing rocks or beating people with clubs. They believed all immigrants should be deported immediately. They'd even beat up whites who didn't look fully Greek, such as Albanians. Police would often look the other way.

Golden Dawn members would shout, "Foreigners, out of Greece! Greece is for Greeks! Blood, Honour, Golden Dawn!"

In the middle of Saint Panteleimon Square, a plaza in front of Saint Panteleimon Church, about a ten-minute walk from where the Antetokounmpos lived, was a message written on the ground that read, "We will clean this square." Golden Dawn wanted to cleanse the country of Black and brown immigrants and anyone else who was not a fully white Greek. Their slogan was "Rid the land of filth." They didn't see Black people as Greek or even as human.

The Antetokounmpos were aware of them, which is why they tried not to walk the streets at night. But sometimes, after a long practice, they couldn't help it, even if they knew it was unsafe. "It was a little scary," Kostas says. "It was something you had in the back of your mind, like when you're walking by yourself late at night, you gotta be careful. You just *know*. You could sense it."

So they kept their eyes straight, shoulders back. Heads on a swivel. Alert. Always alert. They weren't afraid to leave their home—they felt safe and loved and respected by many of their peers—but there was always this threat. Always this fear. "They tried to put fear in people," Kostas says.

Nikolaos Michaloliakos, a twenty-two-year-old Greek man, founded Golden Dawn in 1980. His father, Georgios Michaloliakos, was a member of a security force called Tagmata Asfalias, which was armed by the Nazis. He was also an officer of the Greek Gendarmerie, which was a kind of provincial police.

The young Michaloliakos grew up in a subculture that praised the hanging of Communists. He began building bombs at twenty, leaving them to detonate in cinemas where Soviet films were played, according to Konstantinos Georgousis, Greek filmmaker of the 2012 documentary *The Cleaners*, about Golden Dawn.

Michaloliakos had served thirteen months in jail in 1979 before starting Golden Dawn, which sympathized with the military dictatorship that governed Greece from 1967 to 1974. Golden Dawn had swastikas on the cover of its magazine. It praised Hitler and white supremacists.

The group registered as a political party by 1993 but still hovered around the fringes of Greek politics. It barely made a dent in the national-election vote as late as 2009, getting just 0.3 percent of the vote that year; Syriza, a leftist party, won 4.6 percent of the vote. But things were changing. Greece, like many countries in Europe, was turning to the right. Golden Dawn became more visible the following year, in 2010, when Michaloliakos was elected to Athens City Council. He was seen on camera doing the Nazi salute. When asked if he believed that the Holocaust happened, he said, "I think all history is written by the winners."

Golden Dawn began calling itself the party of "nationalists," refraining from outwardly praising Nazi ideology in order to appear more palatable politically. But it was clearly motivated by Nazism. At the group's rallies, members sang "Horst-Wessel-Lied," a Nazi anthem banned in Germany. They sold *Mein Kampf* at their official headquarters. They had a symbol resembling a swastika on their flag. They incited arson attacks on mosques and synagogues while calling themselves the "party of order."

"What many Greeks got wrong was that they thought Golden Dawn was just an extreme group, that they were not really violent," says Georgousis, the filmmaker. "Violence was the main part. You cannot be Golden Dawn and not be violent. It's like saying you can be a basketball player and not be playing basketball."

Georgousis embedded with Golden Dawn, observing them during the summer leading up to the 2012 elections, when Golden Dawn gained an astounding eighteen seats of the three-hundred-seat parliament, coming in third with about 7 percent of the vote.

At that time, unemployment stood at a whopping 25 percent, and over 50 percent for young people. The government allowed supermarkets to sell expired food at discounted prices; the price of home heating oil had tripled since 2009. Golden Dawn blamed Greece's economic troubles on Jews and migrants, calling them "parasites."

"The financial crisis will be solved once we get rid of three million immigrants. These parasites drink our water, eat our food, and breathe our Greek air," said Alekos Plomaritis, a Golden Dawn candidate running for office in 2012. "They are primitive, miasmas, and subhuman. . . . We will turn them into soap.

"We will make lamps from their skin," he added.

Tensions were exacerbated by the evolving migrant crisis, as Greece was a popular entry point both for asylum seekers and those planning on moving to northern and western Europe. Golden Dawn's views became more accepted in working-class areas like Kos, which, like Sepolia, was filled with refugees. A fifty-year-old Greek woman living there at the time told the *New York Times* that immigrants were "filthy." "Soon enough, the Greeks will become a minority in our own land," the woman said.

Georgousis captured footage of party leaders saying, "[Immigrants] will hear Golden Dawn, and they will tremble with fear." Georgousis recorded Golden Dawn members intimidating Bangladeshi voters, tearing up their ballots, taunting Afghani immigrants on the street in neighborhoods close to where Giannis grew up and calling them "baboons."

As Golden Dawn won 7 percent of parliament that year, Georgousis filmed supporters cheering on a dark night as Michaloliakos stood on a balcony and exclaimed that they were fighting "for a Greece that belongs to Greeks!" He grew louder: "Next time it will be seventeen percent, twenty-seven percent, and one day we will govern the whole country!"

Immigrants made up only about 10 percent of the country's population in 2012, according to the Migration Policy Institute. But they were constantly targeted. One afternoon, about fifty Golden Dawn members on motorbikes, armed with heavy wooden poles, stormed the city of Nikaia, one of the Golden Dawn's biggest strongholds. Flashing shields that resembled swastikas, they screamed at immigrant business owners, "You're the cause of Greece's problems. You have seven days to close, or we'll burn your shop—and we'll burn you," Mohammed Irfan, a legal Pakistani immigrant who owned a hair salon in the city, recalled to the *New York Times*.

In another instance, forty Golden Dawn members, led by Giorgos Germenis, marched through the town of Rafina at nighttime, ordering "dark-skinned merchants" to show permits, according to the *Times*. Such incidents were not uncommon, as a Human Rights Watch report at the time noted, warning that xenophobic violence had become an "alarming phenomenon" in parts of Greece.

Favor Ukpebor, a young Black Greek basketball player, who knew the Antetokounmpos (he was friends with Alex, his sisters were friends with Giannis, and his mom sold shoes alongside Veronica at outdoor markets), saw Golden Dawn up close. Ukpebor remembers Golden Dawn marching through his neighborhood in Kypseli many times, shouting, "Blood, Honour, Golden Dawn! Greece is for Greeks!"

Ukpebor's mother, a migrant from Nigeria, was scared for him to go outside because she heard that Golden Dawn was murdering migrants. "I was really scared too," Ukpebor says. He was almost always the only Black player on his teams and was bullied at school for his skin color. He felt lucky, though, that he wasn't attacked by Golden Dawn. A Golden Dawn member, however, tried to attack his sister on a public bus. She was seventeen. Fortunately, the bus driver intervened and helped her escape, but it was terrifying.

Giannis tried not to let the fear of night consume him after a long day of practice. But he saw Golden Dawn a few times. And sometimes the fear was too close to shake.

* * *

Gkikas, one of Giannis's close friends, is hesitant to share Giannis's stories. "If I tell you the real story, there will be problems," Gkikas says. "Let's just say it was not a friendly city for these guys." Meaning Giannis and his brothers. Black people.

"Giannis has buried it deep inside," Gkikas says, "because he loves Greece."

Because telling those stories could generate backlash. Challenge the truth that some Greeks deny: Greece can love Giannis deeply and still treat people who look like Giannis terribly. Acknowledging that Golden Dawn was not a mere fringe group and that racism and antimigrant sentiment existed then and still exist today would mean accepting an uncomfortable reality.

"In every country, there are racists. That's for sure. But here in Greece, there are very few. Very, very few," says Kostas Missas, who would later coach Giannis on Greece's U-20 national team in 2013. "So no problem with that."

That seems to be a common refrain within Greek basketball circles: "No problem with race."

"We don't have a big problem [with racism] in Greece," says Kostas Kotsis, the Greek Basketball Federation general manager. "Giannis never complained. He never said anything about it. We are very proud of Giannis. All Greek people are proud of Giannis. With Giannis, we can hope that everything is possible. Giannis is our hero."

Back then, he wasn't considered a hero. Gkikas remembers Giannis telling him about a time when he was walking with his family and a car stopped in front of them, impeding their path. They all froze but then immediately started running. "Because most of those guys [Golden Dawn]," Gkikas says, "would go out and hunt them down."

Gkikas thinks of what Giannis would think recounting that story. "He would laugh. Even then he would laugh," Gkikas says. "Everybody else would have been scared like crazy or say, 'What the fuck am I doing here?' But Giannis would say, 'Fuck them.' If he was scared, he would never have come from Sepolia to Zografou. He was risking his life every time."

But another time, Giannis was walking back from practice and saw Golden Dawn sympathizers just in the distance, protesting, shouting. He bolted toward another route, running home safely. "Christos, I'm really afraid of them because if they see me on the road, what will happen?" Saloustros remembers Giannis telling him. "He was anxious about it . . . thinking that maybe one time if he finds himself alone, and if he goes by these guys, he was a little bit afraid."

Saloustros was careful not to ask Giannis too many questions. He wanted Giannis to feel comfortable. Accepted. Because he was. His teammates didn't discriminate against him. "Every teammate respect him," Konstantinos says. The only name anyone was called on Filathlitikos was *loukoumás*, which means "doughnut"—a name Coach Melas called any player he was arguing with, in a sweet way, so as to soften the criticism.

"I didn't want to remind him of the problems," Saloustros says. "I wanted him to have his mind on basketball and to be happy."

But Saloustros couldn't change the way some people viewed Giannis. "There are many Greek people that are afraid of Black people," says Yannis Psarakis, a Greek sports journalist. "Many people are afraid of being in touch with Black people or to go out with Black people, and this is for many decades in Greece. This is not something that happened now or ten years ago. This is very, very common for many Greek people."

There were only so many Black kids in Sepolia playing organized basketball. And like Giannis, those players could feel isolated at times. "It wasn't something usual—you know what I mean?" says Fotios Katsikaris, Giannis's former national-team coach. "For sure it was a little bit uncomfortable sometimes for those kids. How will the community and society accept them?"

Other Black Greeks could relate, especially those who migrated in the 1980s or earlier, before the Antetokounmpos. Nikos Deji Odubitan, founder of Generation 2.0 for Rights, Equality & Diversity, a group that advocates for legal protection and citizenship for second-generation migrants in Greece, grew up in Kypseli in the 1980s in one of the few Black African families around.

Like Giannis, Odubitan was also born and raised in Athens by Nigerian immigrant parents. Odubitan was actually one of Velliniatis's first players. Odubitan felt accepted—until he became a teenager. Until he discovered what discrimination felt like. He was stopped by the police and asked for his papers. "Just being Black and with my friends," Odubitan says. "This is when I started realizing that I'm different."

He hadn't even known what that phrase meant: "Show me your papers." He was confused, thinking about the phrase, sitting in the police car. He spent the night at the police station until his parents picked him up in the morning. "I was kept there until they proved that I am not a young criminal," Odubitan says. "This was very common. It happened to all young kids of Black backgrounds."

His own experience being detained by the police changed things for him. Made him realize that he was born in a country that did not recognize him. "I was raised stateless," Odubitan says. After graduating high school, he would be detained five more times.

Odubitan was someone who could understand what might happen to Giannis.

"Greeks, we have a problem with race, to be honest," says Stavrou, the Greek sports journalist. "Giannis never said anything. He just focused on playing the best basketball he could."

What else could the teenager do? What else could he say? He was trying to survive. Gain acceptance, climb the ladder of a Greek basketball system that was made up primarily of players who did not look like him. Managers, coaches, who did not look like him. Some of whom denied the experiences of people who looked like him.

Giannis was proud to be both Greek and African. He dreamed of carrying the Greek flag, which he would finally get to do a few years later, in 2013, on March 25, when Greece celebrates its independence. Filathlitikos was looking for a player to carry the flag. Giannis volunteered, smiled brightly when he asked his coaches if he could do it.

"My opinion is that he wanted to prove that he felt Greek as much as the other white Greeks," says Melas, the Filathlitikos assistant coach. Wearing his team's red jacket, with black pants and white-and-black Nikes, Giannis walked in front of his teammates, all a foot shorter, clutching the staff of the Greek white-and-blue flag with both hands. The flag whirled in the wind as Giannis looked ahead, proudly, back straight, and marched.

Giannis didn't know that there was one person who idolized him watching from the crowd: Emmanuel Godwin, seven years younger, who was also born in Athens to Nigerian parents, who was also trying to get by without citizenship papers. Godwin had just started to play basketball. His mother also sold clothes to survive.

Godwin proudly watched Giannis carry the flag. And then he heard whispers in the crowd: "Wow. Why is this Black guy there? Why don't we have a white kid hold the flag?"

Godwin wasn't surprised. He was used to the stares, the racist comments, often hurled at himself. Once, when he was sitting on a train, a ticket attendant told him he should leave the country. He remembers white Greek girls clutching their purses tighter when he walked by on the streets. "You see it every day," Godwin says. "It still happens. You might sit on the train and somebody will just stand because he doesn't want to sit with a Black guy."

So even though Giannis was starting to gain attention for his basketball skills, Godwin wasn't surprised to hear Giannis faced the same treatment he had. "Giannis was treated like the way they treat all Black people here. If you're not famous, if you're not a famous Black dude, it's just tragic. They'd be like, 'Why is this Black dude here? Why is he breathing the same air as me? Oh, this guy is Black; he's going to stain my chair.'"

Godwin went to nearly every game Giannis played back then. He'd just sit in the stands, marveling at how someone who looked like him had a chance to make it out of this gym, this city.

"I was always watching him," Godwin says. "He doesn't know that he was my motivation."

Godwin's older brothers were friends with Giannis and Thanasis, so Godwin got to tag along to the workouts. He and Alex became teammates, playing for Zivas and the younger Filathlitikos team. All the boys would hang out after practice, playing pickup games before resuming training. Thanasis and Giannis would insist on giving Godwin the rice they had even though it was their only meal for the day. "They had one rule: even though we don't have, we have to share," Godwin says.

Even Charles was kind to Godwin, once telling him, "If you love something, keep doing it. Keep working at it."

"[Charles's] work ethic—he tried to give it to me," Godwin says, "even though I wasn't his child."

One day, Godwin mustered up the courage to say to Giannis, "I'm going to reach you one day." He really wanted to tell Giannis that he was his inspiration, but this was all he could manage.

"Just keep grinding," Giannis replied.

With Giannis's encouragement, Godwin practiced harder. Giannis could understand him in a way that others couldn't, not just because he was Black but because he was undocumented.

"It was a period of, like, fifteen years that we didn't have any rights," says Afolayan, the Nigerian Greek rapper who goes by MC Yinka, who played for Velliniatis. Afolayan was once detained by police for eight hours. He eventually got an ID that allowed him to travel, but it took years. "It was a marathon to go through for your papers," Afolayan says.

White nonimmigrant Greeks didn't have to live with the gnawing fear that Afolayan, Godwin, Giannis, and every other child of Black migrants did: at any moment, their parents could be deported.

*   *   *

As a child, Giannis feared that one day he would wake up and his parents would not be there. Police may have stopped them. Taken them. Deported them.

When Giannis was a teen, if he came home from school and his mom was late, his mind would run wild with possibilities, running through every awful scenario as if it had already happened. He'd think, *Is this the day my mom, my dad, is going to get deported?*

Giannis wasn't worried about *himself* getting deported, because he didn't actually have a passport. Not a Nigerian passport, not a Greek passport. *He* couldn't get deported, because on paper, he didn't belong anywhere.

It was terrifying, contemplating *what if.* He'd cling tighter to his brothers, but they had similar nightmares too. What to do in the aftermath: How would they know where their parents were? How would they take care of themselves? Who would they call? Where would they go? The anxiety would seize them.

Anytime he and Rana were walking down the street and they'd see a policeman, Giannis's sweet, goofy disposition would vanish. He'd grab Rana, also undocumented and fully aware of the perils of being a person of color in Greece, and say, "Let's go! Let's go! We have to go! Police will stop us! Police will beat us up! Are you crazy!" Giannis would make them completely change course, no matter how much it delayed their trip, Rana recalls. All it would take was one encounter for him or his parents to devastate their lives.

Giannis and his brothers were lucky in that they had friends. But it was much harder for their parents to make friends. They always had to be cautious of where they were, what they were doing, who they were with. They couldn't trust a lot of people, because they were illegal immigrants. Giannis was aware that people could call the cops and say, "Come get them." A neighbor could tell the cops that their home was making too much noise, the cops would show up and ask for their papers, and that would be the end.

His family did get stopped by police a few times. When that happened, Veronica would say she left her papers at home. The cops always took pity on her and let her go. Giannis felt God was with his family.

The boys learned they were stateless at a young age, watching their friends receive IDs and passports. As kids, Giannis and his brothers would ask their parents, "Why don't we have passports? Why don't we have IDs? Why can't we travel as our friends do?" They couldn't understand what was happening.

Charles and Veronica tried to not show worry. "They were the best at making you feel like there was never anything wrong," Alex says.

They instilled a sense of Nigerian identity in their boys as well. Not just by cooking fufu and other favorite Nigerian dishes but in their manner of dress. Veronica loves fashion, loves braiding her hair in black and white, and often wore her favorite outfit—a white traditional Akwa-Ocha dress of the Ubulu-Uku people of the Delta State, Nigeria.

But not having papers started to affect Giannis on the court.

Once, Filathlitikos had to travel for a game to Thessaloniki, a port city on the Thermaic Gulf of the Aegean Sea. They would have to fly. Giannis was excited for the chance to travel for games but in the end couldn't go because he didn't have an ID or passport. The team had a practice that morning, and before leaving for the airport, Saloustros told him, "I'm sorry. Next Saturday, you're going to play again. Don't worry about it."

But Giannis was devastated. Saloustros kept telling him that it was OK, he would get to play again in a week, but Giannis couldn't be consoled. He started crying. Saloustros embraced him, assured him that this would not harm his chances of playing professionally. "You're going to play a lot of games in your career. It's just one game."

It wasn't just one game to Giannis. Not knowing what else to do, he grabbed a ball and started dribbling, started shooting, as his teammates left for the airport. Giannis stayed on the court for almost two straight days. Tried to outshoot his pain.

But he wasn't the only one. Etinosa Erevbenagie, a Black Greek basketball player and friend of Giannis's back then, also struggled with not having papers. He migrated to Greece from Nigeria with his parents when he was nine. Like Giannis, he dreamed of playing A1 Division basketball in Greece.

He and Giannis played against each other, as Erevbenagie played for Panathinaikos's youth team. Erevbenagie, one year younger than Giannis, was explosive on the court. He had court vision, intelligence. Erevbenagie didn't have Giannis's length—he stood about six feet even—but he was skilled and had a passion for the game. "Basketball gave me an identity in a white man's world, which is Europe," Erevbenagie says.

He considered himself African Greek, fully immersed in both cultures, but it wasn't long until he started being treated differently than his white Greek peers. When he was thirteen, during a game, parents started shouting racist things from the stands. He didn't quite understand what they were saying at first. But he remembers the feeling. The pain, the humiliation. "The feeling that I was being attacked for arbitrary reasons, which is the base for racism," Erevbenagie says. "It was really hurtful."

His coach told him to not worry about it, that those parents would be watching him play ball somewhere prestigious one day. But not having papers made it difficult as Erevbenagie began to pursue that dream. At the time, he and Giannis faced similar obstacles: they had talent and determination but didn't have opportunity. Their parents worked seemingly every hour of the day, but it didn't seem enough to pay the bills.

Erevbenagie thought Giannis was talented. "He had this tenacity and aggressiveness," Erevbenagie says. "Like, 'I'm gonna bully you. I'm not gonna back down from anything.'" They started to feel a sense of kinship playing pickup ball outside. The two had mutual Black Greek friends, which brought them closer. "All Africans of our generation, in Athens, we knew each other," Erevbenagie says.

Every time something happened during pickup—a funny moment, a loose ball, an argument over a foul—the two somehow would catch eyes and make a face or communicate in Nigerian Pidgin, an English-based Creole language commonly used in Nigeria. For example, "How are you?" would be "How you dey?" in Pidgin.

It had a specific purpose for Erevbenagie and Giannis: "So white people wouldn't understand what we were saying," Erevbenagie says. Given that there weren't many Black Greeks in Greek organized basketball, finding another Nigerian Greek basketball player like Giannis who could communicate in Pidgin made Erevbenagie feel seen. Understood. "I could relax a little bit," he says. "These words were spoken from the heart."

Especially when the two would say the phrase "See yourself" to each other during games. Anytime one found himself in a funny, awkward situation, the other would say it, which meant "Look at what you did—are you happy?" The more they hung out, the more Erevbenagie realized that Giannis would do things that reminded him of Nigerian mannerisms or behaviors. "It was like, 'Oh, don't get it twisted; we are both Nigerian *and* Greek.'"

Communicating in Pidgin with Giannis made Erevbenagie feel connected to his own African heritage, something he didn't always feel while constantly navigating white spaces. "Like it or not, I am cut from my roots," Erevbenagie says. "Having that reminder of home, of that language, it was special."

*   *   *

Zivas was a coach who was compassionate, welcoming, to immigrants. "He was a guy that loved minorities," Gkikas says. "If it was other teams, they would have kicked them out." Gkikas remembers Thanasis telling him about a coach. "[The coach] said that he was a monkey, that he would never make it. 'You are not for basketball; go play something else.'

"They were not interested in building up some Black guy they know whose background is bad," Gkikas says, referring to the family's financial situation. "Nobody would invest so much time as Zivas did."

Zivas let Giannis be a playmaker, and that wasn't an easy sacrifice. The team would lose some games while Giannis adjusted, but Zivas was focused on Giannis's development and not necessarily wins or losses. That allowed Giannis to make mistakes, to learn.

Zivas wouldn't give up on Giannis. He understood what Giannis's family was enduring. The fear they carried with them. He continued to ask Giannis before every practice, "Did you eat today?"

"In every other team, Giannis would have quit basketball because the coaches would have told him, 'Come on, man—why you skip practice? Because they were hunting you with rocks?'" Gkikas says, referring to Golden Dawn.

Sofoklis Schortsanitis, a legendary Greek basketball player, nurtured Giannis too. Known as "Baby Shaq" or "Big Sofo" for short, Schortsanitis was born in Cameroon to a Greek stepfather and a Cameroonian mother. The family moved to Kavala, Greece. Schortsanitis eventually sprouted to six feet ten, 345 pounds, and played for the Greek national team, helping Greece capture a silver medal at the 2006 FIBA World Championship and a bronze medal at EuroBasket 2009.

He was a member of the historic Greek team that stunned the star-studded USA team of LeBron James, Carmelo Anthony, and Dwyane Wade in the 2006 FIBA World Championship semifinals. It was an embarrassing loss for the US, whose coach, Mike Krzyzewski of Duke, couldn't even refer to the Greek players by name afterward, using only their numbers, claiming he didn't want to disrespect anyone by mispronouncing names.

Giannis and his family watched that game. Giannis was eleven, mesmerized by this player who looked like him. Baby Shaq. Giannis was surprised. *A Black guy was part of that! We can do it!* And to beat *America*? Sofo gave Giannis hope. Maybe he, too, could be a professional athlete and represent Greece.

Sofo had met Thanasis after returning to Athens after his first year playing with Maccabi Tel Aviv. Thanasis asked Sofo to help him practice, and given that Sofo dislikes working out alone, he obliged. Later, Thanasis asked if he could bring Giannis. Sofo was shocked when he first saw Giannis; the kid was so focused he looked almost sullen.

Sofo had also played for Olympiacos, one of Greece's most storied A1 teams. Playing in A2, Giannis wanted to be like Sofo and jump to A1. "Sofo was like a god to Giannis," says Stefanos Dedas, the Greek coach now coaching Hapoel Holon.

Sofo was different from many Greek players, not just because he was Black but because of his size. He was much heavier than his opponents and could post anyone up. Joining the national team was historic. "It was a big thing," says Fotios Katsikaris, Giannis's former Greek national-team coach.

Giannis and Sofo became friends. He encouraged Giannis to keep working. Giannis was in awe of how beloved Sofo was. "Sofo was a fan favorite," says Stefanos Triantafyllos, a former Greek basketball analyst who is now an assistant coach with Olympiacos. "Everyone loved him."

Well, not *everyone*.

"We don't think that Schortsanitis is Greek, according to the ideals of the Greek race," Elias Panagiotaros, Golden Dawn's public-relations representative, told the local Extra 1 channel in 2012.

The host responded, "Are you racists, or do you just fight illegal immigrants?"

"Believing that races are distinct is not a bad thing," Panagiotaros said.

"Forgive me, but this is the doctrine of the Aryan race."

"For God's sake. What do you want us to be? We shouldn't confuse Pekingese dogs with Labradors. God made them like this, and they should remain as they are. Being black, yellow, or red is their honor, but we don't regard them as Greeks. They are not Greeks."

Michaloliakos, Golden Dawn's leader, doubled down when asked about Sofo. "Greeks have never been Black." Soon, Michaloliakos would target Giannis too.

*   *   *

Stubborn. That's the only way Giannis's family and friends know how to describe the mentality Giannis was developing on the court. "It's a family trait," Alex says. Stubborn meant that Giannis wouldn't give up, even if he was losing badly. Even if he was still not physically capable. Stubborn meant that he believed himself equal to every person on the court.

What makes you more special than me? God made us both, he'd think to himself, remembering Thanasis's words: "Nobody is untouchable. The tallest towers in the world can still get torn down."

And he'd grind and grind, motivated by the belief that he was worthy. He'd tell his brothers that too. "If God made us the same, therefore we're equal. The only thing that truly makes me better than you is my mindset. If my mindset is a constant point of stubbornness, then you can't really beat me."

"What's the best part about Giannis? Stubborn," Alex says. "What's the worst quality about him? Stubborn." Giannis had that same tunnel vision as a child. "It was, like, cute stubborn," Alex says. If the boys were playing a game and they'd get to the final round, Giannis would *have* to be the winner, or they'd have to start over.

His teammates started noticing: Giannis was no longer a punching bag. A beanpole. Now he would push back when pushed. Sometimes he'd throw the *first* punch.

Around that time, Giannis was playing one-on-one with Nikos Pappas, one of the best players in the area, who'd later become a star for Panathinaikos and now plays for Stelmet Zielona Góra. "I bet you're not going to score," Pappas said before the game.

Giannis responded, "No, that's not happening."

Well, it did. Pappas destroyed Giannis. It was *ugly*. But Giannis was so stubborn he wanted to keep playing and playing until he got a point. He never did. Pappas won 33–0. It was humiliating for Giannis, struggling in front of all his friends. "He was crying after the game," says George Kouvaris, a Greek sports journalist for Gazzetta.gr.

In another instance, Giannis was facing a player who was about fifty pounds heavier than him. The guy was torching him. Giannis started crying because he was losing, but he battled and battled. "Giannis almost started a fight because he couldn't accept that he could be beaten like this," Gkikas says.

Gkikas took Giannis to the side. "Come on, bro. Don't lose yourself in this situation, OK?" Gkikas told him. "Don't let this take you down. Don't be crazy like this. You cannot act like this."

"You are right," Giannis said. "This was my fault."

Giannis calmed down. Took a few breaths. Wiped his eyes. But it wouldn't be the last time he wanted so badly to succeed that he cried.

Crying wasn't weird or out of the ordinary. That was just how passionate Giannis was. How frustrated at himself he'd get for his inability to master a move or a dunk, and he'd do it again and again and again until it was perfect. Sometimes he felt like he wasn't measuring up to the player he wanted to be. "He's been hard on himself since he was a kid," Alex says.

He would cry after many games too. He would ask Zivas for the stat sheet, and if he saw too few rebounds, too many missed shots, and *especially* if his team lost, he'd retreat to the corner and shed a few tears.

* * *

One day, Giannis was absent from class. An afternoon philology course at 53rd High School, a public school in Sepolia. The classroom building was a three-story courtyard structure with a clear view of the adjacent basketball court.

His teacher, Alexandros Mistilioglou, surveyed the room looking for him. Then he realized there was probably only one place Giannis could be. Mistilioglou looked outside, and there was Giannis, alone, shooting in the sun. The other students started shouting for him to come inside.

"What to do here if he comes?" Mistilioglou said to his students. "Maybe this ball will save him one day and he will achieve something."

In letters, he will not find a solution, Mistilioglou thought. *In basketball, maybe.*

Mistilioglou had Giannis as a student in his second and third years of high school. He thought Giannis was prudent, mature. Humble. Kind. He never complained, always smiled. But he didn't seem to apply himself much as a student.

Mistilioglou could sense that Giannis's family had financial issues. He knew that was part of why Giannis was missing class. One afternoon, Giannis came to the school and stole candy from the office, sneaking as many pieces as he could. Mistilioglou saw but didn't say anything. He could tell that Giannis's mind was always somewhere else.

"Surely poverty prevented him from being a good student because he did not even have the basics to live," Mistilioglou says.

Giannis was reserved. So reserved he was hard to read. He hardly said a word, but he was popular. "The other children loved him," Mistilioglou says. "The teachers loved him."

They always had, even as a child in grade school years before, at 62nd Elementary School, a two-story modernist stucco structure with deeply recessed white windows.

Afrodite Pandi, the assistant principal of 62nd, remembered Giannis and his brothers as being modest, shy, focused on sports. Respected and well liked, never causing trouble. Ioanna Zacharopoulou, an instructor of language, math, history, and environmental studies who taught Giannis in the fourth grade at 62nd, remembered Giannis as being ambitious.

"Giannis is very Greek," says Basileios Motsakos, who taught mathematics at the high school. But in some ways, he didn't fit in. Giannis's high school physics teacher, Vlasis Drakoulakis, used to make Giannis show the length of his hands by placing his fingers next to a protractor. Giannis's nails would extend over. Students would laugh and laugh at the sight.

It wasn't his fault he was long limbed. Different. But sometimes that stung.

* * *

In some ways, Giannis's life was improving: Filathlitikos helped him and his family move to Zografou so they could be closer to the gym. Many locals were helping him, making sure he had some food. Giannis started to believe a different life was within reach. That if he worked hard enough, if he had a little bit of luck, he could make it.

But he couldn't relax. He couldn't let anyone see weakness in him. He would teach his brothers that what separates players, what separates people, is the ability to recognize when the mind relaxes. "It's human nature," Giannis would tell his brothers. But the mind has to return to "killer mode," as he calls it, as soon as possible.

Giannis told them they needed to be stubborn. He would think of his parents while working out. Think of the food he would share with his brothers. Think of how Veronica would plead with Charles to eat. "Charles, you gotta eat also," she'd say. But he'd shake his head. "No, let my kids eat first."

Giannis didn't want to let him down.

"Giannis was one hundred percent focused," Saloustros says. "He thought, *Even if I'm going to be chased by Golden Dawn, even if I will be hungry, even if I don't have shoes to wear, I'm going to be the best*."

Veronica needed him to be. She had some health issues, partially because of the cold and damp in their home. Giannis, now about seventeen, was scared. Charles made sure the family was OK, but Giannis tended to his brothers even more, making sure they were on time for school and practice.

Veronica went to the hospital to get checked out, and although visitors weren't allowed to stay overnight, Giannis hid in the bathroom until everyone left, then came out and slept on a chair outside her room. He wasn't going to leave her.

He was growing ever more determined. He told his parents he was going to make it in basketball to make sure they had a better life. Make sure that Veronica didn't have to walk on eggshells, afraid of being stopped by police. Afraid to make friends.

"I'm going to make it for *you*," Giannis told her, "so you can be better and enjoy life more."

She struggled some days while recovering. Little Alex would come near her bed and sing to her in his sweet voice. He'd gotten his singing voice from her, after all. He had enjoyed doing theater and plays in school, and if singing would make her feel better, at least for a few hours, he would do that.

"He made a song, and he was singing it for me," Veronica says, smiling. "Even how many years later, I remember this. I tell him, 'Alex, do you remember when you sing for me? When I was not feeling OK, when we were in Greece?' He knew Mommy was not feeling fine."

Giannis prayed that his mom would be OK. He started paying even closer attention to Alex, who was just starting to play basketball more regularly himself. Alex was chubby and slow at first. He once hit the side of the backboard on a corner three. They'd laugh at how he'd be out of breath after playing just a few minutes. "We used to make fun of him," Giannis says. "Everybody had a skinny frame, my dad and my mom and older brother, and Alex used to be chubby, and he used to be slow and couldn't keep up."

Sometimes little Alex struggled to hop over the gate to the court itself. It would be locked during summers, so the only way to play was to climb over. It was eleven feet high. Alex was terrified of heights but hopping over was a rite of passage. "When you was able to climb the gate on your own, that was a big thing for us," Kostas says.

Alex would struggle to climb over, time and time again. He'd cut his arm on the gate's wire, which more than once left him bloody and scarred. "You see this?" Alex says, pointing to his arm. "It's kinda faded away. It would skin me." He is still proud of those scars.

But back then, he was simply trying to not embarrass himself. Trying to let his brothers know that he wasn't weak, that he could handle whatever they asked him to do. So he'd climb the gate, day after day, failing to hop over on his own. His brothers had to help him. The day he finally climbed over by himself, he was so proud of himself. His brothers were proud too. "OK!" they screamed. "Alex, you coming!"

He was still a runt, though. Still a half step or two behind his brothers. But he had heart. A lot of heart. He'd dive on the floor. Pull shirts.

Foul if he couldn't catch someone on a fast break. He'd cry when he'd lose. Friends called him emotional, but he was just passionate, like his big brother Giannis. He had handles but couldn't shoot. He'd pull from the corner, swear the ball was going in, lean back like it was going in. *Clank.* The ball would ricochet off the top of the backboard.

He didn't stand much chance in the family's two-on-two games: Kostas and Alex versus Giannis and Thanasis. Alex wanted Thanasis on his team because at the time Thanasis was the strongest and most athletic. But those were the teams; those were the rules. Giannis and Thanasis would always win.

"Alex couldn't really hang," Kostas says, "but he was really competitive." And nervous. So nervous for his first game in Greece that he passed the ball off every time he caught it. Wouldn't even *look* at the basket. "Terrible," Alex says. "I tried to overdo it because I was so scared to mess up . . . because I knew I was going to be playing basketball for a long time."

Because of his brothers. Because he didn't want to disappoint them. Because he wanted to be them. Because even though the world didn't know about them yet, they were already famous in Alex's head. They were his heroes. His motivation, his measuring stick. He'd watch Thanasis hammer a thunderous dunk and wonder if he'd ever possess that kind of athleticism. He'd watch Giannis jab step with such force, such precision, and he'd question whether he'd ever attack with that kind of tenacity. He'd watch Kostas time a blocked shot so perfectly on a fast break and wonder if he'd ever be quick enough, smart enough, to defend like that.

But Alex was driven. Mesmerized by the way Kostas spun a ball on his index finger, eight-year-old Alex spun and spun, day after day, failing so many times his fingernail broke off one afternoon. He kept trying. Wouldn't stop until he could spin.

* * *

Giannis would need a passport to play for Olympiacos and Panathinaikos, Greece's two top teams, since they traveled all over Europe for Euro-League games. If either team signed him, it'd have to count him as a foreign player since he was not recognized as Greek. Foreign slots are usually reserved for talented, experienced players, as well as American players who might not quite be NBA caliber but who are elite nonetheless. Handing a foreign spot to someone as inexperienced as Giannis? "They didn't want to do that for a young kid," says Kostas Missas, Giannis's U-20 national-team coach.

Those spots are highly coveted given that both teams were usually in the hunt for a EuroLeague crown. Plus Giannis was still essentially unknown. His A2 games weren't televised. He wasn't seen as a standout. "Giannis was not much more than a nobody at that point in time," says Nikos Papadojannis, a Greek journalist who has covered basketball since 1987 and a current columnist at the Greek website Gazzetta.gr. He's covered Giannis and Thanasis for years.

"Don't for a second think that anyone in Greece thought Giannis would be a star, let alone immediately," Papadojannis says.

Trigas, the former Panathinaikos U-18 assistant coach, remembers the older squad having interest in Giannis. "The coach of Panathinaikos really liked him, but it wasn't easy, because of his papers problem," Trigas says.

A formal offer was never made. Even if Giannis *did* have papers, he wasn't necessarily good enough or strong enough to play in A1. "In Greece, we lack patience," Trigas says. "We need instant gratification. No matter how big a talent is, nobody would make patience."

Greek teams usually wait for a player to develop before allowing him to move up. "To invest, let's say, a young guy in a EuroLeague team, it's a very big risk for the team," says Kostas Kotsis, the Greek Basketball Federation general manager. "The first priority is to get the win, not to invest."

So Giannis stayed in A2. The level of play was poor. Players were thirty, thirty-five years old. Some would smoke cigarettes outside before games. Many were overweight, out of shape. "The level is not good at all," says Katsikaris, the former national-team coach.

Still, Giannis improved by playing in that league. Refs hardly called fouls, so players had to find more creative ways to score while getting pushed around. "They will beat you up," says Ioannis Papapetrou, a friend of Giannis and current captain of Panathinaikos. "For a kid that is young, to be able to play with thirty-year-old guys that are experienced, he needs to find a way to survive. I think that really helped Giannis realize he needed to get much stronger."

Few showed up for A2 games. But when the team traveled to road games outside Athens, that's when fans started to notice Giannis. And shout racist epithets at him. "When we go on the road, that's when there was a race problem," Zivas says. "The worst time was in Trikala."

*   *   *

Trikala B.C. wanted revenge after Filathlitikos had beaten them by 17 in the teams' first meeting earlier in the season. Trikala had every advantage: the club had more money; it was a bigger club.

Fans became rowdy during warm-ups, shouting insults, even spitting onto the court. Then Kamperidis heard remarks directed at Giannis. "People were saying racist things," Kamperidis says.

Giannis tried to act as if he didn't hear them and continued to warm up hard. Filathlitikos started the game off cold. Trikala took a big lead, and the crowd shouted louder. Then fans started making monkey noises. Louder and louder.

"It wasn't something new," Zivas says. "He was used to it."

Filathlitikos continued to play terribly, eventually losing by more than thirty points. Players were dejected, hardly said a word. Giannis didn't want to talk about it.

CHAPTER 4

FOUND

Kornél Dávid started hearing the name Giannis from local scouts in Europe around November 2012. Dávid, an NBA international scout, wasn't sure what to make of the chatter. Some whispers turn into conversations, but most remain whispers. Many prospects fizzle out. But it struck Dávid, then working for the Phoenix Suns, a bit odd that he was just now hearing about a prospect who was already seventeen.

Some prospects are identified as early as thirteen. Giannis had only *started* playing basketball regularly around that age. "His name came up later than usual," says Dávid, who ironically now serves as an international scout for the Bucks. "Guys are usually playing in youth tournaments or European championships for U-16 or U-18."

Dávid's own NBA playing career included stints with the Cavaliers, Raptors, Pistons, and Bulls. As the only Hungarian to play in the NBA, he knew what it took to succeed in the league. But Giannis? Well, he seemed far away from competing at that level. *Really* far away.

Sometimes Giannis looked like a track star, ready to accelerate and leap up to the rim; other times he looked hesitant, lost, getting rid of the ball quickly, shying away from contact. But Dávid saw things he liked: Giannis's six-foot-nine frame, his athleticism, his basketball IQ.

Dávid couldn't understand why Giannis's opponents in the A2 Division looked like washed-up rec-league players with potbellies and stubbled chins. Why none of Filathlitikos's opponents could even touch the backboard, let alone hammer home with authority. And he wondered why Giannis wasn't playing on a bigger club in A1, like Olympiacos or Pana-thinaikos. "Later on," Dávid says, "I find out it is because he does not have citizenship. And he started late."

For the time being, though, Dávid was intrigued by the tall, lanky kid. He decided to come to Greece to see him in person. *You never know*, Dávid thought.

* * *

Dávid couldn't find the Zografou gym at first. It seemed tucked away, almost hidden. Finally, when he found it, he thought he was in the wrong place because it looked like a high school gym. Tiny, dinky. "*Dirty*," says Dávid, figuring the last paint job must have occurred ten years prior. "It was a terrible place." And it was uncomfortably warm, since there was no air-conditioning. The smell of sweat hung in the air.

Dávid sat down on the creaky stands and looked around. There weren't any fans, and the jerseys didn't have numbers and were all different col-ors, so Dávid wasn't even sure if he was watching a real game. Giannis's teammates looked much older than him, and Dávid saw a few smoking cigarettes outside before tip-off.

"The level of basketball was terrible," Dávid says. "I'd never seen a lower-level Greece league."

Dávid wasn't sure what to make of Giannis. On one play, Giannis whirled by on the fast break, finishing strong at the basket. Dávid noticed that he had incredible length but also that he was uncoordinated. He wasn't necessarily a shooter, though he did take some long-distance shots. Giannis made smart plays; he could dribble, snatch rebounds out of the air. But he wouldn't even attempt to go into the post because he was too frail. He'd get bumped and fall to the floor but always got right back up. Always sprinted back. He never seemed discouraged.

Despite the unevenness, Dávid was impressed. He returned to his hotel, writing in his notebook that night, "Raw talent. Length, athleticism, mobile for his size. Skinny but runs up and down well. Ball skills advanced for his age. Never tried to take over. Unselfish. This guy could be a Magic Johnson. Not sure why he is playing here. Why isn't he around better talent?"

A nobody in a nobody division in a nobody gym is the next *Magic Johnson*? Come on! Even Dávid knew the comparison seemed far-fetched. It *was* far-fetched. But the way Giannis dribbled the ball, towering over his opponents? "He was far away from being a legend," Dávid says, "but I thought this guy could become something."

Dávid was excited, especially since he hadn't seen other scouts at the game. "I was one of the first who tried to find out who he was," he says. Back then, in late winter 2012, Giannis wasn't on any American team's board for the upcoming June 2013 draft. It was as if Dávid had discovered a secret, and he had to protect it before anyone found out.

* * *

Thanasis had recently signed with Maroussi B.C. to play in the top Greek league. The club gave Thanasis a few pairs of free sneakers tucked into a couple of boxes. In one of the boxes was a pair of red-and-white Nike Kobe 4s. But when Thanasis brought them home to show Giannis—the pair Giannis had always coveted—Thanasis said he wasn't going to share them as he always had done.

Instead, Thanasis gave him one of the others, a clunky, ugly pair. Giannis accepted them but still wanted the Kobes. So when Thanasis slept or left the shoes unattended, Giannis would take them to practice, feeling like he was one step closer to his NBA dream. Thanasis was angry at him for taking the shoes; he loved them too and didn't want Giannis to scuff them up.

Charles intervened. "That's your younger brother," Charles said to Thanasis. "You've gotta share shoes with him. If he wants to wear them, he can wear them."

But the glory they all felt, wearing these magnificient shoes, was short-lived. Financial issues wiped out the team before Thanasis could play even a single game for it. Plus Thanasis didn't have citizenship papers, so he was ineligible to play in any event. Watching that sliver of hope dissolve was devastating. "That was the first little bit of success that we'd seen," Alex says. "It put us at the top, then knocked us down."

In the fall of 2012, Giannis first secured Greek agents to represent him: Georgios Dimitropoulos and Giorgos Panou. Panou, a former Greek national-team assistant coach who'd been part of the historic 2006 victory over the US, first represented Thanasis. Panou had been aware of Giannis, spotting him as a fourteen-year-old. He was impressed and asked around, "Who is this kid?"

Thanasis had eventually introduced Giannis and Panou in a downtown Athens hotel over burgers and fries. "You might be an NBA player next year," Panou told Giannis.

"The real NBA?" Giannis said. "The NBA I see on *TV*?"

Like others, as Panou grew closer to the family, he noticed that Giannis wasn't eating much and explained to him that he would need to start eating differently than his brothers and family if he were to have a future in basketball. Panou took him to a nutritionist for medical tests, and the doctor was shocked. Giannis's liver was suffering so much because of his eating habits that the doctor thought Panou had sent him a seventy-year-old who constantly drank.

Panou continued to believe in Giannis, later steering him to agent Alex Saratsis. The group began emailing NBA and EuroLeague scouts, sending Giannis's game footage, a compilation that ran nine minutes, forty-six seconds, writing, "I've got someone here. A secret. Nobody knows about him."

The agents also sent the tape to a few American college coaches, who were not very interested. That was fine: college wasn't really an option for Giannis since NCAA athletes aren't compensated.

Zaragoza, a Spanish team in northeastern Spain's Aragon region, was interested in Giannis. Willy Villar, then Zaragoza's sporting director, essentially the team's GM, exchanged emails with Giannis's agents around October 2012. Then he saw Giannis's game film. "It was very, very bad quality of video," Villar says. But the more he watched, the more he was intrigued. *There's something different about him*, Villar thought.

Maybe it was the way Giannis gobbled up the length of the floor in three dribbles and dunked. That it was so easy for him, natural for him, to cover that much space with so little effort. Villar hadn't ever seen the extraordinary potential that Giannis had for his age, seventeen, combined with his height, six feet nine.

Villar told the agents that he wanted to come to Athens to watch Giannis work out "as soon as possible." The agents explained to him that Giannis was undocumented, but Villar wasn't deterred.

Villar touched down in Zografou a week later. He and Giannis did low-post work, jump shots, and dribbling. Giannis dribbled around cones with skill and ease. Villar was surprised at how someone that tall could be that agile. "It was amazing. Never in my life had I seen this kind of player," says Villar, who is now the GM of Herbalife Gran Canaria, a club in Las Palmas, Spain.

But doubts started to creep in. Villar wondered whether this was some kind of joke; he thought Giannis might be one of those exhibition basketball players who does dribbling tricks and videos on the internet but doesn't know how to play five-on-five basketball. Villar wondered whether he really understood basketball, doubted whether he had control of his body. Maybe he was wrong about Giannis.

He changed his mind quickly once he saw Giannis play against Panathinaikos. Giannis racked up forty-four points and twelve rebounds, and Villar was astonished. His doubts were gone. Giannis played smart. In control. "He fight with great heart," Villar says, noticing how Giannis never ran out of energy. Villar just couldn't understand why nobody else had signed Giannis at that point.

"The feeling for me was, How is this possible I'm feeling this about this guy and nobody in the world thinks the same as me? Nobody in the world realizes the potential of this guy?" Villar says. "I've never seen a player at this age with this potential. With his hands, his body."

At the time, Dario Šarić, a Croatian player now with the Suns, was considered one of the top players in Europe. But Villar swore, after seeing Giannis against Panathinaikos, that Giannis was better than Šarić. As absurd as that sounded to Villar, he was convinced. "It is very strange to think this in this moment," Villar says. "For sure somebody would tell me, 'You are crazy.'"

Still, Villar tempered his expectations. As good as he thought Giannis could be, he didn't truly know what the future held. "I didn't know if he would become a great player. But I did know that he had great *potential* to be one. Believe me—two-time NBA MVP, difficult to imagine for sure."

All Villar knew at the time was that he had to sign Giannis to Zaragoza, especially after seeing how polite Giannis was after the workout. Villar visited the Antetokounmpos' apartment, and though Giannis was shy, not saying much, he said over and over, "Thank you very much. Thank you very much." His gratitude shined.

Villar and Giannis's agents went to dinner that night. "I explained to them that I want Adeto," says Villar, referring to the name he used for Giannis back then, short for his birth name, Adetokunbo, "for the rest of my life." It was October, and they made a handshake agreement that Giannis would sign with Zaragoza in December, once he turned eighteen. But . . . Giannis didn't have papers. "It was a big problem for sure," Villar says. "First, we needed to get the player; then, we would try to find a solution."

For now, Villar let himself enjoy the fact that he had landed the biggest steal in Europe. Giannis signed in December 2012, a deal worth $325,000 over three years, with a club option for a fourth season at another $325,000.

Giannis was both excited and nervous, telling Zivas the news. Zivas felt Giannis still had more options to consider. "There's no need to worry," Zivas told him. "Because you'll surely play in the NBA."

If an NBA team were to draft Giannis, they'd have to buy his rights from Zaragoza. But for the moment, Giannis was stunned that a team would give him an opportunity. He rushed to Kivotos Café to tell Tzikas.

"I'm so happy!" Giannis screamed. "I'm leaving! I'll be making more than three hundred thousand! They will give me a car! They will give me a house, and I will take my family with me!" Tzikas was so happy for him he nearly cried. Giannis didn't even have bus money that day, so the thought of $300,000-plus seemed like a fairy tale.

Later that day, Panou and Dimitropoulos told Giannis that if he did end up playing in Spain, he'd have to find a place to live by himself.

"Excuse me? What do you mean *I* have to go there? *We* will go," Giannis said, referring to his mom.

"You're a young guy," his agents said. "You'll have fun there. Why do you want to take your mother with you?"

Giannis started crying, tore up the contract. "I'm not going anywhere."

The agents were flabbergasted. They all climbed into Panou's Fiat. Veronica, in the back seat, was trying to soothe Giannis as he continued to cry. "Don't cry. Don't worry about it," she told him. "You're gonna help everybody. We know you want to help everybody. Don't worry about it; just play." But she was sad too, thinking of him leaving.

Giannis insisted he would not go without her. He said to Panou, "You think that now I've got money, I will forget my mother and my family? You must never forget that."

Panou apologized and said he was joking and to not worry about it. But Giannis couldn't help but worry. It didn't matter if his dream was within reach. Without his family, it meant nothing.

* * *

John Hammond, Bucks general manager at the time, was sitting in his office when Jeff Weltman, assistant GM, walked in.

"Hey, there's a young player in Greece that's getting a lot of attention," Weltman said. "I think it would definitely be worth the trip for us to go see him."

Hammond can't remember if it was Weltman or Dave Babcock, a.k.a. "Mr. Buck," the Bucks' longtime vice president of player personnel, who was the first to identify Giannis. Other staffers at the time remember Babcock as being the first, bringing Giannis's game tape back to the scouting department. Nonetheless, both men were instrumental in bringing Giannis into their field of vision.

Ross Geiger, a Bucks assistant video coordinator, was in charge of breaking down draft film that year. Geiger remembers meeting with Jonathan Givony, draft guru at DraftExpress; Hammond; Weltman; and Jon Nichols, then manager of basketball analytics, at a Chipotle in Milwaukee. Givony gave them discs containing four of Giannis's games. "Givony certainly expressed how intrigued he was when speaking on Giannis but didn't go overboard," Geiger says.

Givony conducted the first media interview of Giannis in June 2013. "My name is Giannis Antetokounmpo," a baby-faced Giannis said into the camera. Looking up the entire time as Givony asked him questions,

Giannis had a curious sparkle in his eyes. Dark brown and glittering, they hardly blinked. He seemed sure of each word, though his English was not great.

"What kind of basketball player are you?" Givony asked.

"I'm an all-around player," Giannis said. "I can jump; I can shoot; I can pass the ball. I can do everything on the court."

"What is your goal for your career?"

"I want to be an NBA player."

"What kind of player will you be in five years from now?"

"I'll be . . . I'll be . . ." Giannis said, thinking, pausing. "Much stronger. I'll be much better—in everything that I do on the court."

Though the Bucks had some game tape of Giannis, they didn't really have much. There weren't any advanced stats available or any track record of other prospects coming from Greek A2. "It was uncharted territory," says Cody Ross, former Bucks video coordinator. "He stuck out. He had this unique X factor. He was like a gazelle. That's what really captivated us."

But since Giannis's opponents were nowhere near NBA level, scouting him was difficult. "I had to project, and it was nearly impossible with him," says a former Bucks staffer now working for a different NBA team. "There were so many unknowns."

Still, the Bucks were impressed with what they *could* see, even if Giannis was occasionally crashing into three defenders or unable to physically hold his own. "You could see immediately that he had a great feel for the game," Hammond says. "He had that gift."

It wasn't love at first sight. It was *intrigue* at first sight. "We knew he was a huge risk," says the former Bucks staffer. "It *was* a swing." But the Bucks needed a swing. Hammond's (and the Bucks') philosophy was "We're the Milwaukee Bucks. We're not going to sign the next LeBron. Stars aren't going to try to come to Milwaukee. Every once in a while, we're just going to have to get lucky. And, at some point, we're going to have to take a swing at the draft."

But before Hammond could take any swings, he had to come to Greece to see the kid for himself.

* * *

Hammond arrived in Zografou on a quiet morning in March 2013. He saw a coach outside the gym on a scooter smoking a cigarette. Some windows were cracked. He entered the gym and thought Giannis looked even taller in person. Then he saw the kid's hands. They seemed freakishly long. Ten-inch-diameter long. Those hands allowed Giannis to control the ball like a floor general, whirl downcourt for layups.

Hammond took a seat. A local coach tapped him on the shoulder: "Look up—there's his family." Hammond craned his neck and saw Veronica, Charles, Kostas, and Alex cheering from the top of the stands. *My gosh, the whole family's here*, Hammond thought. "You could feel this amazing family connection," Hammond says. He found Zivas, Giannis's coach, and started asking about Giannis's family—where they lived, what they did for work.

Hammond started to brainstorm which NBA player Giannis could morph into. He thought of Kevin Garnett. *Could Giannis become that?* Strength-wise, intensity-wise? He didn't know. Truly didn't know. "It was hard to forecast his potential," Hammond says. He's conscious of the ways others have framed Giannis's story in the coming years as a fairy tale, describing Hammond as having had some kind of clairvoyant power to see that Giannis was MVP material. That wasn't the case at all. Not even close. "I'm not going to make myself sound better or smarter than I am and make the story more than it is," Hammond says.

Hammond wasn't the only NBA GM in the gym. Word had spread since scout Kornél Dávid had visited, as other scouts alerted other teams. Zivas remembers twenty-eight representatives from NBA teams showing up, many of them GMs: Danny Ainge, president of basketball operations for the Boston Celtics; Daryl Morey of the Houston Rockets; Danny Ferry of the Atlanta Hawks; Sam Presti of the Oklahoma City Thunder; and Masai Ujiri of the Denver Nuggets.

Filathlitikos didn't have room for all of them at first. The coaches brought out chairs but still didn't have enough; they had to go buy extra chairs. "You couldn't believe it—like, how is this possible?" says Asterios Kalivas, then an assistant coach for the Greek national team. "We have guys in the A1 Division, and nobody's coming to see them. It was *crazy*."

Giannis didn't believe his agents at first when they told him the guys watching him were truly NBA scouts. It was almost surreal.

"For Greek standards," Zivas says, "that was something extra special."

"It was something that I think will never happen again in Greece," Saloustros says.

"It was very unusual," says Kostas Kotsis, the Greek Basketball Federation general manager.

"This was the fucking *NBA*!" Gkikas says. "There were, like, twenty guys with clipboards. There's a guy with fancy glasses, and after the game finishes, this guy gets out of the court into a limousine that is, like, fucking ten meters. We are looking, like, 'What the fuck is this shit! What are we watching? It is like a movie. A movie!'" (Gkikas later found out he was a GM.)

Georgios Diamantakos, the former Panathinaikos player who was destroying Giannis on the block a few years back, was starstruck too. "It was a dream for me," Diamantakos says. "I thought, *I have to play good here, because if I block Giannis, maybe the scouts will see me also*."

Scouts came to see Giannis because he was athletic and his game fit more into American basketball than the more fundamentals-based Euro-League. If there's talent abroad, international NBA scouts will come to see a prospect—wherever he is. Even in a dinky Zografou gym where one backboard was missing a rim.

The scouts do their homework; they know talent when they see it. Word travels fast. "Hey, have you seen this kid?" turns into a plane ticket, even if that ticket might not lead to a draft pick. "A lot of times, it's the boy who cried wolf," says Bob Donewald Jr., former NBA assistant coach who has coached in Russia, Ukraine, and China and is now an assistant coach with Texas Tech.

But with Giannis, the decision makers weren't flying to Greece to try to discover something. The scouts had already identified him as talented, even if he was still largely a no-name. The question was, *How* good was he?

"Giannis was a mystery," says Fotios Katsikaris, the Greek national-team coach. "You cannot say he was a super, super talent. You cannot imagine the risk."

Adding to the risk? Giannis wasn't able to come to America and work out with prospective teams since he didn't have a passport. "It's not a common thing, drafting a guy out of nowhere. And he was a guy out of nowhere," Dávid says. "Not having citizenship, delayed passport, all of these circumstances kept him a secret. How can you evaluate a guy that cannot leave the country?"

*   *   *

After the workout, Giannis's agents drove Hammond around Athens. Sitting in the back seat, Hammond told them, "I don't know what's going to happen to this guy. But his life is about to change in a major way."

Alex could sense that too. *Finally*, Alex thought. He always knew Giannis was good, and now others were realizing it too. It was *really* happening. This was the opportunity they had all been praying for, working for. "Giannis was a kid. A kid nobody knew. But *I* knew him," Alex says. He smiles, remembering how the scouts would introduce themselves to him and his family.

Kostas remembers Hammond coming up to him and Alex and saying, "Hey, you guys are talented. Where are you from?" Kostas and Alex didn't speak much English then and didn't know what to say. Kostas managed, "We just play basketball." Kostas laughs remembering his gaffe—his nerves, his excitement. "I ain't got no answer for Hammond," Kostas says. "I remember just seeing these scouts in these little plastic chairs and thinking, *Who are all these American guys?*"

And Hammond seemed tickled with both of them. He watched Alex shoot at the little rim on the side. "Oh maaaan," Hammond said in his thick midwestern accent. "He's gonna be good!" General managers weren't allowed to talk to players, but Hammond whispered to Giannis when Giannis passed by his table to go to the bathroom or get some water, "You look good! You look good! Keep going!"

Giannis was a little nervous. Everything he wanted, everything he *needed*, hinged on his performance in these practices, these games. He tried to ignore the magnitude of the moment and just *play*. And once he started warming up, the nerves dissipated.

"He was focused," Kamperidis says. "He knew that everybody came to see him, but he was giving one hundred percent of himself every day." He told himself to have fun. Be present. Be himself. "He was not intimidated at all," Kostas says. "It's basketball at the end of the day."

Giannis was friendly, acknowledging the scouts with a nod and sometimes more. Eric Taylor, an assistant coach at Saint Francis University in Pennsylvania, who came to the gym to watch another player, remembers Giannis coming up to him and shaking his hand, looking him in the eye. "Nice to meet you," Giannis said to Taylor. "Thank you for being here."

Giannis was grateful that scouts came to see him but worried about what they thought of him. One game, Giannis didn't think he played well. Kostas came up to him in the locker room, seeing that Giannis was on the brink of tears. He looked angry too. "Why you mad?" Kostas said.

"Man, the scouts came from the NBA," Giannis said, "and I didn't play good."

"You scored thirty! You won the game!"

"No. *No.*"

Another time, Giannis scored twenty-one points and grabbed ten rebounds. He cried afterward, thinking of all the things he should have done better. "He knew what he was capable of," Alex says. "That's why he was upset at himself."

Giannis couldn't afford to slip. Relax. Not with everything he had dreamed of being so close. But when he would return to the court with Thanasis, the two of them shooting alone, after all the scouts had left the gym, he didn't have to perform. He could just have fun.

One of those times, Thanasis was practicing dunking when he told Giannis to stand above the circle. Thanasis was going to try to jump over him. Giannis, wearing a tattered Derrick Rose Bulls jersey, covered his eyes. Sure enough, Thanasis leaped over him, his legs splitting into the

Jordan logo, clearing Giannis's six-foot-nine frame to throw the ball down. They just laughed and laughed.

* * *

The more the scouts watched, the trickier they found evaluating Giannis. The level of play was so poor that it was difficult to envision him against NBA-caliber players. Zivas himself hardly looked like he was a coach; he once showed up on a motorcycle wearing faded jeans, a T-shirt, and black sneakers. "I had a scout tell me, 'It's a freaking high school game. It's a joke.' And he [the scout] left," says one former NBA assistant GM who came to Greece to watch Giannis. "Another coach told me, 'We should be college coaches watching this high school kid. He's so far away. Three years *minimum.*'"

Giannis was not dominating play in A2. And he was still rail thin, maybe 196 pounds. Scouts weren't sure what position he would play. "He was a super skinny kid who could dribble well, had a couple of highlights, but wasn't that effective of a player yet," says Austin Ainge, Celtics director of player personnel, who came to Zografou with his father, Danny Ainge, to evaluate Giannis.

"The talent was obvious," Austin says, "but there was a long way to go. If we would've known he could grow three inches and gain forty pounds, that would've made the evaluation easier."

The Celtics staff came back to Greece at the end of March, traveling to Volos, about a five-hour bus ride from Athens, for a road game. As Danny took his seat in the crowd, fans started screaming at him, hurling foul names at him in Greek.

That kind of hostility is normal in Greece, where basketball is religion, especially during Olympiacos and Panathinaikos rivalry games. Flares are often thrown on the court. "At first I was scared shitless," says Nick Cala-thes, a legendary Greek American basketball player who played for Pana-thinaikos. He now plays for Barcelona. "It's wild. Everybody in the gym would be arrested if this was in the NBA."

Kyle Hines, an American forward formerly of Olympiacos, who is friends with Thanasis, has been hit with a firecracker, a piece of a broken sink from the bathroom, and a lighter. "Every game is a game seven," says Hines, who now plays for Olimpia Milano. "Here, when you come out the womb, you're an Olympiacos baby or a Panathinaikos baby."

Former Lakers guard Josh Powell, who played for Olympiacos and is also friends with Thanasis, has been hit with quarters and poked with knives. He remembers a brawl with two hundred policemen before a game. "I've played in the NBA Finals, but I've never experienced anything like playing in Greece," Powell says. "We've had people attempt to rob us."

In 1993, a Panathinaikos fan named Giorgos Karnezis, twenty-five, was stabbed to death in the Glyfada suburb near Piraeus on his way home from the rivalry game for the Greek A1 Finals (game 4). He was spotted wearing Panathinaikos colors, and his car was stopped by Olympiacos fans, and one of them stabbed him. Another instance, in 2007, in Paiania, near Athens, Panathinaikos and Olympiacos fans arranged to meet for a fight, almost four hundred showing up. A Panathinaikos fan, Michalis Filopoulos, twenty-two, was stabbed and beaten to death. The government suspended professional sports for two weeks after.

So it wasn't unusual for fans to taunt Ainge in Volos. It was hilarious why they did: they had mistaken him for a rival Greek GM. When they found out Ainge was with the Celtics, they started chanting, "Lakers! Lakers!" Finally Ainge realized what was happening and started cracking up.

Giannis's teammates couldn't believe Ainge had come not only to Volos but back to Zografou the next day to watch practice. Gkikas was nervous but summoned the courage to walk up to Ainge and say hello. During five-on-five, Gkikas turned down a wide-open three. "The three-point line isn't for decoration," Gkikas remembers Ainge telling him after. "You have to shoot the ball." That was one of the best moments of Gkikas's young life.

But the Celtics moved on from Giannis. "I thought he was absolutely a worthwhile project," Ainge later told the *Boston Herald*. "But never in a million years did I see him becoming a potential best-player-in-the-league type of player."

The Bucks weren't fully convinced at that point either; Giannis wasn't at the top of their draft board for their selection at number 15. But the Hawks, picking at number 17 and number 18, were dead set on Giannis.

Danny Ferry, the Hawks GM, became enamored with Giannis when he visited Zografou in February. Ferry, the number 2 pick in the 1989 draft and former Cavs GM, liked how hard Giannis played. How much energy he had. How much love he seemed to have for the game. His competitiveness. His focus. His humility. That he tried to make the right plays but didn't force things. He did things a coach can't teach: dishing simple passes, diving on the floor, running back after a mistake.

"His physique was special," Ferry says. "You saw crazy amounts of talent. You could see traces of LeBron or Magic because of the size and versatility he possessed. His court vision."

Ferry is cautious about making those kinds of comparisons because even though he *did* see a great deal of potential in Giannis, he had no conception at the time that Giannis would morph into one of the best players in the world. "*No one* predicted this," Ferry says.

Ferry was still unsure how Giannis's game would translate in a more competitive setting, but he thought Giannis could become an NBA starter, maybe even an all-star. Ferry was all in on drafting Giannis and felt like he would fit in with the Hawks' hardworking, high-character players like Al Horford and Kyle Korver.

By April 2013, Ferry told his senior staff to travel to Greece, and several went: Hawks international scout Lojze Milosavljevic, assistant GM Wes Wilcox, director of basketball operations Mike McNeive, and assistant coach Kenny Atkinson.

*   *   *

Giannis didn't know much about what was happening behind the scenes with Atlanta or Milwaukee. He was too busy beating himself up over a championship loss. It was the biggest game of his life. April 27, 2013, against Nea Kifissia B.C. A chance to move into A1, as A2 teams have the opportunity to leapfrog divisions the last game of the season. Twenty NBA scouts showed up to the small arena, Zirineio Indoor Hall, sitting in a section to the far left in a space adorned with ribbons. Young twelve- and thirteen-year-olds watched, one beating a drum. The place could accommodate four hundred people, but so many people were squeezed into the stands that one could feel the body heat of the person next to him.

With two months to the draft, this was a critical game for Giannis to showcase his skills. Kifissia was the more experienced team, but Filathlitikos wasn't intimidated. The game went back and forth, neither team backing down, all the way into overtime.

Filathlitikos eventually lost in triple overtime, 89–81, preventing them from moving to A1. Defenders shut Giannis down: he made a three-pointer and a free throw but wouldn't score more than four points. He struggled to gain a rhythm, managing to grab nine rebounds, eventually fouling out after thirty-eight minutes. "Scouts were a little disappointed, but they understood the pressure he was under. They still saw his potential," says Dedas, the former Greek coach. "Americans see potential; we wait for players to be perfect."

Filathlitikos's players, including Giannis, cried afterward. "Giannis couldn't handle it," Saloustros says. "Nobody could handle it." It still hurts Zivas to talk about it. His voice is barely audible when he says the refereeing of that game was "unfair."

Giannis and his brothers were inconsolable. The game had larger consequences for them. "That game could have really changed our lives," Alex says. "Seeing them lose, seeing their reactions, how emotional they were, it really got to me."

Given that Giannis played with both the men's and the junior team, he had a few more games left with the younger squad. He scored thirty-five points in his next outing but sprained his ankle. His coaches told him not to play in the next game. It was too risky. Giannis was devastated, sitting out when so many scouts had flown in to see him. But he had a future to protect.

"It was maybe the first time he was starting thinking like a pro," Saloustros says, "and no longer a kid."

There was still that nagging problem, though: Giannis couldn't turn pro without citizenship papers.

His agents and coaches and the Greek Basketball Federation had been lobbying aggressively on his behalf, especially Giannis Ioannidis, legendary

Greek player and later coach of Olympiacos as well as the Greek national team. Ioannidis, largely considered the best Greek coach of all time, was serving as the deputy minister of culture responsible for sports at the time. He approached Giannis's citizenship just as he would a problem on the court: with care and precision, trying to break it down step-by-step.

Antonis Samaras, then Greece's prime minister, remembers Ioannidis telling him that Giannis could have an international career, with the Zaragoza contract hovering in the background, but that getting papers was "taking forever."

Samaras vaguely knew who Giannis was. "I kept hearing rumors about this young kid of Nigerian descent that was playing basketball somewhere in the second division, and rising fast." But there was so much red tape; it would be a "Herculean task," Samaras says.

When characterizing the government's response to Giannis's request, Samaras avoids the question. He mentions the history of immigrants coming into Europe. How thousands were coming into Greece in transit, trying to move through to the rest of Europe at that time. "At a time when many deep structural changes were happening in the country," Samaras says, "the public sector could not serve the average Greek citizen, let alone the flood of illegal aliens."

But Giannis was not an "illegal alien" that was "flooding" into the country. He had lived there all his life. And he had the potential to play in the NBA. Still, the process seemed stalled at times. "We pushed a lot to get the Greek passport," says Kostas Missas, the U-20 national-team coach. "We tried to get the passport for Thanasis first [in 2012], but we couldn't do that."

Thanasis had been invited to the national U-21 team of Greece two summers before. He participated in the preparation camp, but because he didn't have a passport and couldn't travel outside of Greece, he never played in any official or friendly game. Giannis felt slighted because Thanasis hadn't received his papers, causing Thanasis to lose out on making younger national teams.

The boys were in limbo and had been for a while. Panos Prokos, the Athens lawyer who had given Giannis's family more time on their rent payments, had been working behind the scenes on behalf of Giannis and Thanasis too.

Prokos had a friend named Giannis Palatos, a basketball lover who hadn't missed a national-team game in thirty years. He also was a marketing executive who was involved with hoops, trying to organize basketball teams in the southern suburbs. Palatos was good friends with two prominent men in the basketball community: George Vassilakopoulos, then general secretary of sports (and current president of the Greek Basketball Federation), and Kostas Politis, legendary basketball player and coach, largely for Panathinaikos.

When Prokos sensed how determined Giannis and Thanasis were to succeed in basketball, he called Palatos in front of the family and asked him to do anything possible to help the kids gain citizenship. Palatos hadn't heard of the boys at first but immediately called Politis. Palatos remembers Politis knowing who the boys were and recalls Politis responding, "Yes, indeed, there is a family with a kid who plays basketball, Thanasis, but they also have a great talent, the younger one, Giannis, whom I will help as much as I can." Palatos urged him to stay on the case, as he did with Vassilakopoulos.

Meanwhile, Willy Villar, Zaragoza's sporting director, was working with Giannis's agents to see if there was a way to gain Spanish citizenship. Villar told them he would do whatever it took to get Giannis to Spain, whether that was lobbying the Greek government, the Spanish government, or the Spanish Basketball Federation. "At the beginning, it was difficult to convince the Greek government to get him papers," Villar says. "It was very, very difficult. A lot of problems to get it."

The Greek government continued to drag its feet. It was 2013, and the NBA draft was coming. "The Greek Basketball Federation tried to move mountains in its way to get Giannis a Greek passport," says Stefanos Triantafyllos, the former Greek sports journalist turned coach. "'Forget it. We don't want to risk going to elections because of some guy that plays basketball' was the state's (unofficial) answer to the federation requests."

Other local writers speculated what would happen if Greece didn't give Giannis papers: "It would mean that beyond any shadow of doubt, that

Greece eats her own," one writer wrote at the time. "And Greek basketball has lost the biggest talent it ever laid its hands on."

Local players could see the bureaucracy at work too. "Kids like Giannis were never promoted by their own country," says Tasos Garas, who played in the same circles as Giannis back then. "Almost no one in Greece ever believed in this two-time NBA MVP. That's unbelievable."

Time was running out: without a passport, he wouldn't be able to apply for a US visa to participate in the NBA draft, or go play for Zaragoza. Ioannides was trying his best to push the government, recognizing that Giannis was a unique talent. George Koniaris, the Greek Basketball Federation's lawyer, kept pushing too. But what was largely underreported was that the Greek government began to speed up the process only once they realized that not only did Giannis have NBA potential but that Giannis and his team had reportedly turned to the embassy of Nigeria, hoping to gain citizenship there.

Giannis had applied for a Nigerian passport in September 2012, though his preference still was for Greek citizenship, because, as Giannis told Gazzetta.gr in 2013, "I could become formally Greek."

The possibility of him playing for Nigeria's national team—and not Greece's national team—and playing for Zaragoza as a Nigerian player may have added more pressure. Still, it was the potential NBA career that largely motivated the government to finally fast-track Giannis's (and Thanasis's) citizenship, given that Giannis performing well in the NBA could benefit Greece. "The fact that he had a realistic prospect of playing in the NBA helped a lot," Samaras says.

Villar realized that too. That Giannis's potential to become a star changed the government's tune. "Once they recognized the potential of Antetokounmpo, the process was very quick," Villar says.

Giannis and Thanasis were granted a "special exemption" and received citizenship papers on May 9, 2013. In the process, Greek officials changed their last name from Adetokunbo to Antetokounmpo, a more traditional, Greek-sounding name. Though Charles, Veronica, Kostas, and Alex were not granted citizenship, it was a thrilling moment. Not just because that would enable Giannis to play for the national team and potentially the

NBA but because the papers validated what they had felt their entire lives: they were unequivocally Greek.

But the irony—granting him citizenship purely for athletic reasons—was not lost on some, who saw the hypocrisy in the government treating Giannis one way and other Black Greeks another. "If Giannis was an Einstein or a scientist, he would not be getting Greek nationality because there are 100,000 kids, at least, with the same problem," Velliniatis later told OnMilwaukee. "The problem still stays for 100,000 kids trapped."

"Giannis was," Velliniatis said, "the exception."

Nikos Papadojannis, the Greek sports journalist, later published an interview with Thanasis, stating the obvious: "You only got the Greek passport because you are good at basketball."

"The passport is the least," Thanasis responded. "Why shouldn't a little girl who is capable of painting have a right to life? Or someone who has no particular skills? How is it possible that someone who was born here, went to kindergarten, school, university, received a Greek education, is not considered Greek?"

Giannis couldn't say any of those things. He had to keep his head down. The Hawks were on his tail. The draft was around the corner.

* * *

The Hawks hid their interest in Giannis. They were worried about word spreading to other NBA teams. Aside from then Atlanta coach Mike Budenholzer, hardly anyone within the Hawks organization knew. "We didn't want *anyone* to know," Ferry says. "It was clear that he was the player that we would want."

The level of secrecy was unusual. "There was an intentional effort not to let anybody know within the organization how interested we were," says Alex Lloyd, then a Hawks player-development assistant. Lloyd, now an assistant coach with the G League's Memphis Hustle, hadn't known about the interest in Giannis back then.

The Hawks arranged two secret meetings with Giannis, the first in Paris, where Giannis was playing in a tournament that May. Kenny Atkinson, who used to coach in France, went to watch him. Afterward, he met

Giannis in the lobby of a hotel. Taking out his laptop, he pulled up clips from a Lakers-versus-Atlanta game, peppering Giannis with questions such as "What would you do in this situation?" Giannis kept answering "pass the ball" to every question. Atkinson sensed that he liked to facilitate and was a selfless player.

The other meeting was held near Treviso, Italy, in early June, as Giannis and the U-20 Greek national team were playing in the European championship in nearby Jesolo. Every June, NBA executives scout the best draft prospects in Europe at Eurocamp in Treviso. But Giannis wasn't invited to Eurocamp. He was in Jesolo, near the coast. So after Eurocamp, a hoard of scouts, about fifty of them, traveled on a long narrow road to see this unknown Greek player named Giannis.

Giannis and his teammates were facing off against the U-20 Croatian national team. Giannis impressed: he showed off a nice jump hook. He chased his defender on defense. He looked relaxed, in control, dropping crisp bounce passes. He blocked shots; he played point guard. He had turnovers too, off screen and rolls, but always sprinted back.

While staying in Italy, Giannis also met with Villar, from Zaragoza, and the late José Luis Abós, who would have become his coach with Zaragoza, in Treviso. "We are so excited to have you," Villar told Giannis. "You have so much potential." They talked about him possibly playing point guard for Zaragoza.

But as the tournament wore on, Villar realized he might lose his player. Giannis's stock in America was rising. Villar remembers about four hundred people watching one of Giannis's games in Jesolo, and when Giannis fouled out with eight minutes left in one game, it felt like all four hundred people walked out. "In that moment, I can't believe it," Villar says. "I realize Antetokounmpo will get a high spot in the draft. Everybody is starting to talk about him in that moment."

DraftExpress projected him to be a first-round pick. Analysts liked that he had the ball-handling skills of a point guard but called him a "poor man's Kevin Durant." The word *mystery* kept popping up:

"[He's] a mysterious prospect," said the *New York Times*.

"He is the true international man of mystery," said NBADraft.net.

He *was* a mystery because he wasn't playing for Greece's top two teams. He *was* a mystery because he was an international player. He *was* a mystery because people couldn't pronounce his name. And he *was* a mystery because he had remarkable athleticism and an almost freakishly lanky body, having "absurd length, gigantic hands, and springs in his legs," one analyst wrote. "Throw in a 7'3" wingspan, and it's like allowing a standard-sized wing to play with a broom."

Giannis's official NBA draft profile read, "Antetokounmpo's physical profile and ball skills put his potential off the charts. But it's still just potential. He'll need several years of top Euro-level competition to get him ready for the rigors of the NBA." One insider was a bit more harsh: "He is a high risk, he has no experience at a high level, lacks a specific role and his shot is not very reliable."

The Hawks, however, thought Giannis was a steal, telling him so in that secret meeting in the basement of a hotel near Jesolo. No one could know about the meeting between four Hawks staffers, Giannis, and one of his agents. They huddled around a table. The lighting was terrible, practically dark. One staffer present was concerned that someone could walk in and listen to the conversation, as the room looked like it might be some kind of a lower-level restaurant.

The staffer remembers Giannis looking serious. Still warm, still smiling, but very serious. He teared up a bit, emphasizing how hard he would work if they selected him. His English wasn't that good, but he could string sentences together. The Hawks fell in love with Giannis's personality from that meeting. The staffer wrote in his notebook later that night, "One of the all-time best interviews. Great smile. Humble, thoughtful. Seems to love the game and his family. Comes across as genuine, young, simple, smart. Biggest takeaway is that the two most important things in his life are basketball and family. He wants to move his dad, mom, younger brothers to the States, and his dream is to live in one big house together. He wants his younger brothers to go to high school and college in the States." That dream—to move his family into one house in America—still makes the staffer emotional to this day.

But he wasn't the only admirer. The Bucks, too, were hiding their interest. There was one problem, though. "We didn't have his physical," Hammond says.

Prospects usually participate in the rookie combine in America and take physicals and complete individual workouts. But the Bucks didn't have any of those luxuries, given that Saratsis, Giannis's agent, didn't provide much information because of the nonbinding promise known as a draft-day guarantee that Giannis and Atlanta had. (Both parties agreed that Atlanta would draft Giannis.)

Hammond recalls that Saratsis assured him that Giannis was healthy, but how could Hammond know 100 percent without the evidence of a physical? "That scares you," Hammond says. "Or that doesn't scare you—it just pushes you in a little bit of an uncomfortable position."

It would be a gamble. A big gamble. But Hammond felt comforted by two things: (1) he was selecting at number 15, so there was less risk in the pick, and (2) Saratsis had told him that Giannis wanted his family to come with him to America. Hammond knew how important it was to have family support. He was working for the Pistons at the time of Detroit's disastrous decision to pick Serbian player Darko Miličić at number 2 in 2003. Hammond says one of the factors in the eighteen-year-old not fulfilling his potential was that he didn't have family support around him.

Giannis was the youngest player in the current draft, and he'd be living in a country he had never visited. He would need that support.

The Bucks were on the phone with Giannis's agents a couple of days before the draft, even the night before, according to one former Bucks staffer, trying to smooth over potential concerns.

The Bucks were all in on drafting him, but other teams weren't as convinced. Some felt the pick was too risky, like the Suns, picking at number 5. "They thought there was so many question marks around him," Dávid says. "The risk was a little bit higher to pick him than the rewards."

Milwaukee didn't have much to lose after years of mediocrity. Bucks owner Senator Herb Kohl long had a small-market team mindset of "Just be competitive. Just get to the playoffs." The Bucks weren't gunning for championships. They didn't try to go after championship-level players either.

Kohl had made seemingly ill-advised decisions in prior drafts and in free agency, spending exorbitant amounts of money on older, past-their-prime players who were not in any place to transform a franchise. The Bucks would do just enough to make it to the first round of the playoffs before losing, aside from a miraculous run in 2000–2001, when coach George Karl took a Bucks team led by Glenn "Big Dog" Robinson, Ray Allen, and Sam Cassell to the Eastern Conference Finals, and of course the glory days of the Kareem Abdul-Jabbar (then Lew Alcindor) and Oscar Robertson era, when the Bucks won their only championship in 1971. And the Bucks teams of the 1980s were formidable, winning Central Division titles through the stellar play of Sidney Moncrief, Terry Cummings, and Paul Pressey.

But since? The Bucks stank.

The BMO Harris Bradley Center, where the Bucks played, was freezing cold. It wasn't heated. The cooling system was so antiquated that it relied on a refrigerant that was no longer allowed to be manufactured or sold in the United States.

"Nobody wanted to go to Milwaukee at the time," says Brandon Knight, Bucks guard from 2013 to 2015. "It was one of those things where it was like, 'You're going to *Milwaukee?*' Like, 'Aw, man, that's *terrible.*'"

Besides, Wisconsin loved its Green Bay Packers. Aaron Rodgers. The Brewers. The Bucks were an afterthought, unless you were a die-hard fan who stuck with them through the miserable 1990s, arguably one of the worst decades for a modern professional sports franchise.

Those fans? They were always there. They were always going to be there. Tyler Herro, Miami Heat guard, born in 2000 and raised in Milwaukee, was one of them. He'd remain hopeful for the Bucks and then feel let down when they would get knocked out of the first round of the playoffs again and again. "It sucked as a Bucks fan," Herro says. "Every year it was going to be *the year*, and then it wasn't the year."

Something really needed to change now, because as Milwaukee headed into the 2013 draft, the future of the franchise hung in the balance. NBA deputy commissioner Adam Silver said that the team would need a new arena to replace the aging Bradley Center, which, Silver said, was too small and unable to compete with other modern NBA arenas. Kohl was fighting to keep the team in Milwaukee, as he had for decades since purchasing the team in 1985, though offers would come up to sell the team. Privately, those around him knew he didn't want to have it be his legacy that the Bucks would leave Milwaukee. Still, nobody knew what would happen. If there was ever a time for management to take a swing, it was now.

But Hammond didn't know that the Hawks had secretly flown Giannis (and Thanasis) to Atlanta on June 25, two days before the draft.

* * *

Giannis had refused to get on the plane at first. "My whole family has to come," he told his agents. But that wasn't possible, since they didn't have papers. Charles suggested he take Thanasis, and Giannis finally agreed.

Some Hawks executives were afraid someone would see the two brothers, take a picture, post it on social media, and ruin their chances of drafting Giannis.

One staffer took the brothers downtown so Giannis could get a physical. Giannis was shaking, nervous. He had never had a physical before. The doctor told the staff that his growth plates were wide open, delighting Atlanta even more.

Afterward, Giannis and Thanasis were walking down Peachtree Street, staring at the buildings, smiling, laughing, playing around. This was America! They were here! Of course they forgot they were supposed to keep a low profile. Two super-tall guys speaking Greek in Atlanta? *Super* low profile.

The staffer, horrified, quickly hurried them into his car, hoping no one noticed. "It was a high-stress moment," he says. But Giannis was thrilled, especially when they took him to get a giant meal of chicken wings and Sprite.

The Hawks didn't conduct a formal workout but had Giannis in the gym shooting around. "It was more of welcoming him in," Ferry says. "We were hoping it was the start of a great and wonderful relationship."

Ferry had Giannis and Thanasis stay at his own home, eat dinner with his family. One night they had Italian. Giannis looked so happy, according to Ferry, gobbling the pasta down. He slept in a king-size bed in the guest room. He played chess, Ping-Pong, and cards with Ferry's five kids.

Everything felt like it was coming together. And to be there with Thanasis? That meant everything to Giannis.

Giannis was overwhelmed, staying in such a nice home. *This is what NBA money gets you?* he thought.

Ferry and Giannis headed to the Hawks arena, which was then Philips Arena, the day before Giannis was set to fly to New York for the draft. Standing in the middle of the arena, Giannis looked stunned. He had never been in an arena that big. He had come a long way from the five-hundred-seat gym in Zografou. No more broken windows, no more leaky showers.

Giannis started tearing up. "He could see the life that was in front of him," Ferry says. The Hawks gave him some gear: flip-flops, shoes, socks. He started crying again; no one had ever given him socks before, let alone a full suitcase's worth of shoes. *Wow*, he thought. *They really care about me.*

He has kept the shoes to this day.

* * *

New York was thrilling to Giannis. He bought an I Love New York hat. He had hot dogs, Coca-Cola. They took photos everywhere. The day before the draft, Giannis's agents bought him a suit. Giannis knew so little about the draft that he hadn't even known he had to wear one, thinking that he would just show up in shorts and a T-shirt. They found a tailor last minute. Getting every measurement, Giannis was amazed at all the things that go into a suit, from the collar to the cuffs.

He hadn't had one this nice before: a light gray plaid blazer, black tie, black slacks. He sat next to Thanasis, who of course was a bit bolder with his choice: an extravagant purple-and-navy-checkered french-collared shirt, suit, vest, and tie. That was fitting, given their personalities: Thanasis ever the exclamation point, Giannis the period.

Thanasis beamed, looking at his younger brother. *They* had made it. Together. Thanasis believed in Giannis's potential. Giannis wasn't really nervous about which team would pick him or what would happen next. Or maybe just a little. But he knew that his life was going to change in a matter of minutes. *Please*, Giannis thought. *Please just let me get drafted.*

Ferry was anxious, excited. *Can all of this work?* he thought. *Will we get him?* Giannis thought he was going to be selected by the Hawks. That was the plan, after all. But an hour before the draft, Hammond called him and said they were interested. Giannis had no idea where Milwaukee was. He had never seen the Bucks play before, so he googled "Milwaukee" and saw a ton of snow. That was all he knew about it.

As the draft began, ESPN draft analysts Fran Fraschilla, Bill Simmons, Jalen Rose, Rece Davis, and Jay Bilas talked about Giannis as a largely unknown player with a great deal of upside. One of the big selling points that they had heard from scouts was about what kind of a person Giannis was: his personality, his character, and what he had overcome, all of which made him an attractive prospect.

Fraschilla, an international expert, thought Giannis might have been a top 5 pick if he had come out of high school. "He's the most mysterious prospect in the draft," Fraschilla said. "Think of this young man as a McDonald's All-American that needs a development program. . . . A great talent with a great feel for the game. Can you put him in an NBA game right now? You probably cannot. But in the long-term picture, this kid has as much upside as most anybody in this draft."

Simmons was impressed, thought Giannis had potential as a "huge-ceiling, low-basement" kind of prospect, he says. Simmons spent hours evaluating him on grainy YouTube clips, which made it difficult to understand the caliber of his opponents. "It was hard to tell what he was," Simmons says. "To me, he looked like Paul George. A really good, long-armed athlete who could be a two-way guy, but you just didn't know. You didn't know what the competition was."

Simmons spent hours with Jalen Rose practicing how to say Giannis's last name the day before the draft. They had no idea how to pronounce it. Rose joked that no one would ever call him by his full name, Giannis Antetokounmpo. "They'll just call him Po," Simmons remembers Rose telling him while the two rehearsed. Rose imagined future teammates telling Giannis, "Yeah, yeah, go get my bags, Po."

The draft was . . . strange, to say the least. Analysts didn't know, genuinely, who might be the number 1 pick. At least five different players could have gone first. Simmons heard that if Anthony Bennett didn't go first, he could fall to number 7 or even number 8. "We heard he was falling, falling, falling," Simmons says.

The Cavs did end up selecting Bennett with the number 1 overall pick. Giannis turned to Saratsis. "What's going to happen now? Are we screwed?" He had no idea how any of this worked.

"Don't worry," Saratsis told him. "There's a long way to go before we get where we're supposed to be."

Meanwhile, teams were scheming to make deals. The Oklahoma City Thunder's Sam Presti, picking at number 12, called Saratsis. Saratsis had the sense that he was choosing between guard Dennis Schröder, center Steven Adams, and Giannis and that he was impressed by Giannis. Giannis, however, didn't want to go there, because Presti would likely stash him in Europe to develop. Dallas later claimed they were interested in Giannis too. Meanwhile, Ferry says the Hawks had plans lined up to move higher, but they all fell through. Still, Giannis was available; team after team passed on him.

And then . . . it was too late. After standing backstage with a European teenager and practicing the pronunciation of Giannis's full name, NBA commissioner David Stern walked out into the lights and announced: the Bucks would select Giannis at number 15.

Giannis hugged Thanasis, then walked up to the podium, shook Stern's hand, and flashed a wide smile. He looked so eager, so excited. So young, so baby-faced. He was only eighteen. Giannis doesn't remember much about what happened after that. He remembers being so nervous, saying, "Thank you so much," and hearing Stern say, "Look over here, look over there, look over there, good luck with your journey!" as camera lights flashed. Giannis was so proud of himself. He had been through so much to get to that point.

When Giannis's name was called, Thanasis waved a Greek flag in the air, which was his idea, according to Josh Oppenheimer, the Bucks assistant coach and close friend. Oppenheimer calls Thanasis "Giannis's Flavor Flav" because he is always hyping up and celebrating his baby brother. Thanasis felt waving the flag was the right way to do that, despite Giannis's reservations. "Giannis did not want Thanasis to wave the Greek flag,"

Oppenheimer says, given that Greece had taken a while to grant them citizenship. "Let's claim them for *us*," Thanasis told Giannis that night, according to Oppenheimer.

"Giannis was angry and bitter for how the family and other immigrants had been treated," Oppenheimer says, "but Thanasis knew if he didn't [wave the flag], there would be more struggle after."

Giannis *was* proud to be Greek—and to have made it this far. He never expected to be drafted. Thanasis stood next to him, smiling when Giannis smiled, laughing when Giannis laughed.

But the Hawks were not laughing. They were deeply disappointed. Angry. Someone in the Hawks draft room threw a large plant. A beverage also flew through the air.

The sadness lingered with Ferry. "For a while," Ferry says. Still does. "How do you not feel that way when you watch this kid play?" It took a few weeks of coaxing for him to even agree to talk about Giannis and the draft on the record for this book, as it's still a sore subject with him. "We got through this [the interview] without me crying," Ferry says, managing a laugh.

But another person in the Hawks draft room felt that as a group they hadn't done enough to fight to move up for Giannis. To convince upper management that Giannis was worth giving up anything for. "Maybe we had the highest evaluation on him, but I do know we underevaluated him," that person says. "Ultimately, we loved the player, but we weren't convinced enough. That's the truth.

"It was a huge leap to say the kid could be an all-star," he continues, "which we thought he could be, but to go from that to being one of the best players to ever play the game? We didn't see that. It's just the reality; we didn't get it done."

To Villar of Zaragoza, it was bittersweet. On the one hand, he was happy for Giannis. Proud. On the other hand, he was sad that he was missing out on a great player. A player he'd believed in when very few had. "Five months ago, he was playing second-division Greece, and now he's in the NBA," Villar says.

Hammond and the Bucks were thrilled. The reality, of course, is that had any GM known then that Giannis would grow two more inches, sprouting to nearly seven feet, he wouldn't have fallen to number 15. And even being picked at number 15 was seen as a stretch; he went two, three, picks earlier than some scouts would have thought.

"It really was one of the oddest drafts in the history of the draft," Simmons says. "The fact that Giannis became by far the biggest gem out of that draft? If we had listed thirty predictions for that draft, that would not have been in the thirty." Simmons thought it was a smart pick but that it signified the Bucks were going full rebuild. "That's the kind of pick you took if you didn't really care what happened the next couple of years."

There has been a bit of revisionist history about the 2013 draft in the years since. Giannis wasn't anybody's outright number 1—maybe with the exception of Atlanta. Regarding the teams now claiming to have had more interest than they actually did then, Simmons says, "I think those teams are completely full of shit. I think they do that every draft. There's always some hero. There's eight to ten people in the draft process for every team, so somebody could say in a meeting, 'I really like Giannis.' Then over the years, it becomes 'Oh, I told everyone we should trade for Giannis!'"

After the Bucks selected Giannis, he did his first media interviews. He was both shy and sure of himself at the same time. "It's a wonderful feeling," Giannis told a TV reporter that night. "I can't describe how I feel. It's a dream come true.

"I know I'm not ready. I have a lot of work ahead of me," Giannis said in a conference that night. "But I'm not afraid. I will give everything on the court, in the gym. And I will prove to the Milwaukee Bucks that they made the right choice."

Then Craig Sager interviewed him. Slowly enunciating every syllable of Giannis's last name—"Ahn-te-toe-koon-poh"—Sager let each one hang for an extra second. He asked Giannis whom he modeled his game after.

"People say I play like Kevin Durant," Giannis said, "but you don't look at other players. You just look at yourself. How are you going to improve? I hope I improve. I work hard. I will get ready to play into the NBA."

"You have your choice," Sager said. "You can stay in Europe and maybe come to the NBA later or come right away. What are you going to do?"

"Right away in the NBA," Giannis said, looking him in the eye.

* * *

Giannis and Thanasis returned to their hotel room that night and celebrated by jumping on the bed, giggling like kids. They started praying, promising that their little brothers were going to have a better future than them—that they would go to private schools, receive proper educations. Then they Skyped their parents and Kostas and Alex, telling them their lives were going to change. Everything would be all right.

A group of about fifty friends, teammates, and coaches in Sepolia had joined Charles and Veronica to watch the draft. "Everybody would cheer, like we had made a buzzer-beater," Saloustros says. "We couldn't believe it. It was surreal." They all stayed up to the very end, around 3:00 a.m. Greece time.

Tzikas and his wife, of Kivotos Café, were working fifteen hours that day, so they couldn't attend, but they saw clips of the draft the next day at 5:00 a.m. They broke down crying. "We were very proud," Tzikas says. "The family of the Antetokounmpos is second family for us."

Rahman Rana, Giannis's close friend, was so happy for him he couldn't put it into words. He felt like he himself had made it too. "At least one of us was living the dream," Rana says.

Others were shocked. A Greek African player made it. A Greek African player who was undocumented all his life. He beat the odds.

* * *

The next morning, Giannis, Thanasis, and Saratsis boarded a charter plane for Milwaukee. Hammond was waiting for them at the airport. The headlines that day characterized Hammond's choice as a bold move. A gamble.

"Mystery Man Worth Shot; Giannis Antetokounmpo Is a Project, but Has the Potential to Be a Star," said the *Wisconsin State Journal*.

"Playing it safe was a real possibility. Hammond decided to roll the dice on the youngest player in the draft," said the *Milwaukee Journal Sentinel*.

"No team swung for the fences quite like the Bucks," said *USA Today*.

"Give the Bucks credit: They aren't afraid to take a chance. It may be several years before we know whether the Bucks wasted their pick or struck gold with Antetokounmpo," said ESPN.

The pick *was* risky. And a little odd. No one in Milwaukee media had even heard of Giannis before. The pick seemed to be a departure from Kohl's "just be competitive" mandate, as Hammond seemingly drafted a player for the future—a player who needed time to develop rather than contribute right away to help lock in another lackluster season and number 8 playoff seed.

Hammond acknowledges that there had been safer picks, but none with Giannis's upside. The Bucks had needed a guard, but Hammond didn't feel the need to select a traditional point guard. Though Giannis's Greek coaches viewed him as someone who could play multiple positions, including point guard, Hammond viewed Giannis as more of a wing.

Scotty Stirling, longtime NBA scout and former NBA vice president of operations, once told a young Hammond, in Hammond's first year working in the NBA, that the way to determine a player's position is "You are what you guard." So while Giannis handled the ball like a point guard, had a great feel for the game like a point guard, he couldn't guard a Kyrie Irving kind of point guard. Therefore, Giannis would start out as a wing. A mobile, versatile wing. When Hammond talked about Giannis with staff, his voice lifted a note higher. Sometimes he almost squealed. Giannis was his new project.

When Giannis landed in Milwaukee, the two made small talk. Hammond then broke the unfortunate news to the rookie: "It gets really cold in Milwaukee." Giannis nodded, but he didn't own a winter coat.

*   *   *

Hammond dropped Giannis and Thanasis off at the Pfister Hotel, where Kohl had breakfast every morning. The Bucks had booked Giannis and Thanasis in two separate rooms. The brothers didn't understand why anyone would do such a thing. That seemed *crazy* to them. Way too extravagant. So Thanasis stayed in Giannis's room, and they slept in one bed. Just as they always had.

Hammond joined them in the morning, spotting Kohl with JoAnne Anton, Kohl's assistant, in the hotel coffee shop. "Giannis, there's the owner of the team, right there," Hammond said, waving Kohl and Anton over. Anton smiled and then started speaking Greek, as if it were the most casual thing in the world to do. Hammond was floored: he had no idea Anton was Greek, let alone fluent. *This has to be right*, Hammond thought. *What are the odds?*

They all headed to Giannis's introductory press conference. Beat writers weren't sure what to make of Giannis, this tall lanky teen walking into the media room. They asked him how to pronounce his name, and he sounded it out slowly, phonetically. For many, it was the first time hearing his name. Some were skeptical. "There was no buzz on this guy," says Tom Oates, former *Wisconsin State Journal* sports columnist of thirty years. "I thought, *Man, that kid is going to get broken in half.*"

Giannis was immediately endearing: baby-faced, humble yet confident. "He had a sense of humor," says Lori Nickel, *Milwaukee Journal Sentinel*'s sports columnist. Everyone laughed when Giannis was asked about his biggest challenge: "It will be a little bit difficult, but I will have my family together with me, and it will be easy."

CHAPTER 5

AMERICA

Six days later, Giannis returned to Greece for a brief visit with his family and friends. He went to a club with Kamperidis, Rana, and some other former teammates to celebrate. The DJ gave him a shoutout: "Giannis Antetokounmpo, drafted to the NBA!" Giannis smiled shyly. It was the first time he really let himself dance in public. He knew how to dance, but he and his teammates were always so focused on basketball that experiences like this were rare. "We were not used to this life," Rana says.

Samaras, Greece's prime minister, invited Giannis and his family to visit him at Maximos Mansion, the official seat of the prime minister since 1982. The Antetokounmpos couldn't believe it: the *mansion*. Invited by the prime minister. The same government that dragged its feet on granting Giannis and Thanasis citizenship.

The mansion was in downtown, near Syntagma Square, a short distance from the store Giannis and his buddies used to frequent to play video games. The building was built in the old classical style, with an imposing terrace and garden. Maximos was a rich Greek entrepreneur, after all.

Walking up the ten steps to the mansion's entrance was exciting. Strange. "Now I go to the palace. People used to draw pictures of us as monkeys," Oppenheimer remembers Giannis telling him. "He hasn't forgotten that."

When the Antetokounmpos arrived, around 3:00 p.m., Samaras gave Giannis a gift: a copy of Axion Esti, a revered holy icon of Orthodox Christianity. Historically, it has been associated with a string of legendary miracles, and it has strong emotional connotations among the Greek Orthodox. Samaras hoped it would keep Giannis safe in America. "I told him that it was my personal gift to him, with the wish that the Holy Mother would always protect him," Samaras says.

Samaras could tell the family was shocked to even be there. He tried to make them feel at home. He asked if they'd like any coffee or orange juice; they preferred water. They were polite but reserved. Samaras was impressed by Giannis but equally impressed by his parents. "They are among the most decent people I have ever met," Samaras says. "They won my heart."

Samaras said at the time he was proud to see Giannis get drafted and wave the Greek flag, eager to see how he'd represent Greece. Giannis was grateful but understood the hypocrisy. "Now that I am in the NBA, they can use me for the national team," Giannis later told *Sports Illustrated*. "Now they want to accept me."

Of course, not all did. Shortly after Giannis was drafted, Nikolaos Michaloliakos, Golden Dawn's leader, said on national television, "If you give a chimpanzee in the zoo a banana and a flag, is he Greek?" And when Giannis visited the mansion, Michaloliakos called for Giannis and his family to be arrested and deported, saying that Giannis being drafted by Senator Kohl was part of a plot by a "fanatical Jew and Zionist but also a big and active antifascist activist."

Rana, watching this on TV, was terrified for Giannis. Scared that Giannis would make a mistake, or get injured, or not play well, and give the racists even more ammunition. *What will the Greek people say about him?* Rana thought. *Oh, he's just another Black kid? Will they still acknowledge him as Greek?*

Giannis said he wasn't angry. Couldn't control what others thought about him. "I can't click a button on them so they change their opinion," he told *Sports Illustrated*. "Some guys say, 'He's Black. Greeks are not Black.' You try to explain to them that it's not about the color. If I'm not Greek, what am I? My parents grew up in Nigeria, but I have never been there. If I am not Greek, I don't know what I am."

He let the slurs go. Focused on the task ahead: representing Greece's U-20 team that summer in Tallinn, Estonia, rather than competing in the

NBA Summer League. Giannis didn't expect reporters to follow him in Estonia at hotels, at practices, at games, but "suddenly everybody cares about him," says Kostas Missas, the U-20 national-team coach. "He didn't like this so much."

* * *

One morning, Kamperidis, Filathlitikos teammate and now fellow U-20 teammate, came up to Missas at breakfast, looking weary. "Coach, I couldn't sleep last night."

"Come on," Missas said. "Why?"

"Giannis was doing push-ups and sit-ups all night."

Missas confronted Giannis about it. "I'm sorry, Coach," Giannis said. "But that's the only way I'm going to play in the NBA."

First, though, he had to crack the U-20 lineup. His teammates didn't know what to make of him. They had been playing at the highest levels; he hadn't. "He wasn't the best player back then," says teammate Ioannis Papapetrou, now a star for Panathinaikos, "but you could see the potential and work ethic."

Giannis wanted to play, sure, but he also wanted to collect the five euros Missas promised each player for each win. After four wins, Giannis asked Missas, "What's going on with the euros? That's four games, twenty euros!" Missas laughs, remembering how serious Giannis was: "Twenty euros to him then was one hundred million dollars."

Giannis didn't play much but contributed in key moments—for example, in the final eleven seconds against Germany, when he scored four points and drained two critical free throws, even blocking a shot. "He made the difference for us," says Petros Melissaratos, U-20 teammate. "He was working harder than anyone."

That impressed Larry Drew, his new Bucks coach. Drew had traveled to Estonia to meet Giannis, to let him know that he really cared about him. "I wanted him to know that this was not just about basketball; this was about him as a person," says Drew, now an assistant coach with the Clippers.

One play in Estonia in particular captivated Drew: Giannis grabbed a rebound and dribbled full court, faking out the first defender before muscling through defenders in the lane, then dropping a crisp bounce pass to an open teammate.

Soon after, Giannis participated in a question-and-answer session with Sport24.gr, a Greek website. One reader asked a question that sounded absurd: "How many years before you get an MVP?"

"Haha, too soon for that," Giannis said. "First, I got to earn playing time, gain experience, and get adjusted to the new lifestyle."

"We are expecting so much from you. What do you think you need to improve in?"

"My goal is to become one of the best, and in order to do that, I need to improve in everything."

He did one final interview with Triantafyllos, the sports journalist turned coach, who drove him home after. "It's your first time going to live in America," Triantafyllos recalls saying to Giannis, staring ahead at the road. "Are you scared?"

"Look," Giannis said. "This year I will get one million dollars. This money will help me and my family for the rest of our lives. Why should I be scared?"

* * *

Hammond made sure that every Bucks staffer was prepared for Giannis's arrival. Someone would always need to be there for the rookie. Hammond enlisted Ross Geiger, the assistant video coordinator, to look out for him on a daily basis.

Geiger picked Giannis up from Chicago O'Hare International Airport in September, about two weeks before training camp, showing up in a limo that the Bucks had rented. Neither Geiger nor Giannis had been in a limo before. It was awkward. Weird. Giannis was quiet. Tired. Geiger tried to ask Giannis about music, but Giannis managed only a few words, mostly looking out the window.

Milwaukee was so different from New York. Giannis saw so many houses, trees. Lots of green. That surprised him, because he thought all of America would look like New York, with skyscrapers on every corner.

They finally arrived at the Pfister Hotel, where Giannis would stay for a short time. Everything was white, immaculate. The bed had so many pillows. Extra fluffy. He was grateful, but it felt strange, like the room belonged to someone else. *Why are they spending this kind of money on* me? he thought.

He missed his brothers—missed sleeping next to them, warmed by bodies, not blankets. He tried to sleep, but this uncomfortable feeling gnawed at him. This was too nice, too much. He pulled the mattress off the bed and put it on the floor. He curled onto the mattress, shut his eyes, and dozed off.

*   *   *

On the eve of training camp, reporters asked Giannis about expectations to perform well. "I don't feel pressure or anything else but my friends, my family, and basketball," Giannis said. "Nothing else can pressure me. So they can't touch me."

They. He was referring indirectly to Michaloliakos. To Golden Dawn. Later, he admitted so. "Anything they say, even if it was in the past, people that say bad stuff about me or my family, they can't touch me." Perhaps realizing his words were too direct, he added, "I love my country. Greece is my country."

He wouldn't talk much about race or racism in the coming months. Years. He had made it, but he hadn't *made it*. One comment could threaten his family's safety back home. Especially the way things were back home.

That same month, antifascist hip-hop artist Pavlos Fyssas, known as Killah P, had gone out with friends to a café called Coral, in Athens, to watch a sporting event. About fifty people, many of them Golden Dawn members, armed with bats, surrounded him. Giorgos Roupakias, a Golden Dawn member, stabbed Fyssas twice in the chest, killing him.

Fyssas was thirty-four.

Samaras addressed Greece on national TV, condemning the murder. Protests against Golden Dawn began in Athens and spread to Barcelona, Brussels, Paris, Amsterdam, London, and Nicosia. This time many more people cared, because Fyssas was neither an immigrant nor a person of color; he was white.

* * *

That world seemed far away as Giannis lined up across the baseline with two of his tallest teammates, six-foot-eleven Larry Sanders and six-foot-nine John Henson, the first day of training camp. They stretched their arms out, fingertip to fingertip, comparing wingspans. Giannis looked giddy just *being* on an NBA court. Energetic. Three-cups-of-coffee energetic.

When pairing up players for a drill, Drew told him, "Giannis, you're gonna be with O. J." That would be O. J. Mayo, the former USC playmaker who was at one point the top prep player in America.

Giannis turned around, looked confused. "Who's O. J.?"

Mayo smirked, cursed under his breath. "This dude don't know who I am?" He'd have to show him. And he wasn't the only one. Everyone took turns at Giannis in the next drill. A player from the opposite wing would drive hard to the basket, and the defensive player had to slide over and take the charge. It's called the "Two-Nine Drill," but it really should have been called the "Knock-Giannis-Over Drill."

The rookie stood above the circle, legs slightly bent, arms high, looking like a very long toothpick. Teammate after teammate plowed into him, knocking him down as if he were hollow. Caron Butler, a six-foot-seven, 228-pound veteran from Racine, Wisconsin, who would work out in the snow in shorts and a tank top if you asked him, laid on some heavy bruises. "Weight room!" Butler would scream, banging into the rookie.

Then Zaza Pachulia, a six-foot-eleven, 270-pound center, had his turn. Then Stephen Graham, a six-foot-six, 215-pound guard and roster hopeful. "Just so he could get tougher," says Graham, now a player-development coach with the Nuggets. "We all had to let him know: welcome to the league, *rook*."

Graham hit Giannis so hard that Giannis slid across the baseline. He popped up but clutched his chest as if he had been wounded. "Oh my god," Giannis said under his breath, wheezing.

Graham was worried. "I thought I broke his sternum or something." Drew stopped practice to make sure *rook* was OK. The vets laughed. "Giannis wasn't ready yet," Graham says. "He looks like he's pretty much a Greek god right now, but back then? There was no way he was going to make it. If you blew on him, he'd fall over."

He was a super-skinny scrub but an endearing scrub: he got up quickly each time, not looking discouraged. Butler turned to Nate Wolters, another rookie, and smiled. "The kid's gonna be special."

*   *   *

At the end of the practice, Drew handed every player a playbook so thick that it would take hours to comb through. By dinnertime, Giannis texted Drew and told him he noticed an error in one of the offensive plays.

Drew blinked. The rookie had corrected him? His first NBA coach on his first day in the NBA?

But it would become clear: Giannis was studious. A stickler for the details. He wanted to make an impact. But for now he was a mere punching bag.

The next day, the veterans pummeled him again. They'd toss him out of the paint if he dared go inside. He was a teenager competing against grown men. "It was a very, very, very tough transition for him," Drew says. "Most players would try to just go *through* him." Giannis wouldn't back down, using his length and quickness to compensate, but he looked like a puppy. Everything was happening so fast. "You could tell he was lost," says Ersan Ilyasova, Bucks forward from 2006 to 2007, 2009 to 2015, and then 2018 to 2020.

Giannis's coaches couldn't get angry at him because they saw that he was trying so hard. But there was *so* much to learn: if he got a defensive rebound, he'd try to outlet the ball. Drew had to correct him constantly. "Push the ball! You have to push the ball. You're too long, too athletic, to give it up. *Go.*"

Giannis's body just couldn't execute what his mind told him to do. His teammates mocked his thin frame, calling him Baby Giraffe. Gumby. Stop Sign. They told him he was built like Shawn Bradley, the uncoordinated seven-foot-six center who had most recently played for the Mavericks. Giannis didn't know who Bradley was. Once he consulted Google and realized it was an insult, he fumed to himself.

Oppenheimer, the Bucks assistant coach, nicknamed Giannis Bambi. When Giannis would trip and fall on himself, players would howl in laughter. "There goes them Bambi legs!" Giannis knew Bambi didn't sound like a good thing, but he didn't understand what it meant. He was still learning English. "Coach," Giannis asked Oppenheimer, "what is Bambi?"

"It's a baby deer," Oppenheimer said.

"No, Coach. No! I am *not* baby deer. No. I am *not* Bambi!" He started speaking in Greek, which he did when he'd get pissed off. But the veterans' plan was working: they wanted to get in the rookie's head, make him angry. "We were trying to get him to be that aggressive Giannis, the one y'all see now all the time," says Chris Wright, a Bucks forward that season.

Even then, Giannis wasn't soft. He was going to *compete*. But coming from Europe, being as skinny as he was, as young as he was, and speaking in a voice that was as *squeaky* as it was, he came off as adorable.

Giannis was scared of Geiger's family's goldendoodle, London, because the dog kept jumping all over him when he visited Geiger's parents' home. At one point Giannis refused to go in the backyard for a good couple of minutes before Geiger reassured him that London was harmless and just wanted to play.

He said he loved *The Ellen DeGeneres Show*. Justin Bieber. The classic Eddie Murphy comedy *Coming to America*. He seemed so innocent.

But Giannis was in no position to lead. He was just trying to crack the lineup, show that he was not Bambi. Show that he could absorb hundreds of plays in a new language. One practice, the team was practicing a common NBA play called "Floppy." The coaches noticed that Giannis looked agitated. Oppenheimer pulled him to the side. "What's wrong?"

"Coach, Coach, I know I am skinny. I know I need to get stronger," Giannis said, "but, Coach, I am *not* floppy. I am not floppy!"

"What are you talking about?"

"Everybody, they just keep looking at me! Yelling at me, 'Floppy, floppy, floppy, floppy!'"

"Giannis. 'Floppy' is a traditional NBA play. They're just saying it so that you know it. They're repeating it, trying to help you learn it."

"Oh. So it is a play?"

"Yeah. It's a play."

"He really was a blank slate," Oppenheimer says. "He knew nothing about the NBA other than superstars. Nothing about coaches. He knew nothing other than 'I want to go straight at you, I want to prove myself, and no matter how many times I fall, I'm going to get up and go right back at you.'"

Giannis listened. Sought out advice. He was different from many first-rounders with astronomical egos. "He was like a piece of clay," Oppenheimer says. "Whatever you told him to do, he wanted to do it. And if he couldn't do it, he did it until he could do it."

The two became close, as Oppenheimer was his first shooting coach. They'd stay for hours working on Giannis's form and competing in shooting competitions. (Oppenheimer is known as the "Shot Doctor"; Giannis rarely beat him.)

No one spent more time in the gym after practice than Giannis. Jim Cleamons, Bucks assistant coach, who had previously coached Michael Jordan and Kobe Bryant, winning nine championships over his coaching career, would notice how frustrated Giannis was with himself when he made a mistake. He'd labor on the same move over and over. "He had heart," says Cleamons, who would often tell Giannis, "Giannis, you're going to be a wonderful player someday; just don't become Americanized."

"What are you talking about?" Giannis said.

"I mean: Don't become Americanized. Don't forget those work habits. Don't forget what has gotten you to where you are."

Cleamons would see glimpses of greatness: a Eurostep or a dazzling finish. But Giannis was still adapting. His English wasn't terrible; he just didn't understand certain phrases or words, especially basketball terminology. Drew always explained concepts twice to Giannis, breaking down plays on a granular level. "I knew I had to be patient," Drew says. Oftentimes, Giannis would respond with a blank face. And that's when Drew knew the rookie had no clue what was going on.

He knew basic phrases like "pin down" or "back pick." But he looked lost hearing more complex lingo like "pick the picker," "flare with a rescreen," or even "crashing the glass." As a result, sometimes film sessions that were ordinarily one hour took three. "Giannis spoke more English than I did when I came here," says Ilyasova, who came from Turkey. "When you come from a different country, it's really hard to get transitioned."

Sometimes Giannis would accidentally scream out the name of the play—"Red!" or "Blitz!"—so that he could remember what to do. Butler had to pull him aside. "Giannis, you're not supposed to say the play out loud! You can't tell the other team what our plays are! Keep it to yourself, man!"

There was so much to learn it was overwhelming. "I think his head was spinning," says Wolters, the fellow rookie. "It's hard enough to transition to the NBA when you *do* know the language."

Sam Reinke, a Bucks team attendant that season, once asked Giannis what color shoes he wanted.

"Uh . . . gray," Giannis said.

Reinke held up a pair of gray shoes. "You already have those; do you want a different color?"

"Black."

"You have those too. Is there something else?"

Giannis was quiet for a minute. Then Reinke realized Giannis didn't know the English words for other colors. Reinke pulled out two red shoes. "What do you think? Red?"

"Oh. Yes. Red."

That stubborn part of Giannis, who wanted to get every move perfect, was the same way with learning English. He worked hard. He didn't want anyone to feel sorry for him. "He understood it was only a matter of time before he got it," says Alex, who would Skype his big brother constantly, asking him what America was like.

When Giannis would learn a new word, he'd get so excited he'd repeat it over and over, cracking his team up with his high-pitched voice and Greek accent. The day he learned the expression "Yo mama!" he ran around the locker room screaming, "Yo mama! Yo mama! Yo mama!"

Henson taught him what ice cubes were after Giannis asked, "What are those little square things?" Then Giannis kept repeating it: "Ice cubes! Ice cubes! Ice cubes!"

When he learned trash talk, specifically the word *bitch*, he'd scream "*Bitch!*" when he'd miss a shot.

Another favorite saying he adopted: "Where they at, though!"

He'd walk into the locker room. "Where they at, though!"

Walk onto the court. "Where they at, though!"

Walk into the showers. "Where they at, though!"

He'd watch American movies—specifically movies such as *Friday* or his eventual favorite, *Coming to America*—in order to learn English and to learn more about Black culture. He'd repeat his favorite line "Sexual chocolate!" in that high-pitched voice. Then he discovered TV shows like *Martin* and *The Jamie Foxx Show*. "These are staples in the African American community, so he put on all those to watch, to catch up," Henson says. The movies also made Giannis feel like he had something in common with his teammates. "He would love to think he's American," Wolters says, "getting cool or whatever."

One night, long after all his teammates had left after the game, Giannis took a long shower, taking his time icing afterward. The only other person left was Dave Weber, an equipment manager for the team from 2010 to 2017. Weber and Giannis were friends, but Weber kept making fun of Giannis's thick accent. A few days earlier, Giannis had warned him, "Dave, if you make fun of me again, I will put you in that trash can!" referring to the large gray bin near the locker-room entrance.

So that night, Weber again poked fun at Giannis's accent, testing the limits. True to his word, Giannis lifted him up and dropped him in the can. Fortunately for Weber, the trash can was empty. After letting Weber stew a bit, Giannis came back a couple of minutes later and pulled his friend out.

Giannis made his teammates laugh when he'd speak quickly; his cadence sped up the more excited he got about something. Luke Ridnour, the team's point guard that season, would be explaining something to him, and Giannis would respond, "YesOKlet'sgo." It always came out as one word: "YesIgotyou." "YesOKnoproblemIwillrebound."

"He was hearing you, but he wasn't hearing you," Ridnour says. "He'd go out there and mess up, and we'd talk to him again. He was frantic." Still, he ran hard. Rebounded hard. Never gave lip. His answers always began with *yes*.

* * *

Geiger and Giannis were close friends. They'd hang out every day—go to the movies, watch basketball games, play video games. Geiger started viewing Giannis as his little brother, given that he was five years younger (though a foot taller), driving him around in his '97 maroon Subaru Legacy Outback.

Once, on the way to Bucks practice, Giannis looked out the window, saw a man on the side of the street, and pointed. "Hey, do you see that guy over there?" Giannis asked Geiger.

"Yeah," Geiger said, slowing down. "What about him?"

"He's wearing bigger clothes. That reminds me of being back home."

"Oh, really? Why?"

"Well, in Greece, I used to always give all my older clothes away. So there would be a lot of Greek people that I would see from time to time randomly just in my clothes."

Giannis wasn't able to forget those things. They reminded him of his purpose. Who he was. And nothing reminded him more of the gulf between his old life and his new life than moving into his first place, a three-bedroom, two-bath condo about two minutes from the practice facility.

Geiger took him to Walmart to get furniture. A treat—Giannis *loved* Walmart. It was cheap, and he could ride around the aisles in the shopping carts. The first time Giannis walked in, his eyes darted to the carts. Somehow Giannis stuffed his gangly legs inside the cart and rode around the aisles, squealing, "Ha! Ha, ha, ha! Look at me!" Geiger tried to get him to calm down; they needed to find bedding. But Giannis wouldn't stop; his lanky arms would stretch to the tops of shelves, pulling down items without stepping off the cart, giggling like a kid.

Finally, they returned to Giannis's place. Giannis showed Geiger the master bedroom. "This is going to be for my parents."

"You're not going to take the master?"

"No, man, my parents get the master." They kept walking. Giannis next pointed out the room he planned for Alex and Kostas. Then the farthest bedroom. "This will be mine, but if they want to sleep in here too," Giannis said, referring to his brothers, "that's OK." Even though there was no set date for his parents' arrival in the US, he kept the master spotless for them.

A few minutes later, Giannis Skyped his family. "Look at this place!" he said. "This is *our* new place!" But Geiger knew the Bucks were having difficulties getting visas for the family—difficulties Giannis wasn't aware of yet.

The rookie had so many new things to handle, like installing cable and internet. Given his precarious upbringing, Giannis didn't trust the cable workers. He wanted someone from the Bucks to be there. Geiger was busy the morning of the installation, so Dave Dean, Bucks vice president of basketball operations, asked Daniel Marks, who worked in the scouting department, to come instead. Marks arrived at 9:00 a.m., and by 4:00 p.m., the installation was not completed. Marks was starving. He went into Giannis's pantry and snuck three Oreos out of Giannis's cookie jar, gobbling them quickly.

The next day, Giannis came up to Marks at the practice facility. "Hey, man, did you eat my Oreos?"

"What do you mean?"

"Well, when I left, I had thirty Oreos, and I come back, and there's three missing."

Marks didn't know what to say. He was shocked that someone would count their Oreos. *A millionaire NBA player* who counted his Oreos, at that. But *of course* Giannis counted his Oreos. It didn't matter that he had made the NBA. Inside him was still the child always conscious of food running out.

*   *   *

The first thing Robert Hackett noticed about Giannis was his skinny 196-pound frame. It seemed apparent to the Bucks' strength-and-conditioning coach that the rookie wasn't eating three full meals a day. To get to know each other better, the two went to the Mayfair Mall in Wauwatosa to hang out. Hackett bought Giannis a chicken sandwich at the food court. Giannis devoured it in a couple of bites.

"This is the best thing in the world!" Giannis said.

Hackett laughed. "Dude, that's not even really that good."

Giannis couldn't believe that one sandwich was only five dollars. He bought two more. "Man, we can eat *dinner* off of this!"

Hackett soon realized that he needed to make sure Giannis ate throughout the day. Load him up with strawberry protein shakes, his new favorite, and nutrition bars, making sure the rookie knew it was OK—more than OK—to eat throughout the day. Giannis struggled to put on weight at first because his body was still adjusting. He wasn't used to eating that much or practicing at that intensity. He had never weight-lifted before, which was uncommon for a first-round NBA draft pick. Most prospects start weight lifting as early as freshman year of high school. "Everything was new to him," Hackett says. "He was a sponge."

Hackett had to teach him the mechanics of weight lifting: where to put his hands, his fingers, on the ninety-pound bar to bench-press. Giannis couldn't even bench-press the lowest amount at first, 130 pounds. The first attempt, he struggled to lift the bar. Hackett was right behind him, telling him to keep his balance on both sides, but the bar just trembled.

Hackett taught him how to squat properly, without putting his knees over his feet. How to push his hips back. How to position his shoulders for the shoulder press. Giannis didn't even know what a muscle-up was. Teammates Brandon Knight, Khris Middleton, and Chris Wright showed him, each completing five in a row. Giannis couldn't get his chin over the bar, his feet still touching the floor. His teammates were laughing so hard as Giannis struggled, twitching. "He almost flipped over the bar," Wright says. "He was just really uncoordinated, but you could just tell he was working at it *so* hard."

Hackett tried to teach the rookie patience: he wasn't going to get stronger in one day. But Giannis wanted results *now*. He wanted to get bigger *now*. During fitness tests, like the foot-quickness test, Giannis would ask Hackett what the top mark was. He needed to beat it.

He enjoyed spending all day working out. "He was possessed," Hammond says. Giannis would lift his shirt up, parade around the facility, showing off. "Hey! I got *abs*!" (He had one ab.) He would also check himself out in the mirror after training sessions, looking at his pulsing biceps to see if they had increased in size. He'd flex his squiggly arms; then he'd turn back to his teammates to see if anyone was watching.

"Watch! Watch!" Giannis would say to anyone in the room. "I'm going to get bigger!"

*   *   *

Giannis loved electronic dance music and artists like Avicii and Alesso, but his teammates introduced him to hip-hop, rap—Drake, Rick Ross. Pachulia, a fellow European, who hailed from Tbilisi, Georgia, wanted Giannis to broaden his taste. "Giannis, you were raised in Europe," Pachulia said. "You should listen to house music." Pachulia played him Calvin Harris. Giannis started dancing, shaking his shoulders, but the team shut it down. Back to hip-hop. In quiet moments, Pachulia would turn on house music and whisper to Giannis, "Giannis, it's our time now."

Geiger would tell Giannis which songs were appropriate to sing in public and which were not. "He thought he could just sing whatever he wanted as loud as he wanted, dropping f-bombs," Geiger says. Giannis enjoyed learning dance moves, practicing his Dougie in Cali Swag District's "Teach Me How to Dougie." The Bucks filmed Giannis dancing to Drake's "Best I Ever Had" as the rookie ran his hands up and down his body, trying to look seductive. Giannis *loved* filming it. In between takes, he'd ask to redo certain moves. "You've done it five times," said Geiger, watching. "How's it going to get any better?" Giannis was a perfectionist— even in a music video.

Giannis was starting to develop a sweet tooth. He could eat anything, and it would go right through him. He and Geiger would eat candy at the movies, which they frequented because they thought it would help Giannis with his English. (Giannis loved gangster movies; he liked to act tough in the parking lot after seeing them, walking around shouting, in his most menacing tone, "Yeah! Yeah!") They'd get popcorn, and Giannis would open his mouth, waiting for Geiger to toss a kernel. "Hit me, Ross! Hit me!" Giannis would sip a red or blue Icee and have such a sugar high, cracking so many jokes, Geiger would have to settle him down. Geiger had to explain to him that one had to be quiet during movies.

The two often ate at places that were open late after games, like Giannis's two favorites: Applebee's and the Cheesecake Factory (he considered Cheesecake his "fancy meal," where he would get chocolate milkshakes). He fell in love with chocolate milkshakes and burgers. A true American meal.

Riding to his beloved Walmart in a limo (yes, a limo) made him happy. So did the toy machine at Red Robin. He enjoyed maneuvering the crane for a stuffed animal in between his shake and burger. Giannis would always insist on splitting the bill, even if they ate at McDonald's.

Geiger took Giannis to the Cheesecake Factory for Giannis's birthday. The waiter gave him a free slice of birthday cake. "Ross!" Giannis said, his smile growing wide, candles flickering in front of his eyes, "I think I got this because of my three magic letters: N-B-A!"

Geiger started cracking up. "No, man, that's like a customary thing. They give you a dessert on your birthday! They come sing at the table."

The first time Giannis went to Chipotle, he was astounded at the number of choices, the concept of putting so many items into one bundle. "I want *everything*," Giannis told Geiger. Chicken, steak. Black beans, pinto beans. Guacamole. Cheese. He chose so many items that the server had to use two tortillas. It looked like a football, but in a matter of minutes, it was gone.

Soon Giannis discovered chocolate custard. Costco's pizza and hot dogs. He loved Costco; it's where he had his infamous first smoothie, a dual mixed-berry $1.99 smoothie that was so good he tweeted, "I just taste for the first time a smoothie . . . MAN GOD BLESS AMERICA ☺"

When Giannis had his first taste of peanut butter, trying out Bucks assistant general manager David Morway's wife's homemade peanut butter bars, he cooed, "Ooooohhhh" in delight. When Oppenheimer would order shrimp cocktails at dinner, Giannis would ask, "What is this? What are shrimps?" When shopping at grocery stores, Giannis would linger along the aisles, picking up item after item, just reading the labels, figuring out what everything meant.

The first time he tried pancakes, he became obsessed. He had pancakes for ten days straight. The first time he tried an Auntie Anne's pretzel at the Southridge Mall in Greendale, he thought it was the most delicious thing. He couldn't get over that they made it right there, so quickly.

People were starting to recognize him, walking around the mall with his pretzel. He was so delighted, so shy, he didn't know what to say. He kept waving to people, so proud, thinking it was so cool to walk through Southridge.

People in Milwaukee fell in love with Giannis. And he was easy to love: a big kid in a small city, fascinated with every new adventure.

Giannis couldn't get over the concept of a buffet—unlimited food for a fixed price. The first time he saw one, Drew told him, "Get whatever you want." Giannis put some food on his plate, some of which he didn't even recognize.

A few minutes after they sat down to eat, Giannis saw his coach get up and head back to the buffet. "Coach!" Giannis whispered to him, alarmed. "What are you doing? You can't do that."

Drew looked at him strangely. "It's a buffet. You can do that. You can go as many times as you want."

Giannis was taken aback. He felt the same when the team traveled to road games and he saw that there was food on the plane or in the hotel fridge. Or that a whole meal from Perkins Restaurant & Bakery, a Wisconsin staple, cost five dollars. Once, carrying a couple of frozen pizzas at Target, he went outside the store to find a basket before paying; security quickly stopped him. A fan kindly intervened, explaining Giannis's mistake.

The first time he got his check from the Bucks, he asked Butler, "How do I get them to not take taxes out?"

Butler laughed. "Welcome to the NBA."

When Butler and Mayo went to a local furniture store and picked out nearly an entire apartment's worth of furniture and had it delivered to Giannis, he was truly touched. The veterans who kicked his ass for a week straight to begin the season really cared about him. Were looking out for him.

Giannis had to learn how to manage money. How to tip at restaurants. How to use AirDrop on his phone. And he had questions: Why did he have to pay taxes in America if he wasn't American? Why was this street name so long? Milwaukee was his playground, and each day brought something exciting. Even something as small as learning that he could pause and rewind game film on a TV.

"He was just shocked that this was his life now," Wolters says.

Before a game against the Jazz in Utah, Giannis's coaches tried to explain to him that he might get tired because of the altitude. "Don't panic," they told him. "Your body will figure it out."

But Giannis had to see it for himself. After pregame shooting, he walked up to Oppenheimer. "Coach," Giannis said. "I want to see altitude!" Giannis then sprinted to the top of the stands. Stood there for five minutes, waiting for something to happen, to seize him.

One practice, Cody Ross, the video coordinator, remembers Giannis coming up to him and Oppenheimer, saying, "Guys, I need a haircut. I want a haircut like Cody." Ross's brown hair was always either smoothed back perfectly or freshly buzz-cut. Giannis wanted Ross's best look: a low fade. "He was so concerned with having a cool American haircut," Ross says. So he went to Gee's Clippers, a Milwaukee haven for hoop heads, which gave him his first cut.

Giannis became close with Bucks assistant coach Nick Van Exel. They'd trash-talk each other. "You're too small!" Giannis would say. At first he didn't know who Van Exel, a storied point guard, was. Then he googled, came back to practice the next day, looked at Van Exel, and said, "Ah-ha! Ah-ha! Oh, I know. I know."

Van Exel started laughing. "What do you know?"

"I know, Nick. Nick the Quick! Nick the Quick! Nick the Quick!" Giannis couldn't stop repeating Van Exel's nickname, proud of himself.

Giannis was eager to complete rookie duties. Butler would ask him to fetch some Mountain Dew or McDonald's. "That was something just to keep him humble," Butler says. "But honestly we didn't have to humble him because he never took anything for granted." He *happily* did the chores, like it was a big deal that Sanders entrusted him to get Dunkin'

Donuts for him at 6:30 a.m. before practice. Or when Ridnour asked him to get muffins or drop off laundry to teammates' rooms on the road.

Butler, who was turning into a mentor, kept him on his toes. After Giannis played well against the Nets, in front of a large crowd of Greek Americans, he received a standing ovation. Butler looked at the rookie, checking to see how he handled the praise. *Yup, rook's feeling himself a little too much*, Butler thought.

Afterward, teammates took Giannis out to a nightclub. Giannis thought they were celebrating his great performance, but Butler's birthday was coming up, and the veteran had one wish: to humble the rookie. But-ler asked Giannis to drop and give him thirty-some push-ups in front of everyone in the club—one for every year of Butler's birthday.

Giannis didn't flinch. He dropped to the floor, his chest rising and fall-ing with every push-up. Everyone was laughing at him, including women nearby, but Giannis wasn't bothered. "If you asked him to run through a brick wall," Butler says, "he would really do it."

Giannis was respectful of elders. He would call everyone Mister: Mr. Luke. Mr. John. Mr. Larry. He kept his locker clean and organized, tak-ing pride in how it looked. "Everything he did, he did it with a level of enthusiasm that I haven't seen," says Bob Bender, Bucks assistant coach that season.

Most rookies would balk at being sent to freezing Milwaukee; Giannis loved it. He was grateful for this dream world where Skip Robinson, then Bucks vice president of community relations and player development, would pick him up in his Escalade. "Skip, this is *niiiiice*," Giannis said the first time riding in Robinson's car.

Giannis seemed to always be smiling. Hammond came up to him one afternoon and told him his smile reminded him of a certain leg-end. "Giannis, you know Magic Johnson? You know one of his greatest attributes?"

Giannis had seen highlights of Johnson, had wanted to model his game after him, but he didn't really know much about him. So Giannis nodded when Hammond asked him about Johnson's best attribute but didn't *truly* know the answer.

"It's not his dribble. It's not his no-look pass," Hammond continued. "It's not his hook shot. It may not even be the championships. It's his smile. Giannis, you got *that*. You got that warm smile. Keep that smile."

There was an innocence to Giannis. A naivete. A goofiness, a sweetness. Much of what he said, did, was hilarious. When he learned to do a bicep curl, Reinke, the former team attendant, would be in the locker room with him, and he'd say, "Giannis, getting those muscles all big! You getting big for the women?"

"Oh yes!" Giannis said. "Very big biceps! The women love the biceps!"

Then he realized curls rhymed with girls, and a new saying was born. "Curls for the girls! Curls for the girls! The girls love the curls!" he'd say while looking at himself in the mirror doing bicep curls.

Another time, teammates called Giannis over for a cameo in a team video that would play on the jumbotron. They gave him a foam finger as a prop to use. "Giannis," Oppenheimer screamed, "stick it up your nose!" Giannis tried to stick the foam finger up his nose, and when he tickled his nose with it, he giggled so hard he fell over against the wall. So did Oppenheimer.

Giannis was warm with whoever he encountered. On planes, when his teammates would sleep or have headphones on, Giannis would always be talking to the flight attendants, asking them about their day. "Flight attendants loved him," Wolters says. "He just makes people feel good. People gravitate towards him."

When the Bucks played the Grizzlies, there was a Bucks poster of him that said "Greek and Still Growing." Giannis stared at the photo of himself on the poster. "Let me see—I think I am very handsome!" he mused. When he picked up a technical foul against Toronto and realized the tech came with a hefty fine, he ran to the referee and begged him to take it back.

Fans started calling him *adorable*. He would deepen his voice during an interview, letting them know he had to use his deep voice, his serious voice, because they were filming. He became an internet sensation. A social media darling. "His naiveté and willingness to be forthcoming about how exciting new experiences are for him have turned him into a mix between an athletic marvel and a cat meme," a local writer told ESPN in 2014.

Kurt Leitinger, longtime fan and Milwaukee native, loved Giannis so much he named his car, a GMC Sierra 1500, Giannis. "I even had it lifted so it sits right around six foot eleven to seven feet tall and got 'Giannis' on my license plate." He remembers a fan account on Twitter, @GreekFreak-Alert, that would notify fans when Giannis checked into the game. "He made jaw-dropping plays where you couldn't help but think, *That's not normal. That's special*," Leitinger says. "Bucks fans believed in him right away."

As Giannis's fame grew, he encountered more and more fans, more and more requests. But when asked to do a one-on-one interview with local reporters, he'd often ask the Bucks PR team, "Why do they want to talk to me?"

He was sweet to those he knew. When Melissa Mangan, a strength-and-conditioning intern whom fellow interns suspected Giannis had a crush on, made a protein shake for Giannis, he was so touched he politely asked her if it would be OK if he followed her on Twitter.

A couple of interns, including Mangan, would mix the powder Gato-rade together for the team before games and would have players test to see if it was too sweet. It turned into a competition to see who could mix the Gatorade best.

Giannis always wanted to be the tester, taking pride in the task. He was serious about the technique: one had to stir it *perfectly* because it's a big gallon of powder and water and ice, and the ratio of flavor, mainly grape, had to be just right. He would take a sip, put his pinky up, pretending to be fancy, cracking everyone up, telling everyone the qualities he liked and didn't like from each creation. "Ohhhhhh, this one is a little too sweet!" he'd say.

He'd somehow always pick Mangan's. "He'd say it before even trying it," she says. It got to the point where they made him do a blind taste test, with a blindfold over his eyes, so he wouldn't automatically pick hers. He was so tickled with himself when he settled on the right mixture that he'd run, cup in hand, to Middleton. "Khris! You *have* to try this! It is sooooo good. Try this one!"

You couldn't *not* like him. Unless you found him annoying, as kid broth-ers can be. One afternoon, some players were eating lunch at the practice facility, and despite not having played many minutes at that point in the season, Giannis came in and said, "I'm the Greek Freak! I'm Giannis! Someday I'm going to be the best in the league!" Miroslav Raduljica, a center from Serbia, reading a book, looked *pissed*. "This kid is *so* fucking annoying," Raduljica said under his breath.

Another time, in the players' lounge, some players and staffers were talking about NBA players who spent their entire careers with one team. Giannis blurted out, "I love Milwaukee! I wanna be in Milwaukee forever! I'm going to be here for twenty years! By the time I'm done playing in Milwaukee, everybody will be sick of me!"

Raduljica rolled his eyes. "I'm already sick of him," he said quietly, walking out of the room.

"Everyone was laughing," says Michael Clutterbuck, Bucks director of basketball analytics from 2013 to 2017. "Giannis was just young and naive and didn't understand the way of the business."

Staffers contemplated how best to portray Giannis over social media, concerned that his joy for discovering new American things could be perceived in a negative light. "There was a sensitivity, on the business and marketing side, to portraying him as being overly naive," says Theodore Loehrke, former Bucks senior vice president and chief revenue officer. The Bucks didn't want him to seem unsophisticated. "There was a conscious effort *not* to play up the smoothie thing," Loehrke says, "even though it was a fun story. We just wanted to make sure that people understood him as a person and not as a caricature of a *Coming to America* story."

* * *

There was also a very serious side to Giannis, a burning desire inside him to prove that he belonged. He wanted to be *great*. He didn't care that his first regular-season game was against the New York Knicks and Carmelo Anthony, at that point one of the best players in the league, at Madison Square Garden.

Giannis, the youngest player in the league at eighteen years and 328 days, asked Drew if he could guard Anthony.

The morning of the game, October 30, 2013, Giannis kept exclaiming to Butler, "The Knicks! The New York Knicks! Carmelo Anthony!" Giannis kept looking around, as if he was trying to freeze the moment. Remember every detail. It was still shocking to him that he had NBA socks. An NBA uniform.

One Greek journalist, Nick Metallinos, living in New York at the time, arrived a few hours early just to catch a glimpse of Giannis. He was standing on the baseline when Giannis noticed him and walked over. Metallinos told Giannis, in Greek, that he was Greek too. Giannis showed respect by speaking in the plural: "τι κάνετε" (How are you?). Giannis was floored— another Greek, speaking Greek, in New York City.

He turned his attention back to the court and began shooting around. Butler sensed the rookie was in awe of Carmelo and probably had nervous energy. "Don't go for the shot fakes," Butler told Giannis. "Stay down on defense."

"Giannis was hyped; he was ready to go," Henson says. "He didn't know any better. He's like, 'Carmelo? It's just another guy to me.'"

Giannis quickly found out how strong, how powerful, Anthony was. Anthony finished with nineteen points and ten rebounds. Giannis played only four minutes, forty-three seconds. He didn't attempt a field goal. Didn't grab a rebound. He finished with one point: a free throw. But Anthony saw how badly the rookie wanted to shine. Giannis worked hard to deny Anthony the ball. He always had a strong sense of where the ball was going to be. And if he wasn't near it, he'd give everything to get to it.

"He was scrappy," Anthony says. "I knew, 'OK, he's not backing down. He wants it.' You saw his competitive nature and how he wanted to be great.

"He was a raw, raw talent. You could tell he just had so much upside to him," Anthony says. It was clear, though, that Giannis had a ways to go physically. "I don't think he knew how to use his body at that point in time."

The Bucks lost, 90–83. Giannis was quiet after the game. It didn't help that public announcers fumbled his name throughout the game, as journalists would for the next couple of months, with some variation of the following:

"Gee-Ahnnis."

"Antenna-koompo."

"Ant-tekoompo."

"Ahntay-ti-koonpo."

Sports Illustrated declared that his "five-syllable surname has flummoxed every P.A. announcer in the NBA." The *Milwaukee Journal Sentinel* said, "You still struggle to consistently pronounce the name without stammering." Yahoo said, "Man, this is going to be rough."

"The Greek Freak" nickname began to stick; Giannis *was* freakishly athletic and talented, able to handle the ball surprisingly well for his size. Ted Davis, the Bucks radio play-by-play announcer, coined the nickname "the Alphabet," but Giannis liked Greek Freak. To this day, Giannis doesn't know where the nickname came from, though; neither do those closest to him.

Earlier in the season, at the state fair in Wisconsin in August 2013, the Bucks digital team had Giannis play a game with fans to see if they could pronounce his name. "Everyone was saying it wrong," says Mike Grahl, former Bucks vice president of digital platforms, now the chief marketing officer with the Timberwolves.

A woman in a pink tie-dye shirt said, "Gee-ah-nay-us Ant-te-toe-kenopio." It got worse as others made dozens of cringeworthy attempts:

"Giannis Antay-ti-no-no-koo-poo."

"Jannis Ante-to-kwampo."

"Ate-no-koonopoe."

"Guiness Ante-kwanpo."

"Giannis Anten-te-ko-no-poh-poh-poh."

Grahl remembers how Giannis smiled, didn't seem bothered, despite participants laughing after each attempt. "He embraced it, being the optimistic, fun free spirit that he is," Grahl says.

The Bucks weren't sure whether to call him the Greek Freak at first, unsure whether the rookie found the name offensive. Eddie Doucette, the legendary Bucks broadcaster and a Wisconsin Broadcasters Association Hall of Fame inductee, who had been with the team since its inception in 1968 until 1984, didn't like the nickname Greek Freak. He still doesn't. "I personally think 'the Greek Freak' is defamatory," Doucette says.

He would know. He's an expert at creating basketball terminology, like Kareem Abdul-Jabbar's "skyhook," and bestowing nicknames on every Bucks player. "I wanted to make basketball fun for people," says Doucette, now eighty-three. His best nicknames? The Cement Mixer (Dick Cunningham), the Greyhound (Bob Dandridge), and Captain Marvel (Greg Smith). He was responsible for so much of the new basketball lingo that he'd get calls from teachers complaining that their students were "talking a different language," shouting, "Bango!" when shooting wads of paper into trash cans.

So although Doucette is no longer with the organization, he has an idea for a new nickname for Giannis. "Who's a bigger cheese in Milwaukee, or even in the state of Wisconsin, other than Aaron Rodgers?" Doucette says. "When he's [Rodgers] out of season, it's all about Giannis and the Bucks. If there isn't a bigger cheese than Giannis, why not call him the Big Feta? Everyone loves a piece of feta cheese."

*   *   *

Most days, Giannis was exhausted. He'd spend hours on the court in practice, hours in the weight room, then hours at night, by himself, trying to become stronger. "He wanted to become someone who earned his stripes, not be given his stripes," Cleamons says.

It was frustrating, though, that the results weren't showing. And he was barely getting off the bench during games. A few minutes here, a few minutes there. He had a nice game against Miami, scoring a then season-high eleven points; then he struggled again, scoring just two against Oklahoma City. He was inconsistent. And so were his minutes.

That was partially because he was a liability on defense. He was late on defensive rotations because he was overrotating. He'd reach, hack somebody. Foul. He wasn't used to the speed of play. The awe-inspiring things he did—a monster block, a near impossible finish at the rim—would be erased by out-of-sync moments. He'd try to bump somebody, only to fall down himself, his arms and legs sprawled on the court. He'd look at referees, like, *Where's the foul?* But the whistle wouldn't blow. The Bucks were losing nearly every game, and Giannis was a no-name.

When subbed out, Giannis seemed visibly frustrated. Butler and Ridnour would try to coach him through, tell him to relax. "You're going so fast—just calm down," they'd say. "Breathe." Drew was patient with Giannis, giving him some leeway with mistakes. "Our biggest concern was his development," Drew says.

But Giannis was hard on himself, beating himself up to the point that he'd start crying. In front of the team. One home game, Drew took Giannis out in the fourth quarter, mainly because it was a possession game and the Bucks were about to play defense. Drew called a time-out. Giannis sat next to Drew and stared him down. Then Giannis's eyes started to get watery. "I could see his eyes welling," Drew says.

After the play, another time-out was called, and Drew put Giannis back in the game. Drew tried to explain to him that sometimes players are subbed out during these situations, but the rookie couldn't be consoled. "No, you leave me in the game," Giannis told his coach. "You leave me in there offensively; you leave me in there defensively."

Drew loved that Giannis wasn't afraid to say that. It reminded Drew of another player he had coached: Kobe Bryant. Drew recalls the Lakers' first-round playoff series against Portland in 1997, when Portland's Isaiah "J. R." Rider manhandled LA's guards, including eighteen-year-old Kobe, winning game 3. Afterward, Drew told players they had given their best efforts. Kobe just stared at Drew, angry.

"LD," Kobe said, "I swear to you. That will *never* happen again." Drew asked him what he meant, and Kobe talked about how Rider physically beat him up. "That will *never* happen again," Kobe repeated. Sure enough, the Lakers won game 4 and moved on to the Western Conference Semifinals, and the following fall for training camp, Kobe's body had been transformed. He put on a ton of muscle. Drew thought of that whenever he saw Giannis berate himself. "Kobe was the ultimate competitor, and I saw that same competitive drive in Giannis," Drew says. "He's driven."

When Giannis would cry, Drew realized that the kid wasn't quite a man yet. He didn't yet know how to control his emotions. "He's still a kid, and he's going to have kid reactions to some things," Drew says. "That's something we had to understand."

Even in late summer, when Giannis first came to Milwaukee, when playing casual games of one-on-one with his new teammates, he'd make a mistake, or someone would get the best of him on a possession, and he'd run out, just take *off*, stopping in the tunnel area. He'd ball his fists up, trying to control himself. "The emotion was such that you would say, 'Yeah, he might be having a meltdown in there,'" Bender says.

Giannis always sprinted right back, didn't let the emotion affect his play, but he couldn't stomach not living up to the expectations he set for himself. "He was always working—almost *too* hard," Henson says. At the end of practices, the team would usually scrimmage, and if Giannis didn't feel like he'd made the shots he wanted, he'd go to a side basket and shoot.

Drew would come to check on him. "I missed too many shots, Coach," Giannis would say apologetically. "I gotta make those shots."

When Giannis would miss a free throw, he would be so upset with himself—"like it was the end of the world," Butler says—that Butler had to tell him, "Don't be so hard on yourself."

"But it's *free!*"

"You gotta have a short memory. On to the next play."

Hackett noticed Giannis crying in the weight room on several occasions when the two were alone. Hackett wondered if his public display of emotion might be a cultural difference. Boys and men in the States are oftentimes taught to hold in their emotion. "We won't let it out, especially as a Black male," says Hackett, who is Black. "We're going to hide it. But he could probably care less."

Giannis wasn't raised to hold in his emotions on the court in Greece. "He used to cry after every game," says Zivas, his former Filathlitikos coach. But when Giannis came to America, some of his coaches and teammates were taken aback by it; it's just not something one sees in the hypermasculine NBA.

"You can't cry," Hackett told Giannis. "Just don't do that."

But the more it happened, the more Hackett sensed how badly the rookie ached to be great. Anything less was a failure. Because failing wasn't just failing in the weight room. Failing would mean failing his family. And failing his family would mean returning to Greece. And returning to Greece would mean hustling on the streets again.

"He would think about it, like, 'I'm a rookie; I'm hours away from my family; my whole family is left behind; did I want to just come here to go through the motions? No,'" Alex says. "Did we go through two-hour bus rides, go through all that stuff, to go over to America to just be average? No. That's not how it goes."

Even right before games, Giannis would go through a full on-court workout, asking Oppenheimer to hit him harder with giant cushions. "Sometimes it felt like we had to shut the gym down in order for him to stop working," Butler says.

Giannis would return to the practice court right after games. He wasn't able to let go of his mistakes. He'd grab a ball and try to outshoot his disappointment. Once, Giannis had finished his own workout and was taking off his sneakers when Butler teased, "Bet you can't dunk with no shoes on."

Giannis called for the ball, white socks and all. Starting at the three-point line, he took two gargantuan steps and hammered the ball home so hard the rim shook.

*   *   *

Though he was hard on himself, he was also sure of himself. Those closest to him could tell *he* knew he was going to be really good. Every so often, he'd tell Wolters, the Bucks rookie, about his master plan: "Next year I'll be averaging ten points a game," Giannis said. "I'll keep getting better and better, and then the next year after that, I'll be averaging closer to twenty."

Then he'd tell everyone, "I want to be the best. I'm going to be the man." And they laughed, like, *OK, kid, sure. Those are lofty goals.* "He really believed he was going to be one of the best players in the NBA," Oppenheimer says. No matter how far-fetched his goals seemed at the time, Giannis used to randomly say to teammates or staffers, "I am the Greek Freak! I am the Greek Freak!" Then he'd flex his muscles, as if to prove it.

He would have a modest stat line after a game, and riding in the car with Geiger to Applebee's afterward, Giannis would say, "Yeah! Yeah! Did you see that? Yeah, I'm the Greek Freak!"

He used to tell Cody Ross, "Cody, I am the LeBron James of Greece." Giannis understood the influence James had in America; he planned on being the Greek equivalent.

The first time Giannis met Chris Wright, the Bucks forward, Giannis said, "I'm Giannis. The Greek Freak. The Greek Freak, bab-ayyyyy!" When Giannis met Greg Signorelli, an athletic-training intern that year, who ended up staying six years full-time, Giannis said, "You can call me champ. I'm the champ!"

People still couldn't pronounce his name—some didn't even try—but the first name Giannis stuck more than anything. "He became a first-name household name," says Lori Nickel, the sports columnist, "almost like Madonna or Pele."

Skip Robinson, the Bucks staffer, noticed the influence Giannis *did* have when he walked into a room. Shoulders back. Chin up. "He walks proud," Robinson says. "He walks like a king."

*   *   *

But the king needed a driver's license.

After several months of staffers driving him everywhere, Giannis decided he wanted to learn how to drive. One afternoon, Dave Dean, the vice president of basketball operations, was sitting in his office, listening to Giannis and a driver's education instructor read the rules of driving. Giannis was so excited he belted out every instruction. "*Oh*, that is . . . *hydroplaning!*" Then he'd get quiet, listen—then belt out another revelation. "Bald tires are bad!" Giannis was convinced he knew it all. "I want to take the test right now!" he said. "I am ready!"

He still had a lot to learn. Geiger, Hammond, Dean, and Jon Horst, then director of basketball administration and current Bucks GM, decided to teach him rather than have him continue driver's school. Geiger spent the most time with Giannis, letting Giannis drive his Subaru. Giannis would stuff his six-foot-nine frame into the small station wagon, cranking the seat all the way back. His knees still perched over the steering wheel as he drove. It was an old car; Geiger had gotten it when he was sixteen, and the engine made a loud noise when it started. But that didn't matter to Giannis: he was thrilled. A little *too* thrilled.

Geiger would have to remind him to focus. "See the car on your left?" They'd approach a stop sign, and Giannis wouldn't slow down, and Geiger would think, *Does he see it? Does he know he has to stop?* Or when Giannis wanted to turn, he wouldn't turn on his blinker. They'd get closer to the turn, and Giannis could sense Geiger getting nervous, with a serious face.

"Indicator, indicator!" Giannis would say, flashing a big smile. "I know. I know. Don't worry, Ross. I got this!"

Geiger taught him to pump gas too. And when Geiger would insist on helping, Giannis would say, "No, I'm pumping my own gas." That made him feel cool, responsible. Like he was a real adult, handling adult things.

Hammond, Dean, and Horst would sometimes take Giannis for a spin in the team car, a Ford Edge. Giannis pushed the seat so far back that Dean and Horst barely had room to sit in the back seat. They'd all practice parallel parking in the practice facility. Giannis's teammates refused to get in the car with him, though. They felt he drove too fast. Once, Henson was headed to the airport after a game and saw an SUV zoom past him, weaving in and out of traffic. "I'm like, 'Is that Giannis?'" Henson says. Henson got to the airport, called Giannis: "You can't drive like that. What are you doing?"

Giannis had to learn how to drive on ice and snow. Once, a Bucks staffer and Giannis went to the grocery store, and Giannis wanted to drive them home. The staffer was in a rush and didn't want to let Giannis drive his car. Giannis got out of the car, in freezing snow, opened Google Maps on his phone, and started walking home. It would take about two hours, but Giannis was stubborn. He'd rather walk than sit in the passenger's seat. A couple of blocks in, the staffer caught up with him. "OK, you win. You can drive."

The best times? Giannis would turn the volume up full blast in Geiger's Subaru, rolling down his window, dancing to the people who would come up next to the car. They'd look over, and Giannis would shimmy harder. Geiger's car didn't have the best air conditioner, so Giannis would stretch his two arms out both the driver's and the passenger's windows, reach across Geiger's face while the car was moving, and flap his wings like a bird to generate more air.

"It was, like, *unhuman*," Geiger says. And those pulling up next to them would laugh and stare. "He was this big kid, dancing, with humongous hands," Geiger says. "These people would look over, like, 'What is going *on* in that vehicle?'"

*   *   *

Another cold day in November, maybe fifteen degrees, Giannis didn't have anyone's car to borrow. It was a Saturday. Game day. Giannis had gone to Western Union to send his paycheck to his family but lost track of time.

At the same time, a woman named Jane Gallop was shopping at Glorioso's, an Italian grocery store, a block or two away, on Brady Street. When she got back in her Honda Fit with her partner, Dick Blau, she saw a very tall, very thin Black man running by. *This guy looks familiar*, Gallop thought.

Gallop, a professor at the University of Wisconsin–Milwaukee, has been a Bucks fan since 1999. She *loves* the Bucks. In a flash, she realized: the man running by her was Giannis. And he was wearing a thin navy windbreaker and blue jeans in fifteen-degree weather. "My maternal response was 'Oh my God, it's way too cold to wear a windbreaker. He should be wearing a winter jacket,'" Gallop says. She turned to her partner. "Can we give him a ride?" They caught up to the rookie, rolled down the window, and asked, "Hey, do you want a ride?"

Giannis paused. "Are you going to the Bradley Center?"

"We'll take you there."

Giannis hopped into the small car, said thank you twice, his usual practice. He sat sideways, head bent down in order to fit. He didn't say much. They were all nervous in this incredibly strange moment. "I couldn't think straight," Gallop says. All she could say was "You need a winter jacket."

"Yeah. I don't have any money. I just sent all my money to my parents at Western Union."

Gallop was fangirling so hard inside she forgot to ask for a photo and regrets not finding a store and buying him a jacket. She did manage to ask for an autograph. Giannis wrote it in both English and Greek and gave her and her partner a hug and thanked them again upon arriving at the Bradley Center.

When Giannis found Hammond, told him what happened, the general manager was horrified. "If you ever need a ride," Hammond said, "you call any one of us. Don't get in the car with a stranger."

Giannis didn't know any better. After all, this was America. And all he was thinking about was getting money to his family. Wishing they were in Milwaukee with him.

*   *   *

Lately, though, his teammates and coaches had started to sense that something was off. The bright, charismatic Giannis was not as smiley, not as bouncy. He had lost some sparkle. His laugh seemed manufactured, as if it took effort from somewhere deep down. His tweets, filled with exclamation points about his newest smoothie discoveries, masked deeper pain. Pain that few understood: he felt alone.

CHAPTER 6

LONELY

Each morning, Giannis would take one last look at the master bedroom in his apartment. He'd make sure the pillows were perfectly fluffed, just in case his parents might somehow arrive in the States later in the day. He'd head to the Cousins Center for practice, hope humming inside him.

Maybe today my family will be approved, he'd think, walking from the parking lot into the building. He'd lace up his sneakers next to his cubby, which was always immaculate, organized, as if his parents might turn up and inspect it.

Then he'd find Hammond. "Any word on my family?" Giannis would ask. "How long until they will be here?" Before Hammond could respond, two Giannis questions blossomed into two more: "What about this month? Is there anything else we can do to get them here?"

Hammond assured him that the organization was doing everything it could to bring the family to America—and he was being sincere. Immigration officials had denied the family's visa request twice by this point, but Kohl and his assistant, JoAnne Anton, kept pushing. Hammond told Giannis that he didn't have an answer yet. Giannis would have to keep waiting, keep being patient.

But every day without his family pierced him. Made him rethink everything he'd endured up to this point. He wondered if it was all worth it: the grueling hours in the weight room, adding at least thirty pounds of muscle in mere months, getting smacked in the paint day after day, crumpling to the floor.

"It killed him," Alex says about Giannis being away from the family. "He was calling us all the time. He missed us and was constantly thinking about how he was going to bring us over there."

The dream Giannis had constructed in his head, mesmerized by the braids of Iverson, the jumpers of Durant, didn't look like this, didn't feel like this. He had always imagined being *here* but never once considered his family would be *there*.

Without him.

He had never been without any of them for more than three days, unless he was traveling for a youth tournament. He had never not slept side by side with his brothers. He'd never not had to take two buses with them, just to run up and down a court for a few hours, coming home to their parents, who would ask, "Did you make the most of your time today?"

He was more than homesick, more than frustrated. For the first time in his life, he was deeply lonely. Lost.

*   *   *

Most days, Giannis kept to himself. Milwaukee was still a new city; he didn't know what to do or where to go. He missed the old food back at Kivotos Café, complaining to Tzikas that the food on airplanes and in hotels was mostly processed. "All he wanted was some homemade food," Tzikas says.

Giannis would Skype with his family early in the morning or late at night because of the eight-hour time difference. The internet made them feel near, but after logging off, he'd realize they were so very far away. Everything had changed so *quickly*. He was sending them most of the money he was making, hardly concerned whether he had enough for himself.

One night over Skype, around November 2013, frustrated with his family's inability to obtain visas, Giannis told them, "I'm going to do this for as long as I have to, but if y'all can't come, I'm coming back."

His brothers were floored. They didn't know whether he was just frustrated or genuinely at a breaking point, genuinely considering giving up.

But he meant it: he might leave the NBA. "Obviously we didn't want him to come back," Alex says, "but it meant the world to know that he's loyal to us."

Giannis relayed a similar message to his agents, telling them that the only reason he wanted to play in the NBA was to provide a better life for his family. Without them, what reason was there to remain in America? "Take me back," Giannis said. "I'd rather be with my family than just being over here."

His agents were trying to help with the visas as much as they could. With the family having been declined twice already, the situation was growing more tenuous by the day.

Giannis felt a little guilty. Guilty at all he was enjoying, all he was learning, when people back home still didn't have much. Wherever he was, his mind often traveled: here, there. Here, there. America, Greece, America, Greece.

He always played hard, never sacrificed a possession. That was never in question. "He didn't just show up and let his God-given ability take over. He worked at his craft," says Bender, the assistant coach. "There's a saying: 'Good, bad, go to the next play.' He probably never even heard of that expression before, but God, he was an example of that. A poster child of 'Good, bad, go to the next play.'"

Giannis could compartmentalize well, from years of masking his pain. Pretending that his stomach was not growling. Pretending that he wasn't unsure where he and his family might be sleeping the next month. But Milwaukee was a different challenge. "Being scared to walk in the streets because, you know, the culture is totally different over here," Giannis later told *60 Minutes*. "I was scared. I was lonely."

He was supported. Cared for. He had Geiger taking him for late-night chocolate milkshakes to make him smile; Oppenheimer battling him in shooting contests every day; Coach Drew texting him regularly, making sure his rookie felt valued; Robinson showing up in his Escalade to take him to the mall, just to get him outside his head.

Then there was Hammond, checking in on how he was feeling every day. He was the perfect GM for someone like Giannis because he was compassionate and patient. He didn't expect Giannis to play perfectly right away. But when Giannis would do something exciting on the court, Hammond would scream, "Oh mannnnnnn! That's a bad, bad man right there!"

Hammond was a different kind of GM. He had empathy for players. His Midwest upbringing, his subtle humor, made him relatable. He gave interns rides home. He talked to anyone shooting late at night. He came to staffers' rec basketball league games on Sundays. If someone needed to attend a wedding, they could expect Hammond to say, without hesitation, "*Go!*"

No job was too small for him; if players left bottles on the floor, he'd pick them up. It wasn't uncommon to see him wiping up the floor, wet from the leaky roof, with a towel. On snowy mornings, he'd shovel snow and lay down salt near the practice facility entrance, all in dress shoes, slacks, and a dress shirt. He related to Giannis because he knew what it was to dream big—and to suffer.

The Zion, Illinois, native had survived a near-fatal motorcycle accident in 1971, suffering injuries that prevented him from playing at either of his dream schools, Illinois and Notre Dame. Then, attending Greenville College, he would mourn the loss of his best friend, Scott Burgess, who died of a brain injury after colliding with a player in practice.

Hammond continued to grind, starting as a high school basketball coach in Pawnee City, Nebraska, before becoming a small-town college basketball coach at Southwest Missouri State. He worked his way up in the NBA in various teams' scouting departments, eventually ascending into management with the Pistons.

And even with a limited budget with a small-market team in Milwaukee, Hammond wanted everyone on staff to feel valued. "His words to me were 'I want these players to walk into this locker room and feel like it's a Hollywood premiere in here,'" says Mike Sergo, Bucks staffer of more than twenty-five years, who also serves as the equipment manager for the G League affiliate Wisconsin Herd. "The TVs had to be on *SportsCenter*. Every towel had to be folded. Nothing could be lying in the laundry bins when players walked in."

Had Giannis been drafted to a big-market team like Miami or LA or NY, he might not have had as much one-on-one support that would help him stay afloat when he was so down.

One road trip, Brandon Knight sensed that Giannis was withdrawn, barely leaving his hotel room. Knight caught Giannis in the hallway, on the way to his room to Skype his family. "Yo, what are you doing?" Knight said.

"Oh, I am just going to my room," Giannis said.

"Come here—get your hair cut, man."

"My hair cut?"

"Yeah! A bunch of us are getting them in a different room. Come on."

Giannis agreed, though a bit reluctantly. When he sat down in the chair, greeting the barber, he grinned wide. This was so exciting: a special hotel haircut with American teammates. For a moment, his sadness softened. He had teammates who cared about him.

But then he returned to his room, to the reality in front of him: this was not really *home*. His teammates weren't his family. Milwaukee was nice, but it didn't have the scent of fufu floating through the air, enveloping him like a warm embrace.

It was a strange feeling: clutching more cash in his palm than he ever thought possible, feeling emptier than he ever thought possible.

*   *   *

To make matters worse, the Bucks were awful. Will-we-even-reach-double-digit-total-wins-this-season awful. They were a young team, with many players in their early twenties. Team morale was at an all-time low. "I was so excited to get traded to Charlotte halfway through," Ridnour says. "It was just depressing. Everything was bad."

All hell broke loose when Sanders broke his thumb, getting into a fistfight in a nightclub, throwing a champagne bottle, adding to the perception of the Bucks as completely dysfunctional. It was humiliating for Sanders, who had just signed a four-year $44 million contract extension. With a seven-foot, seven-inch wingspan, he was at one point one of the best shot blockers in the NBA. He could cover the length of the floor in six strides, and in his prime, when he dunked, backboards would shake for thirty seconds, or so it seemed. He turned out to be the Bucks' biggest disappointment that year, getting suspended for drug use by the end of the season.

"What an absolute waste," says Scott Williams, Bucks assistant coach that season.

Injuries mounted. D. J. Stephens, a reserve, remembers someone saying on the bench, "There's sixty million dollars just sitting there at the end of the bench. Can't even play because they're hurt." He had to laugh—things were so bad.

"Whole season was a blur," Cleamons says. "We suffered. And I use the word *suffered*."

"It was chaos," says Pachulia.

It didn't help that it was the year of the Arctic polar vortex, the coldest on record in two decades in Milwaukee. The temperature dropped below zero twenty-four times, and the wind chill was characterized as "life-threatening," with values as low as sixty degrees below zero. Experts warned of potential frostbite to anyone who stepped outside with uncovered skin.

One day, Williams was coming back from practice and the battery mechanism on his garage door failed, and he thought to himself, *I have to get out of this car, or I will literally die. They'll find me on the sidewalk literally frozen.* Williams used to show up first at practice just because he wanted to get the prime parking spot to avoid the windchill walking from farther away. "We didn't have underground parking," he recalls.

The cold was a big adjustment for Giannis. He didn't own warm clothes at first. He had only the Bucks sweat suits, which he wore every day. Ilyasova gave him a pair of jeans, as did Mayo and Butler. But he would wear just a light down jacket or sweatshirt and sweats on those frigid Milwaukee days. Sometimes Giannis would hold on to Geiger's arm when walking because he was shivering, wearing Nike slides with socks rather than snow boots.

One night, as they were leaving the Cheesecake Factory near 11:00 p.m., a heavy snow was falling, the beginning of a blizzard. Inches and inches of snow had already piled up outside as Giannis and Geiger headed to the car. Geiger drove, going just thirty miles an hour on the freeway with headlights on, fog lamps on, air-conditioning running to clear the windshield. The windshield wipers furiously whipped back and forth, but the snow pelted down so hard Geiger couldn't see. *At all*. He was scared. *What if something happens to Giannis?* he thought.

Geiger pulled over.

"Don't pull over," Giannis said. "We keep going."

"Dude," Geiger said, "I can't see."

"OK, bro. Where's that towel?" Geiger always kept a towel in his back seat to wipe melting snow off the leather seats.

Giannis grabbed the towel. "Open the window."

Geiger opened the passenger window. Giannis, still buckled into his seat, took his right arm, towel in hand, and lunged forward and stretched his massive wingspan all the way over to Geiger's side, serving as a human windshield wiper, cleaning each side every thirty seconds. Geiger could see enough to make it home.

"We can't ever do that *again*," Geiger said.

* * *

Giannis was still growing. He had sprouted more than an inch—from 6'9" to 6'10 1/4"—from the start of training camp to December 2013. But by that point, he was struggling on the court, roughly halfway through his rookie season. He tried to stay upbeat, bringing cupcakes for the team on a road trip for his nineteenth birthday on December 6.

But he just couldn't slow down on the court. All that energy, all that *go*, churning inside him, threatening to detonate. He'd foul someone inadvertently. Turn the ball over off his knee on the fast break. He was trying so hard to *be* somebody that sometimes he seemed all over the place.

"His mind was going a million miles a minute," Ridnour says. Giannis had to succeed. He had to be great. *Now*. But he wasn't anywhere near great. Anyone watching could tell he was going to be *really* good at some point. Some future time. He was a Project with a capital *P*, a player who excited, who frustrated. Who dazzled, who disappointed.

He was so young and so earnest, especially on the defensive end, never walking back to the other end after a turnover. It was hard to chastise him, because every error he made contained something delightful: He'd leap to the basket in two dribbles. He'd snatch the ball out of the air and zoom downcourt, finishing coast-to-coast. He'd pull off an unchasable chase-down block.

He just couldn't put all his skills together yet. His body wouldn't allow him to. He felt like he was making *at least* twenty mistakes a practice. One night Giannis shined; the next night he looked lackluster. Confused. Against the Celtics, he dropped a pass out of bounds, and instead of taking responsibility, he responded with a *welp* shrug, like, "Who me?"

Up. Down. Up. Down. He couldn't catch a rhythm. Drew would remind him he had to focus on being more consistent. Giannis knew his coach was right, but it was easier said than done. Because the team was losing so much, Giannis was allowed to play through his mistakes. That meant, however, his youth was on full display; he couldn't hide from his weaknesses.

After one of those nights, Geiger and Giannis returned to Giannis's apartment. Geiger lived in the same apartment complex, just a short walk away. It was around 11:00 p.m., and Giannis was exhausted, sprawled out on the couch. He barely fit: his feet dangled over the armrest of a nearby chair. Geiger realized he had game film to analyze that night for the coaching staff before practice the next morning.

"I gotta go break down film," Geiger said. "Have a good rest of your night."

"Come on, man," Giannis said. "Don't leave, man."

"I have to break down this game. The coaches want it for tomorrow."

"Well . . . go get your computer!"

Geiger sensed something innocent, something soft, in his friend's insistence. So Geiger relented, went back to his own apartment to retrieve his computer, and started breaking down the game in Giannis's place. Around midnight, Geiger sent the video to the coaching staff, relieved to have made deadline. He was working twelve-hour days, and looking after Giannis felt somewhat like a full-time job. He enjoyed it immensely, but like Giannis, he was working to the bone.

"You going to get to bed?" Ross asked. "We have practice pretty early."

Giannis paused. His voice grew thin, barely audible. "Will you just . . . like . . . stay the night?"

"What do you mean?"

"Come on, man. I got, like, two beds in the other room," Giannis said. "I don't want to sleep alone anymore."

"All right. I'll stay." Geiger took a pillow, went to another room, and dozed off. Giannis went to his own room, feeling a little less alone.

The next morning, as the two hopped into Geiger's Subaru for practice, Geiger realized he had crossed a threshold: he had gained Giannis's trust, something Giannis still allows few to do. As a child, Giannis learned that trusting people was dangerous. Trusting people could get his parents deported. Trusting people could let others see that there was vulnerability in him. Fear in him. And he could not, would not, let anyone see that.

But maybe it was OK that Geiger saw that. Maybe it was OK to truly let someone see *him*.

Giannis kept letting bits of himself spill out as time wore on. Once, he and Geiger were walking to see a movie at a local mall and Christmas music was playing. Giannis broke out in song, singing each word perfectly.

"How do you know the words to this song?" Geiger said.

"What do you mean?" Giannis said.

"It's all English. How do you know the words to this song?"

"Oh. Growing up, me and my brothers would go door-to-door and Christmas carol for extra money."

Memories like that would prick Giannis at random moments. When he would be walking down the street. Warming up for practice. Putting on his worn-down sneakers. For a moment, he was back in Sepolia. Back on the side of the road, a child trying to smile, hoping the sunglasses he dangled in the wind would go for three euros instead of two.

*   *   *

The more Drew watched Giannis, the more compassion swelled inside him. He'd grown concerned. Protective, even. He knew his rookie missed home. Felt like every day was *heavy*, bringing new challenges, new concepts to learn. And Drew began to view Giannis as one of his own.

Drew had three, his oldest around the same age as Giannis. Every time Giannis would fumble a pass, miss a play signal, Drew would think of his oldest son, Larry II, who was playing professionally at the time, also struggling to adapt to a new situation. Drew would remember their phone conversations, how he'd listen patiently on the other end, thinking to himself, *Man, I wish they had somebody there for him to talk to about whatever things he was dealing with.*

He vowed to be that person for Giannis. Whatever he was dealing with. On the court, off the court. He gave Giannis his cell number early and told him he would be there for him if he ever wanted to talk. The two did text often, late into the night.

"Sometimes you need that father figure to sit down with him and talk to you, and that's all I tried to do with Giannis. I didn't try to do anything that I wouldn't do for my own boys," Drew says. "I know the importance of having a person there that you can really confide in, a person that you can really trust in, a person that you know that has your best interests at heart."

Some days Drew would deliver criticism harshly, but more often than not, the critiques were delivered in a calm, nurturing tone. He saw the way the rookie was suffering. "His family not being there, it can be a very, very traumatic experience for him," Drew says. "Loneliness, that's one of the worst feelings in the world. I know what that had to be doing to him."

Drew was frustrated himself. His team was dreadful. Everyone was miserable. Everyone was learning on the job. "It was a trying year for me," Drew says. "I mean, it *really* was." He had no choice but to play Giannis. And he felt Giannis would get better by learning while in high-pressure situations. "He [Drew] was really flexible. Really patient with Giannis," Butler says. "He needed to be, because Giannis needed somebody to take the time towards his development."

Drew began to view coaching as teaching, trying to imagine how his own sons would feel during each moment. Drew would automatically repeat his phrases twice, understanding there was a possibility Giannis didn't understand. "I didn't want to overwhelm him," Drew says.

Giannis was more than a *project* to him. Giannis was a person who needed love. Care. His emotional well-being was a priority for the organization.

"Having another Black male figure for him that's older, Giannis needed that," says Hackett, the former strength-and-conditioning coach. Hackett could spot *lonely* on anyone. He had spent the past eleven years with the Mavericks, around older players, younger players. Quiet players, gregarious players. And he knew the truth: when they went home, rested their heads on their pillows at night, they were vulnerable. More vulnerable than they'd ever let anyone glimpse.

Hackett knew, no matter how cheery Giannis was, how much he raved about a new food or song, he was hurting inside. His past was tugging at him, motivating him but threatening to pull him down.

"You get to a certain point in your life, as a Black male, where you're living a double life from where you come from and who you are with your family, than what society sees you as," Hackett says, "because they look at you as you're just the NBA superstar player. You're not supposed to have any problems, and they do. They're human. They have problems just like everybody else."

*   *   *

One bright spot was that Thanasis had moved to the States to play for the Delaware 87ers of the then D League, the NBA's development league (now called the G League). Whenever Giannis could, he'd fly Thanasis to Milwaukee for one or two days. It made both of them feel some sense of normalcy.

Thanasis came to Milwaukee for Thanksgiving. When he arrived at Giannis's apartment, Giannis came down to the lobby and paused, looking at his brother. They had endured so much change in such a short period that both nearly broke into tears. They embraced, hugging tightly, neither wanting to let go.

The brothers were both still adjusting to American restaurants. They had gone to Morton's The Steakhouse for a team dinner. Opening the menu, Giannis was shocked: *Sixty dollars? How could a steak, a piece of meat, be sixty dollars?* He could have bought a lot with sixty dollars. Sneakers. Three shirts. Paid a utility bill.

Thanasis experienced a similar moment on another occasion while in Philadelphia, after the Bucks had played the Sixers. He and Giannis found themselves in a fancy restaurant, skimming the menus, when Giannis told Thanasis, "Get whatever you want to eat."

Thanasis kept silent.

"Whatever you want," Giannis said again, trying to fill the awkward silence.

They continued to stare, and stare, until Thanasis ordered a salad. Giannis did too. As they ate, the distance between their past lives and their new lives never seemed greater.

* * *

The day after Thanksgiving, the Bucks were in Charlotte for a matchup against the Hornets. The team had a Thanksgiving dinner at a local convention hall. Giannis sat at a table, scrolling on his phone while sitting next to Oppenheimer and Cody Ross, the video coordinator.

"What are you looking at?" Ross asked.

"Black Friday deals."

"Giannis," Oppenheimer said, "you're an NBA player now. You don't need to be looking at deals."

"Nope," Giannis said, shaking his head. "No matter how big I get, no matter if I become a superstar, I will always be looking for deals. I am always going to be *me*."

* * *

What if we all went to sleep and woke up and we were back where we started?

The thought would pop into Giannis's head at any moment. His brothers' too. They would often joke to each other about the possibility, laughing hard over Skype. But underneath the laughter was fear. Real fear. It was almost terrifying, contemplating the way things could be taken away quicker than they came.

It didn't help that people back in Greece began to look at the family differently. Alex remembers people looking at him strangely, thinking, *Oh, he's acting different because his brother got drafted.* They'd text him to play basketball, and if he missed the text or wouldn't respond in time, they'd text him, "Oh, you can't hang out because your brother's in the NBA?" It infuriated Alex. "I was the same person as I was before," he says.

His friends didn't understand how precarious Giannis's situation felt. Yes, he was in the NBA right now, but what about tomorrow? Tomorrow was always tenuous. Always to be determined.

What if we all went to sleep and woke up and we were back where we started?

That was particularly terrifying for Giannis, because the second he signed his contract with Milwaukee, he became the patriarch of his family. His dad always would be, in essence, but Giannis became the *provider*. Everything that happened to them from then on was on his shoulders. His back. His wallet.

He wanted that responsibility. So Giannis was hesitant to spend money and thought deeply about each purchase. "He didn't want to spend a dime," says Knight, the Bucks guard. Once, Giannis turned on his TV, and it wouldn't power on. He called Geiger. "My TV's not working." Geiger figured it out: Giannis hadn't paid his cable bill. "My bill?" Giannis said, surprised. "How much is it?" It was only twenty dollars a month. "Oh, I'm not paying that," Giannis said. He didn't.

Giannis was the only Bucks player to not set up direct deposit that season. "He insisted on a check," Oppenheimer says. He needed to *see* the evidence of money in real life, *feel* the physical paper in his hand, in order to believe it. To trust it.

He hesitated to let other people pay for him. When he'd go to dinner with Skip Robinson, the Bucks staffer, Giannis would say, "Are you sure? This OK? Too much?"

Robinson would just smile, assuring him it was fine. "He was just *so* polite," Robinson says.

Robinson sent him a fancy sport coat with a collar, tailored just for him. Giannis quickly called him. "This is crazy! Skip, this is *crazy*."

"No, no, it's not crazy," Robinson said.

"No. No. This *is* crazy. This is *crazy*."

Robinson had to convince him to keep it. When surviving had been his mentality for so long, he found it unfathomable to consider gifts or excess. When Sanders bought him a custom business suit and matching Gucci shoes, Giannis said he couldn't accept the gift. "He didn't want to take it," Sanders says. "He was looking at me like I just got him a new house."

Sanders explained to him that this was the NBA; vets are supposed to take care of rookies. Besides, he had gotten the suit custom made. The tailor kept asking Sanders, "Why are his pants so damn long?"

"Take it," Sanders said, reassuring him, smiling. "It's OK." Giannis finally agreed, grateful his teammate would think enough of him to buy him a gift. Sanders knew, though, there wasn't a chance the shoes or the suit would ever see the light of day. They were too fancy for Giannis. He wore a gray or black Bucks sweat suit every day of the year. Even on the rare occasion he would go out to dinner or a club with his teammates. They joked that he didn't own a pair of jeans. "He didn't care about jeans or shoes," Sanders says. "He just wanted to *play*."

When Sanders would give Giannis his $190 per diem (compared to the $400 a *month* Giannis was making in Athens his final season), Giannis screamed to Geiger, "Larry gave me his envelope!" Another time, he ran up to Geiger, after completing rookie duties to buy doughnuts from Dunkin' Donuts for the team. "Ross! You're never going to believe this! Caron let me keep the change!"

Giannis couldn't believe that the Bucks provided tables of food before and after practice. Platters of pasta. Energy bars. Chicken. Gatorade. Chips. For *free*. After everyone had taken theirs, he would fill up four or five plastic containers of the food to take home. His teammates would look at him strangely, unsure why he was hoarding food.

"Giannis," Hackett would tell him, pulling him aside. "Don't worry. There's more."

But how could Giannis be sure? *More* was wishful thinking. He had always aimed for *enough*. One bad selling day, one mishap, could lead to not enough. He couldn't turn off that fear of not enough.

He tried to save every cent he earned. He had planned to hang out with Geiger for his birthday, along with Geiger's mother, who was in town. "Giannis, I heard you just got a car," Geiger's mother said to him.

"Yeah, *real big* car," Giannis said, gushing with pride.

"Well, Ross's friends are coming; they're all staying here for Ross's birthday. Of course, you're coming. Do you want to drive us?"

Giannis lit up. "Yeah, I drive. I drive us!"

They headed to a restaurant nearby. Geiger, sitting in the passenger seat, looked over at Giannis's speed and saw that his gas tank was nearly empty. "Giannis," Geiger said. "You have five miles until empty."

"Oh."

"Yeah . . . We're not going to make it to the restaurant. We've gotta stop."

"OK, OK. I stop, I stop."

He pulled into a gas station, and Geiger stepped out of the car to help him. "No, no, I got this," Giannis insisted. The car probably held about twenty gallons, but the pump stopped after twenty seconds.

"What's going on?" Geiger said. "There's no way it's full."

"No . . . but I'm out of money."

"What do you mean you're out of money?" Geiger was confused—how could Giannis be out of money when he didn't spend any money?

"Well, I only put so much on this card for a certain period of time. The rest goes to my parents." He hopped back in the car and reassured Geiger's mother, "We'll be fine! We have enough gas to get there and back! I'll worry about it later! It's OK!"

Once, Giannis asked Sal Sendik, former team attendant, who later helped out the equipment team from 2011 to 2015, to go to the grocery store with him. When Sendik came to Giannis's place to pick him up, he walked into Giannis's room and saw him digging through a suitcase. Giannis pulled out four envelopes; they were his weekly per diem.

"Giannis, dude, you saved all of these? Why didn't you spend them?" Sendik asked.

"Oh. I saved them for my family to give to them at the end of the season when they come here hopefully," he said. "I don't really need it."

There were a lot of things he didn't think he needed. He would give away new gear if he had multiple sets of something, like socks or shirts, to the Bucks ball kids. He rarely spent anything on himself.

Which is why he felt guilty, seeing a new PlayStation at a Best Buy one afternoon. It was nearly $400, but he wanted it. *Really* badly. And he could afford it. He kept staring at it, trying to decide what to do.

You know we can't get that.

He was back in Athens. Back on the street. A child again. Sunglasses in hand, suppressing *want*. Focusing on *need*. Reminding his younger brothers: *You know we can't get that.*

But on an impulse, he bought the PlayStation that day in Milwaukee.

The guilt suffocated him. He chastised himself for the rash decision. How could he be so frivolous? What was happening to him? He hadn't earned anything yet. "He felt like he was spending too much money," Alex says.

He returned the PlayStation the next morning.

*   *   *

Meanwhile, Giannis's sneakers were falling apart. They started to show the wear and tear of bulldozing his way to the basket. Falling down some possessions. He had been wearing one pair of sneakers the entire time, the first five months of the season.

Yes: a single pair. A plain-Jane Nike sneaker: white with a red swoosh and red heel. Not a pair of Kobes. Not a pair of KDs. Most NBA players wear a different pair every game. Hell, every *practice*. They had fashion statements to make, brands to endorse. Giannis was just grateful to have a pair *at all*. One he didn't have to share with Thanasis.

That was different. That was exciting. That was also something he took deep pride in. The sweat that would soak up in the heel? His. The jagged tears down the seams? His. The worn, faded gray laces? His. So he was going to use the pair until it couldn't be used anymore.

Jay Namoc, the Bucks equipment manager from 2012 to 2017, gave him that first pair of Nikes and kept trying to give him new pairs, especially when Giannis started to slide on the court when the shoe began to age. Giannis might as well have been playing on a dust-ridden court, given how little grip remained on his soles.

Namoc was worried about Giannis's safety, so he asked Oppenheimer, who was growing closer to Giannis, to try to convince Giannis to give up the shoes. Just as Hackett had told him there would be more food, Oppenheimer insisted there would be more shoes.

But Giannis wouldn't budge. He didn't want *more*. He wanted *this* pair to last forever. He became emotional when the shoes were so decrepit, so thin, that he finally accepted he could no longer use them. "He would look at those shoes with a lot of sadness," Namoc says.

Namoc tried to comfort him: "Look, man—you have a bunch of new pairs. I can get you more. Don't even worry!"

Giannis's voice grew shaky, his eyes pleading, as he said, "Is there any way . . . any way you could fix them?"

"Bro," Namoc said. "Just get a new pair . . . We'll get you a new pair . . ."

Giannis would wear only two pairs his entire rookie season. He was given plenty—eighty-two, to be exact, a pair per game. Though he didn't want to wear them, Giannis wanted to take all eighty-two home with him. Oppenheimer found the rookie shooting on the court one day to confront him about that choice. "They're not going to fit in your apartment," Oppenheimer told him. "Why don't you leave some here? Wear a few here and there at practice?"

"*No,* Coach," Giannis said, leaning closer to Oppenheimer, lowering his voice as if he were about to spill a secret. "I want them all at my house."

"Why?"

"I want my house to look like *MTV Cribs*."

Truth is, he was saving the shoes for his brothers. Hoping they'd one day obtain visas, one day be able to come to Milwaukee. Run up the court, know the exhilarating feeling of breaking in a brand-new shoe.

* * *

The Bucks approached the new year with a tough stretch of road games in Phoenix, Oklahoma City, Toronto, Houston, and San Antonio. Giannis wasn't playing consistently, but he moved to the wing as Ridnour moved into the lineup at guard.

Giannis was extra giddy for the Oklahoma City game, on January 11, 2014. There was his idol: Durant. Giannis studied him before the game, pulling up a chair, tracking Durant's movements, from his fingertips to his toes. He was captivated by how serious Durant looked shooting. Not smiling, not once.

The first time the two teams had met, back in November, Giannis was terrified. *Oh my god*, he thought to himself as the game started, *I'm guarding Kevin Durant!*

He was still in awe this time around. Durant guarded Giannis tightly the whole night, harassing him when he brought the ball up court. Durant finished with thirty-three, leading his team to a 101–85 blowout win, but the rookie held his own: thirteen points, eleven rebounds, and five assists, two blocks, two steals. He played his heart out. He even posterized Kendrick Perkins, who had seventy pounds on him.

Durant was impressed. "He's just sneaky athletic; he's quick. He's very long in that wing position. He plays extremely hard," Durant said after the game. "I can definitely roll with a player like that."

Giannis beamed afterward, telling his teammates, "Kevin Durant said I'm going to be good! Kevin Durant said I'm going to be good!"

Then Giannis fell into a slump. The Bucks suffered a bad loss to the hot-shooting Raptors. Giannis managed a solid line of eleven points and seven rebounds but got a technical foul in the third. Drew reminded him to be patient. He wasn't going to play well every night; he had to come to terms with that.

But Giannis couldn't. He was frustrated with himself. He wasn't playing as much as he would have liked. So he did the only thing he knew to do, the thing he did most nights: head to the gym. Take his frustration out on the rim. Shoot and shoot and shoot until his arms felt like jelly.

The Cousins Center was his refuge at night. Deep into the morning too. "I'd see him in there in the middle of the night," Sergo says.

The court was comforting. Giannis would often tell Oppenheimer, in all seriousness, "I could sleep here." And sometimes he did. Just like he had back in Sepolia. Shutting his eyes, shutting out his troubles.

Whenever he'd finish his workout, he made sure to clean up all the water bottles around the Cousins Center court, even ones he had not left behind. Trash he hadn't left either. He always did things like that; telling the staff that he would empty out his own ice bucket, he would wrap his own ice bags. He didn't want anyone to feel obligated to wait on him, pick up after him.

So on those lonely nights, back in the gym by himself, he'd take one last look at the court, making sure nothing was left on the ground, before turning off the lights.

What if we all went to sleep and woke up and we were back where we started?

CHAPTER 7

HOPE

Around midnight, after players had left the Cousins Center practice facility, Sergo, the longtime Bucks staffer, would grab a ball and shoot. He loves heavy-metal music, so one night he blasted Metallica.

Suddenly, a frail old man walked onto the court. "Can you turn that down!" the man asked Sergo. Turned out, the man was a priest. The Cousins Center was located in the back of the offices for the Catholic Archdiocese of Milwaukee. Every day, a group of ten to twelve priests would play basketball before Bucks players arrived for practice, a routine dating back to the mid-1980s.

By Giannis's rookie year, some of the priests were fifty, sixty, seventy, even eighty years old, defending hard, crashing into the lane, sporting bright-colored shirts, official NBA headbands, and elbow pads. Sometimes they'd play shirts versus skins, not caring who was watching.

They *lived* for these games. Sometimes three-on-three, sometimes even five-on-five, full court, for about an hour. "Play could get intense," remembers one priest, Rick Stoffel. "We could have some arguments about 'You fouled me!' 'No way that was a foul!'"

They'd slap hands, point to the passer on the assist. Every possession mattered. The best shooter was a priest named Jerry Brittain. He was also known for having the boniest elbows—he could knock someone *out* with them. "I'm not particularly big. I'm not particularly well coordinated, so

I was an in-your-face defensive guy. Right up against you," says Brittain, who still plays every day now at eighty-four.

Hammond was friendly with the priests, giving them Bucks T-shirts. Once, Hammond asked the priests to stand together for a photo.

"Why?" one priest asked.

"I'm going to post it in the Bucks locker room," Hammond said, according to Stoffel, "and let our players know that these are the people waiting in the wings to take their places if they don't play up to standard."

If the Bucks were practicing in the morning, the priests would stand in the doorway, looking at the players as if to say, "It's time to get off the court. We've got the court now." There was a mutual understanding, though, that if a Bucks player wanted to shoot, the priests had to leave. Not with Giannis, though. He respected elders, especially clergy, as his mom had taught him. "When Giannis would come out," Sergo says, "he didn't say to the priests, 'Get out of here.'"

Since these interactions usually happened during the day, Sergo found it odd to see a priest in the gym so late at night. Sergo apologized profusely to the priest and promised to turn Metallica down. Well, sort of: "I kept the music at a numbing level. Not a *mind-numbing* level."

That was life for the small-market franchise: it didn't exactly have state-of-the-art facilities like other NBA teams. Its gym, well, its church *with* a gym, had an old swimming pool the nuns would often use, one time making a couple of Bucks players wait to do pool rehab for fifteen minutes until they finished their own swim.

Sometimes former Marquette coach Rick Majerus would swim there. *Naked.* Scott Williams, the assistant coach, "saw his big white ass doing laps in the pool" and asked him to put on shorts. "Hey, man," Majerus said, "you're just lucky I wasn't doing the backstroke."

The court wasn't slippery, but it wasn't polished either. It was functional. *Fine.* Even with the occasional roof leak. Players would huddle at half-court, and a few drops would trickle down on someone's head. Staffers would have to place small plastic trash cans strategically on the court to catch the water while players ran up and down in drills. One leak had disastrous consequences, as Middleton injured his hamstring while slipping on a wet spot.

"The place looked like it had been there since the forties," Ridnour says. Anyone could walk in. There was little security, except for a mannequin named Art, dressed like a policeman, sitting at the front window. Art looked terrifyingly real. He'd scare players who hadn't been there before.

It was eerie. One light would flicker on and off. Hallways were dark and narrow, including a tunnel that was no more than five feet high; one had to practically double over to get through. The ventilation system hadn't been used in years, so any noise, from the wind outside to a door creaking open, could be heard. Some players thought the place was haunted. They'd hear a door suddenly swing open when no one else was around.

"It was creepy. It was a really weird place," Wolters says. "And priests playing at lunchtime? Like, *what*? It's the NBA, and we have priests playing there!"

The Bucks didn't operate like most modern NBA franchises. It was more like a mom-and-pop shop, with one of the smallest staffs in the league. It has always been like that. Sharpshooter Jon McGlocklin, who had scored the first-ever basket in Bucks history in 1968 with a baseline jumper against the Chicago Bulls, used to have to find high school gyms to work out at during off-seasons. "We didn't have anything," says McGlocklin, who went on to become the Bucks color analyst from 1976 to 2018.

He made $10,000 a year as a rookie. He negotiated his third NBA season contract in a phone booth in Fort Leonard Wood, Missouri. The Bucks still flew charter, as did every other NBA team. He could barely fit his six-foot-five frame in the showers on the road, had to sleep crossways in order to fit in the beds. Only one thing mattered: "It wasn't about money, because we didn't have any money," McGlocklin says. "It was just about winning a championship."

John Steinmiller, Bucks executive vice president of operations, who has been with the organization for more than fifty years, was the lone publicity department contact for five years in the 1970s. There were only ten full-time staffers in the front office. Every ticket had to be dealt with by hand.

The Bucks were still making the most of what little they had when Giannis joined in 2013. There were hardly any sales staffers. So few people attended games that ticket representatives would secretly hand out free tickets to staffers' family members.

The Bucks' main challenge, it was argued, was Kohl's unofficial mandate: "Just be competitive. Just get to the playoffs."

Kohl was a short, bald, soft-spoken man. He never married. He was extremely wealthy but preferred to buy his suits off the rack and his reading glasses from Walgreens. He drove a modest early-2000s Buick sedan. When he ran his family's grocery stores in the 1960s and 1970s, he sometimes bagged groceries when lines were too long.

He never wasted words. Buying the Bucks for $18 million in 1985, he felt that a small-market team needed to operate frugally to avoid financial collapse. So for years, the Bucks ambled along, clearing a low bar, never aiming to set it higher.

"Nobody in the organization ever talked about winning a championship," says a former Bucks employee. "Every decision made on the business side and basketball side was kind of in survival mode. It gave you short-term buzz, but there was no view of ultimately building a championship franchise."

The Bucks had the league's lowest average attendance in 2013–2014, Giannis's rookie year. There were so few fans walking around the city wearing team gear at the time that marketing staffers, in hopes of luring fans to games, would walk around the city and hand out wooden tokens that could be redeemed at the Bradley Center. "I'm proud of and embarrassed by this at the same time," says Theodore Loehrke, former Bucks senior vice president and chief revenue officer. "That's how dire the state of Bucks fandom was at the time."

It was frustrating supporting a franchise that often traded away promising young players, not wanting to make big splashy moves to land superstars in order to improve. There were talented players, like Michael Redd and Brandon Jennings, but there were so many head-scratching moves it was hard to feel confident the team could land talent who might . . . stay.

Trading away superstar Ray Allen is a wound that *still* hurts Bucks fans—a wound that made losing in game 7 of the Eastern Conference

Finals in 2001, and dissolving the Big Three of Allen, Robinson, and Cassell, even more painful.

The draft was equally dispiriting. Dan Bilsky, a Milwaukee native and die-hard Bucks fan, threw his remote control at his TV, shattering the device, during the 1998 draft, when the Mavericks selected Robert "Tractor" Traylor and traded him to the Bucks in exchange for Dirk Nowitzki and Pat Garrity. Bilsky was furious the Bucks didn't select Paul Pierce. "I stormed upstairs and out of my house," Bilsky says. The draft has always had a sad aftertaste for Bilsky, who remembers experiencing the Bucks' first lottery pick of his lifetime, when the Bucks picked Todd Fitzgerald Day at number 8 in 1992. When Day was drafted, cameras picked up his reaction, which was one of disappointment. "Oh, man. Milwaukee. Damn," Day appeared to have said.

It didn't help that the Bradley Center, where the team played, resembled an old warehouse, with its drab exterior and concrete walls. It looked like it was on the verge of falling apart, though it was built in 1988. The roof leaked, and the occasional cockroach could be spotted around the locker room and hallways. It was freezing inside because there was ice underneath the court; the arena had been built to lure a hockey team. But fans could sit courtside for fifteen dollars.

"It was an old, dilapidated arena, but it was *our* old, dilapidated arena," says Doug Russell, sportscaster at Milwaukee's 97.3 the Game and 1130 WISN.

Workers would put the basketball court over the ice instead of letting the ice break down and refreezing it. One 2013 preseason game in particular, against the Raptors, the surface of the court was so slick from the ice below that players slipped all over the court. Referees had to cancel the game with 5:58 left in the first quarter, the score 14–9. "Welcome to the circus," one longtime staffer remembers telling a new intern.

The arena was so cold that walking from the bus to the court and into the locker room was "the walk from hell," Sergo says. One game, it was so frigid that Bucks staffers began handing out hot chocolate and coffee to fans, informally calling it "The Hot Chocolate Game."

The Bucks didn't have an indoor parking garage, so staffers would start players' cars in the fourth quarter so they'd be warm when players came out.

However, on multiple occasions, players who were not as fastidious about maintaining their vehicles would pull up with the gas gauge pointing to empty, and the cars would run out of gas before the game would come to an end.

Giannis became accustomed to the cold. He would always be the first one at shootaround, sounding chipper. His breath would be visible as he shouted to his teammates, "Morning! I'm making all my shots today! I'm ready!" Despite the cold, coming from where Giannis came from, the Bradley Center was *perfect*. A dream come true.

* * *

The Bucks' lack of a modern NBA arena, one that could attract thousands of fans, stood at the heart of the franchise's biggest challenge: whether or not it could survive in Milwaukee. The threat of leaving was omnipresent, something Wisconsinites were always forced to reckon with. *Especially* heading into Giannis's rookie season.

He arrived at a seminal moment, when the team needed a new arena if it was going to stay in the city. "We have to find a way, and we will find a way," Kohl said at a press conference before the 2013 season, regarding finding a new facility. "The question is when and how." Kohl acknowledged how urgent the matter was for the organization to catch up to its counterparts: "Milwaukee and Wisconsin need a twenty-first-century sports-and-entertainment complex."

But as the 2013–2014 Bucks flatlined into a franchise-worst record, the threat of leaving the city seemed more pressing. *Something* needed to change. Milwaukee needed a savior who could transform the team into something fans could be proud of again. Abdul-Jabbar was Milwaukee's last great hope. And then he left. To a bigger city, to the Los Angeles Lakers, after demanding a trade.

Leaving, leaving, leaving.

It set a precedent that would be felt for decades to come: that stars don't belong in Milwaukee. They might start there, but they will eventually leave. "Milwaukee is a city that's had its soul snatched a lot of times," says Myron Medcalf of ESPN, a Milwaukee native. "It's like, we'll produce you, but you'll never claim us years from now."

"As a fan," Medcalf says, "you felt like you were less than. You weren't Los Angeles, you weren't New York, and you weren't Chicago with this young dude named Michael Jordan. It was just like, 'Nobody's going to want to come here. And if they do, they definitely don't want to stay here.'"

To love the Bucks was to contend with a decades-old wound of being abandoned. First in basketball, when the then Milwaukee Hawks left for Saint Louis after playing four seasons in Milwaukee from 1951 to 1955. Then in baseball, when the then Milwaukee Braves left for Atlanta in 1966, just over a decade removed from long lines of snake dancers whirling down Wisconsin Avenue celebrating the arrival of the team in 1953, and even a World Series title in 1957.

That left a hole in the heart of Wisconsinites. Many called the owners who took the team to Atlanta "carpetbaggers." Fans felt rejected and betrayed, insecure and heartbroken. Then Milwaukee mayor Henry Maier said that the loss felt like a "black eye." It was, in the words of Bud Selig, who, four years later, brought the Brewers to Milwaukee, "a terrible, terrible trauma."

But watching Giannis fly up and down the floor all those decades later was to feel something other than trauma. For Milwaukee basketball fans who have continued to love its team through years of agony, Giannis represented possibility. Hope. Excitement. He wasn't yet the Messiah, not even *close* to the player Abdul-Jabbar was, but the fantasy of what Giannis could *become* was tantalizing. To watch him was to wonder, Could this goofy, nearly seven-foot wunderkind from Greece rescue this small-market city from oblivion?

* * *

Around that time, an online group called Save Our Bucks was created by a longtime fan and season ticket holder who chose to remain anonymous under the Twitter account @Paulpressey25. The group was born out of a Bucks forum on RealGM.com and included four other key members: Paul Henning, Kurt Leitinger, Paul Cousins, and Engel Martin. They loved the Bucks. They rallied for ownership change after years of mediocrity under Kohl. "The Bucks were always a kind of running joke after a while," says Henning, a Milwaukee native. Henning hated seeing how far his beloved franchise had fallen since his childhood, when he'd watch Moncrief, his favorite player, encapsulate everything the city was: hard-nosed, hardworking.

Henning's parents were season-ticket holders in the early 1970s, sitting in the second row behind the basket, back when the Bucks played at the MECCA. With superstars like Abdul-Jabbar and Oscar "Big O" Robert-son, the Bucks were thrilling. Henning's dad, Randall Henning, owned a Volkswagen shop, MoFoCo Enterprises, and he happened to work on custom seats for several of Abdul-Jabbar's cars—a Rolls-Royce, Jaguar, and Mercedes-Benz, among others—cutting and welding seats far back to fit his seven-foot-two frame so his knees wouldn't rest against the steering wheel.

Once, Abdul-Jabbar picked up McGlocklin in his Cadillac Fleetwood, "a car as long as a block," McGlocklin recalls. When McGlocklin got into the car, he turned to talk to Abdul-Jabbar, but all he saw was his team-mate's legs. McGlocklin cranked his neck back, seeing that Abdul-Jabbar had taken the back seat out in order to move his seat all the way back.

Abdul-Jabbar never fit in: in hotels, he had to put a chair at the end of the bed to catch his feet. Showerheads seemed to hit him at his belly. But he was a generational player whose creativity, grace, dominance, and finesse transformed the game. His dunks, his unstoppable skyhook, were innova-tive. He handled the ball like a guard, and no one had seen anything like him before. "He is as close to a meld of Wilt Chamberlain and Bill Russell as you can be and remain human," *Sports Illustrated* wrote in 1969.

That year, Abdul-Jabbar, then Lew Alcindor, was to be drafted out of UCLA, and the Bucks had a chance to land him in just its second year of operation since restarting its franchise after the Hawks had left fourteen years earlier.

It was an uphill battle to even *bring* basketball back to Milwaukee. Mar-vin Fishman, one of the team's original owners, wasn't even thinking about basketball at first. The Milwaukee native who made his money in real estate was originally trying to bring a professional football team to Milwaukee. But negotiations fizzled, since, as he later put it in his book, *Bucking the Odds*, "Milwaukee had spent a year sucking its thumb and holding on for dear life to the Packers."

Knowing that Alcindor's draft prospects loomed on the horizon, Fishman moved on to bringing hoops back to Milwaukee, steeling himself against a counterargument he often heard: "Milwaukee isn't a big-time basketball city. If the Hawks couldn't make it here, why should anyone think another pro basketball team could make it here?"

But he bought a four-dollar one-way Greyhound ticket to Chicago to try to convince J. Walter Kennedy, the NBA commissioner at the time, that the NBA needed a franchise in Milwaukee. And he succeeded. "I was delighted!" Fishman wrote. "What a coup this little Milwaukee group had pulled on the big time sports people!" Still, reporters asked him, "Do you really think you can cut it in pro basketball? You didn't do much in baseball." This was the chance Fishman had been waiting for to prove that Milwaukee *was* a basketball city.

Alcindor, however, made it known his preference was to play in a big market: New York or Los Angeles. Not a smaller city like Milwaukee. Kennedy flipped a coin—a 1964 Kennedy half-dollar—into the air to determine where Alcindor, the obvious number 1 pick in the 1969 draft, would go. The Suns and Bucks were vying because of their dreadful records the previous season. The winner would get Alcindor. Jerry Colangelo, Phoenix Suns GM, called it a "monumental, once-in-a-lifetime flip of a coin."

John Erickson, Bucks general manager; Wes Pavalon, principal owner of the Bucks; and Fishman sat in the Bucks office on Seventh Street and Wisconsin Avenue on the morning of March 19, 1969, anxiously awaiting a phone call from Kennedy with the results of the flip. The three men brought good-luck charms: Erickson, who couldn't sit still, wore a kibbutz medal his wife had brought from Israel; Pavalon, who was chain-smoking cigarettes, wore a Saint Christopher medal that he called his "Italian good luck piece"; and Fishman kept a Winston Churchill silver dollar tucked in his left shoe. They were all praying, audibly enough that Fishman was sure others could hear them.

The Suns went with "heads" based on a fan poll. The toss went tails. The Suns were demoralized, the Bucks elated. So elated that Pavalon jumped up and accidentally jammed his cigarette into Erickson's right ear when he was about to hug him. It stung, but Erickson laughed it off: "I didn't care, once we had Lew," Erickson told *Sports Illustrated* in 1970.

Eddie Doucette, the Bucks' iconic broadcaster, describes the feeling in that room as a sense of "euphoria." "It was like somebody had turned the lights on. It was a magical moment," Doucette says. "It lit the city up. Everybody was crazy: 'We're going to get Lew Alcindor, the greatest basketball player of our time, coming to Milwaukee!'

"It gave the city an identity," Doucette says. "The Milwaukee Bucks hoisted the city on its shoulders when they drafted Lew."

They also had coach Larry Costello, a basketball mastermind who always kept a yellow legal pad to jot down notes. "He was extremely old school," says Mickey Davis, who played for the Bucks from 1972 to 1976. Costello would send players a five-page document of the drills they needed to practice to be in shape for training camp, like running a mile in five and a half minutes. And he'd include a test in every playbook; those who got the highest marks would play, he'd tell his players.

Alcindor ended up helping the Bucks win twenty-nine more games than they had the previous season, and ticket prices increased from five to seven dollars, but the Bucks fell to the Knicks in game 5 of the 1970 Eastern Division Finals. Alcindor left the floor in New York with fans taunting him, singing, "Goodbye, Lewie; goodbye, Lewie; goodbye, Lewie; we're glad to see you go." That was painful, given that Alcindor was born in Manhattan.

He was determined to come back to New York for revenge, as he told Erickson that night: "We'll be back, Mr. Erickson." The next day, the Bucks traded for Robertson, ten-time NBA All-Star, who brought his particular kind of leadership. Sometimes if a player wasn't where he was supposed to be, Robertson would throw the ball where the player was supposed to be. It would roll out of bounds, and Robertson would just *glare* at the player.

The next season, with Robertson in place, plus sharpshooters McGlocklin and Bob Dandridge, the team felt confident. "We knew we were going to win it," McGlocklin says. "Even though we knew the Knicks were still pretty good, we just knew it was our year."

The Bucks finished the 1971 regular season 66–16, beating the San Francisco Warriors and Los Angeles Lakers and, finally, sweeping the

Baltimore Bullets in four to win the championship. Milwaukee had proven to the skeptics that it belonged in the big leagues. That basketball *could* succeed in Milwaukee.

Alcindor, who legally changed his name to Abdul-Jabbar in fall 1971, after converting to Islam in 1968, was named league MVP and Finals MVP. "You know," Robertson said, clutching a champagne bottle in the locker room afterward, "this is the first champagne I've ever had, and it tastes mighty sweet. We won the title in high school, but it was soft drinks then. This is the big leagues, man."

Some of his teammates were less demonstrative. Abdul-Jabbar was drinking a Coke and chewing gum before finally having a small glass of champagne. The lack of exhilaration was probably due to the fact that, as guard Lucius Allen told *Sports Illustrated* at the time, "people expect us to win."

When asked about building a Milwaukee dynasty, Abdul-Jabbar said, "I don't know about dynasties, but right now we're on top of the world."

There were no parades then, but about ten thousand fans crowded the airport when the team returned from Baltimore, blocking the exiting players. It took four policemen to escort McGlocklin and his wife and son to their car. But once they were safely inside, fans mobbed the car, pressing their faces against the windows. McGlocklin was afraid to drive, for fear of running someone over. "It went from exhilarating to scary," he says. "We were trapped." Somehow he managed to drive over a curb and a lawn to escape.

Abdul-Jabbar solidified his reputation as the best player in the world, but he shied away from media. He was perceived as being standoffish, cold. His teammates knew a different side: Abdul-Jabbar was quite funny, often playing pranks on people. "You had to be on the lookout for him," says Terry Driscoll, who played for the Bucks from 1972 to 1974.

One afternoon, returning to what was then known as General Mitchell Field Airport after a road game, players met up with wives and children who came to pick them up. Unbeknownst to Pam McGlocklin, Jon's wife, Abdul-Jabbar had put their toddler son on top of a tall locker that no one but Abdul-Jabbar could reach. Abdul-Jabbar just laughed and laughed before finally pulling the kid down.

"He did have that side to him, that side he didn't want the world to see," McGlocklin says. But he wasn't happy in Milwaukee. On October 3, 1974, over a dinner of beef wellington, red wine, and assorted cheeses in a suite at the Sheraton Hotel in downtown Milwaukee, Abdul-Jabbar told executives he no longer wanted to play in Milwaukee.

He wanted to be in a larger city that was more in tune with him culturally, with Black culture, with Islam. With jazz. "I'm not criticizing the people here," Abdul-Jabbar told the *New York Times* in 1975, "but Milwaukee is not what I'm all about. The things I relate to aren't in Milwaukee."

He never grew to like the cold. He had a window in his home that faced north, and he kept the curtains closed. But one day, he opened the window and was greeted by a solid sheet of ice.

He faced racism on a daily basis. Every day brought new microaggressions: people would stare and gawk at him, as if he were an exotic animal. "Live in Milwaukee? No, I guess you could say I exist in Milwaukee," Abdul-Jabbar said earlier in his career. "I am a soldier hired for service, and I will perform that service well. Basketball has given me a good life, but this town has nothing to do with my roots."

His tone grew harsher. The media felt he was distant, rude. He described the city as merely "where I work." The reaction was swift: "Everybody in Milwaukee was mad as hell," Chuck Johnson, former sports editor of the *Milwaukee Journal*, told the *Los Angeles Times*. "He had put down the city."

When Abdul-Jabbar was traded to the Lakers in 1975, in one of the most monumental trades in NBA history, something fundamentally changed in Milwaukee. The trauma of losing not just the city's star player but a generational player, after having achieved unimaginable success, was brutal. It hurt. Some felt insulted. Bitter. *We're not good enough for you? We're too small for you?*

He had been the city's hope. And now he was gone. "Everybody was devastated," Doucette says. "They thought, *How are we going to make up for this?* But people became understanding of the fact that life changes." They tried to get excited about the fantastic players they were getting, like Junior Bridgeman and Dave Meyers.

The Bucks would still go on to win multiple Central Division titles, led by Moncrief's stellar play, Paul Pressey's poise, and Don Nelson's never-back-down approach to coaching. Those Bucks teams were formidable. And fun: they played disco music in the locker room. Nelson sported his trademark fish ties.

The Bucks battled. Seemed like they were always on the cusp of greatness, especially in duels against the Celtics, though they oftentimes came up short. Those games were intense. In 1983, Celtics president and former coach Red Auerbach told reporters, "This is the first time I've ever lost a series that I won't go to the winners' dressing room. If it's the last thing I do, I'll get back at the Bucks."

Every game felt like an *event* at the MECCA. Games often sold out. Pop artist Robert Indiana painted the court bright yellow in 1977. It was not exactly a popular move at the time, as it cost $27,500, a price that the *Milwaukee Journal Sentinel* said should result in "something akin to the ceiling in the Sistine Chapel."

It was so bright that Nelson said at first he thought he had to wear sunglasses to see.

"It was so unique and peculiar," says Andy Gorzalski, longtime Bucks fan and producer of *MECCA*, the ESPN 30 for 30 documentary about the building. He would later put down a whopping $20,000 on his credit card to protect the iconic court. "You would think hiring a pop artist to do the court would happen in New York or Los Angeles," Gorzalski says, "but no, it happened in a Rust Belt place."

No other NBA court was as cool, as flamboyant, the effect highlighted by the fact that it was dark inside the building and the ceiling was low. Fans sometimes left the MECCA with gum stuck to the bottoms of their shoes—but that *court*. Those *colors*! It was incomparable. And it made sense: the Bucks had to do *something* to stand out since they still had the smallest venue in the league.

Former Bucks swingman Marques Johnson remembered when the Lakers would travel to town, his buddies Norm Nixon and Jamaal Wilkes, the epitome of Hollywood, would stroll into freezing Milwaukee with fur coats, cowboy boots, and fancy caps. "We just knew that if we jumped on 'em early, and really put the pressure on 'em early," Johnson told *CBS Sports*, "they'd be ready to get back to the warm weather in a hurry."

Seats were so close you felt like you could touch players. "I always remember such a warmness when I was there," Henning says. The Bucks had a section where fans could sit with favorite players and take pictures. "I still have my Polaroid," says Sharonda Robinson, Milwaukee native. "Dave Meyers, Junior Bridgeman, Brian Winters. I loved, *loved* that team."

The MECCA was formerly the Milwaukee Arena, a lackluster red brick venue thought to resemble an old train station. It accomodated just 11,052 fans, the smallest arena in the NBA, but "it was booming," Doucette says. "It was the most electric place in the city at that time." But because it was so small, Jim Fitzgerald, Bucks owner, put the team up for sale in 1985. "This team couldn't be kept in town by any sane person unless there were more seats," Fitzgerald told the *Milwaukee Journal Sentinel* that year. But Fitzgerald was adamant that someone from Milwaukee purchase the team and keep it in Milwaukee: "We feel this is where they belong."

Milwaukee *needed* a new arena. Jobs in the city were dwindling, the economy in tatters. Wisconsinites worked hard, but opportunity always seemed just out of reach. An exciting new venue could help, but politics and bureaucracy often stood in the way. Milwaukee mayor Henry Maier seemed averse to helping fund an arena. He maintained that the city didn't have any money to do so. Once pressed for action to save the Bucks, he quipped, "It's not the end of the earth if they leave."

Fans were losing hope. Again.

Meanwhile, Kohl eyed the franchise. The Milwaukee native, whose family owned a chain of department stores, Kohl's, loved hoops. He was a regular at Marquette basketball games. He was one of the original ten investors in the Brewers too, as he is a childhood friend of Bud Selig.

When Kohl eventually bought the Bucks and maintained that he was committed to keeping the team in Milwaukee, reporters called it a "miracle," an end to the "hysteria."

Leaving, leaving, leaving.

Kohl understood that sentiment: "We couldn't afford to lose them," he said at his introductory press conference. "Psychologically and economically, it would have been a disaster." How he'd get a new arena to replace the MECCA, though, was a mystery. But then a local couple, Jane Pettit and her husband, Lloyd Pettit, announced they'd donate $90 million toward the construction of a new arena, naming it the Bradley Center after Jane's father, Harry L. Bradley. "It doesn't cure the city's financial problems," Selig said at the time, "but it certainly gives it a boost sociologically and psychologically."

But the arena, completed in 1988, couldn't change the fact that the Bucks were . . . horrible. The 1990s were brutal. Attendance plummeted. "The Bucks were just giving tickets away," says Andy Carpenter, longtime Bucks fan. "It really sucked how bad they were all the time. The pain was very deep. It almost seemed systemic."

In the words of Vin Baker, Bucks all-star, after the team had lost twelve of the last fifteen games during 1997—a particularly awful season where the Bucks were on pace to miss the playoffs for the sixth straight season— "Lots of expectations and no results."

But fans continued to love their team, *always* loving their team. "You had to *really* be a fan to watch; you had to really love basketball to support Milwaukee," says one such fan, Matthew Smith.

Another fan, Jim Kogutkiewicz, learned how die-hard Bucks fandom was, growing up on the south side of Milwaukee watching games with his grandmother. When a Bucks player missed the free throw that could have won the game, his grandmother smacked her fist in her hand, shouting, "You gotta make your free throws!"

Once Kogutkiewicz got to high school, in the 1990s, during peak Bucks malaise, he wore an Air Jordan shirt to school, and his friend, a fellow Bucks fan, scolded him for selling out: "Real nice fuckin' shirt." The Bulls were beloved; the Bucks were mocked. "Other NBA cities think we should just be grateful that we let other stars come here and kick our team's ass," Kogutkiewicz says. "That we should just be thankful we have a team."

That changed in 2001, as Ray Allen, Glenn Robinson, Sam Cassell, and coach George Karl turned the Bucks into a winning team again. Milwaukee played a high-octane offense that was exciting. Fun. Players were trigger-happy; anyone could get hot. "Light It Up," the team's rap anthem that year, would blast through the Bradley Center:

"Yeaaaaah, yeeeah, yeaaaah, yeaaaaaaah. Milwaukee! Milwaukee! Milwaukee! Milwaukee! The word around town is we're lightin' it up, so who's gonna win it? The Bucks, the Bucks! Straight from the Central Division, the team that's swishin, runnin,' and dishin', the Bucks on a mission!"

The Bucks wore goofy but endearing purple-and-green jerseys. Karl got a standing ovation every time he emerged onto the court for home playoff games. "It was basketball heaven," Karl says. "A party on the streets every night. It was really powerful and enjoyable for a small market to get back into the big time."

Karl, known as Furious George for his temper and toughness, was the perfect coach. He had an underdog mentality. He had gotten thrown out of games for technicals. Over a lifetime, he's had one hundred stitches. He was the one player on Dean Smith's North Carolina team from 1969 to 1973 who Smith thought dived on the floor *too many* times. And when he got to the ABA, playing for the San Antonio Spurs, *Sports Illustrated* noted, "You went to see George Karl play, and a hockey game broke out."

The Bucks carried themselves with a swagger Milwaukee hadn't in a while. "No matter who he is playing against or what the odds are, he thinks he can win," says his son, Coby Karl, coach of the G League's South Bay Lakers, "and I think his teams embodied that." The Bucks were one missed jump shot away from reaching the NBA Finals that year, losing to Philadelphia and Allen Iverson in the Eastern Conference Finals.

Hope gone. Again. It was painful. Some fans were almost angry at themselves, knowing that, being from Milwaukee, they weren't *supposed* to set their expectations too high. They weren't *supposed* to let themselves dream. They had been conditioned to prepare for the fall. Expect disappointment.

"It was just gutting," says Raj Shukla, a longtime fan who grew up near Milwaukee. "Gutting, gutting, gutting, gutting." But Shukla refused to give up on his team. Dealing with loss is part of his identity as a resident of this city. "Milwaukee is this place with its ever-present inferiority complex. It's this sense of resignation that underlies everything. Even as you're pouring your heart into this team," he says, "you're half waiting to get your heart broken. I don't know if it's just a Rust Belt town dealing with a lot of hard times, but it's just always there."

The Bucks descended into obscurity again, trading Allen for an older Gary Payton and Desmond Mason, who struggled to live up to expectations. That was how management seemed to operate: they were content in getting a recognizable face who was at the tail end of his career in the NBA, and they thought that would be enough to maybe put a few more fans in the seats and make the playoffs.

But it didn't work. And Milwaukee went back to being a place few wanted to visit, let alone play for. "When I was on other teams," says Luke Ridnour, the former Bucks point guard, "Milwaukee was the road trip you didn't care about—just get in and get out of there."

The threat of the franchise leaving increased. Kohl had turned down numerous offers to sell the team since purchasing it, but that threatened to change in 2003. It was reported that Michael Jordan and his investment group would be purchasing the Bucks the night of the 2003 draft, but Kohl decided to pull out of selling the team in the end because he wasn't convinced that the new ownership group would keep the team in Milwaukee.

Kohl truly loved the Bucks. He was awful at managing the team but determined to at least keep it there. "I've never had an owner that would come to as many practices as Senator Kohl would," Karl says. Kohl just didn't invest in the long term. His goal was to merely be *good*. But coaches don't play to just be *good*. Players don't play to just be *good*. They play to be great. They play to win championships.

And when the SuperSonics left Seattle before the 2008–2009 season, it seemed like the writing was on the wall for Milwaukee. "It was weird to a lot of Bucks fans because the Sonics had a more prominent fan base and team than the Bucks," says Dan Shafer, a Milwaukee journalist who covered the arena debate. "I think it was just like, well, if Seattle could lose its team, Milwaukee could *definitely* lose its team."

The diehards continued to stay loyal to the team, especially in northwest Milwaukee. You could see people there walking around in Brandon Jennings jerseys. Milwaukee is a prideful city. A city that continued to celebrate the 1982 Brewers—and that team *lost* the World Series.

By 2012–2013, the season before Giannis was drafted, the Bucks finished 38–44 and were slaughtered by the eventual champion Heat in the first round. Paul Henning knew things were bad when someone offered him tickets behind the tenth row because that person didn't feel like going. Not even a Heat squad with LeBron James and Dwyane Wade could lure fans to the Bradley Center.

Kogutkiewicz had never called his senators before, but with the Bucks looking like they might leave, he picked up the phone for the first time. "We gotta keep the team here in Milwaukee," he pleaded, leaving messages for his representatives.

But as miserable as the Bucks were the next year, fans finally had something to look forward to: *Giannis*.

When they saw him play, they felt *understood*. When they learned his story, they felt *seen*. Like many of them, Giannis had come from nothing. Like many of them, Giannis worked all his life for a mere slice of the pie. And like many of them, Giannis hoped for better.

Giannis *was* Milwaukee. A bright light in a dark, dreary winter.

*   *   *

Hours before Giannis's first start, against the Knicks, he walked up to Oppenheimer. "When I get in," Giannis said, "I'm going to bust Carmelo Anthony's ass."

It was late December. At nineteen years, twelve days, Giannis was the youngest player to start an NBA game since 2006. And it *showed*: he picked up two fouls in less than six minutes, returning to the bench without any points.

When Giannis subbed back in, he hounded Anthony on defense. In overtime, with under a minute left, Giannis smothered Anthony so hard that the veteran fumbled the ball out of bounds. In the second overtime, Giannis stole the ball from Anthony, forcing another critical turnover.

New York beat Milwaukee in the end, but Giannis finished with ten points and seven rebounds before fouling out. Anthony still dropped twenty-nine points, but Giannis held his own. It was his best game yet.

"The reason was Carmelo," Giannis said after the game. "I respect him. He's one of the best players, but he can't come out and start bullying my teammates and me."

Anthony had talked smack to Giannis at the start of the game. "Of course he is going to get in my head," Giannis said, "because last year I was watching him from the TV." But Giannis dared to start talking smack back. "You can't guard me!" Giannis said. "I got you! I got you!"

Anthony looked surprised, like, *Who is this young guy talking to me?* At the same time, he respected it. It made him play harder: "He really wanted it," Anthony says. "It was good for both of us."

A referee came up to Drew and said he was giving both Giannis and Anthony a warning. "I don't care who you are," Giannis said, referring to Anthony. "For me it's just a jersey. Sometimes you've got to respond because you can't be like a chicken."

Some reporters chuckled at the word *chicken*, but Giannis didn't laugh. He didn't care how famous a player was; he was going to go at him, even if he failed. "All the superstars got the best out of him," Butler says. But "he always got done up because those guys were just better. Let's face it."

On defense, Giannis was a step behind. He'd reach and shove because he just couldn't catch up physically. He'd look over at Drew as the coach motioned for a sub: "Coach, no," Giannis would plead, "I still want to stay in. I still want to guard him."

"Giannis, I can't afford you getting a third foul."

"No, Coach, I'll be fine. I'll be fine, Coach."

Sometimes when Drew didn't let him guard the big names, the rookie would look upset. "I guess he felt we were trying to kind of hide him a little bit, which he took offense to," Drew says. "He didn't care if they scored thirty on him; he was not going to run from that matchup."

The rookie wanted to stay in so he could help his team win, but Milwaukee basketball that season became more than depressing; it seemed dysfunctional. Weeks would pass without a win. *This might be the end of the Bucks in Milwaukee*, Henning thought.

It was clear that a considerable swath of the fan base was disillusioned. Angry. One longtime Bucks fan succinctly characterized the mood in a 2014 *Grantland* feature: "Just wait out the clock. Then they get moved to Seattle and who gives a shit."

Henning felt he had to do something, so he helped mobilize with Save Our Bucks. "There had to be a complete revamping. An ownership change," Henning says. The group crowdfunded enough money to place a billboard at I-43 and McKinley that said, "Winning Takes Balls."

"The location was picked so all the execs and players who lived in the nice northern suburbs of Milwaukee would see it every day on their way to work," says Kurt Leitinger, a longtime fan who was also part of Save Our Bucks. "It took off because it was a grassroots movement and purely crowd funded. Fans will rally hard for the team they love. We felt like we couldn't stand by idly anymore."

They met with ownership too. "They didn't like us at all. They wanted to get rid of us as fast as possible," Henning says. "They wanted us to shut up, and we weren't going to do that."

Pressure mounted on Kohl. Even Hammond focused on the arena issue, albeit in a different context. A few hours before the Bucks were to play the Magic in Orlando, Hammond sat next to Giannis, who was eating his pregame meal.

"Giannis," Hammond said, "that arena right there, it's beautiful. Superman built that."

Giannis cocked his head. *Superman?*

Hammond explained that that was Dwight Howard's nickname. "Without him, they may not have that arena."

Giannis smiled.

"Giannis, maybe you can build one of those someday here."

Hammond meant what he said. He felt a deep-down certainty when it came to Giannis's potential. Hammond had taken a lot of grief over the years, doing Kohl's bidding at the draft, adhering to his negotiating limits, not being empowered to make big splashes. To change things.

But in drafting Giannis, Hammond departed from tradition for the first time. It's not that he knew something about Giannis that others didn't. It's that Hammond had the guts to take a swing. The guts to draft for the future.

And even though the Bucks were 8–33 by the midway point of Giannis's rookie season, Hammond's swing seemed to be paying off. Around

February, Kohl called a meeting with coaches and management. "Well," he said to the group, "who's our best player?"

Drew didn't hesitate. "Giannis."

Kohl craned his neck around in disbelief. "*Giannis?*"

Drew nodded. Bender, also in the room, nodded.

"*Giannis?*" Kohl repeated. "*Giannis* is our best player?"

Giannis was averaging just seven points a game. Sure, there were impressive moments, a competitive, no-backing-down mentality. But *best player?*

The coaches stood their ground. Nobody was as aggressive as Giannis. His defense was improving too. "Kohl didn't really accept it," Bender says, "but Giannis *was* our best player."

The rookie gave Milwaukee hope. A feeling the city hadn't felt in a long time.

CHAPTER 8

REUNITED

Veronica, in her white puffer jacket and gray sweatpants, and Charles, in his black puffer and blue sweatpants, opened the door of the limousine and looked around. It was jarring; they were in America. *Finally*.

Hammond had arranged for the limousine to pick them up at Chicago O'Hare International Airport, along with cake and flowers, on that day, February 3, 2014—a day etched into Giannis's mind. It was one of the happiest days of his life. His parents stood in front of the limousine, proudly, taking a picture; Veronica was so happy she wouldn't let go of the door handle as the photo was snapped.

Giannis's spirit seemed to have lifted overnight. "His whole attitude changed," says Nate Wolters, the fellow rookie.

JoAnne Anton, Kohl's assistant, labored for months to help the family secure visas. She spent hours researching, talking to state and federal officials. Kohl's political ties as a senator were crucial too. A person familiar with the situation says John Kerry, then secretary of state, may have been involved. It was an arduous process, with seemingly never-ending paperwork.

Giannis was able to obtain a P-1 visa as a foreign athlete employed in the US; the US embassy in Greece issued a P visa for support personnel to Charles, given that he would be providing emotional support and help in developing Giannis in basketball. Veronica, Kostas, and Alex qualified on the same support visa.

The next day, a Monday, the family headed to the Bradley Center to watch Giannis and the Bucks face the Knicks. Alex and Kostas were in awe watching players come onto the court. "Oh my god!" Alex said to Kostas, spotting Carmelo Anthony. "That's Melo! That's Melo!" Alex noticed how many thousands of people were in the stands. "I was scared," he says. "I had never seen so many people in one place. It was *crazy*." He was shocked at how skinny and small his big brother Giannis looked. "He definitely had to put on some muscle," Alex says, laughing.

Alex remembers Giannis being nervous before the game, playing in front of his family in America for the first time. He wanted to impress them. The family clapped quietly when Giannis subbed in for the first time. But as time passed, they became more animated, jumping out of their seats when Giannis would score or make a big play. Giannis was dominant in the fourth quarter, scoring eight of his fifteen points, battling Anthony, his favorite foe. Both were trash-talking. "Giannis was *fighting*," Kostas remembers. "Even though he had a lot of work ahead of him, he was just trying to fight and show he belonged in the NBA."

With ten minutes left, Giannis hammered home a putback dunk to give the Bucks a ten-point advantage. Charles high-fived some fans around him, including Bango, the Bucks mascot, who happened to be nearby. Charles was so proud of his son he was practically shaking. They all were. Alex was screaming so loud he tilted his head back and just looked up toward the sky. Thankful, grateful. In complete shock. Charles kept putting his hands over his head, as if he couldn't believe what was happening. Veronica was smiling, laughing, taking it all in.

Brandon Knight drained a three-pointer in the final 1.4 seconds to seal the Bucks' 101–98 win. The Bucks were just 9–39, but Giannis's spirit couldn't have been higher.

"My parents were here, my brothers were here, we won, the crowd goes crazy. So I'm happy," Giannis told reporters afterward. "I don't have to worry about nothing anymore."

Veronica, Charles, Kostas, and Alex stood at midcourt, jumping up and down and hugging each other.

They had made it.

* * *

Adjusting to America wasn't easy. Especially for Alex, twelve, who attended Saint Monica School, an affluent private school in Whitefish Bay, and Kostas, sixteen, who attended nearby Dominican High School. Neither spoke English well, and they struggled at first to make friends. Giannis tried his best to make them feel comfortable, but he wasn't in the hallways every day at school; he couldn't help them feel less shy, less intimidated.

"You're either going to work extra hard to understand what people are saying, or you're going to be left out," Alex says, looking back at that time. He and Kostas had to adjust quickly to new surroundings. Everything was much bigger. A McDonald's every couple of miles (Alex remembers two in all of Athens). Wide roads with GMCs and Escalades. Life began to accelerate. Really fast.

The brothers had to get used to the cold weather. In Greece, it rains a lot, gets hot in the summer, but it almost never snows. Acceptance of the frigid Midwest came in stages. "You like it at first. Then you hate it. Then you get used to it. Then you deal with it," Alex says. He finally understood why Giannis had worn earmuffs and gloves during family Skype sessions earlier in the season.

"What are you *doing*, bro?" Alex would ask his brother on Skype. "You look like a clown, bro."

"It's *so* cold, man."

The condos where Geiger and Giannis lived had a small media room with a seventy-inch TV. Geiger and other staffers would invite Giannis's family to join them for pizza from Trattoria di Carlo, a local Italian restaurant, to watch Giannis's games when the Bucks played on the road. Bucks management wanted Giannis's family to feel welcomed, supported.

During the first pizza-and-game gathering, when the Bucks were playing at Denver, Charles and Veronica barely said a word. They just sat there, polite, smiling. They were cheering for Giannis, but quietly. It was awkward. It would take time for them to open up. They were in a strange city, in a strange country, not speaking much English themselves.

"It's tough for them to have friends," Giannis later told *Time* magazine, "because for 25 years, they've lived without having friends. It's tough to trust somebody."

When Veronica first came to America, she would ask Giannis to give her the names and numbers of whoever he was hanging out with so she could google them. As the season wore on, she was still protective, but she and Charles became more animated in the condo pizza gatherings. Charles would complain about the refs; couldn't they see players hounding his son in the post? If Giannis would get a deflection, not even a full steal, Charles would scream, "Let's go! *Yeah!*"

His pride was palpable. He and Giannis were particularly close. Charles would often wear Giannis's black sweatpants. And when Giannis was on road trips, Charles wanted to make sure everything was pristine, so he'd straighten up Giannis's things. The apartment was almost always spotless. Teammates could sense how much Charles loved his son.

"Charles was so proud, seeing the direction his son was going," says Zaza Pachulia, the center.

The Antetokounmpos would sit in the same place at the Bradley Center every game: section A, two rows down from Kohl's seat, on the same side as the players' bench. Other families sat *across* from the players' bench, but Giannis requested his family sit closer. He needed to see them, *feel* them.

Giannis constantly talked about his brothers with his teammates—how good they could be, how much they motivated him. And he'd always bring them to practices. Afterward, they'd all work out, with Giannis shuffling his brothers through drills. Every cut was hard; every pass was crisp. "This is how hard you need to work," Giannis would tell them, demonstrating a move. "Like *this*."

Then they'd play two-on-two or three-on-three with anyone left in the gym. Alex was a chucker. Some might even say a ball hog. He'd launch from thirty-five feet, no hesitation. Kostas, who had made varsity at Dominican, was more thoughtful with his decisions. He saw how seriously Giannis (and Thanasis) approached the game and knew he was next in line. He had to focus. But in these games, the only rule was to have fun. They'd laugh and laugh. Almost as if they were back in Sepolia, just without the eleven-foot gate, without the bloody cuts.

Hammond gave each member of the family a key to the gym. Often-times, Veronica would be in the gym, around eleven o'clock at night, pass-ing the ball to Giannis. She'd grab the ball out of the rim, pass it to him, over and over.

She'd watch him lift weights, watch him run suicides. Giannis needed her there, but she needed him too. Giannis became the decision maker of the family. Even though Charles was still head of the household, Giannis now understood American bills and taxes in ways his dad did not. Giannis would sit at the dining room table, sifting through documents, keeping tabs on how much they spent or owed. He would check on his brothers' grades at their schools. He wanted to make sure everyone felt OK.

For the first time in a while, *he* felt OK. Grounded. He finally bought a new PlayStation.

*   *   *

Alex was very mindful of money. Even though he was receiving a pri-vate school education and Giannis assured him the family had more than enough money, Alex couldn't shake flashbacks to Sepolia. He weighed every purchase, trying to ensure he was getting the best deal. Kostas was still that way too. "Our biggest pet peeve," Alex says, "is, Why get it if you don't really need it?"

He was amazed how quickly his classmates would decide they wanted to buy clothes or shoes at the mall and then just buy them. "It was crazy," he says. "The biggest jump in social class ever," referring to his family's changed circumstances in America. One of his new friends had a full basketball court in his backyard. "How can one country have one or two courts in the whole area and then in the US somebody can have a court at his house? You don't see that in Greece. At all."

What if we all went to sleep and woke up and we were back where we started?

The brothers would continue to say the phrase to each other, laughing, thinking of how far they had come. But that fear, lurking just beneath the surface, persisted. The phrase motivated them, especially Giannis. If he messed up, if he didn't perform up to standard, everything his family had gained would be gone.

"Whatever is given to you can also be taken away from you," he'd remind his brothers. They felt that feeling of impermanence acutely. "We didn't feel secure yet," Alex says. In some ways, they hadn't left Sepolia.

*   *   *

Giannis found that playing for an awful team had its perks: he got to play more and more minutes, breaking into the starting lineup here and there. When he found out that he had been selected to play in the Rising Stars Challenge at the upcoming 2014 All-Star Weekend in New Orleans, he glowed.

"You've been smiling since you walked in," said Jim Paschke, longtime Bucks television broadcaster, standing on the Bradley Center baseline with Giannis. "This is fun, isn't it?"

"It's very fun," Giannis told him. "I'm very happy." With 21 starts, and averages of 6.9 points and 4.5 rebounds (third among rookies), he was more productive than anyone could have anticipated. "I'm ready to go against the big guys," Giannis told Paschke that day, referring to Anthony Davis and Damian Lillard.

Giannis ended up scoring nine points with two rebounds and two assists in seventeen minutes, including a miraculous sequence where he needed just two dribbles to get from one free throw line to the other, finishing with a double-clutch reverse dunk.

But he remained on the bench for most of the game. "He was considered, out of the players that we had, maybe the tenth or eleventh guy," says Nate McMillan, his coach for the game. McMillan thought Giannis had a great deal of potential. He noticed the way Giannis was full-court pressing, denying, every second he was on the court, never taking a second off. But teammate Andre Drummond happened to be playing very well that night.

Sitting on the bench, watching, Giannis grew more upset. Finally, he decided to speak up in the second half of the game. Not in a disrespectful way but in an earnest tone. "Coach," Giannis said, reaching over to McMillan, "what about me?"

McMillan was surprised. "I was focused on winning the game," McMillan says. "I had lost track of substitution." Giannis then played a bit more, but not much. After the game, Giannis told McMillan, "I'll be back."

Giannis was practically seething when he told Oppenheimer what had happened. "Coach, I will never forget Nate McMillan," Giannis said. "He will pay for this."

Oppenheimer laughed. "Pay for what?"

"He did it on purpose. He tried to embarrass me."

That was Giannis: remembering every slight, every comment. He still felt like he had so much to prove. Not just at this game but in the NBA. The world. He was conscious that Dario Šarić had been considered a better player than him. He was conscious that the Knicks were rumored to not have sent a scout to see him in Zografou the year before. "He took things so personal," Oppenheimer says. "He stored them as fuel. I really believe he had people, things, in his mind that were really important for him to conquer."

But he was also grateful that he was even in the position he was in. Alongside fellow rookie Steven Adams, Giannis served as co-coach in a pickup game for international media members the final day of All-Star Weekend.

Giannis walked into the pickup game bright, energetic, at 9:00 a.m.—not hungover like many other young players participating in their first All-Star Weekend. He walked up to all the international reporters, asking where they were from, spending five, ten, minutes with each. He'd ask if they'd been to this city, that beach. "He made us feel comfortable," says Antonio Gil, a reporter based out of Madrid, Spain.

Gil was on Giannis's team but didn't help much: he was ice cold from the field. "You're a Spanish guy!" Giannis called out to him. "You're supposed to go out there and shoot!" They both cracked up. Gil continued to miss, and they lost.

*   *   *

The next week, in late February, Giannis purchased his first car: a used black GMC Yukon truck. He *insisted* on buying a used car; he couldn't stomach buying a new one. Ridnour, the Bucks point guard, tried to explain to him that he didn't have to pay a dime and that players could get free cars from certain dealers.

"They do that?" Giannis asked Ridnour. "They will give me one? For *free?*"

No matter how many times Ridnour assured him, he couldn't be convinced. "He was just so innocent to what you can get in the NBA," Ridnour says. "Free cars, free cell phones. He didn't know about any of that stuff. He was just ready to hoop."

Giannis brought Geiger to pick up the Yukon. Given that it was a special day, he wanted his best friend there with him. The two posed for a picture in front of the truck, Giannis wearing a white Nike hoodie and black sweatpants, clutching the key, smiling wide, and Geiger wearing a black Bucks sweat suit, reaching up to rest his fist on Giannis's shoulder. "I followed him on his first drive home alone," Geiger says, laughing, "which I was a bit worried about."

He wasn't the only one with reservations. A few weeks earlier, Giannis's family had hesitated to get in the car with him. They were accustomed to taking buses most places. "I was scared," Alex says. Charles was the first to ride with Giannis. Giannis was eager to show his dad he was a good driver. Geiger went with them, because Giannis had only his learner's permit, and if there was an accident, Geiger wasn't sure what kind of documents Charles would need. They drove around the Saint Francis area, and Giannis made sure to turn on his indicator this time around.

Giannis was ecstatic when he finally got his license. "Excited as any sixteen-year-old would be," Oppenheimer says. Giannis was so proud of himself he even bragged to a reporter, "I got my license already. Yeaaaaah! First try! Come on, man! Talk to me!" Horst, Dean, Hammond, Morway, and Geiger all beamed as if Giannis was one of their own. "It took a village to teach this guy how to drive," Hammond says.

About a month later, Giannis insisted on driving Geiger to an electronic dance music concert. Now that he had his license, he always wanted to be the designated driver. Deorro was playing at the Rave, a multihall concert venue in Milwaukee, on a Saturday night, and Geiger had tickets. "You don't have to be out in the mosh pit with the other kids," Geiger told him. "We can just go check it out. If you don't like it, we can leave."

Giannis had never been to a concert before, but he loved EDM. "Oh, I know this beat," Giannis would often say when driving with Geiger, predicting the song within seconds. "This is the music they play in Mykonos. One day, me and you are going to go to Mykonos."

Giannis agreed to see Deorro but told Geiger he had one reservation: "I have to ask my mom."

Geiger laughed. An NBA player asking his mom? *Really?*

Really. Veronica still struggled to trust people, but she said yes this time. Giannis called Geiger immediately with the news: "Ross! I can go to the concert! We're going to the concert! She said yes!"

Giannis arrived at Geiger's place in a crisply ironed button-down shirt with nice jeans, a fresh pair of Nikes, and plastic glasses. It was the first time Geiger saw him in something other than sweatpants. "Dude," Geiger said to him, "we're not meeting up with anyone here." Geiger could tell Giannis put a lot of thought into every detail of the outfit. "You would have thought I said, 'Hey, we're going on a double date; I know these girls that want to meet us,'" Geiger says.

About halfway to the Rave, Giannis turned to Geiger in the car. "Man, this is big. This is *big!*"

"What? That you're going to a concert?"

"No," Giannis said, smiling, "that I asked my mom if I could go with you, and she knew it'd be late at night, and she *still* said I could. That's big, bro. Like, she *trusts* you."

*   *   *

The Bucks' disaster of a season was winding down. With a 102–98 loss to the Raptors in early April, the sixty-third defeat of the year, the team had its worst season. It had been so miserable most just wanted the season to end. Players had missed a total of 277 games to injuries or illnesses.

Hours before the final game against the Hawks, Kohl announced he was selling the team to Marc Lasry and Wes Edens, two New York billionaires, for $550 million and that Lasry and Edens were committed to keeping the franchise in Milwaukee. "I wasn't going to live forever," Kohl, then seventy-nine, told reporters at the time.

It was a stunning moment. Kohl had arguably been a terrible owner in basketball terms, but he did the one thing that mattered more than anything: he kept the team in Milwaukee. Through years of tumult, years of offers, he held on. He took pride in that, even if the Bucks had accomplished little. "Somebody could have offered me $5 billion, and I couldn't do that," Kohl said, referring to selling the team out of Milwaukee. "How could I still live here? How could I live with myself?"

Kohl said he would contribute an eye-popping $100 million toward a new arena in downtown, and the new ownership would add $100 million. "Milwaukee fans deserve a winning team," Edens, a cofounder and chairman of the board at Fortress Investment Group, told the Associated Press. Lasry was chairman and chief executive officer of Avenue Capital Group. Edens's mother was born and raised in Wisconsin, and both he and Lasry loved basketball. They aimed to win a championship.

Still, nobody knew what to expect. Some were skeptical, a bit slow to embrace the new owners, dismissing them as "New York hedge-fund billionaires" and fearing the team would eventually leave Milwaukee regardless of what Kohl or the new owners had promised.

On the bright side, Milwaukee secured the number 2 pick in the upcoming 2014 draft. Finally, a chance to land a franchise player. Staffers wasted no time preparing, compiling three six-hundred-page binders to give to the new owners. Jabari Parker, a six-foot-eight forward out of Duke, and Andrew Wiggins, a phenom from Canada who played for Kansas, came to Milwaukee for workouts. The Bucks weren't able to secure a workout with Joel Embiid, a promising big man from Cameroon, due to medical reasons.

The more the Bucks watched Parker, the more they fell in love. Parker was tough and hardworking, having grown up on the south side of Chicago. Selecting Parker was a huge deal for the Bucks: he was the first elite player since the Bucks landed Glenn Robinson, the number 1 pick in 1994, and Andrew Bogut, the number 1 pick in 2005.

Jabari could be the cornerstone they had been searching for.

Not Giannis.

Giannis was viewed as an important piece of the puzzle, a player who could *complement* Parker. Naturally, Giannis wasn't exactly thrilled. He wanted to be the best player on the team; he wasn't just going to hand that title off to someone else.

The day after the Bucks drafted Parker, reports surfaced that Milwaukee's new owners sought permission from the Brooklyn Nets to interview head coach and Hall of Fame point guard Jason Kidd. Kidd had a messy divorce with Brooklyn, essentially forcing his way out. He had been a rookie coach, having led the Nets to a 44–38 record and a playoff berth. Lasry, a partial investor in the Nets, built a relationship with Kidd when Kidd played for New Jersey.

Most Bucks staffers hadn't known the new owners were pursuing a coaching change in secret. Coach Drew had been in the Bucks draft room, helping select Parker. He talked glowingly about Parker's future at Parker's introductory press conference. Then, three days later, Drew was fired and Kidd was hired. Drew says the Bucks had hired Kidd without telling him first, and that didn't sit well with him. "I didn't think that was tastefully done," Drew says. "I wasn't really in the mood to talk to anyone, and I didn't."

In addition to his new coaching position, Kidd had lobbied to take over Bucks basketball operations and become team president, a power play that made many uncomfortable. The new owners denied his request, but the attempt made things awkward between Kidd and the holdover executives. Some feared he'd try to become the alpha of everything, as he had attempted in the past.

Meanwhile, Giannis was processing the loss of his first coach. The coach who was patient with him, nurturing to him. Giannis posted a picture on Facebook of him and Drew at Madison Square Garden before his first game against the Knicks. Drew had smiled, put his arm around Giannis. Giannis remembered how Drew had sensed he was stressed, a bit lost, heading into the game and told him to relax, to just play basketball.

Drew didn't talk to Giannis after being fired. "I don't know if it was the right thing to do or not," Drew says. "I did not want to have any connection with anybody in Milwaukee at that point."

He moved on to coach the Cavaliers. "I've coached Kobe; I've coached Jordan," Drew says. "And now I can say I've coached Giannis."

* * *

Giannis and his family waited to see if Thanasis would get drafted that summer. Thanasis wasn't as skilled as Giannis. And compared to top-tier Euro-League talent, Thanasis was undersized. Seen as a hustle player, a great defender, but not quite polished or athletic enough to succeed in the modern NBA game that values fundamentals and outside shooting. "Thanasis was in the shadow of his brother," says one European agent who has clients in Greece.

Giannis advocated for his brother publicly. "I know he's capable to play in this league," he told the *Milwaukee Journal Sentinel* that summer. Fortunately, Thanasis was drafted by the Knicks in the June 2014 draft, selected fifty-first overall. He and Giannis hugged in the stands of Barclays Center. "I think I'm happier today for Thanasis than I was last year in the draft for myself," Giannis told reporters that night. "Hopefully our brother [Kostas] will follow our footsteps and make it too."

Giannis had much to do, preparing for his sophomore season. He had led all rookies with sixty-one blocks, making All-Rookie second team, but was critical of himself. He graded his season performance a "D-minus," telling local reporters he needed to work on everything: shooting, dribbling, strength. "At the beginning it was hard to believe. I was thinking, like, 'Whoa, I'm playing with these guys now? I'm on the same court as these guys?' But as the season went on and on, I began to believe, and I said to myself, 'I belong here.'

"I am happy with myself," he said, "but I am not satisfied."

Milwaukee's quiet small-town environment was perfect for him. He could focus on developing his game without distractions. "I love Milwaukee," he told the *Milwaukee Journal Sentinel* that summer. "I hope I'm here for a long time." When thinking about the way fans had embraced him, he said, "It makes my heart feel great. I'm glad they like me as a person, and I hope in the future they like me as a player, too."

He still wasn't the player *he* wanted to be. He finally completed his first muscle-up, though. He was so proud of himself he checked himself out in the mirror, flexing his biceps, to see if his body looked any bigger. "He's like, 'I'm really starting to grow into this,'" says Chris Wright, the Bucks forward.

Wright and Giannis grew closer that off-season, often playing one-on-one and six spots, a shooting drill where a player launches from different spots with defense covering him. One day, Giannis missed all his shots and didn't win any spots. He was angry at himself. Didn't want to talk to anybody. He just walked out of the gym.

The next day, Giannis told Wright, as well as Wolters and Middleton, who were there shooting around, "I'm gonna whoop *all* your asses today."

Everyone laughed.

"Whatever, man," Wright said.

Giannis guarded Wright on the wing. Wright drove hard left, dunked it. Giannis looked angry again. He wasn't whooping *anyone's* ass. Middleton taunted Giannis: "You ain't gonna win no spots today. Again!"

Giannis then caught the ball and made every shot, winning all six spots. He tossed the ball into the air, then started running around the Cousins Center, screaming, "Yes, baby! *Six!* Jordan, baby, *six!*" alluding to Jordan's six championships. He then jumped on top of the scorer's table, beating his chest, screaming louder, "*Six! Six!*" looking at the empty bleachers as if fans were screaming for him, pointing his finger at invisible faces. "*Yeahhhhh!* Y'all see me!"

"Run it back!" Wright said, protesting the result.

"No, no," Giannis said. "We're not playing anymore." He declared himself the winner. No more getting punked. "Coach," Giannis said to Hackett, who was sitting nearby, "I'm telling you: next year, I'm going to be better. I get better every year."

Giannis needed to get better, given that he'd be suiting up for the Greek senior national team for the first time in a matter of weeks. He was the youngest player on the roster, which was filled with Greek standouts like Nick Calathes, Nikos Zisis, and Kostas Papanikolaou.

Once again Giannis was the baby. The scrub. But the Greek national team didn't have time to bring him along slowly, the way the Bucks had. Greece was expected to medal. Giannis had to show up ready.

"If I want them to respect me," Giannis told Missas, his former U-20 national-team coach, right before leaving for Greece, "then I must win their respect."

*   *   *

When the nineteen-year-old landed in Athens for training camp, he met with his new coach, Fotios Katsikaris. Katsikaris, a veteran European coach who later served as an assistant with the Utah Jazz, wasn't sure what to make of Giannis on the first day because Giannis was so *serious*. He never smiled, never seemed to relax the muscles in his face. One veteran player on the team was offended by the apparent snub. He took Giannis's seriousness for rudeness. The vet came up to Katsikaris and said, "Tell this kid to change his attitude because I'm going to punch his face."

That's how hard Giannis competed. "Giannis wasn't acting like a kid his age," Katsikaris says. Some veterans on the team, ten years Giannis's senior, thought the young player was cocky just because he was coming from the NBA. It didn't make sense to them how a second-division mystery had ascended to the highest league in the world, while many of them would never get that kind of opportunity.

"He was a high draft pick, but we didn't know how his game would fit," says Nick Calathes, teammate and Greek star. "We didn't know if he could help us."

The first time Giannis met with Katsikaris, Giannis asked if Thanasis, his oldest brother, could join the team. Katsikaris was taken aback—that a player who had just earned a coveted spot would ask not about his own role but about a family member. Katsikaris tried to be diplomatic, told Giannis it wasn't possible at that point.

Giannis then asked Katsikaris, "Where do you see me? What can I do to improve?" He looked Katsikaris in the eye. The coach hadn't seen that kind of focus in a young player before. "He absolutely wasn't ready to play, but he was a real diamond," Katsikaris says. "Greece is a small country, and of course we have a great culture in basketball, but we never had a player like him. With his characteristics, with his raw talent. We needed to work with him."

Katsikaris wanted two things from Giannis that summer: strong defense and physicality. Giannis struggled offensively but shined at times. His first practice, he received the ball and didn't see an outlet pass on one side, so he drove downcourt, faking out two defenders and dunking. He started gaining the respect of the veterans. "He was one of the hardest workers that I've played with," Calathes says. "He was just a little raw."

The first preseason game of the 2014 FIBA Basketball World Cup, though, Giannis didn't play a minute. Instead of being discouraged, he shot for hours after. Then he went up to assistant coach Asterios Kalivas and said, "If I make three out of four three-point shots, can you please tell Coach to let me play a little bit more for the next friendly?" Giannis made two of four, but the sentiment stood: he wanted his coaches to know he would do whatever he could to get in the game.

After practices ended at 7:30 p.m., when everyone else went to shower, Giannis would tinker with his shooting form with Kalivas. Giannis wouldn't leave until 9:00, refusing to shower until he returned to the hotel. "If you would have told me then, in 2014, that Giannis in 2019 would be the NBA MVP, or you buy me a coffee—I will take the coffee," Kalivas says. "I put all my houses, my fortune, on this. But I have never seen anybody work so hard. If he could practice all day, he would do it."

Giannis started to become friends with his teammates, even open up to them. "I remember he was saying that 'I want to be one of the all-stars in the NBA one day,'" says Zisis, team captain and Giannis's roommate during the preseason. Zisis, thirty at the time, had heard about Giannis over the last few years. "There's this Black kid here in Greece, running up and down like crazy," he'd hear. "He can take two dribbles from half-court and dunk the ball."

The more Zisis, one of the most talented players in Greece, played with Giannis as the summer tournament in Madrid unfolded, the more he noticed that Giannis was willing to do the dirty work of defense and rebounding. "His energy was incredible," Zisis says. Occasionally Giannis would do something exceptional, like a tomahawk dunk. "We never saw that, even in Europe," Katsikarsis says. "And you see immediately, like, '*Oh shit*, this kid—he's special.'"

Tzikas, the Kivotos Café owner, and his wife, Katerina Drimpa, came to Madrid to surprise Giannis and watch him play. They knew Giannis's own family couldn't make it. They stayed in the same hotel as Giannis, too, to make him feel as if he were home.

Giannis beamed seeing them—especially Tzikas. The man who'd given him a sandwich and fruit juice when he didn't have to. And now, Tzikas would get to see him wear the blue-and-white Hellas jersey, represent the team Tzikas so loved.

The two of them hugged, then just looked at each other. Tzikas was so proud, explaining to Giannis why he'd made the trip to Spain: "I wanted you to know you had someone there for you."

* * *

Giannis didn't play much throughout the tournament. He struggled with decision-making. He struggled getting to the basket, as it was difficult for a player of Giannis's size and athletic ability to find space in the packed European paint. Referees didn't recognize him, so he didn't get the benefit of the doubt for calls either.

Still, Greece went 5–0 in group stages before losing, 90–72, to Serbia. Giannis played much more than he ever had against Serbia, and played well, but Greece lost. Everyone wanted to leave immediately.

"Don't worry, guys; you tried your best, and we still love you!" some Greek fans who had traveled to the game said to the team as they walked to the team bus. Giannis trailed behind Zisis, who started crying. Giannis grabbed Zisis and hugged him. "Don't worry, don't worry," Giannis told Zisis. "We got this next year. Don't even worry."

It meant a lot to Zisis that a young player would care about him enough to say that. When the team landed in Athens, Giannis had tears in his own eyes, hugging his teammates. They had all grown close, giving their all for two months.

A week later, Zisis found an interview Giannis had given about the tournament. Giannis mentioned to the radio host that he learned what love truly means by wearing the jersey of his country and that he learned that lesson from Zisis.

Zisis cried listening to the interview. "A nineteen-year-old kid, whose parents are not from this country, and he really loves this country," Zisis says. "He really understands."

Giannis has always understood.

CHAPTER 9

MEAN

Giannis would stand in front of the mirror and practice his scowl. He'd squint his eyes, suck in his teeth. His nose would wrinkle; his forehead would tighten. His lips would curl, and then he'd let out a grunt.

He was trying to look more aggressive, less adorable; more intimidating, less innocent. He needed a new identity heading into his second NBA season—one vastly different from the goofy, endearing rookie discovering smoothies for the first time.

He needed to get *mean*.

"He had to practice it because he's not that guy," Robinson says. "He's a lovable guy. A nice gentleman."

Giannis didn't want to be seen as a *nice gentleman* on the court; he wanted to be seen as someone who would tear your heart out. He tried to pattern his scowl after Russell Westbrook's scowl. Giannis *loved* Westbrook: his demeanor, his speed, but *especially* his scowl. Giannis came into practice once, scowling and grunting. "This is my new thing," Giannis told his teammates.

They ignored him. Laughed a bit. But Giannis insisted on impressing them: he flexed his muscles after bench-pressing and flashed his scowl again, hoping his teammates would appreciate the intensity of his grunt. "Bro," Knight told him, "you still don't have any muscles. Relaaaaax."

Giannis's teammates found it hilarious when he'd attempt the scowl after a dunk, something he started doing toward the end of his rookie season. The first time he did it, against the Pistons, he ran back to the other end of the court with so much aggression even Butler was surprised. "I didn't know where the hell that came from," Butler says, laughing.

Afterward, his teammates asked him, "What *is* that? Where'd you get that from?" They assumed he'd learned the scowl from YouTube—where he learned everything in those days.

Giannis laughed. "Oh," Giannis said casually in a "this old thing?" kind of tone, "I took it from Westbrook."

Giannis's scowl seemed out of place. Manufactured. "We'd be like, 'Oh, he must have practiced that at home today,'" Knight says. The scowl *was* coming along, but it still wasn't loud enough, mean enough. *Convincing* enough. "You gotta work on your roar," Knight would sarcastically advise Giannis. "You gotta work on your yell. We gotta get you right, man."

*   *   *

On the first day of training camp to open the 2014–2015 season, Giannis wouldn't crack a smile. Not for a second. He couldn't, since Parker was the new star; Giannis was still the curiosity. The two would eventually come to like each other, even become friends, but not at first. Giannis felt like the Bucks were supposed to be *his* team. He had earned that after the way he played his first season. And he was going to prove that *he* was the leader.

Some fantasized that the pair could become the Batman and Robin of a potential new era in Milwaukee, but Giannis didn't want to be Robin. He needed to be Batman. "He wasn't on the throne," Oppenheimer says, "but the chair was empty. And he wasn't going to help somebody get there when he thought he had the same amount of ability to get there."

Giannis and Parker went at each other in every drill. Kidd was happy about that; he demanded that competitiveness from everyone. He wasn't going to accept another humiliating fifteen-win season.

Only about a year removed from his own playing career, Kidd was very much a player hiding in a coach's suit. "Even on the sidelines you can just see the competitiveness bleeding out of his skin," says Kerry Kittles, Kidd's former Nets teammate. "You can see him trying to suppress it."

Kidd huddled his new team at half-court about midway through the first practice. "Who thinks we're a playoff team?"

Players looked at each other, paused a second, recognizing there was only one right answer.

Everyone raised his hand.

"Good," Kidd said. "We're going to practice like it."

Drills began, emphasizing physicality, driving to the hoop, taking contact. Kidd kept telling Giannis to drive to the basket: "Don't settle for jump shots." One play, Giannis drove coast-to-coast and took the ball strong to the hoop but got pummeled inside. The ball hit the backboard and bounced out of bounds.

"You know, a feather can blow him over," Kidd said, turning to his assistants. They laughed. Kidd didn't. He was dead serious. "A couple times up and down the court, you breathe on him, he's falling over. We gotta get him stronger."

Then players scrimmaged. One play, Giannis grabbed a rebound, dribbled in and out to beat his defender, and then dribbled the ball behind his back to fake out another defender, sprinting downcourt all the way to the cup for a dunk. It took him just four dribbles to get from one end to the other. Wright and Oppenheimer looked at each other. "Yo," they said at the same time. "*Yo*."

Another play, Giannis received the ball at the top of the key. He stumbled, barely recovering his balance. He managed to dribble left, hard to the hoop, taking off for a windmill. Four players stood in his way, but Giannis rose over them and slammed the ball down.

Everyone in the gym stopped for a second. The dunk was surprising. Vicious. For the first time, Giannis looked really, really *mean*.

* * *

Kidd wanted Giannis to operate like an assassin on the court. A true killer. Meaning he needed to not only carry himself with a certain swagger, a certain meanness, but he needed his game to back up that kind of demeanor. Kidd saw star potential in Giannis and wanted him to maximize his gifts: his length, his athleticism in the open court.

Kidd and assistant coach Sean Sweeney would work out with Giannis multiple times a day. They'd teach him moves, challenge him out of his comfort zone. Kidd would make Giannis do a drill over and over until it was perfect, as he would with all his players.

Kidd was known for playing *mind games*. He wouldn't yell; he wouldn't act overly aggressive. Far from that. He was more delicate, soft-spoken, getting under someone's skin, knowing the *thing* that made each player explode. He never gave players answers, wanting them to figure it out on their own.

His coaching style with the Nets, and then with the Bucks, was described as "psychological warfare" by one former player. When asked about Kidd, players and coaches often say, "On the record or off?" Kidd was loved, hated. His coaching style was described as follows:

"Jedi mind tricks," Oppenheimer says.

"Mind fucks," says one former teammate, a bit more bluntly.

"Machiavellian," says a former Bucks staffer. "He kind of relished that combativeness in people."

But also: "He's a winner. Naturally a winner. He's a competitive moth-erfucker," says Chris Copeland, Bucks forward from 2015 to 2016. He played with Kidd on the Knicks in 2012–2013.

"He'd just brutalize people," says another ex-player. "There's plenty of teammates that I had that didn't like him, not even as a coach, like as a person. He'd pit people against each other."

"I think he may have had rocky relationships with a lot of players," says Johnny O'Bryant III, Bucks forward from 2014 to 2016. "But one thing he did was he laid the tradition of a winning team. Sometimes the way he went about it, being straightforward, he was just an *asshole*, but I think it paid off in the long run."

"I'd never call Jason Kidd an asshole," says Nicholas Turner, Kidd's exec-utive assistant from 2014 to 2018, "but he was a player too, so he also has an ego. . . . There's definitely some things that people misunderstand about J-Kidd. Ultimately he wants to win. He has good intentions."

There was also a cerebral aspect to Kidd. "He was like a professor," says Jason Terry, Bucks guard from 2016 to 2018, who also played for Kidd in

Brooklyn in 2013–2014. "Instead of telling you what to do, he engages you, empowers you, by asking, 'What do you see?'"

"Jason had a brilliant mind," says Nixon Dorvilien, Bucks assistant trainer from 2014 to 2016, "but he kind of made you uncomfortable around him."

"When players go through it and it's uncomfortable, they like to say, 'He's playing mind games with me,' but it's not that," says Greg Foster, Bucks assistant coach from 2014 to 2018, now with the Pacers. "He's trying to get you to do something you wouldn't normally do. That's *coaching*."

Knight searches for the right words. "I don't want to sound negative," he says. Knight explains some of Kidd's methods, such as how Kidd would embarrass the culprit of an error by making everyone *but* that person run sprints for his mistake. "He just had his way of getting his point across," Knight says.

Little things were made to be a big deal: at one point center Thon Maker didn't have an iPhone, messing up the team's blue-bubble iPhone group chat. Kidd was upset about it and made the team run because Kidd felt that Maker not getting an iPhone was an example of the team not being united.

But there was another side to Kidd, one that held players accountable, gave them confidence, raised the level of play. If players were doing the drill wrong, Kidd would grab the ball and hop in the drill and show players how to do it perfectly. Kidd would sometimes dominate and say, "Guys, this isn't that fucking hard!"

Kidd hated when players were not on time. Or when he had to go over something again. He was a perfectionist—and thought players should get it right the first time. He had this look, this death stare, that was piercing.

His mind was several steps ahead. The things he saw, few could. "It was like being around Einstein," Oppenheimer says. "Giannis realized that and wanted information, and Jason found a way to feed him information."

Kidd poured hours into helping Giannis but was less sympathetic with other players. "I don't think he could identify with the average player," says another ex-player. "There's a reason Hall of Famers are Hall of Famers, especially point guards. You see things that no one else does. I think he would just take it out on players and just verbally go at them. Just make them feel like shit, that they couldn't be as good as *Jason Kidd*, who could just step on the floor and do this fancy thing."

Kidd would challenge players by calling them out during film sessions—not by yelling but by asking the player in front of everyone, "Tell me: What were you doing here? What were you thinking here?" It was humiliating.

"The frustration was," Copeland says, "he's fucking Jason Kidd. One of the best point guards of all time. He's like, 'Why don't you just do this?' It's like, 'Bruh, you're *Jason Kidd*; *you* can do that.' He was hard on a lot of guys because his level and his IQ was so much higher than everybody."

Kidd would ask Giannis to explain what he did wrong during film sessions. There was no right answer, but a nod wasn't acceptable. He had to say his mistake out loud. That was difficult for Giannis, who wasn't a vocal player. Though gregarious off the court, he was still quiet on the court, still trying to fit in. He *hated* speaking up on the floor. He'd rather show leadership through action, through work ethic.

Kidd pulled Giannis out of his comfort zone by pointing out flaws verbally, seeing how Giannis would respond. It was part of Kidd's plan to transform his new project into a *point guard*. For point guards, talking is like breathing—instinctive, necessary. Because in Kidd's eyes, Giannis *could* be that point guard. He *could* become a superstar.

Kidd was sure that there was something special about Giannis. It was the way Giannis saw plays ahead of plays. The way he could push the ball up the floor like a natural ball handler. And given that he had miraculously sprouted two inches, to six feet eleven, since arriving in the NBA, Giannis, Kidd felt, could morph into one of the most versatile players in the league.

Still, that was a ways away. "We knew at the time that Giannis had the ability to handle the ball," says Joe Prunty, Bucks assistant coach from 2014 to 2018, "but being able to handle the ball and being able to run the team are different things."

Kidd flirted with having Giannis at point guard beginning in 2014 Summer League, though Giannis's official position was listed as center in two of four of the games. Kidd knew Giannis could play all positions; he could become a hybrid point forward, like Scottie Pippen was. Privately,

Kidd told his coaches that Giannis might never morph into a point guard, but he could turn into the next-generation big man, because, truly, what five-man could guard him?

Kidd told the press that he envisioned Giannis, at nineteen years old, being like Magic Johnson, Grant Hill, *and* Pippen after Giannis played thirty-two minutes as the primary ball handler against the Jazz in Summer League. "I remember writing the story," says Charles F. Gardner, *Milwaukee Journal Sentinel*'s Bucks beat writer at the time, "and thinking to myself, *This is crazy.*"

It *was* crazy. Giannis still, more than anything, resembled a toothpick. His body wasn't developed enough, his skills weren't honed enough, to merit a comparison to any of those legends, let alone all three. But he had a unique skill set, an intriguing build—one that people didn't yet know how to define. He was, as *Grantland* put it, "a human wormhole—all infinite limbs and impossible strides, twisting our conception of space inside out."

Giannis played well at the point in that Jazz game, dropping fifteen points, five assists, four rebounds, and three steals despite committing four turnovers. He looked comfortable. "He viewed himself as a point guard," Oppenheimer says. "He was one of those guys that was like, 'It's great if I score, but if I get an assist, I'm happy.'"

Still, Giannis didn't quite know how to control the tempo of a game. He'd often dribble into double teams, turning the ball over. Sometimes he was just going too fast. That became clear during a preseason game at Cleveland. Kidd started Giannis at point guard. The *Milwaukee Journal Sentinel* called the move "the Giannis Antetokounmpo experiment."

Cleveland's Matthew Dellavedova, known for full-court, suffocating defense, smothered Giannis. Giannis looked hesitant, timid. He went 0-for-5 for four points and zero assists in twenty-three minutes. He continued to struggle in the preseason finale against Minnesota, going 0-for-7, turning the ball over a damning eight times.

The coaches realized Giannis would need to be brought along a bit more slowly. He needed more experience. He needed to learn to play under control. The coaches had given him too much, too soon. The experiment had to be reevaluated.

"It was a reminder," says Sweeney, the assistant coach, "of, 'Hey, we've got some of these skills, but we're not quite ready for that responsibility.'"

* * *

The coaches created "Night School"—optional, but not *really* optional, nightly workouts. Most players showed up; Giannis *always* showed up. He and Sweeney would shoot, go over plays, and complete defensive drills for hours. Usually 8:00 to 11:00 p.m., sometimes even to midnight, every night. The two were inseparable. Both had a workaholic drive that few understood.

Sweeney hardly laughed. He looked so serious, so focused, that players would joke, "Yo, Sweeney, why are you so grumpy? What's wrong, Sweeney? Are you having trouble, Sweeney?" Pachulia made it one of his season goals to make Sweeney smile.

Sweeney's steely demeanor fit perfectly with Giannis. But Sweeney didn't take it easy on Giannis; he pushed him. Told him when he was messing up. The two would go at each other sometimes, yelling, fighting like brothers might, but it would end with "We good? OK, let's get back to work." Both valued work above everything else. "One of the things that Giannis did that set himself apart from the others," Sweeney says, "was that he had in his mind that 'I want to be the hardest-working player in the world.'"

Giannis would head straight to the gym after returning home from road trips too. He'd often bring his brothers, incorporating them into his drills. Giannis worked out just as intensely as he played games—maybe even more intensely. "He put in time others weren't willing to do," Sweeney says. "He wanted to be pushed past where he thought he could be pushed."

One night, forward Johnny O'Bryant, who had recently celebrated the birth of his first daughter, stayed a little bit later with Giannis after the two worked out. They talked as they gathered their bags.

"J-O-B," Giannis said, referring to O'Bryant's nickname, "I could never have kids right now."

"What do you mean?" O'Bryant said.

"If you have kids, you can't really put as much as you want into basketball. At some point, you have to go home and be with your kids."

O'Bryant smiled. He knew Giannis was right. He also knew Giannis was still a kid himself. Giannis wasn't really even dating. It was family, basketball, Bucks. Family, basketball, Bucks.

He also wanted his brothers to be better than him. "He wanted to be the best at all times. But he also wanted us to be the best too," Alex says. "That kept us pushing—because he wanted it so bad for us."

Kidd had introduced Giannis to legends like Dikembe Mutombo and Hakeem Olajuwon. Olajuwon told Giannis to stay focused and to stay away from what he called *temptation*: no women, no drugs. Nothing but basketball.

It wasn't clear what Giannis's role would be on the court, though. Start or come off the bench? Point guard or small forward or some combination? He was still working to get stronger, bigger. Sweeney and Kidd put him on a healthier nutrition plan—no more milkshakes, burgers, Cheetos, fries, Cokes—all of Giannis's favorites. Giannis switched his diet to protein and greens. He'd leave the practice facility with five Rubbermaid containers filled with chicken, eggs, nuts, fruits, and vegetables, consuming more than he ever thought possible.

As the season began, he was mostly playing small forward and would excite with a play or two, a big rebound, a loose ball dive, but his coaches wanted *more*. "His effort and hustle plays were always there," says Josh Broghamer, Bucks assistant coach from 2017 to 2018 and video coordinator from 2014 to 2017, "but sometimes he would forget an assignment or be in the wrong spot on offense or make the wrong read."

Giannis started to figure out how to use his quickness to get around guys who were much bigger than him. Kidd experimented with his position often, throwing him onto the court at power forward and even center at times.

Against the Grizzlies, Giannis targeted Zach Randolph, the Grizzlies' 250-pound terror. Randolph's body was like a concrete wall; just *watching* him yank a rebound out of the air made you flinch.

Not Giannis. Giannis had bulked up a bit but still looked flimsy, elbowing Randolph in the back, hitting him, shoving him. Randolph dominated him, which was Randolph's plan all along. "I was trying to put him under the rim," Randolph recalls. But Giannis kept fighting. "He had no quit in him."

Giannis boxed out Randolph one play, managing to push the veteran out of the way. "Oh?" Randolph said out loud, surprised.

"Come on," Giannis said, clutching the ball, swinging his elbows out.

"OK, OK, young fella."

That's when Randolph realized: "He got heart. The young fella *wanted* it." Giannis, who scored a then career-high eighteen points, twelve of which came in the fourth quarter, reminded Randolph of a young Pippen: long, athletic, all over the court, good knack for the ball. He just hadn't put it all together yet.

Giannis was gaining more confidence. He could see over the defense, throw critical passes. Sometimes he'd sink a little hook shot. He looked much improved from his rookie season, though he was still playing too fast, too out of control, with too many turnovers.

He looked brilliant at times, as when he took off from the three-point line and after one dribble softly laid in a finger roll against the Pistons. Or when he held his own against Serge Ibaka of the Thunder, no longer the punching bag he'd been his rookie season.

Giannis was honored with his own bobblehead by the end of November, against the Timberwolves. The first ten thousand fans received the smiling Giannis bobblehead. "It doesn't look like me," Giannis told reporters after the game. "I'm more handsome. But it's a nice feeling."

Ever since he saw the Bucks hand out Larry Sanders bobbleheads his rookie year, Giannis had dreamed of having his own bobblehead. *When is it going to be my turn?* he thought then. Now that he had his own, he stashed a few away to bring back to friends in Greece. "I didn't think I was going to have one," he said that night, smiling. "But I was always dreaming."

* * *

The coaches wanted to tweak Giannis's shooting form. He was never known as an outside shooter. It wasn't necessarily discussed as a glaring weakness, as it would be in the coming years, but it just wasn't something he needed to do much of throughout his youth. He was always so long and so athletic that he could just stretch his legs a couple of steps and be at the rim, so there was never a *need* to develop a jump shot.

He didn't shoot poorly from the field as a rookie, by any means. He even looked *comfortable* letting a three or two fly, his footwork and follow-through somewhat fluid. But the coaches continued to work on his form. Oppenheimer spent time helping him release the ball higher. Giannis's release was low, almost below his eyes and off his shoulder. They worked on his footwork, his base, slowing down the movement of catching the ball, gathering, and shooting.

Kidd, however, didn't want Giannis to shoot from long distance much at all at first, especially threes—or, according to several of his assistant coaches, he didn't want Giannis to get consumed by, or obsessed with, shooting. Kidd had been a fast guard, a wizard who could make split-second decisions on the move. Kidd wanted Giannis to do just that: get out in front of the defense, push the ball, score inside. In Kidd's eyes, why should Giannis surrender to the three-point line when he had the size and mobility to quickly get to the rim?

Giannis, however, wanted to be an all-around player, wanted to incorporate that fifteen-foot jumper into his game. It was never one or the other for him—inside or outside—he just wanted to do *everything*. Be everywhere. He was learning to adapt, following his coach's advice. He was getting to the free throw line frequently, from driving to the hoop aggressively.

But at one point that season, Kidd told Giannis not to shoot any more threes. He was trying to give Giannis confidence in the best parts of his game, instilling a mentality in his young player: "They can't guard you from driving." Kidd assured Giannis that he would get his time to shoot, but he wasn't ready yet. Not this season.

Initially Giannis was upset—he wanted to shoot threes; how could he not shoot threes? But Kidd would sub him out for launching an outside shot, later telling Jared Dudley, a veteran forward on the team, "I gotta put the mentality in Giannis when he's younger, before he becomes a superstar."

Frustration was building. Giannis didn't like getting picked on during film sessions, didn't like having to speak up. One practice, Giannis got a little animated. He wasn't being disrespectful; he just wasn't doing what Kidd wanted him to do. Kidd told him to leave: "You're done for the day."

That was what some of Kidd's former players meant by "mind games." Kidd continued to incorporate them, not playing Giannis (or Parker) in the fourth quarter early on because the team played better without them. "That really burned Giannis up," says Nicholas Turner, the executive assistant. "He always got better from that."

Kidd's tactics were working. Giannis was working harder than ever, coming back to the Cousins Center right after games upset at himself, working to correct his mistakes late into the night, at times cursing out loud for no one to hear.

"You're not going to break this kid," Hammond says. "Jason would challenge him, and Giannis would come right back at him for more. Look—Jason's a tough guy. He's a real tough guy. But so is Giannis."

Once, during a closeout drill in practice, the defender couldn't leave the floor until he stopped his man from scoring. Kidd made Giannis go eleven times in a row because Giannis couldn't stop his man from scoring. Giannis had a big smile on his face: he was *loving* it. He wanted to keep going.

"Giannis was a guy that you had to put your arm around him perhaps at times," Sweeney says, "but more than anything, you could go at him however you wanted because he had that innate toughness and that innate desire."

Giannis would pepper Dudley, the veteran teammate who was becoming a mentor to him, with questions on how he could improve. During time-outs, Dudley would in turn challenge Giannis with questions: "What do you see? What's going on here?" Dudley would tell him how to handle a certain coverage or how better to attack the lane. Giannis never argued or talked back. He was grateful for the advice. Dudley morphed into a big brother. He set rules. "No partying," Dudley told him.

Dudley became Giannis's biggest advocate, telling Kidd to start Giannis over him, something few veterans would do. Giannis wasn't even the best offensive player; Brandon Knight clearly was. But Giannis had the most potential. He'd make beautiful passes. He'd snatch the rebound and kick out the ball and run like someone was chasing him. "We all knew Giannis was going to be good," Dudley says. "But I don't think anyone knew he was going to be *this* good."

Dudley loved that Giannis didn't think he knew everything, as many young players do—and that Giannis was willing to make hustle plays, always sprinting back after a turnover even if there was a chance he'd get embarrassed.

"Unlike Americans, he had no ego," Dudley says. "He was always that guy that didn't care about getting dunked on. I respected him for that. I respected his hunger."

That didn't mean that Giannis didn't still believe in himself. Know his worth. The following year, before tip-off at Charlotte, Giannis sat on the sideline with Oppenheimer. They watched Charlotte's Nicolas Batum, a six-foot-eight forward having an all-star kind of season, warm up.

"You see Batum?" Oppenheimer said to Giannis.

Giannis nodded.

"Look at him," Oppenheimer said. "Really *look* at him. He's a *really* good player. If you work really hard, you might be able to be a Nic Batum type of player."

Giannis stared at his coach for a second, not frowning but looking surprised. A bit offended. "Coach," Giannis said, "if I become Nic Batum, I'm going back to Greece."

* * *

As a former point guard, Kidd was trying to get his players to *think* like point guards. Kidd created short quizzes for players before every shoot-around, posing five questions meant to improve basketball IQ: questions about certain coverages, plans for the opponent, or even just the history of the game. The last question was always a random basketball trivia question. "It was like we were in class," Dudley says.

Giannis *had* to get every question right. And most times, he didn't. But being the prankster that he was, he would creep around the gym and look over teammates' shoulders and cheat, especially off guard Michael Carter-Williams or Khris Middleton. "He kept looking at people's answers," Carter-Williams says, laughing. Guys would start to guard their papers from Giannis; the quizzes created a sense of both competition and pride.

There were times Giannis forgot to put his name atop the quiz, but his coaches would be able to tell it was his quiz because his English handwriting was still a work in progress. But he kept striving to get a perfect score.

The coaches told each player to keep a notebook to jot down information and plays, an idea that came from Sweeney's former boss at Evansville, Marty Simmons, who now coaches at Clemson. "Most guys didn't stick with it," Sweeney says. Giannis became *obsessed* with it. He still carries the little black college-ruled, spiral-bound Mead notebook wherever he goes today—even if he's nowhere near a basketball court.

"I'm not gonna lie—I don't know what he writes in that notebook," Kostas says. The two will be talking, and then Giannis will pull out the notebook, write something down. Kostas will look at him funny, ask him what he's writing. "I'm just writing," Giannis will say, his hand moving quickly. He's deeply private, and he doesn't show the notebook to anyone.

When Giannis first started using the notebook, he'd write before a game, after the game, even during the game. He'd write down the smallest of details: about angles, cuts. What he didn't do well. What he wanted to do well. Then he'd reflect on bigger goals: his hopes, his dreams. Giannis wrote everything down not just for himself but for his brothers. He didn't want to forget any detail that could potentially help them. "He learns something and writes it down so he can try to teach me and Alex immediately," Kostas says. "That's the bigger purpose."

By that point, Kostas, sixteen, was a junior at Dominican, and Alex, thirteen, was an eighth grader. Giannis was trying to help Kostas reach his goal of playing Division I college basketball and prepare Alex to play at the high school level. And when they would make a mistake, Giannis would correct them, as if they were his teammates.

After practice, Giannis and Alex would play NBA 2K, and when Giannis would see himself in the actual video game, he'd beam with pride

Thanasis, Giannis's oldest brother in Greece, far right, and Giannis, third from right, pose for a team photo with Filathlitikos. Thanasis is Giannis's role model. *Grigoris Melas*

Giannis, far right, and his friends and teammates, Rahman Rana, middle, and Andrian Nkwònia, left, take a picture after visiting Mount Lycabettus as fourteen-year-olds. *Rahman Rana*

Giannis dreamed of carrying the Greek flag, which he would finally get to do on March 25, 2013, when Greece celebrated its independence. He volunteered on behalf of his team, Filathlitikos. *Grigoris Melas*

Giannis competed in an all-star game in Athens when he was around seventeen years old. He was determined to make the NBA.
Grigoris Melas

Giannis shakes the hand of NBA Commissioner David Stern on draft night, after being selected fifteenth overall.
Mike Stobe/Getty Images

Giannis would show tremendous athleticism his rookie year, dunking with authority.
Christian Petersen/ Getty Images

Giannis was so excited to purchase his first car, a used black GMC Yukon truck. He asked his close friend Ross Geiger, Bucks video coordinator, to come with him to pick up the keys in February 2014.
Ross Geiger

Giannis has always been hard on himself. When he missed a free throw in his rookie year, he'd feel upset, telling his teammates: "But it's free!"
Greg Nelson/ Sports Illustrated

Giannis visits his hometown in Sepolia in summer 2015, playing pickup with old friends.
NurPhoto

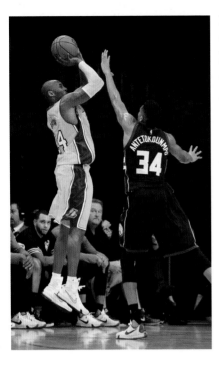

Kobe Bryant was one of Giannis's biggest inspirations. Notching his first career triple-double on this February 2016 night was special for Giannis. *Sean M. Haffey/Getty Images*

Giannis used to shy away from contact his rookie year. By 2016, he was dunking on opponents with ease. *Mike McGinnis/ Getty Images*

By 2019, Giannis was more determined than ever to bring a championship to Milwaukee. *Gregory Shamus/Getty Images*

There is always joy when Giannis plays. He is still the kid who loves to play basketball. *Streeter Lecka/Getty Images*

The Antetokounmpos pose for a photo before Giannis wins his first MVP in 2019. Veronica, his mother, and Mariah, his girlfriend, stand with the brothers on stage. *Cassy Athena*

Giannis gives an emotional speech after winning MVP in 2019. He thanked his family, teammates, and Milwaukee. *Kevin Winter/Getty Images*

Giannis's main goal is to have all his brothers make the NBA. Here, he chats with his brothers Kostas, middle, and Thanasis, right.
Kevork Djansezian/Getty Images

Giannis enjoys the launch of his first sneaker, the Nike Zoom Freak, in 2019.
Rodin Eckenroth/Getty Images

Giannis can play
any position on
the court, often floating
through them all.
Dylan Buell/Getty Images

Giannis used to practice his scowl in the front of the mirror as a rookie
and second-year player. Now, he intimidates opponents nightly.
Aurelien Meunier/Getty Images

Giannis is the savior the Bucks have been waiting for since Kareem Abdul-
Jabbar. He is their hope to finally bring a championship back to Milwaukee.
Rich Fury/Getty Images

and look at his brother. But Alex was too in awe of the fact that Giannis was in the game to even acknowledge his brother's glances.

Giannis started attending Alex's rec-league games, sitting in the crowd, tracking every play like a hawk. He'd even come down to the court, give him feedback midgame. He could sense his little brother was nervous. "Try not to be stressed," he said to Alex one game, placing his hand on Alex's small orange jersey. "Look at me. Just play the game." When Alex returned to the game, he looked much more relaxed. *Giannis* looked much more relaxed. "Bravo, Alex! Bravo!" Giannis screamed from the wooden bleachers.

Giannis felt like Milwaukee was home and staffers were like family. He developed a relationship with everyone in the organization. Sergo taught him how to throw a football, making fun of how Giannis looked like a "Martian" for the first few weeks trying to grip the ball. When Giannis chose the number 34, Namoc, the equipment manager, would say he had big shoes to fill and call him "Olajuwon."

Giannis even made interns feel special; when athletic training interns would tape his ankes, he'd shout them out by name before thanking them.

Giannis was still goofy, still kid-like. Sometimes he would pretend he was the coach, call Sweeney over, grab the clipboard, and draw a play. "This play will work for me!" Giannis would say, breaking into a big smile. The play was pretty much Giannis, with the ball, running from one end to the other, scoring, nobody else touching the ball.

Giannis's English was much better than the year before, but he was still learning new phrases. He became obsessed with saying the word *bro*. "Bro, bro, bro, bro, bro, brooooooooooooo," he'd say. He continued to make bold proclamations. Giannis was sure he was going to grow to seven feet. "I can be like Kareem Abdul-Jabbar!" he said one day.

His teammates laughed at his superstitions. He didn't wear head-phones and didn't listen to music before games or before practice because it brought emotion to the game, and he wanted to play without emotion. He tried to sleep for two hours and forty-five minutes before games and then eat a little bit of pasta as the game got closer. He had to have two ice bags and a foot bath after every game. He began shooting with a shooting sleeve because, one practice, he made shot after shot with the sleeve on, so he believed the sleeve was responsible for his good shooting.

He was like that off the court too. "He'll take an Advil and, like, five minutes later, he'd be like, 'Bro. I *feel* it. I feel fresh; I feel new,'" says Carter-Williams. "I'm like, 'OK, bro, it was only an Advil.'"

When Carter-Williams joined the team, something in Giannis loosened. He seemed more comfortable. The two became best friends. "I saw Giannis change," O'Bryant says. "MCW made him come out of his shell."

Carter-Williams would joke with Giannis about how Giannis only wore sweatpants. Didn't even *try* to dress up. "Bro," Carter-Williams would say, "how come Thanasis got so much swag and you have no swag? I don't get it."

Carter-Williams understood Giannis's tunnel vision, his excitement. "Come on, bro—let's go to the weight room!" Giannis would tell Carter-Williams. "Bro, we gotta get *big*. Look at LeBron. *Look* at him! We gotta get like him."

Carter-Williams introduced Giannis to J. Cole. He played him the song "Love Yourz," which became Giannis's favorite song. "He thought it was like heaven going through his ears," Carter-Williams says, resonating with the idea that, in some ways, it's easier to "love yours," love what you have, when you don't have money. But with fame, money, you have more responsibilities. More pressures: "It's beauty in the struggle, ugliness in the success," J. Cole rapped. "No such thing as a life that's better than yours."

Giannis started opening up to Carter-Williams about his family, about his life in Greece. His fears. Money. Giannis told him he wanted to stay as frugal as possible.

"Bro," Giannis told Carter-Williams, "we're rich, bro. *Rich*." It was as if saying it out loud made it somehow more real.

Before a game, a friend had given Giannis his first pair of Jordans, the Jordan Xs. Giannis took them out of the box and paused. These were fancier than any shoe he had ever held. He touched the soles, staring at them, realizing they were his. Really *his*. The soles on this pair listed many of Jordan's milestones: "85 Rookie of the Year," "89 All Defense," and "92 MVP/Championship," to name a few.

Giannis read them out loud, unconcerned with who heard him. Jay Namoc came over to Giannis's cubby. Namoc picked up Giannis's regular sneakers, the ones he'd be wearing that night, and flipped them over, scanned the soles. "Ain't shit on these," Namoc said.

Giannis nodded, a little deflated.

"Hey, man," Namoc said, sensing Giannis's disappointment, "you work hard enough, maybe they'll put these kinds of accomplishments on the bottom of your shoes one day."

*   *   *

Dudley would always sit next to Giannis on bus rides on the road. Dudley was aware that Giannis was still living with his parents and younger brothers, all in one apartment. That surprised him.

"Hey, man, I know you're only twenty years old," Dudley said to him on one ride, "but next year you're gonna be twenty-one. You gotta move out. You gotta get your own apartment."

Giannis was floored. "No, I can't; I'm gonna stay there." Giannis couldn't imagine not living with his family but didn't want Dudley to think he didn't value his advice. He told Dudley he'd think about it. Dudley suggested living in the same building but having his own apartment within the complex.

"You need your privacy to grow as a man, to get away," Dudley said. "It'll help your basketball game. You can still see your mom and dad every day."

Even the slightest bit of separation seemed unfathomable to Giannis, who still was adjusting to this life. So were his parents, his brothers. All of it still felt a bit strange. Giannis confided in Dudley about how hesitant he felt to spend money. The two daydreamed about the money Giannis might make one day.

"The *bread*!" Giannis would say, impressed with himself, having recently learned the colloquial term for money. "One day I'm going to get the *bread*." That word became an inside joke to the two of them. But the more they talked, the more Dudley realized that Giannis wanted more than money or security. He wanted a family of his own one day.

"I remember him talking about, he didn't want to marry an American girl: 'They try to steal your money,'" Dudley recalls. He laughs, thinking back to those bus rides, when he was just trying to nudge Giannis gently—not give him too much adulting to contemplate at once.

*   *   *

Parker was having a decent rookie season until it ended in a heartbreaking fashion. During the third quarter against the Suns, in late December, Parker tore his ACL in his left knee. Grimacing, he couldn't walk, had to be helped off the floor by teammates. It was a huge blow for the Bucks, who were finally starting to look competitive. And now, the future of the franchise would be sidelined at *least* a year.

That created room at the power-forward spot for Giannis, who was thriving with a *wow* play every night: a loose ball on one end, and in a blink, already at the other end dunking. His Eurostep was ballet-like: graceful, precise, powerful.

But the Bucks were struggling, dropping a game to Charlotte on December 23, right before Christmas. Players returned to the locker room dejected, silent. Everyone was ready for the next two days off with their families.

"Zaza," Kidd said, turning to Pachulia but addressing the group, "do you think this was a winnable game?"

"Yes, it was a winnable game," Pachulia said.

"And do you think we deserve the next two days off?"

Pachulia couldn't believe Kidd had put him in that situation, threatening to ruin Christmas. Pachulia tried to strike a diplomatic tone: "You know what, Coach—I understand the frustration. We're all frustrated because this was a game we were supposed to win. We didn't give enough effort. But at the same time, this is a holiday. Christmas is important to our families. It's not about us; it's about our families. Guys have made plans."

Kidd then turned to Dudley. "What do you think? Should we take these next two days off?"

Dudley, too, gave a diplomatic answer.

But Kidd wasn't satisfied. "See you guys tomorrow at 9:00 a.m."

"Whoa, whoa, whoa," players said. "What do you mean?"

"We're going to have practice tomorrow."

"We booked flights to different places!"

"I don't care. You guys get paid to do a job, so you're doing your job tomorrow. Things change."

Practice the next morning was *ugly*. Kidd *went* at Sanders. Called him a "piece of shit," a "terrible player." The team ran and ran and ran and ran, like a college team would. "I don't think I've done that since I left J-Kidd," Knight says. "It was not normal."

Players had to finish a fast-break drill in twenty-two seconds, but twenty-seven was the team's best record. They did it over and over until they made it. Some were bent over, panting, cramping. Practice lasted three hours, and then Kidd made players lift weights and do pool exercises. Half the team didn't know how to swim, but Kidd made everyone run in the pool.

"Everybody was so tired that nobody was thinking about Christmas," Pachulia says. "We didn't have energy left to open gifts."

Kidd continued to berate Sanders, though, calling him "pathetic." Sanders couldn't handle it. Where he was in his life, his career, this *practice*, all his mistakes, all his frustrations, he felt his entire body stiffen as he cramped from head to toe. "I had a full-body convulsion," Sanders says. "My body broke down. Physically I couldn't take it, and mentally I really couldn't take it."

Sanders asked to be excused to go to the bathroom. "Oh, don't worry," Kidd said as Sanders walked away. "We'll wait, then run some more." Sanders left the facility and took himself to the hospital, spending the night there. Few knew what happened in the aftermath, and he didn't have the energy then to talk about it.

"I don't think he's a bad person," Sanders says about Kidd, "but mentally, he kinda, like, brain fucked me a little. It was a lot of, I love you, kiss you on the cheek, now it's all about money, who cares about your mental health, your body breaking down.

"I'm happy. I'm in a much better place now," he says. "I'm sorry it had to go out the way it did."

*   *   *

Without Sanders, and without Parker, Giannis played even more minutes, looking dominant at times. He had a remarkable play against the 76ers: he chased an opponent down, blocked him, hit the ground, got back up, blocked another shot, hit the ground, got back up, tried to take the charge.

Playing the three, four, and five, Giannis took the majority of his shots in the paint, shooting 57 percent at one point. Kidd's plan was working; Giannis wasn't testing out the outside jumper he had been working on in private.

Bill Simmons saw him play in person for the first time that year. "It was so clear that he was special," Simmons says. "His arms were so fucking long; his steps were so fucking long. I was all in." He wrote in *Grantland* that year, "Seeing the Greek Freak in person is like seeing Young Scottie Pippen crossed with Young Kevin Durant crossed with an octopus. He's only 20, takes 10 yards per step, plays four positions, has Freddy Krueger arms, might pass the 7-foot mark soon and basically doesn't have a genetic parallel."

Giannis showed promise against the Lakers, scoring a career-high twenty-five points. In overtime he made two shots, then missed the third, and attempted one final shot, which also missed. Still, that type of shoot-again-no-matter-what confidence showed maturity.

The next day, Giannis enjoyed his first In-N-Out burger. The team toured UCLA's campus and then Hollywood. Giannis smiled so wide, as if a celebrity were just around the corner. "Coach," Giannis said to Sweeney, "this is the *real* America!"

On the way back to Milwaukee, sitting next to each other on the plane, Sweeney and Giannis did what they always did: broke down film. While everyone else dozed off, the two of them continued to work, a faint light shining above them, a laptop, and of course Giannis's notebook.

Sweeney froze a play, then explained to Giannis what he should have done in the sequence. Sweeney was a master of nuance, of details. He'd explain to Giannis little things—the trajectory of the ball, the precision of a pass, how to most efficiently slide over to the midline on defense.

Talking, freezing the frame, talking, freezing the frame—that was the rhythm of their relationship. They'd go for hours, until Sweeney called it a night. But Giannis stayed up, writing in his notebook, too many swirling thoughts to sleep.

*   *   *

Giannis was again selected to play in the Rising Stars Challenge at All-Star Weekend, this time in New York. Once again, he was fully focused, as if it were a real game. When opponent Mason Plumlee took off for a breakaway dunk, Giannis didn't just let him have the easy bucket; he sprinted down the entire length of the floor and blocked Plumlee, smacking the ball out of bounds. A time-out was called.

"Hey, man, it's an all-star game," Alvin Gentry, Giannis's coach for the game, told him.

"Coach," Giannis said, "all I know how to do is play hard."

That was obvious even before the game, when Giannis sprinted through layup lines. "He's just a guy that you can hit him once, hit him twice, hit him three times—just understand that he's coming back for the fourth," says Gentry, now the associate head coach of the Kings.

After the game, the Bucks made a surprising move: trading Knight, the team's leading scorer, to the Suns. The Bucks had thirty wins at that point, fifteen more than the entire previous season, thanks to smothering defense. The trade was shocking, especially to Giannis, who was learning the business of basketball, learning that friends could leave at any moment. Geiger had left to work for the Suns. Wolters had been waived. Morway had gone to work for the Jazz. It was a lot to deal with.

Giannis still looked lost at times. His biggest problems were consistency and taking care of the ball. His potential was tantalizing, his mistakes frustrating. NBA reporter Zach Lowe described the dynamic best: "On any given possession the Greek Freak can look like he knows nothing and everything at once. He is an empty vessel, and in a blink, he is one vision of modern basketball fulfilled.

"He's learning on the job," Lowe continued, "and the results range from the sublime to the embarrassing."

About five games before the playoffs, Giannis became frustrated in practice. He kept screwing up in a one-on-one closeout drill. It was one of Kidd's hardest drills: a defender started at the foul line and closed out on an offensive player, who stood at the three-point line. The defender had to cut off the dribble, not allowing threes (or any bucket, really). Players would go and go until they got a stop.

Giannis *killed* on offense, scoring twenty-eight straight times. On defense? *Everyone* scored on Giannis. He couldn't get a stop. He was exhausted and stopped closing out hard. At one point, he stood on the free throw line, catching his breath, not moving, not trying. He was *pissed*. Realizing Kidd wouldn't bail him out, he began moving his feet. His closeouts were still weak, half-hearted. It took him fifteen minutes to get a stop.

Kidd just watched. Didn't yell, didn't call him out. Just *watched*. Waited until film the next day to expose him. Kidd turned on footage of the drill, showing Giannis failing to close out hard. Giannis was forced to watch how lackadaisical he was, in front of everyone. Kidd didn't say anything. He didn't need to. The embarrassment hung over Giannis. He understood, apologized to Kidd. Told him it wouldn't happen again.

The next day, the Bucks played Cleveland. Kidd told the team before the game, "Giannis isn't going to play tonight. If we're going to be the best team we want to be, *that* can't happen."

That meaning the drill. Giannis's lack of intensity. Giannis had hit a wall, as many young players do. He was *tired*. And Kidd was old school: he wasn't afraid to sit his best players down.

One January game, at Philadelphia, the Bucks messed up a defensive coverage. Kidd thought Giannis had made the mistake. Giannis respectfully insisted that it wasn't his mistake. They went back and forth, but Giannis stood his ground, diplomatically saying, "Coach, I promise—it wasn't me."

Then, at halftime, Kidd pulled up the play on film. "Show me," Kidd said, confident he was right. But Kidd was actually wrong: the film showed it *wasn't* Giannis's mistake. Kidd still benched Giannis for the second half.

The Bucks were blowing the 76ers out, so Kidd didn't necessarily *need* to put Giannis back in. He was making a point, as if to say, "Yeah, you're getting better, but I'm still the boss."

Kidd hoped benching Giannis against Cleveland would be another teachable moment. An opportunity for him to refocus. The message was "We need you. We need you to be better."

But Giannis was upset. He decided to look up Kidd's NBA stats, thinking, *What did this guy do in his career, anyway?* When he saw Kidd's résumé—NBA championship, USA gold medal—he realized he'd better keep his head down.

"Giannis was really, really angry," Oppenheimer says. "It was an opportunity to play against LeBron."

The Bucks lost, 104–99. Giannis had played so well up to that game, starting sixty-seven of the team's last seventy-seven games. By practice the next day, Giannis was still fuming. He came in with his head practically shaved. His teammates were concerned. "Bro, are you all right?" they asked. "What's going on with you?"

"Yeah," Giannis said, shrugging. "I'm just going through it."

Tyler Ennis, a guard who had joined the team in February, knew what was *really* agitating Giannis: "You could see how much it bothered him, that he had to miss the game."

The next day, the Bucks played the Knicks at Madison Square Garden. Before the game, Giannis told Sweeney his plan: he vowed to play *angry*. Rebound angry. Score angry. Pass angry.

"Why angry?" Sweeney asked him.

"I didn't play."

"Well, if you do it for that game, you gotta keep doing it in all the games."

The game started, and Giannis blocked a shot, yanked the ball out of the air, zoomed downcourt. New York's Cole Aldrich was just ahead, and as Giannis sprinted toward him, dribbling behind his back, Aldrich instinctively ran out of the way, allowing Giannis to hammer home a dunk. Giannis did the Westbrook scowl. Well, the Westbrook-*Giannis* scowl he had been practicing all year.

The arena erupted. Kidd tried to hide a faint smile. "That was part of what J-Kidd was trying to do," Ennis says, "just make him channel that anger into the game, and it came out on that play."

Giannis finished with twenty-three points and nine rebounds to help the Bucks win, 99–91. Afterward, Giannis told reporters he had played "angry." Then he showed them what he meant, showed them his scowl. He scrunched up his cheeks, tightened his nose, dubbed it his "ugly face."

Then he softened, unwrinkled his forehead, and smiled. He laughed, and reporters did too. "The ugly face was prettier today," Giannis joked. "I had *swag* too." Then he stiffened back up and explained his approach from there on out: "I try to be angry when I play," he said. "I try to be mad. *Mean*, man!"

*   *   *

The Bucks had clinched a playoff spot as the number 6 seed in the East, something that had seemed impossible the year before.

The number 3 seeded Bulls, first up against the Bucks, were stacked, with Derrick Rose, Jimmy Butler, Pau Gasol, and Joakim Noah leading the roster. They played tough, physical. They were far more seasoned than the Bucks, which was the youngest team in the playoffs.

Butler hounded Giannis in game 1, making it difficult for Giannis to find any kind of rhythm. Giannis kept fouling, kept looking out of place, shooting 4-for-13 from the field. He was still icy in game 2, going 2-for-11. The Bucks lost both games.

The Bulls' strategy was to be physical with Giannis. Slow him down in the open floor, take away his driving lanes. Foul him if he got inside. Make him resort to jump shots, which were his biggest weakness. With so many defenders suffocating him, Giannis had never attracted that much attention before.

"It really, really pissed Giannis off," O'Bryant says, "the way they guarded him. The things they did to him."

His teammates told him to not second-guess himself. Let the game come to him. Attack the rim. He did just that with a breakout performance in game 3, as Kidd shifted him to power forward, scoring seventeen of his twenty-five points in the first half—adding twelve rebounds. Carter-Williams had nineteen, but the Bucks lost again, this time in double overtime as Rose dropped thirty-four.

No team had come back from a 3–0 deficit to win a playoff series. "We can come back. We can win this series," Giannis told Carter-Williams, "even though the odds are small."

Carter-Williams nodded. "The odds were small for us to even make it to the NBA in the first place," Giannis said to him. "We're not quitting."

The Bucks won game 4. And in a game 5 win, Giannis swatted four shots, including a critical block on Rose, who charged down the lane with thirty seconds left. "I remember being in awe," says Doug McDermott, Bulls forward who now plays for the Pacers. "Like, Giannis is fearless. There's not a lot of people in the world that would take on that challenge."

Giannis started gaining more confidence as the Bucks fought to keep their season alive.

"It was Giannis's coming-out party," says Aaron Brooks, former Bulls guard. "I could just see him progressively getting better in each game in the series."

Game 6 was brutal. Bulls guard Mike Dunleavy Jr. punched Carter-Williams in the jaw in the first quarter. Officials didn't see it, but TNT's cameras did. Carter-Williams chipped a few teeth and later had to seek dental assistance.

That was Dunleavy: competitive, cold-blooded. Once, a water boy didn't have a towel for him. He flipped out, yelling at the ball boy. Another time, Dunleavy got ejected from a game, took his jersey off, tossed it into the crowd. His Bulls teammates used to watch that video of him on YouTube to fire them up.

Giannis was infuriated. Carter-Williams was his best friend, and *nobody* was going to do that to his best friend. Giannis was about to explode as the Bulls' lead ballooned to thirty. With Carter-Williams out, Giannis looked directly ahead, as if he was about to scrunch his face. Then he ran. So hard, seventy feet downcourt, making a beeline for Dunleavy. He body-slammed

Dunleavy so hard Dunleavy landed in the front row of seats. Giannis was ejected from the game, drawing a flagrant 2 foul and earning him a one-game suspension that would start next season.

It was a side nobody had seen from Giannis before. No longer happy-go-lucky, smiley—he finally looked *mean*.

"Giannis almost killed him," Oppenheimer says. "But that's how he was: he had a loyalty to his teammates. He wasn't a punk. But it did surprise me, the aggressive nature of it. It surprised everybody."

"I wasn't shocked," Sweeney says, "but I remember thinking to myself, *Wow*."

"I got a lot of respect for Giannis, going after him, to be honest with you," says Foster, the assistant coach. "You don't see that much in today's game."

Milwaukee fans had a lot of respect for Giannis in that moment too. "That made Giannis a hero forever," says Jim Kogutkiewicz, the longtime fan who was at that game.

Fans began to boo Dunleavy. It was a startling sound for the forward, who had grown up in Milwaukee. His dad, Mike Dunleavy Sr., had both played for and coached the Bucks. "We gave him so much crap for that," McDermott says. "He thought that Milwaukee was kind of *his* city. But after that night, we made sure that we let him know that that's *Giannis's* city now."

Nobody tried to leave early, even after it was clear the Bucks were going to lose by more than fifty points. As the final seconds of the 120–66 loss dwindled away, fans began a loud, defiant chant: "Mil-wau-kee! Mil-wau-kee! Mil-wau-kee!"

So many fans—fans who had been quiet, almost dormant, for years, struggling through decades of despair, through the still-painful Ray Allen trade, through the once-great-hope Andrew Bogut shattering his elbow, through the signing of journeyman Drew Gooden to a ridiculous $32 million deal, through trading a promising future franchise player in Tobias Harris—were now proudly screaming at the top of their lungs, "Mil-wau-kee! Mil-wau-kee! Mil-wau-kee!"

They weren't going to leave quietly, no matter that they were down fifty-four. No matter what would happen with the upcoming arena deal. They needed this team to stay in Milwaukee.

"Mil-wau-kee! Mil-wau-kee! Mil-wau-kee!" fans chanted after the final buzzer, as if to say, "We're still here. We still matter."

CHAPTER 10

STAR

During a drill at the start of 2015–2016 training camp, a defender had to help and recover before playing one-on-one. Giannis dominated. At one point, his entire *head* was above the rim, having dunked on a teammate so badly that players are still embarrassed to name the victim to this day.

Forward Chris Copeland stood in line, noticing that Giannis didn't seem to feel sorry for any of his victims. Didn't pause to let them catch a breath. *Giannis is a killer—a real killer*, Copeland thought.

Copeland didn't quite know what to make of Giannis, until he felt a stiff elbow in his back when it was Giannis's turn to play defense. Giannis guarded him tightly, refusing to concede any space. "It was one of the few times I felt uncomfortable," Copeland says. "Like, bruh, back *up*."

In nearly a decade playing pro, Copeland wasn't used to a player playing that intensely in practice. Even with little things, like stretching and warming up—Giannis *had* to be first. "It's not an insult, but Giannis is like a *creature*. Like, what is *this*?" Copeland says. "Mobile *and* huge? He's a different type of human. He's like a seven-foot Russell Westbrook."

Bo Ryan, the legendary University of Wisconsin–Madison coach, was watching, as camp was held at Madison that season. Ryan watched the way Giannis's eyes trailed Kidd's demonstrations: every movement, every cut. Giannis never took a possession off. That made sense to Ryan, who had previously coached a USA basketball team at a tournament in Serbia; Europeans didn't take many breaks.

"Some people just have it. Giannis had it from day one," Ryan says. "You could just see it hadn't all come together yet, but it was going to." Ryan remembers talking with other coaches and scouts who were there, including Rod Thorn, the Hall of Fame executive and former coach who was hired as a special consultant to the Bucks that year. Ryan recalls everyone being excited about Giannis's potential. "Watch out for this guy! Look what he can do!" Ryan remembers hearing. "Just think when he gets older. Just *think* when he starts shaving!"

With Parker still injured, and Middleton having recently signed a $70 million extension as the team's top scorer, Giannis wanted to prove that he himself was the best player. So he showed no mercy during the one-on-one drill. He kept dunking, posting up, at will. Some veterans whispered to the coaches to stop the drill: "We're gonna be here all day!"

Giannis probably couldn't hear any of them. He was so focused all he saw was the defender and the rim. He wasn't going to let anyone get in his way. "He wasn't that good yet, to be honest. He still wasn't our best player," Copeland says. "But you could just see him learning his powers."

Part of that was because Giannis didn't *look* like a kid anymore. He didn't have to *practice* scowling anymore; his lips would instinctively curl, his nose would automatically scrunch. His body was going through a transformation. He was more chiseled, more confident. Stronger, tougher. Bigger than he had ever been, clocking in at 242 pounds.

He was learning how to better take care of his body with better nutrition. The Bucks hired a new team chef, Shawn Zell, who introduced Giannis to hearty foods that were still healthy, such as bison sloppy joes and a "bison power bowl," his favorite (sweet potatoes, mustard greens, corn, bison, peppers). Giannis ordered the same breakfast nearly every day, messaging Zell before he came in with one of two emojis: the egg emoji or the chef emoji. He loved egg-white omelets loaded with veggies—tomatoes, spinach, and onions, plus bacon and a bit of feta. He ate lots of fruit, about six to eight cups per day, mostly pineapple. It was more than he had ever eaten in his life.

Zell taught him about the importance of hydrating the night before, to avoid cramping late in fourth quarters. He helped him find energy-packed snacks, like waffle snacks by a company called Honey Stinger, plus carbo-hydrates like pasta, to eat before tip-off. Giannis had always just played his heart out, never really paying attention to his body, his health. He couldn't, given the way he'd grown up.

"He lived most of his life not making that a priority, in terms of 'I need to fuel and eat and get ready for games,'" says Zell, who served as team chef from 2015 to 2020. "If you would have told fifteen-year-old Giannis that turmeric shots would help with his recovery, he would have looked at you, like, 'What the heck is a turmeric shot?'" That became one of his favorites.

Was there any correlation between Giannis's new dietary habits and his growing two inches since his NBA career began? "Good nutrition helps in all things," Zell says, "but it's not—if I drastically change my nutrition, it wouldn't help me grow two inches. It's all part of a big cog, and [there's] a bunch of working gears in it. [Nutrition is] just a small gear in a huge machine. It's diet, it's how he's working out, it's genetics. There's so many different things that play into it."

Though his body was growing, his vocal leadership had some distance to go. Kidd continued to push Giannis to speak up. He'd put Giannis in drills where he had to talk, or else he'd have to stay in the drill. Or every other player *except* for Giannis would have to run.

"You could tell Giannis was trying to be vocal, even though it wasn't in his nature yet to do that," says Malcolm Brogdon, Bucks guard from 2016 to 2019, who now plays for the Pacers.

But Giannis didn't struggle with communicating when he was joking with his teammates. Just being himself. Once, during a particularly taxing practice, Kidd said that if Giannis hit a three, practice would end. Giannis was so excited he ran to the three-point line, caught the ball.

"Wait!" he told everyone, putting the ball down. "I gotta put on my sleeve first!"

"Bro, are you *serious*?" his teammates said.

Dead serious. Giannis still believed in his shooting-sleeve superstition. He put on the sleeve, bent his knees low, smiled like he had already sunk the shot, and then . . .

He airballed.

Everyone burst out laughing, including Giannis. He started making fun of himself. "That's what I liked about him; he's just a super regular guy," Ennis says. "He wasn't too prideful to laugh at himself. And that's what drew people to him."

When he and his teammates were eating in the team kitchen, they'd blast music. Oftentimes, it was Snoop Dogg's "Gin and Juice" and Marvin Gaye's "Let's Get It On." Giannis would be in the back of the kitchen, swaying, singing, using a utensil for a microphone. "Laaaaaaaaaaaid back!" Giannis would rap. "With my mind on my money and my money on my mind!"

As the season began, he looked relaxed, sure of himself on the court. Something was clicking. Maybe it was adding more muscle. Maybe it was being a little bit older. But after dropping twenty-seven points in a loss against the Wizards, in his first game of the 2015–2016 season, he was clearly showing a new confidence. He looked unstoppable. He told Saratsis, his agent, afterward, "I can do this every night."

* * *

One afternoon, as the season wore on, Kidd said to the group during a film session, "Who's the best player on this team?" It was a thorny question— one intended to provoke Giannis to speak up. Kidd knew Giannis wanted to be the leader; here was his chance to claim it.

Nobody raised his hand, because it was awkward. Then Kidd started spouting off Middleton's stats: "He's leading our team in points, assists." Players knew Kidd would keep talking until someone answered him.

Giannis *hated* those awkward silences in film sessions but didn't try to fill them. He'd just tuck his head down, hoping it would be over soon. "OK, it's J-Kidd's antics. Let's just raise our hands," remembers one former player. A bunch of hands rose in support for Middleton.

Giannis sat still, silent, hands clasped on his lap. He didn't say Middleton *wasn't* the best, but he didn't say he *was* the best either.

"Giannis," Kidd said, "why didn't you raise your hand?"

Giannis didn't answer.

Just say it, bro, Ennis thought. *Say it so we can move on.*

Giannis looked at his coach and finally said it. Several players and coaches remember his words: "I'm the best player."

No one had ever heard Giannis speak up like that. Kidd didn't say anything—moved on like nothing had happened, his face expressionless. Now Giannis would have to lead, if he expected his teammates to follow. And Giannis was inching closer to where he wanted to be: commanding respect, earning his spot.

*   *   *

But his older brother Thanasis was slipping.

The Knicks cut Thanasis in October 2015. "Thanasis was extremely energetic, very passionate," says Coby Karl, then an assistant coach with the affiliate Westchester Knicks, who coached Thanasis. "Almost *too* energetic. He would get out of control."

It hurt, given that Thanasis had come so close to his dream. Now that opportunity was gone.

"It was tough," Thanasis says. "I had to go back home." Of course Thanasis was proud that his baby brother was succeeding, but he had given Giannis the blueprint.

Back in 2013, when Giannis was about to be drafted, he did an interview with the Greek TV station Antenna. The producer, Yannis Psarakis, picked up Giannis and Thanasis in his gray Honda HRV, Thanasis sitting in the front, Giannis in the back, to take them to the studio. Every question, Giannis would turn to Thanasis and ask, "Can I say that? Can I say that?" He had always looked to Thanasis for approval. For guidance.

When Giannis couldn't handle the pressure of ball handlers, back in Greece, and kept turning over the ball, Thanasis blocked the crap out of anyone who stole the ball from Giannis. But when NBA scouts came to see Giannis at the practices, Thanasis was guarding him, beating him up, making it hard for him to score. Not because Thanasis didn't want his brother to succeed but because he was a competitor too.

And now, the younger brother's dreams were sprouting before the older brother's. Thanasis was elated for Giannis but yearned to find his own path too. "The key is patience," Thanasis says. It's a lesson he learned from their dad.

Thanasis remembers a video he saw on YouTube, where three men had to cut down a tree. The first man was swinging his axe hard at the tree. But after a few hours, he stopped. The second man whacked the tree for four hours, six hours, then stopped. The third man kept chopping at the tree, nonstop, refusing to quit. The other two men were amazed that he kept at it for hours on end, but when they came closer to him, they realized the man had on a blindfold. He hadn't wanted to see his results, because if he had seen his results, he'd get discouraged. Instead, working blindfolded fostered the mentality that every time he took a swing, he believed the tree would fall.

This entire time, Thanasis had been working blindfolded. "I relate to that video," he says, smiling, then looking down at the ground, "because it's not about the results; it's about what you can do every day to stay ready so when you get the opportunity, you chop down the tree."

He just didn't know if the opportunity would come. He went back to Greece in hopes of finding a EuroLeague team to play for. Giannis stayed in America. Their lives were diverging. Again.

* * *

Giannis began to hold his own against the league's biggest stars. He had a career-high thirty-three points against LeBron James and the Cavs. He guarded not just James but Kevin Love, who was much bigger. James complimented Giannis after the game. Giannis was starstruck: "LeBron said I'm going to be good! I'm going to be good!" he told his teammates.

The Bucks were optimistic. They were young, talented. And having added big man Greg "Moose" Monroe, the Bucks were ready to take another big step forward. Giannis was still learning his body—how to guard bigs and smalls. He had more fouls than anyone in the league by December 1, but Kidd had faith in Giannis. Tried to give him confidence. "We go as you go," Kidd would tell him.

That was a lot of responsibility for a young player. Sometimes Giannis was so hard on himself, thinking he wasn't living up to it. "He takes everything personal," says Jabari Parker, who had grown closer to Giannis. "After a loss, after he doesn't think he plays well, you know not to talk to him."

Greivis Vásquez, a point guard who joined the team that year, was concerned. Giannis looked frustrated. Some teammates shared Vásquez's concern: they thought maybe Giannis was unhappy playing basketball because he looked so serious, so intense, all the time.

"He blamed himself for almost everything," Vásquez says. "'I should have done this; I should have done that.' In reality, he was doing more than enough for us to win. That was something he needed to work on."

Giannis no longer expressed himself by crying, at least not publicly; he tucked his emotions inside. Vásquez worried Giannis would wear himself ragged over an eighty-two-game season. "Most nights, you couldn't recognize if he was happy or uncomfortable. Most of the time, he was uncomfortable because he wanted to be better and he was not satisfied," Vásquez says.

Giannis was obsessed with getting better—and bigger. By 3:30 p.m., he'd already be fully drenched, sweating through a workout, ahead of a 7:30 game. "You know we have a full game in a couple hours, right?" Ennis, the guard, would ask Giannis.

"Yeah," Giannis said. "I know."

Opponents, still tying up their laces, would see Giannis sprinting and ask Bucks players, "Does he always do this?"

The Bucks players would just nod. "Yup. That's Giannis."

*   *   *

After the all-star break, in late February, Kidd walked up to Giannis in the locker room right before a game against Atlanta. "You're going to start at point guard tonight," Kidd told him. "You're going to handle the ball."

"OK, Coach," Giannis said. "I got you." Giannis was a little nervous but didn't show it. He wanted his coach to know that he wasn't afraid. Then Giannis found Sweeney. Double-checked: "So . . . I'm playing point guard . . . tonight? You sure about that?"

Sweeney laughed. "Yup. That's what it is."

"OK."

Putting the ball in Giannis's hands was the ultimate display of trust, and Kidd felt that Giannis was ready for it. "I was kind of forced to be the leader," Giannis later told *60 Minutes*. "It's like when you have a little baby and you put them in the water so they can learn how to swim."

Giannis had nineteen points and three assists against the Hawks, a strong showing, but moving to point was intimidating at first. Giannis wasn't really comfortable. He could stretch his long arms, wrap the ball around bodies, deliver a pinpoint pass anywhere. But it was difficult to do it at the NBA pace.

"Dang, this point guard thing's *hard*," Giannis told Ennis after one practice. "I gotta push the ball; I gotta talk to everybody; I gotta know where everyone is."

"Yeah, bro, it's not as easy as you think," Ennis said. "Instead of yelling at us all day to get you the ball, now you see!"

Ennis would laugh when he'd see Giannis coming off the floor, gassed. Soon, though, with more conditioning, more reps, Giannis was thriving at the point. The move was brilliant. Giannis was more aggressive, stringing together four triple-doubles over the next month, including his first against the Lakers in Kobe's final season.

That game, Giannis was magnificent. He directed the offense, dunked, posted up, looked confident. He had twenty-seven points, twelve rebounds, ten assists, four blocks, and three steals in the Bucks' seven-point win. Afterward, Kobe told reporters that Giannis had the potential to be a great player, and that he had the physical tools and intelligence, but it was just a matter of him believing in himself and going after it.

Kidd then took Giannis into the Lakers' visiting locker room, into a private room to talk with Kobe.

Giannis stared at his idol, this man in front of him who had no idea what it meant to share *one* pair of his Nike Kobes, the red-and-white ones, with Thanasis. The first playoff game Giannis had ever watched in Sepolia, back in the internet cafés with his brothers, was the Lakers against the Celtics, Kobe against Paul Pierce.

Oh shit, Giannis thought, finally meeting Kobe. *Jason Kidd* and *Kobe Bryant? I'm having a conversation with them?*

Kobe gave him advice for about an hour. He told him to work on his jump shot, get in the gym every day, and shoot a thousand jumpers a day.

Giannis vowed to shoot fifteen hundred. Kobe also told him about the kind of mentality it took to be great. "Be serious until the last day you play basketball," Kobe told him, also noting the importance of recovery, of taking care of one's body, of making sacrifices. "You have to have that killer mindset," Kobe continued. "That mindset that you will not be beat. That you will outwork *everybody*."

Giannis couldn't stop smiling. He jogged back into the Bucks locker room and told his teammates, "I got to talk to Kobe! I got to talk to my hero! Kobe told me you just have to work hard! I can't make any excuses!" He was giddy, repeating each line as if trying to memorize it.

"He was just like a little kid," says Nixon Dorvilien, the Bucks assistant trainer, who watched from afar. "Giannis literally changed after that meeting. It was just a light bulb that went off about what it takes to be great."

The Bucks as a team, though, were inconsistent. They had a lackluster offense, including Giannis's own shooting percentages. Teams continued to sag off him, daring him to shoot. Despite this being Giannis's breakthrough season, averaging 16.9 points, 7.7 rebounds, and 4.3 assists, the Bucks underperformed, missing the playoffs. It was disappointing, to say the least. Momentum felt halted. Stalled.

But for the first time, Giannis's mind gravitated toward something other than basketball. Other than getting better, getting bigger.

He fell in love.

* * *

Bucks players had just finished a Summer League game and were about to walk out of the gym when Ennis, the Bucks guard, spotted a friend: a woman named Mariah Riddlesprigger. Riddlesprigger, an NBA intern, was working the Summer League. Ennis's brother and Riddlesprigger had attended the same college, Rice University, and were friends.

Ennis and Riddlesprigger caught up before parting ways. After Riddlesprigger walked away, Giannis went up to Ennis and asked, "How do you know her? Who is she? Can you introduce me?"

Ennis was a little surprised at how eager Giannis was. "Honestly, I'd never seen him talk about anything but basketball and smoothies," Ennis says. Ennis assumed Giannis had dated before but didn't really know. Giannis was so focused on achieving his basketball dream that maybe there hadn't been time for relationships.

But the way Giannis asked about Mariah, looked at Mariah, her bright, big smile, Ennis could tell that Giannis was intrigued. He agreed to introduce them, thinking they might be a good match. They were similar in a lot of ways: hardworking, athletic, bighearted, family oriented, down to earth, and competitive. Riddlesprigger had played volleyball at Rice.

Ennis asked Riddlesprigger if she was allowed to be introduced to a player, because she was technically working for the NBA. Ennis remembers her saying, "I don't know. We're not really supposed to be doing that." Ennis never found out much more, but a year later, he found out they were dating.

She would later become the mother of Giannis's first child, Liam.

"Giannis owes me," Ennis says. "He should have named the baby's middle name Tyler."

* * *

That fall, Giannis signed a four-year $100 million contract extension. Only after, of course, postponing the signing by four hours so he could complete a morning workout. He accepted a slightly lower salary—about $6 million less than the max he could have signed, without any player or team options—in order to help the Bucks build a contender.

He called Wes Edens, Bucks co-owner, who was in Ireland at the time: "I just wanted to say thank you for the money. It means so much to me and my family. I'm going to work very hard for it." Giannis took his family to Capital Grille in Milwaukee. They ordered steak. When the food came, much more than he had anticipated, with appetizers and side dishes, Giannis looked confused. "I don't know who's paying for all this," he said, jokingly but not so jokingly. "Because I only said I'd get the steak."

The reality of the extension set in: it was more money than he and his family could fathom. And yet Giannis told his brothers, his parents, "Just because your bank account changes doesn't mean *you* change."

Giannis was still the same player who'd skip showers and head to the Cousins Center when he was upset with his performance. The first time he ever flew first-class back to Greece was in his fourth year in the league, right after he signed the extension. Still, he had been hesitant; it was Thanasis who had to coax him to splurge: "We can't be sitting back in coach, next to the restroom. We gotta move up front." Up to that point, Giannis wouldn't even pay if an airline charged more to sit in an exit row, always thinking about saving money for the future, never sure of what might happen.

"As a person, he's always been the same; we've always been the same people," Alex says. "It's just the stuff *around* us changed."

The family was living in a modest town house when Giannis, at the advice of Dudley, his former teammate, finally moved into his own space within the complex, a compromise that felt OK to all of them. It was a big step for Giannis. Dudley told him that he was proud of him for making the move. But Giannis, of course, was still not spending *the bread*.

Alex, heading into his freshman year at Dominican, saw the way Giannis remained frugal. He had to be convinced to buy a house. "Are you *crazy?*" Giannis told his friends and family. "It's too big. It's so much. I don't need all of that."

When he visited Carter-Williams's house for the first time, he was astounded. "Bro," Giannis told him, "this is amazing."

"Bro," Carter-Williams says, "you're gonna be able to buy like thirty of these."

Giannis still hesitated. He still bought only what he needed. Before the next season, 2016–2017, Sweeney and Giannis were working out at the Pyramid in Long Beach, California, staying at an Airbnb. "Did you watch the game last night?" Sweeney asked him.

"No, I didn't have a TV."

"You didn't get a place with a TV?"

"Nah, but it's got great Wi-Fi."

Adding a TV seemed superfluous. "He never thought, *The money is good. I'm good. I'm set for life*," says Thon Maker, who played for the Bucks from 2016 to 2019 and considers Giannis a brother. "He was humble enough to say, 'Look at me, look at where I'm at, I'm making one hundred million dollars—can you *believe* it? I can't even believe it.'"

Life began to accelerate. Really fast. More fame, more fans. The family couldn't move as freely as it once had. Giannis had transformed from a lanky, hopeful prospect to flesh-and-blood savior. The Bucks had finally gotten approval for a new multimillion-dollar downtown arena. "It was like he went from 'Oh, you might be that dude' to 'Oh, you're *Giannis*,'" Alex says. "We had to be cautious about who we let in our circle."

Giannis made sure the family stayed the same: "Thank you" and "How are you doing?" "Our parents, the way we were raised, it overpowers what we have now," Alex says. "Deep down inside, we're still the kids that lived back there several years ago."

Not a day passed when Giannis didn't think of those days. Selling. Sepolia. Peddling items at upscale beaches. Not having enough. Pushing a fridge down the road. That had been only five years before. Five years before, when no one knew who he was.

That motivated him. That scared him. He often told Kostas and Alex, "Respect the game of basketball because basketball has given us all we have."

Giannis was a unique emerging star. He didn't care to wear flashy outfits in the tunnel before games like some of his counterparts, like Westbrook and James. Giannis was always most comfortable in his Bucks sweat suit. He was going to the arena to *work*. He wasn't going to a wedding, a party. In his eyes, what reason was there to dress up? To this day, he has still never purchased a pair of sneakers.

"He's not going to be the guy that has ten, twelve, cars. That's not how he was raised. That's how Americans think," says Jared Dudley, former teammate.

Giannis also didn't care to work out with other players in the league in the off-season—not because he wasn't friendly but because he reasoned that when you're friendly with someone, you don't compete as intensely against them, with the same aggression. "Giannis is not a guy that wants to be friends with everybody," Brogdon says. "He's not a guy that's really friendly. But once you get to know him, and break down that barrier, that will, he becomes a friend. And you can talk about anything."

He wouldn't let opponents see that side of him, though. He'd turn down invitations from top-flight private trainers with NBA clients, preferring to stick with Bucks staffers, not wanting to give opponents even a glimpse of his tendencies on the court. "Giannis is a bit of a throwback. You see him after games, there's a cordial handshake and a hug, but he's not getting on the banana boat," says Oppenheimer, referring to the banana boat that James, Chris Paul, and Dwyane Wade famously rode in the off-season in the Bahamas that became a viral meme. "If Giannis is on a banana boat, it's him and his brothers."

He didn't much care about social media. While other players posted their workouts on Instagram, Giannis preferred to keep quiet about his routines. His parents had a saying that they used to tell Giannis and his brothers growing up that came from the catechism: "If your left hand does something, your right hand doesn't need to know."

Milwaukee was the perfect place for Giannis to live. People recognized him on the street, of course, but didn't interrupt him during meals. He liked how quiet Milwaukee was, how serene. "I don't like all these flashy cities like LA or Miami," Giannis told the *New York Times*. "I don't know if I could be the same player if I played in those cities."

But it was clear: Giannis was now undoubtedly the franchise player. And there was pressure to perform. "The people who remembered Kareem thought, *Wow, maybe he's the guy?*" says Eddie Doucette, the former Bucks broadcaster. "*Maybe he's the next Kareem? Maybe this is the guy that's going to carry us to the promised land?*"

With more expectations came more demands. Especially with media. "He doesn't have the free time he once had," Oppenheimer says. "With that, becoming the world's face, you can lose your face."

Giannis kept a sense of humor, though, tried to open up a bit to media, especially when he discovered dad jokes right before the 2016–2017 season. "I have a joke. I'm gonna say a joke," he told reporters at media day that season.

"Knock knock," Giannis said.

"Who's there?" a couple of reporters said.

"Obama."

"Obama who?"

"Ohhhhhhh-baaaaaa-myyyyseeeelf," Giannis sang to the melody of Eric Carmen's "All by Myself."

Another instance, a year later, Giannis asked reporters, "Have you guys seen the new movie *Constipation?*"

"No," one reporter said. "What movie?"

"*Constipation.* That's because it hasn't come out yet!" He then ran away from the media scrum, tickled with his joke.

"Giannis is a big kid," says Tony Snell, Bucks forward from 2016 to 2019, now with the Hawks.

He was a kid dealing with adult responsibilities. And he began to close up more as his fame grew. He'd sometimes leave reporters waiting for more than an hour. "Come on, Giannis," Bucks PR said on one of those occasions. "Just come out there for a second. They're not out to get you."

Milwaukee was probably as friendly as an NBA media scrum could be, but Giannis just didn't want any attention. Life was so simple when he could just play basketball rather than try to explain it. Try to explain *himself.*

One afternoon, Telly Hughes, Bucks TV reporter from 2010 to 2018, told him, "You keep playing the way you're playing, you're gonna have to get comfortable talking to the media."

"Nah, yeah, whatever," Giannis told Hughes. "I still don't like it." He walked away.

"Giannis keeps a lot of things inside," Hughes says.

Thon Maker, too, noticed how much Giannis held within. He noticed the way Giannis would clench his fist when he'd make a mistake, harping on himself. He saw the way, after a loss, Giannis would be so angry, so silent, in the locker room, hands on his head, just thinking, thinking, thinking.

Giannis was trying to prove that he was the team's leader. If there was a new player, he'd play more aggressively. "Not in a selfish way, but he was playing mental games with the player," Maker says. "He'd expose him and really assert himself so that people can see, 'All right, yeah. This is *his* team.'"

Giannis and Maker became close. Giannis saw some similarities to his own game in seven-foot Maker. Maker knew childhood strife too, as his family, members of the Dinka tribe, had fled Sudan's civil war when he was six, moving to Perth, Australia. Like Giannis's, Maker's first love was soccer. They knew hard work; they knew pain. They'd attend chapel together to pray every week.

Giannis became a mentor as the two played one-on-one every day. One day, when Giannis was particularly aggressive on defense, bumping Maker, throwing him out of the post, Maker just looked at him, thinking, *What the fuck?* Giannis explained himself. "I don't want Alex to be lazy," Giannis told Maker, looking over at his youngest brother, who was watching them play. "I want Alex to see that this is hard. I'm working hard, so he got to work hard too."

Giannis meant that. He wasn't going to let Alex coast or even just observe him from afar. Giannis ended up coaching Dominican in fall league (the team went undefeated). "Giannis has never said no to us," says Jim Gosz, the Dominican coach. And Giannis often gave Alex pointers at halftime. Oftentimes, that meant scolding him. One fall-league game, Giannis got really frustrated with Alex for not moving on offense, not moving on defense. He called him out in front of everyone. Alex was embarrassed, but Giannis set the bar high, and if he wasn't happy with his brother's play, he'd let him know.

In a way, it motivated Alex's other teammates as well, seeing that Giannis was watching so intensely. Giannis would talk to them too, give each one advice—even the players who rarely saw any minutes in the game.

Later, in 2018, after Dominican lost in the sectional finals to Kettle Moraine Lutheran, Giannis raced to the locker room. He was the first one in. He was more upset than anyone on the team. And when all the players had filed in, he said, "Remember this feeling. I need you to know what this feels like. What is it gonna take to not feel this feeling again?" Alex just looked at his brother, absorbing his words with the same kind of wonder he's had since childhood.

* * *

Giannis tried to show Alex that same example in his own games. One game, against the Pistons, Giannis fed Maker the ball again and again. Maker was *hot*, drilling a three in transition. Giannis screamed, "*Yeaaaah!*" The next possession, however, Maker airballed. He looked embarrassed.

When Giannis passed him the ball again, Maker passed up the shot, whipped the ball back to Giannis. Giannis swung it right back to him, yelling, "No, shoot it!" Maker gave the ball up again. Giannis was furious.

"Listen!" Giannis told Maker during the time-out. "You gotta shoot it! I don't give a fuck if you miss it! I don't care how many shots you miss—you still gotta shoot! If you hesitate, I'm gonna punch you!"

Maker blinked. Giannis meant it literally—he would punch him. So Maker went back in the game and let the ball fly. He had five points in the overtime period. "It gives you a lot of confidence," says Maker, who scored a career-high twenty-three, "when he trusts you."

Kidd started bringing Kevin Garnett, one of the NBA's all-time best power forwards, to practice to tutor Giannis and Maker. Giannis could see himself in Garnett. They were both intense, passionate. Obsessive. Giannis had played against Garnett the previous season, Garnett's last in the league. One time in particular, the two really went *at* each other. Both were talking trash. Giannis dunked the ball hard—a tip dunk off one of Copeland's misses. "It was *crazy*," Copeland says. "Like, what the fuck? You don't see a lot of seven-footers just on the rim like that."

That was Giannis's statement to Garnett: "I'm here."

The first time Garnett showed up to Bucks practice, he went to the weight room to get a full workout in. By the time Giannis and Maker walked in, Garnett's T-shirt was fully soaked. Then they went onto the court, and Garnett demonstrated how to feel a defender on his back, how to master jump hooks. How to have a countermove, how to shimmy. Low-post footwork. "Look at the back of the rim, not the front," he'd tell them.

Then Garnett walked toward Giannis, who was warming up his shot under the basket. Garnett told him to trust his work ethic. "It's all about your mentality," Garnett told Giannis. "You have to have a warrior mentality. Look, man—if you have that, nobody can stop you!" Garnett told him he had to dominate by any means necessary. Don't have any friends on the court.

After Garnett left, Giannis pranced around to each of his teammates and screamed, "Yeah! Yeah! *Mentalityyyyy*! Yeah! I learned this from KG! Mentality! You can't tell me nothing!"

Giannis had dropped thirty-five points and had nine rebounds and seven blocks against Chicago in late December 2016. Afterward, Brogdon compared him to Kobe, saying that Giannis had the potential to be great. Giannis seemed surprised: "Really, me? I'm Kobe?" Then he admitted that when he hit a jumper in the second quarter, he felt like Kobe. "I'm not going to lie. I was like, 'Kobeeee,'" he said. "I'm not there yet, but I'm going to work as hard as I can."

Two games later, in January 2017, he hit his first game-winning buzzer-beater, backing down the Knicks' Lance Thomas for a fifteen-foot step-back shot in Madison Square Garden. Terry sensed that Giannis was coming into his own. "He was on his way to greatness," Terry says. "He wanted to win every drill, every sprint, every game."

Giannis had 1,059 new messages on his phone later that night after his buzzer-beater. He couldn't concentrate, with interview requests from ESPN, *Sports Illustrated*, and *SLAM*, so he stayed off his phone, off social media, for the next six weeks.

Heading toward the all-star break, Thanasis retweeted hundreds of fans saying they voted for Giannis, trying to increase his brother's vote total. "We all did," says Alex, pulling out his iPhone and showing screenshots of the tweets he saved from that year.

Giannis and the Bucks were in Orlando when the NBA 2017 All-Star selection show aired. It was a Thursday night. He didn't believe he'd be named a starter. When he saw James, he didn't think he'd get picked at *all*. He thought maybe Jimmy Butler, Kevin Love, or Carmelo Anthony would be selected.

Veronica and Mariah showed up at his hotel room to surprise him. As they all watched, Giannis was named a starter. He had made it. Truly made it. A few seconds later, Thanasis, who was playing basketball in Spain, called to congratulate him. It was early in the morning in Spain, but Thanasis made sure he was up because he wanted to be the first to celebrate his brother.

Giannis became the first Greek player to participate in an All-Star game. He was also Milwaukee's first NBA All-Star since Michael Redd in 2004 and the first Buck voted in as a starter since Sidney Moncrief in 1984.

Giannis wasn't celebrating, though. The night before the game, he stepped onto the New Orleans court and had a full-speed workout with Sweeney, who had flown in because Giannis couldn't bear missing one session.

After the team's first practice, Carmelo Anthony, his teammate on the Eastern All-Stars, asked him if he was nervous.

"If I get the first layup, first dunk, I'll be fine," Giannis said.

Anthony was surprised. "You're too big to be nervous."

Too big? *Giannis?* How quickly things had changed. Three years before, Giannis had been trying to put his elbow in Anthony's back, and Anthony had laughed off Giannis's too-eager defense like a kid brother who'd wanted to tag along.

Yet Giannis still acted like the understudy, trying to learn. Anthony gave him pointers, telling him to slow down, gather himself. Giannis always looked him in the eye, always said, "Thank you, thank you."

"He was a very humble kid," Anthony says. "He always listened."

Giannis carried around his black notebook, asking LeBron James questions about moves and jotting down the answers. Giannis was trying to capture every moment, as if it weren't real. "Let me take a picture first," he told reporters before answering their questions in a scrum, holding up his phone to take a selfie. "This is *crazy!*"

Giannis dominated during the game, leading the East squad with thirty points, though his team lost, 192–182. He was one of the few players actually playing hard defense. He stole the ball from James Harden, which turned into a windmill dunk. Stephen Curry lay down on the floor to avoid Giannis, but Giannis posterized him anyway.

Durant had high praise for Giannis afterward. "I expect him to be here every year for the rest of his career," Durant said. "If he isn't, that's on him." Durant admitted he couldn't have predicted Giannis's ascension when they'd first played against each other.

No one could. Maybe except for Giannis's younger brothers. They all hung out in the hotel room after the all-star game, staying up into the early morning, just like the old days. Giannis was finally a star. But Giannis was still just their big brother. Still the same guy who turns to see if Veronica is in her usual seat at the start of the game. He'll wave, feeling at ease knowing she's there. And if she for some reason can't make the game, the first thing Giannis does after each game is look in his phone for Veronica's message.

It is usually the same message, even if the Bucks lose: "I'm proud of you."

*   *   *

That same month, in February, Parker tore his ACL for the second time. It was a devastating blow. Still, thanks to a stellar defense, the Bucks managed a 14–4 record in March to clinch the sixth spot in the postseason, their best month since going 16–2 in February 1971, the year Abdul-Jabbar helped the Bucks to a championship. Giannis became the first player in NBA history to finish top twenty in total points, rebounds, assists, steals, and blocks in a single season.

There was no one at his size, with his athleticism, who could move the way he could with the ball. Of course, positionless basketball existed long before Giannis—especially with bigger, taller players who could stretch the floor, something Giannis had yet to do, given his long-distance shooting woes—but Giannis brought a different kind of versatility, and unselfishness with the ball. He combined power with grace, dunking on people as if they were pins. "Like it's nothing. Like it's just a Nerf ball," says Sterling Brown, Bucks guard from 2017 to 2020, who now plays for the Rockets. The *New York Times* described Giannis aptly: "He has the agility of a ballroom dancer and the power of a bulldozer."

The Raptors, the Bucks' first-round playoff opponent, would try to slow him down. Toronto was the clear favorite in the series; Milwaukee had a running 2–13 record against them. Giannis was nervous before game 1. He's *always* nervous before games, until muscle memory takes over and he settles into his groove. But he came out aggressively in game 1, blocking a shot by DeMar DeRozan. He dunked on Serge Ibaka. The message was clear: Giannis had arrived.

Strong defense allowed the Bucks to steal game 1, though Toronto came back with more physicality to take game 2. Every time Giannis drove, Raptors players clogged the paint, limiting space for him to drive.

Toronto's strategy against Giannis was simple: slow him down in the open floor; bait him to shoot jumpers in the half-court. And it worked, though the Bucks managed to win game 3 at home. The Raptors turned up their defense on Giannis again, winning game 4. Giannis was held to fourteen points and a distressing seven turnovers.

P. J. Tucker smothered Giannis, and Giannis looked like he didn't know how to respond. He played sloppy, unable to get a rhythm. He was so dissatisfied with his performance he responded by scoring a playoff-career-high thirty-four, plus nine rebounds, three assists, two steals, and two blocks, in game 5. It wasn't enough to lift Milwaukee to victory, though, and the team was ultimately eliminated the next game despite a final rally in the fourth quarter.

Giannis played nearly forty-seven minutes in that final game. He was *exhausted*. He looked like he was going to collapse—like every muscle in his body was working to just keep him standing upright. Giannis had given everything. The Bucks had gone further than they had in a long, long time.

"See now, this is how it feels," Terry, the veteran guard, told Giannis after the game.

Giannis was too gassed to speak. He nodded.

"This is what you should feel as a superstar in this league," Terry continued. "Every night you step on that floor you should feel exhausted because you gave everything you have."

Giannis was deeply disappointed. It was a turning point for him. Knowing how different the postseason was from the regular season. Knowing the dogfight it would be just to get *back* to this point. He made All-NBA second team and won Most Improved Player, but those things didn't matter as much to him as a championship did. He would need to change, adapt, get better. Stronger.

Oppenheimer and Kidd knew the next step for Giannis didn't have anything to do with on-court skills. It was something deeper Giannis needed to find, embrace.

Oppenheimer asked Kidd, "What's the difference between Giannis at this stage and LeBron at this stage?"

Kidd didn't hesitate: "Confidence." Oppenheimer remembers Kidd explaining that the two players had the ability to impact the game the same way, though their games were vastly different and they came into the league with different expectations. James came into the league and was expected to dominate; he was given the keys to dominate. Giannis was beginning to find his stride but had never been expected to be *the* guy. He still needed to build that confidence.

"Confidence is everything," Kidd told Oppenheimer.

Oppenheimer nodded. He felt the same way. Giannis was much more hesitant than James. When he tried to make a pass and the seam closed up, he'd hesitate, whereas James could throw a pass, deliver it on time, on target, no hesitation whatsoever.

"Once Giannis grows past that little bit of hesitancy," Oppenheimer told Kidd, "combined with that confidence, that can take him from good to great."

"Exactly," Kidd said. "Once he realizes he's confident, he can be the best player in the league."

*   *   *

A bit later that summer, in early July 2017, Jim Kogutkiewicz, the long-time Bucks fan, was walking around the Third Ward district one afternoon with his girlfriend, Bridgette Wells, a few hours before Summerfest, an annual Milwaukee outdoor music festival. They planned to go, and since the grounds opened at noon, they decided to walk near the lakefront.

They saw three people coming closer to them, from behind one of the nearby condos. It was Giannis, Thanasis, and Mariah, wearing T-shirts and shorts, like the normal people they are. Still, it was jarring for Kogutkiewicz to see them outside of . . . being on TV.

"Oh my god," Kogutkiewicz said to Wells. "It's Giannis!" He mustered up the courage to ask for a picture with Giannis. Giannis obliged.

Later, after looking at the picture, Kogutkiewicz zoomed in on the giant water bottle Giannis was clutching and noticed something written in black Sharpie on the bottle's cap: "MVP."

About a month later, Kobe wrote to players on Twitter with challenges for each of them, as part of his #MambaMentality campaign. Giannis hadn't received one, so he tweeted to Kobe, "Still waiting for my challenge . . . @kobebryant."

Kobe wrote back with just one word: "MVP." From that point on, Giannis was more determined than ever to win the award.

* * *

Later that summer, Giannis was contemplating moving to a different apartment, and he wanted to throw a yard sale in the front lawn of his home. He had items he wanted to sell, like shoes he had never worn.

Bucks management shut down the idea, for obvious safety reasons. Giannis was disappointed. He had been so excited. He took pride in being a salesman. It's as if he forgot he was an NBA player. An NBA *star*. A potential MVP candidate, if he met Kobe's challenge.

But Giannis still saw himself as *Giannakis* (Little Giannis). A child hustling for a dollar, concerned for the well-being of his little brothers.

Giannis had gone to as many of Alex's games at Dominican as his schedule permitted, but most games, Alex didn't leave the bench. It didn't matter to Giannis; he came there to see his brother, not his brother *the basketball player*.

If Alex played or didn't play, he was still Alex with the chubby cheeks. The baby of the family. And now Giannis and Kostas had given him a new nickname: Alex the Great. Alex hadn't lived up to the name yet, though. He had a way to go in growing into his body. He wasn't particularly assertive his freshman year. "He looked like a baby deer," says Gosz, Alex's coach at Dominican, where Alex finished the season averaging about three points a game.

"He didn't look comfortable," says DeVon Jackson, Dominican assistant coach. Alex went back and forth on jayvee and varsity. "He was clueless. When he'd practice with varsity, he'd get dominated," Jackson says. "Those guys would be throwing him around." He'd get fouled or stripped and get frustrated: "Call something!" he'd plead to the coaches. He did things fluidly, like the Eurostep, mimicking Giannis, but struggled to grasp the plays, understanding positions. Still, Giannis believed in his brother, often telling his Bucks teammates, "Alex is going to be the best one out of all of us. He's going to be better than me."

It wasn't hyperbole. He meant it. He never had to tell Alex to hustle. He never had to explain something to Alex twice. But he pushed him. Harder than any of his brothers. "Lock that shit out," he'd tell Alex, sharpening his focus. "It's just me and you."

The Antetokounmpos often sat in the same spot in the bleachers at Dominican for Alex's games. Top left, behind the team's bench. It was their way of dodging attention. "I [didn't] want Alex to get nervous," Veronica says. She knew Alex would be eager to put on a show for Giannis. "Alex would [play] five times better," Gosz says, at those high school games when the Greek Freak was in the building. And when Alex made a good play, he sometimes turned to the bleachers and pointed to his family.

Kostas, meanwhile, was finding his stride, starting to get noticed by recruiters. He wasn't highly ranked—number 102 in the 2016 class, receiving a four-star ranking. Dayton offered, and he accepted. Kostas was known for his defense, his hustle. Then six feet nine, he was gangly, long. There is a framed photo of him in the hallway leading to Dominican's court, stretching his arms out toward the court, screaming. It encapsulates his hustle, desire.

His game, though, needed improvement. He wasn't a shooter. He wasn't particularly quick. And he was always compared to Giannis. "With Giannis being my older brother, people ask me about the pressure all the time, but I don't think pressure is bad," Kostas says. "Pressure is good. Pressure makes you work harder. Pressure makes you scared. And when you're scared, you push yourself beyond a certain point."

Kostas wanted to one day make the NBA too. Seeing Giannis dominate, as well as Thanasis playing at a high level overseas, first for Andorra (near Spain) in 2016 and then Panathinaikos in 2017, motivated him. Thanasis told Kostas, "Go hard but have fun." Giannis was stricter—"Be focused every day."

"I wanted to play with them [in the NBA], but I had to wait for my moment," Kostas says.

Giannis drove six hours to move Kostas into his dorm at Dayton, stopping only at Walmart. Giannis carried bedsheets, helping his little brother move in late into the night.

Alex, unlike Kostas, was far from the Division I level, but he was getting a little bigheaded despite his lackluster freshman season. At times, he'd showboat in games, screw around. Not go to class. Wear gaudy chains. Giannis quickly put him in his place one afternoon.

"Who do you think you are! Do you understand what this family went through to get you here?"

That would be the first of several heat checks. The next came during a summer workout, when his brothers pulled him to the side. They were *not* pleased. "We feel like you're too relaxed," Alex remembers them saying. "You really need to pick it up."

That night, Alex cried. There was no worse feeling than letting them down. Especially because Alex knew they were right. He *was* just going through the motions in workouts. "I believed that I was better than I was," Alex says. "That was the turning point for me. I realized I had to turn this around."

The rest of the summer, he worked on his ball handling, his jump shot. He became quicker, stronger. He humbled himself. Stopped thinking he knew the answer to every question. Then came fall. Alex almost left the game altogether.

Giannis had to keep all his brothers from falling apart.

CHAPTER 11

LOSS

Alex didn't understand why, on September 29, 2017, Mariah showed up in the middle of the day to pull him out of US history and bring him home. Why, when he blasted Drake in the car, she did not bop to the beat with him. All she said was, "Be strong for Giannis."

She looked upset. So did about twenty family members and friends standing inside the downtown apartment when she and Alex walked in. There were large men in black suits too. Alex didn't recognize them, but one came up to him: "Sorry for your loss."

The hell are you talking about? Alex thought. Then Alex finally found Giannis. He was crying. That was another unusual sight—Giannis hardly ever let his brothers see him cry. See any kind of pain.

"You remember what I told you two days ago?" Giannis asked Alex.

Two days before, the family had had a get-together. Alex told Giannis he couldn't make it (he had plans with friends). "That's fine," Giannis said, "but I'm just letting you know: we gotta keep being a family because you never know when Mom and Dad's not gonna be here."

The grief compounded as Giannis reminded Alex of that eerie exchange before delivering the news: Charles had died of a heart attack.

He was just fifty-four.

Giannis, then twenty-two, had been at the Bucks practice facility earlier that day. The Bucks were starting their final day of training camp ahead of the 2017–2018 season. Giannis, Maker, Middleton, and Brogdon were in the locker room, playing "BUTTERFLY EFFECT" by Travis Scott, getting ready for practice, when several coaches came up to Giannis to tell him about his dad.

Giannis just walked out, unable to speak, unable to process. Kidd told the team what had happened, canceled practice, while Giannis headed back to his apartment. Kostas was in Ohio, playing for Dayton. Thanasis was in Greece, where he was playing. They quickly hopped on flights to Milwaukee. But for that afternoon, it was just Giannis and Alex, crying, holding each other in the apartment, trying to keep the other from falling.

Giannis had to be strong. For Alex. For his mom. For everyone. His dad had taught him that: toughness. A "'don't-give-a-fuck' mentality," as Giannis calls it, where he plays hard no matter what the condition—win, lose, anything. A mentality that he needed to maintain off the floor too. His dad had taught him to take care of his brothers. In a way, Giannis was prepared for a moment like this, though no one is prepared for a moment like this.

"Giannis *was* a father-figure-slash-mentor," Alex says. "He kind of skipped the stages of actually being a father and having a kid."

Memories flooded. How proud Charles had been of Giannis when he'd made it to the NBA. When Charles first came to America and watched Giannis in Madison Square Garden, the way he jumped around and high-fived strangers when Giannis scored. How his dad told him to maximize every minute: "Make sure what you give your time to is worth it. You shouldn't wait one more day than what's necessary. If you could accomplish something today, why wait until tomorrow? Go get it today!"

More memories. The way Charles would show up to the gym in Zografou on the rare occasion he was not working and catch a glimpse of Giannis dancing past defenders with the footwork Charles had taught him. Or how Charles would be soft-spoken but kind to all of Giannis's friends back then, always sounding cheerful though he had every reason not to be. "How are you doing?" Charles would ask Giannis's friends. "How are your parents?"

For so long, Giannis's only goal was to survive and make his parents proud. He did that and more. So much more. They had all made a life together, here. In America. A life where Charles had the leisure, the time, to walk around the lake near their apartment, just take in the cool air, let it wrap around his body without worrying about a bill or a meal. He could just enjoy something as simple as thinking, walking. Doing little things to make Giannis smile, like washing his car when he was on road trips.

Time. It spun and spun. Back to the days that Charles had gone without food so Giannis could eat. How his dad would always say, "Don't worry about it. I'm not eating." He'd sit there, bare plate, acting like nothing was wrong.

Giannis always remembered that. And it stabbed at him in this moment. He felt numb. Didn't say much. He was shocked. He couldn't understand it. It happened so suddenly. So out of the blue. There were no signs. Nothing. Charles just left.

The love between Giannis and his father was so pure. That hurt too: their love becoming a *was*. Past tense. Charles becoming past tense. Catching himself flip between *was* and *is* in conversation was a new trauma on its own.

Before Charles's death, Giannis believed nothing could hurt his family after what they had been through. *Nothing* could touch them. If they could survive Sepolia, they could survive anything.

It was cruel for this to happen.

* * *

The night his dad died, Giannis went to the practice facility to shoot. That was the only way to try to make sense of what would never make sense. His world was crumbling, but the gym was intact. Exactly as he'd left it. Leaky roof and all. "That was his sanctuary," says Maker, who was there with him that night.

Maker remembers Sweeney, Veronica, Mariah, and Alex being there. Giannis, Alex, Maker, and Sweeney worked out. It was not a hard workout but a workout to keep Giannis warm. Moving. So he didn't have to think, cry. Sweeney and Maker just kept talking to him—talking and shooting, talking and shooting. Trying to put a smile on his face, though that was impossible.

Giannis was trying to find a way to distract himself. Trying to focus on what gave him joy. And that was basketball. Sweeney reminded him of that, that night. "This is what makes you happy, being out here on the floor," Sweeney told him. "Nobody can tell you anything."

Giannis nodded, kept shooting. His teammates, coaches, and staffers were worried about him. They weren't sure how he was going to handle it as the days wore on. They had to force him to take some time off, telling him to be with his family. Grieve.

The 2017–2018 season was about to start. Charles had come to all his games. Having him there, center section, was something that calmed Giannis. Gave him purpose. And every game he played from here on out would be a reminder of that loss. That empty seat.

"I think it changed him; I think it hardened him a little bit," says Michael Carter-Williams, the former Bucks guard. "When you're that close to people in your family, it's like you can't even imagine losing them."

Giannis turned inward, grew quiet. He thought about it every day but wouldn't say much. He kept looking at a picture of him and his family, the brothers sleeping in the same bed, the parents sleeping in the nearby den behind a curtain; Giannis was maybe ten years old.

"He wasn't talking," says Michalis Kamperidis, the former teammate and friend from Filathlitikos. "He didn't have the willingness to talk, you know? I was trying to not talk to him that much and let him get over, you know? He was really, really hurt. It was really hard for him. But, you know, it's *still* hard for him to this day."

Giannis was concerned about his younger brothers. How they would handle it. Given that Alex lived with him, he had to tend to him first. Alex was still too shocked to speak. Alex remembered Charles driving him to school that morning, just four hours earlier. His dad seemed fine. Perfect. *Fine.* The two had talked about basketball practice. What time his dad would come afterward. "I'll come pick you up," his dad had said.

As Alex leans back on his couch in the basement, recalling this day, the worst of his life, his voice is shaky. Barely audible. "My dad was my best friend," Alex says. Veronica remembers how Alex would ask his dad to take him places: "Daddy, take me to this place! Take me to that place! Daddy, we need to go here! Daddy . . . Daddy . . . Daddy . . ." One time, Alex wanted a certain hat, and they went place to place to find it. Charles would go anywhere if it made his kids happy.

"They were so tight," Veronica says. "They talked all the time like they were friends. They were very close. Very, very close.

"He had never seen anything like it, anything that hard," Veronica says. She tried to talk to Alex about it but couldn't. "You cannot know how it affects him because he don't talk. He is not talking. He is always quiet. But I know it affected him, because it was his best friend. And he was the best dad."

If you could accomplish something today, why wait until tomorrow? Go get it today!

Alex still thinks of those words every morning. Before getting out of bed, he closes his eyes, hanging on to the image of his father a little longer. He sees himself asking his dad to take him to the court or store. He hears his dad cheering for him at games: "Go, Alex, go!" He sees himself arguing with his dad about who will win the 2015 NBA championship.

He thinks about how his dad saw games where he scored twenty, games where he scored zero. His dad loved him just the same. He thinks about how his dad was always calm: "Don't worry about it." How, in his dad's eyes, he was never just the youngest brother. He was his own man. And his dad was the man he wanted to be: determined, protective, kind, hardworking, selfless. He was the one who made Thanasis *Thanasis*. The one who made Giannis *Giannis*. The one who made Kostas *Kostas*.

And without his dad, Alex didn't know how to be Alex. Grief spilled onto everything he touched. His dad was everywhere and nowhere. "We all have shoes, right? Shoes we walk in? Imagine you have shoes your whole life," Alex says, "and then they're taken away from you. Now you have to live without them."

Alex took time off school. He put down the basketball. He contemplated quitting for good. How could he continue playing? His parents were the reason he played, and now half that reason was gone. He kept thinking of the first time his dad had watched him play, back in Greece. Alex was firing from three, stealing the ball. "I'm really proud of you," his dad told him afterward. It was the first time his game was recognized, rather than his brothers'. It was the sweetest moment of Alex's young life.

It hurts thinking about that moment. Thinking about how after that moment, his dad had taken him more seriously on the basketball court. At first, his dad was just enamored with Giannis's and Thanasis's games. "He was like, 'Awww, it's cute that he's trying to do the same thing as his brothers,'" Alex says. "But then when he saw that game, he told my mom, 'Alex is kinda good!' Once I started taking it more seriously, he did too."

His brothers hurt in their own ways as well. Kostas remembered Charles's comforting words when he was having an off day. "The biggest thing he taught me was, if you have a bad day at practice, a bad game," Kostas says, "he'd tell me, 'Tomorrow is another day. Just wake up, try to get better. Take it day by day. Don't try to focus on the past. Just keep working.'"

Kostas remembered the fridge. The way it teetered, almost fell over, when he, Giannis, and their dad pushed it down the block on the little skateboard. The sound of their laughter when they had made it to the apartment. How resourceful they were, how scrappy they were. How *together* they were.

Thanasis felt like he was drowning. Anything difficult in his life he felt he could handle by outworking someone. But this wasn't something to fix, to solve. No "'don't-give-a-fuck' mentality" could rid him of the sinking feeling that he was falling lower, lower.

Thanasis got a tattoo on his arm to help himself cope. It depicts his dad and in Greek lettering reads, "The father holds the hand of his children for a while, but he holds their heart forever."

* * *

Giannis sensed Alex was drifting, and he wanted to make sure his little brother knew he was loved, taken care of. And he didn't want him to quit basketball. Neither did Kostas or Thanasis. When those two finally landed in Milwaukee, they had a talk with Alex.

They told Alex their dad would want him to keep playing, to succeed. They believed in him. "That's the reason I probably push for it now," Alex says. "Me and my brothers, we just want to live out my father's legacy."

Alex points to a large portrait toward the back of the family's basement. Mariah gave it to Giannis for his birthday that year. It's painted yellow, orange, and blue, with the words "I am my father's legacy" sprawled across the canvas. There is Giannis in the center, pointing to the sky, surrounded by Thanasis, tossing a ball up in the air; Kostas, scooping up a layup; Alex, leaning in for a crossover; and Francis, the oldest brother, who lived in Nigeria for most of his life and who has remained close with his brothers throughout, crossing his arms. Charles's and Veronica's names are written in the top right corner.

It was comforting for them to see all their brothers painted, including Francis. Francis had been the only one to pursue soccer instead of basketball. He played semiprofessionally at midfield in Nigeria. Around this time, Francis was receiving interest to play in Greece for the Greek club AE Sparti, located in Sparta, Laconia, Greece. He worked out with the team a bit in 2018, but his career was short-lived. He ended up pursuing music. Musically, he goes by Ofili, which is his middle name, and he now lives in Athens.

Giannis still glances at the portrait whenever he works out at home, as it is on the wall right next to his personal workout room. It reminds them all who they are. Where they come from. Why they must press on.

Alex came back sophomore year still mourning the loss of his father, but like Giannis, he used the court as an outlet, upping his scoring to nearly sixteen points a game that season. "He was all about business," says Jackson, the Dominican assistant coach. "It was a kind of getaway escape for him."

Up to this point, the family had been living in a complex with two separate apartments: Alex was on the fifth floor with Giannis, Charles and Veronica on the fourth. After Charles died, Veronica moved up to the fifth to be with her sons.

And Giannis, somehow, had to keep playing basketball. And not just play but elevate the Bucks to advance deeper in the playoffs. "He came back full speed, rejuvenated with energy," Maker says, "but playing for his father."

Giannis always played hard, always played with a sense of purpose. But that sharpened after his dad's death. "When you walk out there, you have to have that look in your eye," Giannis told Maker one day before a game. "That look that says, 'I'm a dead man. I'm a dead man. I shouldn't be alive.'

"Just focus. Every possession. You can't get distracted," Giannis told him. "'I'm a dead man. I shouldn't be here. But I am.'"

"He used basketball to express his pain, his anger," Maker says. "He just left it all out on the floor every single night."

Giannis averaged 33.7 points, 10.3 rebounds, and 5.3 assists per game in his first seven games.

Losing his father changed the way he viewed things outside of basketball. He was not afraid of anything anymore.

* * *

Hours before a game against the Blazers, about three weeks after Charles's death, in late October, Giannis's face looked frozen. It was as if every muscle clenched tighter and tighter. A bee could have buzzed by, and he wouldn't have flinched. He wasn't talking to anyone.

Jason Terry, the Bucks point guard, looked over at Giannis and could sense the focus, sense the intensity. "Stone-faced killer," Terry says, describing how Giannis looked that day.

Giannis was both full of emotion and bereft. He was there, but he wasn't there. He scored a career-high forty-four for the win, including seventeen points in the fourth quarter. He stole the ball from CJ McCollum, finishing with a massive dunk for the lead with eleven seconds left. Then he blocked a critical shot from Jusuf Nurkić.

"MVP! MVP! MVP!" the crowd chanted, though it was little solace to Giannis, who had poured all his pain, all his anger, onto the floor. And when the buzzer sounded, he was empty again. Hurting again. Basketball was only a refuge for so long.

He returned to the locker room and picked up a Sharpie, scribbling on the game ball, "This is for Daddy. We got a win tonight."

His dad was with him. In his sneakers, in his jersey. In his locker, his water bottle. Giannis sat back in his chair, giant ice bags attached to his knees, and stared blankly ahead. His teammates sensed he wanted to be left alone. Giannis looked exhausted, almost in a daze, staring at the ground.

It was lonely, having a career night without the person who would have loved to see it.

*   *   *

Giannis always wanted a big family. Kids running around. Thanasis always imagined all the brothers having big families too. All in a big living room— kids left and right, wives, Veronica—enjoying the holidays there together. And though Charles would not be there, they'd feel he was there, with Veronica holding everyone together.

When Giannis was interviewed for *60 Minutes* about a month or so after Charles's death, he told host Steve Kroft that he wanted to raise humble kids, in the way that Charles had raised him and his brothers. He told Kroft he wanted eight kids. Kroft asked him why he wanted eight— then asked, jokingly, if he wanted to go for ten kids so they could have enough to play five-on-five. Giannis laughed. "I just want as much as possible," he told Kroft. "If my girlfriend accepts—I don't know if she wants eight kids. But that's what I want."

"Well, she knows now," Kroft said.

"She knows. Probably, she's gonna leave me. She's like, 'Uh-uh. I'm not having eight kids with you.'"

Kroft tried to ask him about his dad's death, but Giannis just wasn't able to talk about it. "He was really sad," Kroft says, "but he talked about it as if it was something in the past." Kroft remembers Giannis as being upbeat, kind. He had a great sense of humor. "There is something really magnetic about him," Kroft says.

It was Giannis's first time really opening up to someone in the media. Allowing cameras to be around his family for that long. Giannis hadn't heard of *60 Minutes* before. He (and his agents) usually turned down requests.

Giannis was a bit hesitant to open up at first. He didn't talk much about how, or why, his family came to Greece in the first place. It was almost like he was protecting something. He wanted to keep boundaries elsewhere too. "He was a little self-conscious about his driving," says Draggan Mihailovich, a producer of the segment. Giannis didn't want them to film him inside his car. They settled on a clip of him pulling out of his driveway.

But once Kroft and Mihailovich told him the film crew had gone to Greece to see his old neighborhood, Giannis loosened a bit. "You went to Greece!" he said, beaming. Suddenly he couldn't stop talking, wanting to know where they'd gone, what they thought of Sepolia. They showed him B-roll of the old Filathlitikos gym. He saw his old coach, Takis Zivas. "Look at him!" Giannis said. "He's still in his old shoes!"

Something about seeing where he came from—rather than talking about it—allowed Giannis to let them into his sacred space: the gym. He invited them to watch him work out at ten o'clock at night. Giannis wouldn't skip his workout, insisting he couldn't let anything—not even *60 Minutes*—interfere with his routine. That was because, as he'd reveal in the aired segment, in a rare moment of vulnerability, "I'm really scared of failing."

*   *   *

About midway through the season, Giannis had to face a different kind of loss: Kidd was fired in January 2018. The Bucks simply underperformed, failing to move into the upper echelon of the East and beyond. They had been inconsistent. Some nights they looked amazing, other nights terrible. The defense was uninspiring, the offense paltry, the record simply not good enough at 23–22.

The firing seemed inevitable, as some players were frustrated with Kidd's harsh, old-school coaching style and discouraged by his tendency to blame the Bucks' youth for the team's problems, often pointing the finger at players rather than himself. One Bucks source at the time claimed—with more than a little understatement—that he was "driving the team a bit hard." Even Giannis didn't always see eye to eye with Kidd's methods.

Giannis had reportedly called Kidd before the Bucks had notified him of his firing and tried to save Kidd's job. However, Giannis was uncomfortable that Kidd had revealed this private conversation to the media.

It was tough for Giannis, dealing with a coach being fired *again*. But not just any coach—a coach who believed in him. Trusted him. Kidd was the first to put the ball in Giannis's hands and say, "You can be a point guard." He was the first coach to think Giannis could be more than an all-star someday; he could be a superstar, a franchise player. In many ways, Kidd helped Giannis grow up. See his own powers. But that was the business. Nothing Giannis could do would change the situation.

Joe Prunty, the Bucks lead assistant coach, took over as interim coach for the remainder of the season. "It was tough," Prunty says. "There's a personal side to it. When it happened, it was 'All right, we have to regroup. This happened, but we have a job to do.' But obviously it was a big change."

Giannis continued to thrive, keeping defenses on their toes despite his lack of a jump shot. In February 2018, he had caught an alley-oop from Middleton, leaped over six-foot-five Tim Hardaway Jr. for a dunk that went viral. He finished second in all-star votes behind LeBron, and he was named a starter for the 2018 all-star game. "It's over my imagination," Giannis said during All-Star Weekend in Los Angeles. "I always had a feeling maybe I can make it in the NBA, but I never thought I was going to be 23 years old, be in my second time in the All Star, having a chance to win the MVP, carrying a team on my back. That's over my imagination."

He played hard during his all-star team's practice, surprising Mike D'Antoni, his coach for the game. Practices weren't really supposed to be practices. "It's a glorified photo op," says D'Antoni, now an assistant coach with the Nets. "And Giannis coming in, stretching, getting ready for practice, while other guys are definitely on vacation, they're like, 'Oh my gosh. This guy is serious.'

"Being different is sometimes hard," D'Antoni says, "but he was different in a good way. You could just tell his desire to be great."

He didn't stop pushing himself as the Bucks struggled over the next month, falling to eighth in the East. The *Milwaukee Journal Sentinel* wrote, "This team has had more ups and downs than a fifth-grade class at a trampoline park."

* * *

Meanwhile, off the court, Giannis and Mariah were getting closer. Giannis knew she wanted a dog—a goldendoodle, specifically. He wanted to surprise her with one, but there was only one breeder in Wisconsin that had the exact goldendoodle she wanted. And there was another problem: the breeder was about four hours upstate, in Stanley, Wisconsin. Given the Bucks' demanding schedule, he didn't have any time to drive and get the dog.

He asked Bucks management for help, who then tasked Chris Rodriguez, a basketball operations intern at the time, with the assignment. It would be the most nerve-racking one in his two-year apprenticeship with the team from 2017 to 2019. Rodriguez didn't tell his fellow interns about the assignment, fearing word could spread and ruin Giannis's surprise.

The plan was to leave at ten in the morning on that day, April 9, pick up the puppy, then arrive by game time so Giannis could give Mariah the puppy after the game.

Rodriguez had never been that far upstate. "All I saw were cows and fields and horses," Rodriguez says. He arrived at the breeder but was told the goldendoodle was actually at another location. Trying to find the second place, he got lost. His GPS stopped working as he drove into an even more rural area. He pulled into a farm's driveway, calling his mom, his friends, asking them to help with directions.

He started stressing out as his service grew even more faint. The stakes were high: What if he got lost? And worse, what if he let down one of the best players in the NBA? Rodriguez kept driving, finally finding the breeder about forty minutes later. "It was the most Amish-looking place you have ever seen," Rodriguez says. "They were wearing bonnets."

He tucked the puppy into his back seat, but she was so hyper she kept trying to squirm out of the box she was in, and she peed and pooped all over the box. The stench was so unbearable Rodriguez needed to roll down his window, but he feared she'd jump out of the car. He settled on leaving the window halfway down as he tried to calm the puppy. "It's OK. We're almost there," he said to her as if she could understand. "We'll be there soon."

Arriving back at the Bucks arena, he had to cover his nose, the car smelled so terrible. The *puppy* smelled so terrible. *Well, at least we made it*, he thought. After the game, he spotted Giannis and handed over the puppy.

"Oh my god," Giannis said, covering his nose. "She smells *so* bad!"

"Ah, yeah," Rodriguez said sheepishly. "Sorry. That's what I've dealt with the past eight and a half hours."

Giannis gave him a pair of Nikes and a nice tip, even though players aren't necessarily allowed to do so. That was huge for the intern: "We make nothing."

Giannis then surprised Mariah with the puppy; she melted at the sight of the fluffy little bundle. They named the puppy Mila. She was theirs.

* * *

The Bucks faced the Celtics in the first round, hoping to finally break through. They hadn't won a playoff series since George Karl and the Big Three in 2001. But the Bucks quickly found themselves down 0–2 to Boston to begin the series.

Milwaukee bounced back to win the next two games to even the series at 2–2, but they lost game 5 and faced elimination. Again. Giannis was limited to sixteen points on ten shots in that game, looking exhausted. He took responsibility afterward, saying that he had to be more aggressive.

Rebounding from his lackluster game 5, he showed up big, helping win game 6 and forcing a game 7. He gave everything, playing forty minutes a game, trying to physically will his team to victory, but it wasn't enough. He didn't have the support. The Bucks looked young and inexperienced, and the Celtics advanced to play the 76ers.

Pushing the series to seven games was a big milestone, and so was finishing above .500 in back-to-back seasons for the first time since 2001, but the season was largely a disappointment—bouncing out of the first round *again*. Failing to live up to expectations *again*. Giannis thought about game 7 all summer. So did his teammates.

"We weren't refined," Brogdon says. "We had a bunch of guys that were talented, but we didn't really have a direction on how to play together."

The clock was ticking to figure that out, to prove that the team could contend for a championship with Giannis in his prime, as the team had three years before Giannis could become an unrestricted free agent. "Fail," the *Washington Post* wrote at the time, "and it might take another 40 years to get another player of his talent level to join the franchise."

The Bucks hired a new coach, Mike Budenholzer, from the Hawks, to help turn things around in the postseason, to break the curse of three first-round exits over the last four seasons. His first task would be getting Giannis more support and maximizing his gifts.

Giannis had leaped into MVP consideration. Winning the award had been a goal of his. But when it didn't happen, Thanasis sensed his brother's disappointment. "I know you played like the MVP. I know you was chasing it," Thanasis told him. "At the end of the day, you're the MVP of life." Giannis realized he had gone the distance to make sure his family was OK. More than OK. He was taking care of his brothers, his mom, his girlfriend. His youngest brother was receiving a private school education. Thanasis was right.

"It doesn't matter if you didn't get it," Thanasis said.

Giannis worked harder than ever, still with that same goal of winning MVP. He had the chance to work out with his idol, Kobe, that summer. Giannis prepared question after question, writing them down in his notebook to bring with him. He showed up for the 2:30 p.m. workout at 11:00 a.m., getting shots up and treatment before Kobe even walked in. He wanted to show Kobe he wasn't there to mess around. He wasn't there for a social media post. He really wanted to learn. Listen, improve. And he took pride in beating Kobe to the gym by more than three hours.

After the two shot jumper after jumper—350 to 400 shots, all the same shots, making 20 at one spot—Giannis was a bit shy about asking Kobe so many questions, telling him he didn't want it to feel like an interview.

"No, no, ask me whatever," Kobe said.

"Are you sure?"

Kobe nodded. Giannis opened his notebook and began asking how to prepare, how to constantly improve. Kobe told him that day that he had to think outside the box. "You always gotta be a kid," Kobe said.

"Be a kid?" Giannis said. "What do you mean?" This whole time, Giannis was trying to show that he was big and strong. Mature. A *man*. A *mean* man, at that.

"No, what I mean is, a kid uses fantasy. You can see a kid being creative, playing with two rocks and playing around with them. When you're a kid, you always wanna learn. You ask questions: Why do I do this? Why am I sitting in the passenger seat? Why am I going to school today? You're always asking questions. Be a kid."

That stayed with Giannis. He told his brothers immediately after what had happened. Kostas especially soaked it up, as he had just been drafted with the sixtieth and final pick by the 76ers in the 2018 NBA draft and was immediately traded to the Mavericks. Alex became a team captain at Dominican, heading into his junior year, and was starting to gain the attention of college and NBA scouts.

The brothers continued to go back and forth to Greece, where Giannis was now considered a hometown star. An icon in his home country. Kids idolized him. Wore his jersey. Greeks constantly affirmed their love for him. How proud they were of him. His home court, where he spent all those years playing outside growing up, was dedicated to him. The Athens-based artist Same84 painted a giant mural of Giannis on the court. The length of his body covers the space, his green Bucks jersey accented by a blue background. Another mural of Giannis leaping into the air, cocking the ball back behind him as if about to dunk, was painted on a tall cream-colored apartment building next to the court, above a car wash.

"For Greece, Giannis *is* basketball," says Nick Calathes, the Greek star and Giannis's national-team teammate. "There's going to be a movie about it one day. He came from nothing. He hasn't changed from then to now."

Many Greek Americans identified with him too, given that he had matured in America but didn't leave his culture behind. Giannis constantly talked about how much he loved Greece.

"It's so much more than 'Local kid makes good,'" says Katy Kostakis, a fan who grew up near Boston but whose aunts and other family members live in Sepolia. She has been to Greece many times. "It's that him and his entire family made it. It just gives us such pride."

And hope. Especially for Black Greeks who grew up in similar circumstances.

Favor Ukpebor, the young Black Greek basketball player who knew the Antetokounmpos growing up, started playing the same year Giannis was drafted. "After Giannis got drafted, more Afro-Greeks believed they could have a chance to play at the highest level of basketball." Including him. "He made a huge impact on me," Ukpebor says. "Almost every kid my age or younger started playing basketball because of Giannis. It was very rare to see a Black Greek kid go to the NBA."

But there are hundreds of Black Greek kids growing up today who may never receive the opportunities Giannis did. Whose citizenship will not be fast-tracked, the way Giannis's was. These kids are not embraced, affirmed, the way Giannis is now. The sad truth is, as beloved as Giannis is, he is still a target of racism in his home country.

CHAPTER 12

IDENTITY

About a month before Charles's death, Giannis's childhood court in Sepolia, the one with his mural painted across the surface, was vandalized with fascist and Neo-Nazi Golden Dawn symbols: a circle inscribed with a cross, painted in white over the portrait of Giannis's face. It was large enough to be seen through the fence surrounding the court.

The vandalism may have been in part triggered by Giannis's decision not to play for the Greek national team earlier that summer in the 2017 EuroBasket tournament because of a knee injury. The Greek Basketball Federation condemned Giannis's decision and accused him of lying about the injury, claiming there was nothing wrong with his knee and that the decision was part of a larger conspiracy by the Bucks and the NBA to keep Giannis from playing for Greece, despite the fact that Giannis had played for the national team for three straight years.

"[This was] an organized and well-staged plan," the Greek federation said in a statement. Then Takis Tsagronis, the federation's general secretary, commented: "What the Bucks claim is not the reality; something else is happening."

Giannis denied the claims. Sitting out was one of the hardest decisions he had ever had to make as a professional athlete to that point. It was the biggest disappointment of his career, he said. Playing for Greece was his dream long before he even knew of the NBA.

Local resentment reemerged later that winter, when Giannis sang the Greek national anthem in Cleveland along with Greek Americans who had come to watch the Bucks against the Cavs. "Enough with the black guy who pretends to be Greek," wrote Evangelos Markopoulos, a Greek-born professor working in London at the time, in a public Facebook post that linked to the video of Giannis singing. He then referenced the EuroBasket tournament: "Enough is enough. We won't forget what happened in the summer. He didn't give a fuck about any of us, or the national team, or our flag."

By this point, in late 2017, several Golden Dawn members, including Michaloliakos, the party's leader, had been arrested in the aftermath of the 2013 murder of Pavlos Fyssas, the local hip-hop artist. Four other members of parliament and at least fifteen other people were also arrested in the police crackdown that began that year. Charges included membership in a criminal organization, murder, racist violence, and weapons possession. One Golden Dawn member shouted, "Nothing will bend us! Long live Greece!" as he was arrested.

The trial was thought to be the biggest case against fascism in Europe since former Nazi leaders were prosecuted in Nuremberg in 1945. That didn't, however, stop Golden Dawn from winning seventeen seats in an election earlier in January 2015, and it didn't stop sympathizers from intimidating immigrants, posting racist slurs on social media, or desecrating Giannis's court in Sepolia. The backlash wasn't surprising, given that Giannis embodied everything Golden Dawn disdained: diversity, immigration, Blackness.

* * *

Even when Golden Dawn had targeted Giannis as a rookie, calling him a chimpanzee, Giannis continued to profess his love for Greece. In January 2017, the same year his court was vandalized, he refused to sign a Greek flag handed to him by a fan in America after playing the Knicks because he felt it would be disrespectful to write on the sacred flag.

He told reporters at the 2017 all-star game that he'd rather win an international gold medal than an NBA MVP award or title because it would be more meaningful to him, because it would mean he would be representing an entire country. *His* country. "Whatever I do," Giannis said that day, "I try to make all Greeks proud."

He completed his three-month mandatory military service, along with Thanasis, the summer before, in 2016. He daydreamed about winning an NBA championship and celebrating with his Bucks teammates by taking them to Mykonos, one of his favorite places, imagining them smoking cigars on the island.

He regularly traveled back and forth between the United States and Greece, embracing his full identity: his Greek side and his Nigerian side. He has long been accustomed to people seeing only one side of him. When he was a child, some Greeks doubted that he was Greek because he was Black. Then as an adult, in America, he encountered the opposite, with some people telling him, "You're not African. You're Greek. You're the Greek Freak."

Nikos Zisis, his national-team teammate, remembers how some people had said Giannis shouldn't play for the Greek national team back in 2014 because, in their words, "he's not Greek." That always bothered Zisis, not just because he knows the pride Giannis feels for Greece but because it is a fact that he was born in Greece. Went to Greek schools, Greek churches. Christmas caroled to his heart's content in Greek coffee shops. "He represents with the best way possible as a Greek citizen," Zisis says.

Giannis regularly gave back to his old neighborhood in Sepolia, with food and charity, not forgetting where he came from. Yet to some Greeks, no matter how much he inspired or gave, ascended and accumulated, he would never truly be Greek. They would only see him as Black.

Adonis Georgiadis, who currently serves as the country's minister of development and vice president of the New Democracy party, and who is one of the country's most powerful right-wing politicians, spoke sarcastically about Giannis on TV in 2018, deliberately mispronouncing his name: "Akenotoumbo, Akenotoumbo . . . Doesn't he play as a Greek? Don't they say he is Greek? He has Greek nationality. The guy was born somewhere in Africa."

A mural of Giannis, located in the Palaio Faliro Municipality outside Athens, was also vandalized with Nazi symbols. Giannis, painted in his Bucks uniform, flexing his muscles and roaring, was tagged with swastikas and the letters *SS* on his right arm in black paint. His head was covered in graffiti too. "We have a far-right element, enormous racist element in our society," says Nikos Papadojannis, the Greek journalist. "And that stems from the fact that this society was never really diverse."

Greece was under foreign occupation for much of its history, mostly under Turkish rule. And historically, most Greeks are, and have been, white. Some Greeks have treated even white non-Greek immigrants—from countries like Bulgaria and Albania—with disdain, in addition to the much more vulgar, and violent, disdain for immigrants of color.

In 2017, hate crimes had more than doubled from the year before. In 2018, young Greeks beat and stabbed Pakistani migrant workers. A Jewish memorial was also desecrated. Krypteia, a Neo-Nazi group, set fire to the Afghan Community Center in Athens. Many Muslims were fearful, especially Muslim women, some of whom had their hijabs pulled off.

That same year, Golden Dawn attacked a social center for immigrants near Piraeus. Six men dressed in black, wearing motorcycle helmets and holding crowbars and torches, shouted, "Today you are going to die! You can't have this place in Piraeus!"

Eleftheria Tompatzoglou, a lawyer representing the family of Pavlos Fyssas, the Greek rapper killed by Golden Dawn in 2013, was inside the center and was one of the victims. She'd need seven stitches for a scalp wound after the attack. As she touched the blood at the back of her head, she heard the men shout, "Blood, Honour, Golden Dawn!"

Meanwhile, Giannis was becoming a global phenomenon. A *Greek* phenomenon. A symbol of hope around the world. And the more he rose, the more some Greeks denied the racism that he encountered. That he still encounters.

"When they saw the success of Giannis, they forgot everything," says Tzikas, the Kivotos Café owner. "Racism is global, but we don't see that we have the problem, the white people. It's very bad."

When talking about how much they love Giannis, some Greeks fail to remember the racist insults hurled at him at Trikala back when he was an NBA prospect. The intimidating presence of Golden Dawn. The glances of customers at Kivotos Café, watching Tzikas give the Antetokounmpos an apple every morning.

Why are you giving to the little Black kids?

Zisis has noticed the shift in the way people talk about Giannis since his time on the national team. The revisionist history that causes people to deify Giannis. "Now, it's easy to be fond of Giannis. It's very easy," Zisis says. "But back then, there were many people that weren't accepting him. And there still are."

That's the less-talked-about part of Giannis's story, one swept under the rug: "Not even one percent of Greek society dislikes him or comments anything bad about him being Black," says Trigas, the former U-18 Panathinaikos assistant coach. "Maybe [now] everybody forgets about his black skin because you're watching his dunks."

* * *

One afternoon early in his rookie year, back in 2013, when Giannis was getting acclimated to Milwaukee, teammate Caron Butler pulled him to the side and explained what it meant to be Black in America. Butler told him not to wear a hooded sweatshirt because of the way Black boys and Black men can be racially profiled—or even assaulted or killed.

The year before, in 2012, Trayvon Martin, an unarmed seventeen-year-old Black high school student, was shot and killed by George Zimmerman, a twenty-eight-year-old white and Hispanic man. Butler explained mass incarceration to Giannis too. Wisconsin had the highest percentage of incarcerated Black men in the country, and more than half of all Black men in their thirties and forties in Milwaukee had been incarcerated at some point in their lives, according to a 2013 study from the University of Wisconsin–Milwaukee.

Butler, who is from Racine, Wisconsin, wanted Giannis to be alert. "I wanted him to have a pulse on everything," Butler says. There was much for Giannis to learn, such as the fact that Milwaukee had the highest rate of segregation between Blacks and whites of the 102 largest metropolitan cities in the country, according to the 2010 national census.

Even Peter Feigin, Bucks president, in 2016 told the Rotary Club of Madison that Milwaukee was "the most segregated, racist place I've ever experienced."

That segregation still manifests itself in nearly every facet of society, including eviction rates. In a city of fewer than 105,500 renter households, Milwaukee landlords evict roughly sixteen thousand adults and children every year, many of them Black people, especially Black women. In a typical month in a Milwaukee eviction court, three in four people are Black, and three in four of those people are women. Black women make up 9 percent of Milwaukee's population and 30 percent of evicted tenants.

Myron Medcalf, the Milwaukee native who works for ESPN, whose childhood home was on Twenty-Sixth and Hampton Street, remembers an increase in violence happening in the city in the late 1980s. He had felt safe growing up, but in 1988, a neighbor named Michael was jumped for his Starter jacket. He nearly died, stuck in a coma for two months. Every night, the local news broadcast updates on Michael's condition. "I just kept thinking that was Chicago. Or some other place. That wasn't Milwaukee," Medcalf says.

But it was. And Black men in particular would be targeted. Killed. Medcalf, who is Black, went to the funerals of seven teenagers before he was seventeen, including that of his fifteen-year-old cousin. Medcalf remembers every phone call. Each body he saw, like the one laid out in front of his church, chalk surrounding the victim's figure.

"Milwaukee swallowed up a lot of people," Medcalf says. "There are educational challenges, if you look like me, specifically. It's a city that can breed a sense of despair, a sense of 'This is as good as it gets.' It's a place where people don't necessarily see a lot of folks achieve their dreams."

Giannis was absorbing so much so quickly. He would listen to his Black teammates talk about their experiences of racism in Milwaukee, like six-foot-nine John Henson. Henson went to a jeweler to browse watches in 2015. When he rang the doorbell, an employee locked the door and told him to go away. They wouldn't let him in and hurried to the back of the store. Police were dispatched.

Jabari Parker felt he was racially profiled when he was pulled over in his car numerous times, driving through the Milwaukee suburb where he lived. Another teammate, Josh Powell, once went with two of his friends to a Milwaukee restaurant, where a waiter refused to serve them and told them to leave. And later, Sterling Brown, another teammate, was arrested by Milwaukee police officers, who tased, tackled, and stepped on him after a minor parking violation. Brown brought a civil rights lawsuit in federal court for excessive force, eventually settling with the City of Milwaukee for $750,000 in 2020.

America was the first place where Giannis saw a Black man driving a nice car. It shocked him. *What's going on here?* he thought to himself, watching it drive past him. It caused him to reflect: *Does my country [Greece] give people of color enough opportunity?*

Many Black Greeks, including those who knew him as a child, were still contending with that question. Still living in Greece, seeking papers, not able to have the same opportunities as Giannis.

There was a brief glimmer of hope for migrants in Greece in 2015, when the leftist party Syriza was in power and the landmark Law 4332 was passed, which gave children of immigrants born and/or raised in Greece the right to Greek citizenship. But the law was undercut in 2020 when the alt-right anti-immigrant New Democracy party imposed new hurdles, including difficult exams about Greek life, language, and culture, effectively denying citizenship once again to children of migrants who were born in Greece.

Emmanuel Godwin, the Black Greek player who looked up to Giannis while they were growing up, who was in the crowd watching Giannis proudly carry the Greek flag on Independence Day, is still trying to gain citizenship despite having been born in Greece. He applied for papers four years ago. "They don't care," Godwin says. "How can I be born here and I *still* don't have papers? How can you do that?"

Sometimes Godwin wishes he was where Giannis is. Playing professional basketball in America. Having a passport. "I still look up to him," he says. Godwin still keeps in touch with the family, sending Giannis funny memes, texting Alex. Godwin is still playing, currently for A.O. Eleftheria Moschatou. But without a passport, a shot at even EuroLeague seems unlikely. But he keeps working, dreaming. And he keeps tabs on Giannis: "Now that he's made it, everybody's like, 'Oh yeah, I used to help him! He was my favorite guy! I love him so much!'" Godwin says. "I'm like, 'Wow, look at these people, man.' This is crazy. It's really sad."

Etinosa Erevbenagie, the former Panathinaikos youth-team player who used to speak Nigerian Pidgin with Giannis back in the day, watched his own basketball dreams dissolve largely because he couldn't gain citizenship. He didn't have a realistic chance of getting recruited to a higher club because there are only two spots for foreign players, which he was considered, despite feeling Greek. "I considered myself Nigerian Greek," he says. "But in terms of the official documents, I was just Nigerian."

Anytime his agent spoke on the phone with a potential team, the team would tell the agent that Erevbenagie was certainly talented enough but then ask about his documents. "Then everything would just stop," Erevbenagie says. He can hear the conversations, still stuck in his head. *It's not you, but it's you. It's not the papers, but it's the papers.* He managed to play in Spain and in lower-division Greece but was never able to move up.

He often thinks about what kind of career he might have had if he had been able to have his papers fast-tracked the way Giannis had. What kind of life he might have now. "Everything would be different," he says. There's pain in his voice. It was frustrating, not being able to change his circumstance. "I cannot fight against the system," he says.

He took refuge in his studies and now aspires to become a psychologist, motivated by the small percentage of Black mental-health professionals in Greece. He feels lucky to have found a route outside of basketball but hurts for his younger sister. It hurts every time he has to explain to her she is excluded from certain activities, places, opportunities, because even though she was born in Greece, she is considered African.

What he wants for her, and for the next generation of Black Greek kids, is "to be able to dream. I want them to have access to things I didn't. I want to create an environment for younger generations to not just think about surviving but to actually dream. And breathe."

When he says that word, he takes a breath. He is happy that Giannis was able to dream—and make it out. Genuinely, Erevbenagie is happy for him. Would never say anything disparaging about him. He just hopes that Giannis will speak up more to help others make it too. "Not everybody is Muhammad Ali or Colin Kaepernick, and that's OK. Perhaps Giannis didn't have the confidence or language when he was younger, but now that he's maybe older, he can finally talk about this," Erevbenagie says. "I know deep down that Giannis knows that he has a huge platform and there is a lot left to be said and done."

* * *

Back in 2013, as an eighteen-year-old, Giannis was asked by Gazzetta.gr if he ever experienced racism. Giannis said, "Never! I have never felt that ever! Everyone regards me as Greek and I am very happy for that!" And in a feature in the Greek publication *ΕΓΩ!Weekly* that same year, Giannis commented, "No, never, at least not from my friends or classmates at school. Only from fans of opposing teams during games. That will unfortunately always happen."

Thanasis, however, has spoken more candidly in recent years. In a 2019 interview with the Greek Sunday newspaper *Documento*, Thanasis said, "I was born in Aretaieio Hospital in Athens. I say this so that no one thinks that they brought us from somewhere or that we came from the moon."

Thanasis continued: "How is it possible that someone who was born here, went to kindergarten, school, university, received a Greek education, is not considered Greek?"

At the beginning of Giannis's career, journalists speculated about the family's origins. Oluwafemi Adefeso, a Nigerian sports journalist living in Lagos, Nigeria, and founder of African Basketball Conversation, a premier symposium about hoops in Africa, was scrolling the website Eurobasket around that time when he saw the name Giannis Antetokounmpo. Then he looked at a picture of Giannis. The name seemed strange to Adefeso; he didn't think it sounded or looked Nigerian. "Not many [Nigerian] people could relate to him at first glance," Adefeso says. "You're like, 'Oh, this guy is brown-skinned and is Greek, so he's definitely not *fully* Greek. He has to be some sort of, how we call it, half-caste.'"

Adefeso wondered, *Maybe his mom is African and his dad is Greek?* "That's what a lot of people thought," he says. "There was a little bit of not being really sure where he's really from and if he's truly a full-blooded Nigerian. So it took a while to become aware and accept him."

When Giannis started to become *Giannis*, and Adefeso learned more about Giannis's two Nigerian parents, he wished that Giannis would play for the Nigerian national team. He continued to cheer him on, as he did other players of African descent who play for other national teams, like Serge Ibaka of the Democratic Republic of the Congo, who plays for Spain's team.

But Adefeso wished there was a deeper connection between Giannis and Nigeria. "People love him as Nigerian, but they are not overly hysterical about how great he is, because the connection is really not there," Adefeso says. "A lot of people want that connection."

Giannis inched a bit closer to that connection in 2015, when he played in the NBA's inaugural 2015 Africa game in Johannesburg, South Africa, for Team Africa against Team World. The six thousand available tickets at Ellis Park Arena sold out in nine minutes. Giannis was in Africa for the first time, and he brought his family with him, making the trip even more meaningful. Giannis and his brothers understand a little bit of the Nigerian languages Veronica and Charles used to speak to them.

Giannis had fun, even going on a safari and to South Africa's Lion Park, petting lion cubs. Still, he was extremely focused on the game itself. He was polite, unusually quiet. Intense. Every drill in practice he sprinted as if it were a real game. Luc Mbah a Moute, Giannis's teammate on Team Africa, walked up to him and said, "You getting ready to play in the finals, huh?" Giannis just nodded. Meanwhile, their coach, Gregg Popovich of the Spurs, was laughing, having a good time, looking laid-back (no joke).

NBA legends Hakeem Olajuwon and Dikembe Mutombo surprisingly showed up in the second quarter of the game, in full uniform, joining in. "It was special," says Boris Diaw, another Team Africa teammate. "You never think you will play with these guys."

Giannis scored a game-high twenty-two points. Players were allowed to put patches of the flags of the countries they were representing on the backs of their jerseys. Giannis picked only the Greek flag to be on his jersey. Diaw remembers Giannis being sure of the decision. "I remember Giannis only wanting the Greek flag on his jersey," says Diaw, who put both the Senegalese and French flags on his own jersey.

Later, in 2017, when Giannis interviewed with *60 Minutes*, the producers asked him which pronunciation of his last name he preferred, the African or Greek. Adetokunbo or Antetokounmpo? "Whichever one you like," Draggan Mihailovich, the producer, remembers Giannis responding. Mihailovich says he had a hunch why: "He just didn't want to make anybody mad."

The producers then asked Giannis about the migrant crisis. Giannis's answer didn't make the final piece, but it showed a more open, sympathetic Giannis. "Those people in the boats, they're just coming over in Greece to have a better life, you know, people that I know, people close to me have done that in the past," Giannis said. "I hear a lot of people [say], they're coming over here to take our jobs. They're coming over here, you know, some people, in the boats in there because they're having war. They're about to get killed. That's the only option they have."

He opened up a little more when he defended Thanasis in 2018. A Greek TV host named Takis Tsoukalas had described Thanasis as an "ape" following one of Thanasis's Panathinaikos games, saying, "They have an ape. That Antetokounmpo guy is an ape. That's what I'm telling you."

Giannis tweeted in response, "I have lost sleep over the last few days over this negative-racist incident which occurred recently. If this happens to Thanasis, who with pride and a permanent smile represents the Greek national team and Panathinaikos, I can't imagine what's happening to other [people of color] in Greece.

"My brothers and I are proud to be Greek-Nigerian," Giannis said, "and if any one doesn't like it, that's their problem."

Interviewing with *The Undefeated* in 2019, Giannis said that he wanted to explore more of his Nigerian roots. "Obviously, a lot of people don't know where I'm from," Giannis told *The Undefeated*. "There are a lot of people that I see and I tell them that I am African. I am not just 'The

Greek Freak.' It doesn't matter what people may believe because of my nickname. . . . Deep down, I know who I am and where I am from."

Even when he rose to become a top-five player in the league, in the *world*, by this point, commentators and fans still joked that they couldn't pronounce his name, laughing, as if it were somehow not possible to do so correctly. Kenny Smith, an *Inside the NBA* cohost, asked Shaq on air in 2019: "Can you pronounce Giannis's last name?"

Shaq responded, "Giannis Ante-ka-noon-po. Is that right, my brother?"

The other cohosts chimed in. Charles Barkley said Shaq's version was "close enough." Ernie Johnson called it "kind of in the ballpark." Giannis, also part of the broadcast, acknowledged it wasn't the correct pronunciation but laughed it off and asked them to call him "Superman."

Giannis didn't publicly speak in depth about his experiences regarding race in America or Greece until a video interview with TNT's *The Arena* in 2020: "Greece is a country of white people, so it can be tough for people with my skin complexion," Giannis said in the segment. "You go through a lot of neighborhoods, and you face a lot of negativity. Racism.

"It was tough—it's always going to be tough—being Black in a country of white people," Giannis continued. "It's going to be times where you feel like you're not who you are. Especially if you're born here [in Greece]. I was born here."

The backlash in some quarters was immediate and intense. Greeks, including prominent politicians, bashed Giannis online.

"What exactly does this monkey do, again? Oh, yeah, he plays basketball," tweeted Konstantinos Kalemis, the Greek Ministry of Education's refugee coordinator, who then called Giannis the "[N-word]" and "the ungrateful one" and "nothing but an illiterate who suddenly is called a messiah. . . . Giannis is not a human being."

"The only real Greeks are those who were born Greek," tweeted Kyriakos Velopoulos, president of the far-right party Elliniki Lysi (Greek Solution), the fifth biggest in the country. "One can learn to love Greece . . . but that's the furthest one can go. Antetokounmpo's quotes are proof of that."

Rachel Makri, a well-known member of the right-wing populist Independent Greeks, demanded Giannis give his Greek citizenship back.

Papadojannis, the Greek journalist, wrote a column about the incident, about how Greece denies its racism: "Those who refuse to look in their mirror, for fear of what they will see. The blind ostriches of the planet," he wrote. Papadojannis wishes he lived in a more inclusive Greece. "Giannis right now is not a sports hero. He is a social symbol for Greece," Papadojannis says. "It makes him a symbol of Greece not as it is but as we would like it to be as a country. At least me, I would like my country to be more diverse, more open, as a society."

He can't help but think that's not a universal opinion, given that, to some, Giannis had turned from hero to foe, now framed as an ungrateful, disrespectful athlete who should be showing deference to a country that granted him citizenship.

A few days after the TNT segment aired and was posted online at Bleacher Report, a sports website owned by Turner, the segment mysteriously disappeared from the website. It was pulled off YouTube too. It can't be accessed online anywhere to this day. It's as if someone wanted to scrub the record clean.

CHAPTER 13

FREAK

A low rumble echoed from blocks away. Plumes of smoke exploded into the air. Debris scattered into the street as a large yellow crane began to tear down the Bradley Center on this morning in early January 2019.

The glass-front atrium had been knocked over, the narrow windy hallways plowed through. Bit by bit, the demolition continued over the next few months as the desolate home of the Bucks over the last thirty years was dismantled.

Aaron Salata, a Milwaukee-area native and Bucks fan since the 1980s, came to watch the first day of the demolition. He couldn't get too close, as a sign—Danger: Demolition in Progress—impeded his path. Salata *loves* the Bucks. He was six years old when his father took him to his first game. His favorite players were Sidney Moncrief and Marques Johnson, back when the Bucks were formidable, playing in the beautiful, bright MECCA. He continued to wear his twelve Bucks jerseys in steady rotation, proudly, throughout the miserable 1990s, sitting in the cold, depressing Bradley Center. He'd never give up on the Bucks: "We've always had a chip on our shoulder."

When Salata watched the demolition of the Bradley Center, he felt something new. Something unfamiliar: hope. He clapped and cheered. He stood next to about a dozen people also celebrating. A man in a green shirt and blue jeans walked by, fist-pumping into the air. Many, too, were sad; sure, the Bradley Center didn't have much atmosphere, and it housed some pretty awful teams, but it was home. It was sacred. It meant something to Milwaukeeans, to love something so deeply that rarely returned the favor.

Salata hoped the demolition would lead to new beginnings: "It was symbolic of the old Bucks hopefully going away." No more *just get to the playoffs*. No more *just be competitive*. No more leaky roofs. No more ill-advised free-agent acquisitions. No more mediocrity!

By this point, about midway through the 2018–2019 season, the Bucks had a new coach in Budenholzer, a new $524 million state-of-the-art arena in Fiserv Forum, an NBA-best record, and, of course, Giannis. He was the generational player fans had been waiting for. He was the reason fans wear Bucks gear proudly throughout downtown Milwaukee, a far cry from his rookie year, when Bucks staffers handed out tokens to the few souls daring to wear purple and green.

If Giannis hadn't come to Milwaukee, it's unlikely the Bucks would still be there.

* * *

A few months earlier, before the 2018–2019 season began, Coach Budenholzer arrived in Milwaukee with high expectations. There was even more urgency to win, given that Giannis's supermax-contract decision loomed in the background. He'd have the opportunity to leave Milwaukee after 2021, when he'd be an unrestricted free agent. The supermax was instituted to help teams keep their top players by allowing them to offer more money than competitors.

Budenholzer had a few things in common with his new superstar: He was a grinder. A perfectionist. A family-oriented person: he and his son, John, work on giant puzzles at home that stretch across the entire kitchen table sometimes for two weeks until they complete it. Budenholzer's also intensely competitive. The fifty-two-year-old and son John would play one-on-one in the family's driveway, and Budenholzer would be out for blood. Didn't matter that his son was barely in high school.

Budenholzer would later dive on the hard carpeted floor in the Bucks locker room before a game against Chicago, full suit, chasing an invisible ball, to show his players what intensity looked like.

He's had that hustle since he was a kid, the seventh of seven kids. He was never the tallest, never the strongest, never the most athletic, growing up in Holbrook, Arizona, a town of five thousand in eastern Arizona, near the Navajo Nation. He got by on hustle and smarts, being a basketball nerd who genuinely loved to work. To spend hours milling over one play. "Bud's got that ground-up, nothing-handed-to-him personality," says Bo Ryan, the legendary Wisconsin coach, who is friends with Budenholzer.

Like Giannis, Budenholzer didn't need frills to play. If he had a ball and a hoop, he was happy. He played on blacktop playgrounds, wherever there was a game. He often played on the nearby reservations against Indigenous players, in Navajo towns like Dilkon, Window Rock, Tuba City, and Ganado.

He was barely recruited for college scholarships and wound up at Division III Pomona College in Southern California. Budenholzer would smother opponents, even in practice. "He was the scrappiest guy on the court," says Bill Cover, former Pomona teammate and the school's second all-time leading scorer. Cover remembers Budenholzer chasing his NBA coaching dream upon graduating, driving his "old, beat-up car" to wherever there was a camp. Wherever he might get closer to his dream.

On one such day, Budenholzer had been driving for a long time, driving down from Oregon to NorCal, and it was nearing midnight. He asked Cover if he could stay at his house (Cover's mother's house, that is, in Palo Alto). Afterward, Budenholzer penned a handwritten thank-you note to Cover's mother expressing his gratitude and telling her she'd raised an amazing son. "She was so touched by that," Cover says. "She still brings up that thank-you note."

Still, like Giannis, Budenholzer wasn't exactly on the short list for the NBA, coming out of a small school. Even for players who *have* played for top-tier Division I programs, it can take years. "Nobody was predicting that Mike would become a two-time NBA Coach of the Year," Cover says.

But when Cover thinks of Budenholzer's work ethic, competitiveness, and ability to communicate—how he'd just come up to anyone and offer a tip, share a drill he knew or a piece of advice that might help a player—it makes sense to him why Budenholzer ended up as a coach.

He'd apply those same skills when he got his start in the video room with the Spurs under Popovich. Budenholzer worked his way up as a film-room guy and an assistant coach for more than fifteen years. He studied basketball religiously, laboring alone for many hours in dark rooms, breaking down video highlights while eating Subway sandwiches—hoping to make it as a head coach one day. Finally, he joined the Hawks as a head coach from 2013 to 2018.

"He was an assistant for *so* many years," says Boris Diaw, who played for Budenholzer on the Spurs, "that he could have had a chance to be a head coach before, but it's hard when you're not a former player to get a chance. He kept learning all those years."

Especially from Popovich. Budenholzer adopted Popovich's attention to detail, becoming obsessive about details when joining the Bucks. Budenholzer would get upset if the font size was one point too small or too big. It would irritate him if an apostrophe was missing or a double dash was inserted instead of the warranted single dash. Assistants would put a sheet of paper up to the whiteboard as a guide because they knew Budenholzer wanted the writing to be perfectly straight. *Every* detail had to be perfect.

Even at home. He'd review film constantly, shuffling hundreds of papers into narrow binders. "He's extremely organized," says Ricky Muench, a Bucks video and player development assistant in 2019–2020 who also spent multiple afternoons a week training Budenholzer's son, John. "Bud goes through the papers like it's all for a finals game."

It became clear to Budenholzer, in his first meeting with Giannis, that Giannis was as much a stickler for the details as he was. Budenholzer took Giannis, as well as Khris Middleton, to breakfast at a Spanish restaurant at the start of the season. While they ate eggs and Iberian ham, Budenholzer explained his new system, one that catered to the strengths of his team, of Giannis: more spacing, more speed, emphasizing three-point shooting, tough defense.

Listening intently, Giannis took out his notebook and started jotting down notes. Giannis asked question after question, writing down each response, such as how practice would be run, who initiated offense, the philosophy on defense.

This was Giannis's third head coach. He was used to adapting, but this time he had a much stronger supporting cast as the Bucks added talented big man Brook Lopez. The strange part, though, was that his new coach wanted him to shoot threes. Yes, he wanted *Giannis*, the non–jump shooter, to shoot threes.

"I don't care if you make it, miss it, hit the backboard, airball—I don't care," Budenholzer told Giannis. "Shoot the ball."

It was the first time someone had encouraged him like that. Asked him to do something other than *just go to the basket*. It was exciting but weird. New. A coach asking him to not just use his natural gifts of exploding downcourt, dunking over people, just because he could, but try the one thing that everyone thought he *couldn't* do? And Budenholzer was serious: he'd yell at Giannis to shoot if he hesitated or turned down a shot. He wanted more of Giannis. And Giannis wanted more out of himself.

* * *

The first day of training camp, Budenholzer outlined boxes in blue tape around the three-point line of the court so players could get used to spacing across the perimeter and spotting up for threes.

Giannis wasn't exactly confident in his shooting, and his opponents knew it. They'd sag off a foot or two when guarding him, daring him to attempt, knowing he'd likely brick. Of course, they also played him that way because they were terrified of giving him an open lane to the basket.

It was still strange, hearing Budenholzer tell him to shoot. Kidd hadn't allowed him to shoot much at all in their first two seasons together. The memory of getting benched for launching threes was still fresh. And that caused him to think before acting at times. But Budenholzer didn't want him to think; he wanted him to let it *fly*.

The hope was that Giannis would gain confidence and not hesitate as much. But his form was slow. Clunky. It looked like he was thinking of what to do rather than just . . . doing it.

Giannis's shooting woes puzzled those around him. Was it a technical problem? A confidence problem? A mix of both? Some wondered if he simply wasn't able to morph into a reliable shooter because of his body. He's an enormously long-limbed person with huge hands, and honestly, people with those proportions can have difficulty catching, gathering their bodies at high speeds, rising up, getting enough backspin on the ball, with their hands stretching across the ball. Yet Kawhi Leonard's hands are enormous, and he's an incredible shooter, an observation that's sometimes made.

It was (and still is) confusing because Giannis wasn't a particularly poor shooter during his rookie year. He even attempted 118 threes that year. Even back in Greece, he launched threes. That wasn't a huge part of his game by any means, but it wasn't discussed with any urgency as it is now. But with every passing pro season, his shot seemed more uncomfortable. His torso would tilt back. He'd palm the ball. His release was higher, but it looked a bit unnatural. Slow. "I honestly don't know what happened to it," says one Bucks staffer. "It's pretty bad."

Earlier in his career, Giannis had a pretty midrange fadeaway jumper. Drill after drill, he'd work on post moves and finish with the midrange jumper. "He had an unbelievable mid-post game," says Eric Harper, former assistant video coordinator from 2017 to 2018. "I mean, that was his *shit*." Harper would walk in at 10:00 p.m. and find Giannis there, laboring on the midrange. But as he progressed in his career, various Bucks coaches have tried to take him farther away from the basket and mold him into more of a pure guard—a guard who shoots threes.

"I just think it's analytics," Brogdon says, "the way the NBA is moving. The Bucks are one of those teams, where Bud wants threes and layups, high-percentage shots."

Budenholzer paired Giannis with Ben Sullivan, assistant coach, who trained under renowned Spurs shooting coach Chip Engelland. Sullivan and Giannis would work for hours on different dribble-shooting combos, trying to replicate game-rhythm shots. Follow-through was a big emphasis—trying to create one fluid motion in which the release point moved away from Giannis's head.

But Giannis could get to the basket so easily. And he'd often do just that instead of settling for a jumper. It was hard to blame him: his body was now so chiseled, so powerful, he looked like a Greek *god*. Especially with how much he was lifting. Giannis looked nothing like the scrawny player practicing his scowl in the mirror. But he still acted like the player afraid of not measuring up, just trying to crack the starting lineup. He was the last person to leave training camp in 2018–2019, asking the Bucks' video-coordinator crew to hound him in the paint after practice, especially Schuyler Rimmer, a six-foot-nine, 240-pound assistant video coordinator who became his designated defender and rebounder.

Giannis wanted the coordinators to try to suffocate him. Not with dummy defense either. All had pads on, shoving Giannis with all their might. Naturally, Giannis would still dunk on all of them. "He's going through us like a running back going through a football line," says Wes Bohn, an assistant video coordinator that season. Giannis would be drenched in sweat after completing a full workout after all his teammates had left, prompting Bohn to always have three towels ready for him.

That made an impression on Tim Frazier, who was fighting for a roster spot. It was jarring to him that Giannis, a global icon, was staying later than anyone, sprinting harder than anyone. "I don't think Giannis knows what a day off is," Frazier says. Not even when he is supposed to be taking a day off.

Giannis loved playing chess with Mason Yahr, who worked with the Bucks medical staff from 2016 to 2020, mostly as a sports science data analyst. Giannis was so intense when the two played. Every time Yahr took one of his pieces, Giannis would look completely disgusted with himself. "He was *so* pissed," Yahr says. One match, Yahr beat Giannis, as Giannis was forced to surrender when Yahr took Giannis's queen. "He always told me he'd get me back," Yahr says. "Giannis didn't want anyone to beat him in anything."

*　*　*

Giannis was virtually unstoppable as the season began, eventually dropping forty-four against the Cavs in December 2018. He was trying to
lead not just with his actions but with words, something he'd learned from
point guard Jason Terry the previous season.

Terry had told him that being a leader was being able to have hard
conversations with teammates. "Leaders have to tell teammates what they
need to hear, not only the praise they want to receive," Terry told him.
"Leaders keep their voices heard. And honesty is eventually appreciated."

Giannis looked at him, a little shy. "Are you sure?" he asked. "I can say
that?"

Terry nodded. Giannis almost needed permission, someone to tell him
it was OK to be that person. Terry would whisper to him during time-outs,
"Dominate the next segment. Dominate the next play."

Giannis began to operate with a different kind of confidence: he knew
there was nobody who could stop him one-on-one, full speed ahead to the
basket. He was making an effort to speak up more too.

"We need to hear you," Budenholzer would tell him. "We need to hear
you as much as we see you on the court."

That wasn't something he had been comfortable with, especially since
Kidd had tried to get him to do that. But he was improving. "It's something he's still growing into," Brogdon says.

Giannis would get on teammates if they weren't giving as much as he
was, but he also listened, offered support. He was never going to become a
rah-rah type of leader, but he'd make sure his teammates knew he believed
in them by giving each individual attention.

One such teammate was Christian Wood, a roster hopeful during training camp. Wood had gone undrafted in 2015 and had bounced around
the NBA and the G League, hoping to find a home. Giannis barely knew
him when meeting him at training camp but respected Wood's work ethic.
He treated Wood like he was a starter. Like he was a focal member of the
team. Giannis gave him a bracelet that featured the words "prove them
wrong."

"He makes you want to compete at his level," says Wood, who now
plays for the Rockets. He was the same way with Frazier, the other roster

hopeful. Giannis would stay after with Frazier, teaching him the plays. Frazier once asked Giannis where he wanted the ball and how he could help get him more opportunities, but Giannis ignored the question and asked Frazier what plays *he* wanted to run. "I was the sixteenth man," Frazier says. "He didn't have to do that."

Giannis was trying to become a better listener. Be more receptive to what his teammates thought.

"He listens a lot more," says Sterling Brown, who now plays for the Rockets. Brown remembers Giannis being so individually focused at one point—"I gotta get better; I'm so determined"—but the last few years he's understood more of the bigger picture. What it might take for the Bucks to win. Which might not even be him taking the final shot all the time. "For him to sit back and listen to his teammates, and take advice, take constructive criticism, that was huge for me to see," Brown says.

The Bucks flourished, taking off for an NBA-best 34–12 start. Giannis was selected as an all-star starter and team captain. He couldn't believe it—a team named after him (Team Giannis), the other after LeBron (Team LeBron). "If you told me that six years ago, I would have never, never, never thought I would be in this position right now," he told reporters before the game.

He led all scorers with thirty-eight points, though his team lost, 178–164. Giannis had eleven dunks, including a play where teammate Paul George tossed the ball off the backboard to him. As he rose up, he saw James under the basket. James instinctively moved out of the way as Giannis threw the ball down.

After the game, James found Giannis. "I love everything about you, man," James told him.

Giannis stood there, shocked. Confused. He was still in awe. Even at this point. "Who, me?" his face seemed to say. *He's LeBron fucking James*, Giannis thought, reflecting after the game. James had been a role model for so long. His measuring stick from afar.

Giannis *was* taking his game to a new level, especially after dropping a career-high fifty-two points at Philadelphia in March 2019. One play, Giannis backed down Ben Simmons deep into the post and turned around and dunked all over him, screaming, "He's a fucking baby!" Giannis was done being nice. He was done being modest.

He continued to be praised for how *different* he was. What a *freak* he was. A near seven-footer who can maneuver up and down the floor like a guard. A bigger player who has uncanny vision. A player who can guard positions one through five, not willing to give up a single play.

"He's a guy that's redefining the game of basketball from the inside," says Caron Butler, his former teammate. "And he hasn't even peaked yet. I think once the jump shot and the things he's lacking in but improving in happen, he's going to be a guy that you cannot tell the story of basketball without mentioning."

We simply don't have language for someone like Giannis, who has been compared to players all across the spectrum, from Scottie Pippen to Shaquille O'Neal. Someone who can miraculously dominate a jump-shooting era without a reliable jump shot. He is, as the *Wall Street Journal* smartly put it, "the basketball equivalent of a tech billionaire communicating by carrier pigeon."

"I don't know what he is," says Alvin Gentry, Kings associate head coach. "Is he a guard? Is he a forward? Is he a center?"

"I don't know anyone like him," says Mike D'Antoni, Nets assistant coach. "If you've got nine things to do to stop Milwaukee, he's eight of them," D'Antoni says. "The preparation it takes to stop him. That's how he's changing the game."

"I think he's a center," says *The Ringer*'s Bill Simmons. "A center in whatever the modern version of the center is." Giannis reminds Simmons of a young Shaq—not Shaq from the Lakers or mid-2000s Suns or Heat, but Shaq the amazing seven-foot athlete who, if he was within nine feet of the rim, was going to score.

"I think the mistake we make in assessing Giannis was comparing him to LeBron or Durant and people like that," Simmons says. "I feel like the people to compare him to are Shaq or Joel Embiid. He doesn't seem like a center, but he is. He should be playing center. . . . He's devastating around the rim. Completely unstoppable. You have to foul him, or he's dunking."

Giannis is leading a new generation of young international players who are emerging as multidimensional stars, like Luka Dončić (Slovenia), Joel Embiid (Cameroon), Nikola Jokić (Serbia), Ben Simmons (Australia), and Kristaps Porziņģis (Latvia). And they're bringing their fan bases. In fact, about 74 percent of Bucks Facebook followers in 2018–2019 were international.

The NBA had 108 international players that season and a record 7 international all-stars, a substantial change from the 1990s and even early 2000s. The 1992 Dream Team, a group that included Michael Jordan, Larry Bird, and Magic Johnson, asserted itself as the best in the world. European teams, however, were improving. And when America lost to Greece in 2006, in that game Giannis watched as an eleven-year-old, it was clear that European teams had caught up. A long list of international players have now starred in the NBA, including Dirk Nowitzki, Hakeem Olajuwon, Dikembe Mutombo, Toni Kukoč, Manu Ginóbili, Tony Parker, Yao Ming, Peja Stojaković, Steve Nash, Pau Gasol, and many more.

The number of overseas-born players has tripled over the past two decades. "They weren't just coming to play," says Ersan Ilyasova, Giannis's former Bucks teammate, who is from Turkey. "They were really succeeding here at a high level."

And changing the way the game is played. Nowitzki, especially, changed things for big men. The way he shot the ball, the way he ushered in new expectations for taller, bigger players to be more mobile and perimeter oriented rather than back-to-the-basket post players, defined a generation.

European clubs were teaching players fundamental skill work from a young age—ball handling, passing, footwork—while American clubs were stuffing players in eight-court gyms and having them play AAU games from morning until night.

"The coaches in Europe are there to develop talent, not to win," says D'Antoni, who had played in Italy from 1977 to 1990 before turning to coaching, "but in the US, if you've got a high school coach, he's trying to win."

Giannis benefited from that development-first mindset, but his story was different from those of other international stars. He didn't come out of a top club. He proved that if a player is talented or has potential, has the physical capabilities and intangibles, the incredibly vast network of American and international NBA scouts will find him.

"It gives a lot of kids back home an opportunity to believe that it *is* possible and that it can be done," says Bismack Biyombo, Charlotte Hornet and vice president of the National Basketball Players Association, who was born in Lubumbashi, Democratic Republic of the Congo. "It just shows how global the game of basketball is. Everywhere you go, kids are talking about the NBA."

John Hammond, now the GM of the Orlando Magic, feels emotional every time an executive or a scout asks him about a potential prospect by saying, "Could he be as good as *Giannis*?" That Giannis, the one people weren't sure what to make of, is now the benchmark. The model comparison. Hammond notices it, too, when asking young players which player they want to emulate. They often tell him, "Giannis."

"He's inspiring players," Hammond says. "They want to be him."

One such prospect is Jalen Green, the prospective number 1 pick in the 2021 NBA draft, who bypassed college to play for the G League's Ignite. Giannis inspired Green, who is half Black and half Filipino, to take his game overseas and explore his roots. "Giannis kind of inspired me to go to the Philippines," Green says. Green enjoyed competing there in 2019. He's become almost a cult figure there, as young as he is. "When I saw Giannis's story, I thought, *Why not go represent for my Filipino side?*"

The more famous Giannis has become, the more he's been asked to explain both of his cultures. His Greek side, his Nigerian side. Even his own younger brothers often made fun of him because he's the only one of all of them who still has a Greek accent.

"When you gonna change your accent?" they'd ask him. "When are you gonna start talking a little bit more Americanized?"

"Nah, this is who I am," Giannis would tell them. "I take pride in who I am."

Giannis has never much cared what people thought of him, but he did read what fans, strangers, said about him, how they questioned whether he could be the face of the NBA because he was, in their words, "not

American enough." Or that he didn't have enough swagger because he's a low-maintenance person. A superstar who doesn't want the attention that comes with being a superstar.

"A lot of people say that I can be the face of the league," Giannis told the *Milwaukee Journal Sentinel* in 2019. "Lately, people have told me . . . the closest people, you know, my family, my girlfriend, my mom, my brothers, [other] people say that I cannot be the face of the league because I'm not American. I don't have the American culture in me.

"I sat back and thought about that. Should I have a little bit more American swag? Should I come with the suit to the game? Should I be more Americanized? But man, if I can't be the face of the league being me, I don't want to be the face of the league."

* * *

A few weeks after the 2019 all-star game, Giannis visited Alex's practice, as he often does when he doesn't have Bucks practice, and started leading players through drills. Some of Alex's teammates were still shocked that Giannis not only was Alex's brother but showed up so frequently—and not just to *watch* but to coach.

And on this particular March afternoon, Giannis wasn't in a good mood. He didn't like the way players were lackadaisically moving through drills. Going through the motions, like they had somewhere better to be. He gathered them at center court and told them about his teammate Eric Bledsoe, who had recently signed a four-year $70 million extension. "Do you think that made him feel *comfortable* because he had the extra money?" Giannis asked the group.

No one said anything.

"No," Giannis continued. "*No*. He's in the gym a lot more now than he was before. And it pushes *me* to be in the gym more and be with him more."

Players nodded. But Giannis wasn't finished. "Who do you guys feel is the best team in the Eastern Conference?" he asked. It was the kind of question players weren't sure if they were supposed to actually answer. Jamari Magee, Alex's closest friend, raised his hand. "The Bucks," Magee said.

Giannis looked surprised. "You think we're better than *Toronto*! You think we're better than *Boston*! You think we're better than *Philadelphia*! No. We're not better than them."

Technically, the Bucks *were* the number 1 seed in the East at that point, had playoff pairings been predetermined, but Giannis's message was clear. "We haven't done anything," Giannis said. "We didn't win a championship. We haven't done anything! You can't ever get comfortable."

Giannis certainly wasn't getting comfortable, even though the Bucks had transformed into a legitimate title contender, something that had seemed inconceivable his rookie year. But Budenholzer challenged Giannis to slow down, to put as much time in his recovery as he did in his work. It wasn't about getting comfortable, but it was thinking more about how he could preserve himself to be at his best.

He'd sub Giannis out when Giannis didn't want to be subbed out. Giannis wanted to play every minute. "We need you later, not today," Budenholzer would tell him. That was difficult for Giannis to accept. Even with the knee soreness that he'd dealt with off and on for the past two seasons, he felt he could play through anything.

Because he had played through anything. He had *lived* through so much—there was nothing on the basketball court that could truly hurt him. In Giannis's mind, he couldn't relax. He always told his brothers that: "It's human nature to want to relax, but you can't relax. You have to get back into killer mode."

Budenholzer, however, knew there were times to kill—and times to recover. With an eighty-two-game season plus playoffs, plus the number of times Giannis was smacked underneath the basket, it all took a toll on his body.

"They've had to pull him back, save him from himself a little bit," Yahr says, "because literally Giannis won't leave the gym if you don't make him."

* * *

The Milwaukee River was dyed green, *Bucks green*, celebrating the Bucks' top seed heading into the 2018–2019 playoffs. It was glorious, the way the city embraced the Bucks. Were *excited* about the Bucks again. Everything had changed in the six years Giannis had been with the franchise. The arena had birthed an entire entertainment complex nearby, Deer District.

It seemed like the Bucks could actually compete for a title. They finally had their first generational player since Kareem Abdul-Jabbar. Their first shot back at that elusive 1971 championship. "You never expected the Bucks to be playing during the prime-time games on ESPN, on TNT," says Tyler Herro, the Heat guard and Milwaukee native. "It's crazy to be seeing it. They've proved they are at the top of the league."

It was surreal for Paul Henning, who'd rallied for organizational change with Save Our Bucks just six years before. "Now, the first thing people think of when they think of Milwaukee is Giannis," Henning says. "He's changed something that's been in place for forty years."

"He is," Henning says, "Milwaukee's son."

So much of Giannis *is* Milwaukee. How blue-collar he is. How he doesn't act like he's better than anyone else. "He treats everybody with the same respect as the next person," says Logan Miranda, a Bucks team attendant who often guards the home locker room. During Miranda's first year with the Bucks, Giannis was putting on sneakers when he noticed Miranda. Giannis then walked up to Miranda and introduced himself. "Hi, I'm Giannis."

As if Miranda didn't know. "What's your name?" Giannis said.

"Logan."

"Cool. Good to meet you."

The next day, Giannis walked by Miranda. "Hey, Logan."

Miranda still can't get over that Giannis remembered his name.

Matthew Smith, a longtime Bucks fan whose two sons now have Bucks posters on their bedroom walls, wasn't sure what the Bucks were thinking when they drafted Giannis. He had never heard of him. Now? "He's a once-in-a-lifetime player," Smith says. "And to have him in *Milwaukee*? You see players like that, but they're in New York or LA or Chicago. To be blessed to have a guy like that in Milwaukee? It's amazing."

But what Milwaukeeans really admire is that it didn't happen overnight. Many of the league's young superstars are identified as eighth graders, on the fast track to millions. Zion Williamson, the number 1 pick after that season, had been destined for superstardom since he was a teen. But Giannis's path was different. He had to watch the bench-press bar tremble in his grip rookie year, not get discouraged that he was so far behind. He had to spend hour after hour in the weight room with Bucks strength coach Suki Hobson, transforming from someone that couldn't do a single chin-up into someone that could bulldoze through three defenders whenever he chose.

And that resonated with some Milwaukeeans who maybe wake up in the morning and go to a job that isn't glamorous but work hard at it. Milwaukee is a proud city. And when people there saw a person like Giannis, who worked from the ground up, they were proud. He was no longer the frail eighteen-year-old just grateful to be in the NBA, enamored by smoothies and buffets and Kevin Durant. He was no longer the overly emotional twenty-year-old who didn't know how to channel his fire during his first playoff series against the Bulls.

Giannis was growing into a man.

"We feel like we've grown up with him," says Raj Shukla, a longtime Bucks fan. "That really means something."

Even people who don't know much about basketball identify with him. With his personality. How humble he is, how funny he is. They like *him* as much as they like *the basketball player*. "There's a level of redemption for Bucks fans," says Dan Shafer, who had covered the arena debate. "You watched all these terrible Bucks teams, and instead of abandoning them, you stuck with them. And you ended up with the most fun, most likable megastar to carry us out of the darkness."

"There's this Shawshank moment," Shafer continues, "where he crawled through the river of shit and smelled like roses at the end of it."

It was exciting but terrifying, the way things were changing in Milwaukee, heading into the playoffs full of expectations. They weren't used to that: being *expected* to win something. At least, they hadn't been for a long time. The city that had been characterized as Not a Basketball City since the team's inception had to constantly prove it was worthy of even having a team.

There was still a sense of self-doubt among some fans, almost as a defense mechanism to protect against future disappointment. They'd been burned before. "It was scary when the Bucks became good again," says Andy Carpenter, a longtime Bucks fan. "There was still a fear that 'The Bucks are gonna blow this because that's just what the Bucks do.'"

*   *   *

The Bucks made quick work of the Pistons in round 1 of the 2018–2019 playoffs. Giannis was aggressive starting in game 1, when he made an and-one layup over Bruce Brown. Giannis pounded his chest and screamed, "I'm fucking unstoppable!"

After a 4–0 sweep, the Bucks advanced to the second round for the first time since 2001.

The Celtics proved to be a much tougher opponent. Boston threw body after body at Giannis, especially Al Horford. Whenever Giannis spun, someone was in his way. When he tried to spin the other way, someone else was in his way. The game 1 loss, 112–90, stung. Giannis was the last one dressed, lingering alone at his locker, feet in an ice-bath bucket.

He was baffled. Truly baffled. He couldn't knock down jumpers, and he couldn't find a rhythm to the hoop. He looked powerless. Thanasis called him afterward. "You need to play harder," Thanasis told him. "*You* have to be the aggressor. *You* have to make the right pass." It hurt, hearing that from his big brother.

The Bucks didn't panic, but Giannis was more vocal than usual. He let the team know: "We can't lose this next game. This is a *must*-win for us." Giannis rebounded triumphantly, dropping twenty-nine and ten to tie the series. The Bucks won the next three games, finishing off the series with a 116–91 win. Something Giannis had said before the final game struck a chord with the team. "A lot of us probably come from nothing," he said. "And we have the opportunity to write our own story now."

It was miraculous, advancing to the Eastern Conference Finals, facing the Raptors, and winning the first two games. Giannis started the second game with a vicious dunk and then a critical block on Marc Gasol. The Bucks legitimately looked like they could win the championship.

Alex had never seen his big brother focus that intensely. "You'd see him, and it was almost like he wasn't a person," Alex says. "From the time he woke up on the game days, to the time the game was over with, he had this blank look on his face like, 'I'm about to go kill.'"

But the Raptors stole the momentum, winning game 3 in double overtime. Kawhi Leonard was phenomenal, defending Giannis, limiting him to difficult shots and causing him to make poor decisions. Giannis fought through double and triple teams, unable to find his touch.

The Raptors torched the Bucks in game 4. Giannis looked exhausted, taking hard fouls, trying to finish through contact. The Raptors knew how to draw him out of the paint and force him into his weakness. At one point, Giannis even airballed a free throw.

He continued to push, but the Bucks crumbled in clutch situations. They had led for over thirty-five minutes of game 5 but had a fourth-quarter meltdown and lost. They had led once again for much of game 6 before losing again, and ultimately losing the series in six after a 26–3 Toronto run in the final game. Worse, Giannis didn't play nearly as many minutes as he could have, which led many to think that Budenholzer underutilized him—a far cry from how Kidd would run Giannis so ragged it looked like Giannis wouldn't be able to stand up without help. It would be one of the many times fans and media would criticize and question Budenholzer's seemingly odd coaching decisions.

Losing the series was devastating. Mind-boggling. To come that far, to have squandered a 2–0 lead and come up empty-handed. It became glaringly clear to Giannis how different the regular season and the playoffs were. How best records didn't mean much if one fell apart in the postseason.

"I think it's just the start of a long journey," Giannis said after the game. "We're going to get better. We're going to come back next year and believe in who we are, believe in what we've built this year."

Some players shed tears in the locker room. Many were in shock. "Giannis wanted it *so* bad," Frazier says. "It was a learning experience for him. Being a leader, everybody is looking at *you*."

"I know Giannis put a lot of it on himself."

* * *

Giannis didn't sleep for two days. He lay in bed at night, wide awake, thinking. Hurting. It was the kind of hurt that lingers. Nothing can be done about it. It would leave when it was ready to leave.

2–0.

It's hard to move on from something like that. You think you have something, and then it slips away. You *let* it slip away. A sixty-win season. You want to be proud for having come that far, but coming far doesn't get you farther.

Always want more, but never be greedy.

Giannis missed his father, his sayings. A lot. Charles would have been really proud of him. Would know exactly what to say in this moment.

Giannis tried to walk around the city that Sunday. He was touched by how many people he saw wearing Bucks gear two days after the loss. How things had changed. Back when Milwaukee sports shops carried mostly Chicago Bulls gear, very little Bucks gear. Back when some people were embarrassed to even say out loud they were Bucks fans.

Some people walking by saw him that day. Smiled. Didn't interrupt his walk, his peace. That he can do that, in this city, is still comforting for him.

His mind drifted. *What could I have done better? What do I need to change?* He started thinking about the summer ahead, the things he was going to work on. How much better he needed to be to make sure he never felt this way again.

CHAPTER 14

MVP

Kostas and Thanasis flew to Milwaukee to stay with Giannis and Alex the week before the NBA Awards, which was to be held in Los Angeles. Giannis's brothers wanted to be there in case Giannis won MVP. On the day of the ceremony, in late June 2019, Giannis, his brothers, and Veronica took a private jet to LA.

Alex kept peppering Giannis with questions on the plane: "What if you win?" The brothers started talking about winning a championship next season too. It still hurt, coming that close. But on this morning, they were just excited for what was ahead that night.

An Escalade greeted them when they arrived. When Giannis wasn't looking, Alex and Kostas whispered to Saratsis, one of his agents, also in the car, about the MVP: "Come on, bro—tell us if he's going to win or not!" Saratsis wouldn't budge. He genuinely didn't know, and he didn't want to predict a win and then end up disappointed. Alex insisted: "Bro, just tell us right now. Does he win or not?"

"I don't know," Saratsis said. "We're just going to have to wait and see. Have faith."

They arrived at the ceremony dressed in striking colors: Giannis in a dark navy suit with a depiction of the Parthenon on the inside lining, his way of honoring Greece; Thanasis in a bright orange suit; Kostas in a light pink suit; Alex in a dark purple suit; Mariah in an elegant black strapless dress; and Veronica in a gorgeous ruby pantsuit with a gold-plated necklace. Veronica did her own makeup, her own hair. She always has. It made sense to her to make sure she put together her entire outfit herself on such a momentous occasion.

They could feel Charles there.

When the ceremony began, Giannis whispered to his brothers, "Aye! If I win, I want you guys to come up with me."

Alex was floored. His gut reaction was no. "We didn't think we could handle it. I knew I would bust out crying," Alex says. Alex kept quiet, but Kostas was a bit more assertive. "No," Kostas said. "We can't go up with you, bro."

Alex started to reconsider. "Maybe we should go?"

Thanasis, being the oldest, made a decision. He looked at Giannis. "It's *your* moment, bro," Thanasis said. "You go by yourself."

"Thanasis was too emotional to even talk to," Alex says.

They all were. But after Thanasis said his piece, Kostas and Alex realized that Thanasis was right, of course. Giannis *should* go up alone. "This is the moment he's going to remember for the rest of his life, and we wanted it to be *his* moment," Alex says. "We were with him, but it's stuff he was going through where *nobody* was with him, and he was by himself, so we wanted him to be by himself when we went up there."

Giannis vowed that if he won, he wasn't going to cry. His brothers couldn't promise the same.

They waited and waited. And then the moment finally came. Adam Silver announced Giannis as the 2019 MVP.

Giannis, the one who, when drafted, some analysts had pondered whether he should play in the development league or in Europe for a few years. Giannis, the one who once said he'd do anything in his power to prove to Milwaukee that he was a worthy pick, a worthy person.

He was the first Buck to win MVP since Abdul-Jabbar in 1973–1974. Silver handed him the MVP trophy, and Giannis took a few breaths, stared at the award he held in his hands, the sheer weight of it making the surreal moment feel real.

"Oh man," Giannis said, looking at the floor. "Man, I'm nervous. OK."

He took a deep breath. "So, first of all, I want to thank God. For blessing me with this amazing talent—I wouldn't be in this position I am today." He paused, trying to compose himself. "Hold on." He took a step back. "OK, OK." Sensing that he was overcome with emotion, the audience cheered.

And then Giannis started to wipe his eyes, tried to prevent himself from letting a tear resting in the corner of his eye fall. "I want to thank God for putting me in this amazing position I am today. Everything I do, I do it through him. I'm extremely blessed, and I realize that, and so I thank God." He kept looking at the floor, shaking his head, the magnitude of what was happening seeping into his body.

"I want to thank my teammates. It takes more than one person to win sixty games," he said. He thanked his coaches for pushing the team, believing in them. "I want to thank the front office, the ownership, for believing in me when I was eighteen years old," he said, finally breaking down. "When I was back in Greece." He could no longer try to speak through his tears. He covered his face one last time before they streamed down his cheeks.

Hearing his name, realizing the years of hard work he had given, the sacrifices his parents had made for him, for his brothers, he felt all of it rush through him.

He thanked the city of Milwaukee; he thanked Greece; he thanked Nigeria. All these places that have made him, *him*. He recalled childhood days of waking up at 5:00 a.m. to watch the NBA when it came on in Sepolia.

"I want to thank my dad. Obviously my dad is not here with me, but . . ." His voice trailed off. Veronica clapped. It was impossible to not feel his pain. How far he had come: a little boy sleeping in the corner of a run-down gym, determined to become somebody. "Two years ago, I had the goal in my head that I know I'm going to be the best player in the league. I'm going to do whatever it takes to help my team win, and I'm going to win the MVP. Every day that I step on the floor, I always think about my dad—and that motivates me and pushes me to play harder and move forward even when my body is sore. Even when I don't feel like playing.

"I want to thank my amazing brothers, you know—I love you guys, man," he said, patting his chest, his heart, through tears. Kostas and Alex covered their eyes, put their heads down, as they too cried.

"You guys are my ride-or-die. You guys are my role models, man. I look up to you guys. Thank you for everything you guys do. And I want to thank my amazing mom. She's my hero." Veronica wiped a stray tear on her cheek. "When you're a little kid, you don't see the future, right? Your parent sees the future for you," Giannis continued. "She always saw the future in us; she always believed in us; she was always there for us; she is the foundation of this family. You are my true hero.

"At the end of the day, this is just the beginning. My goal is to win a championship," he said. "We're going to do whatever it takes to make that happen." He took one last look at his brothers before leaving the stage.

Alex always knew his big brother was great—but now the entire world knew. "I'm lost for words," Alex says. "Knowing that's your brother, somebody you live in the same house with, someone you work out with, is the greatest player in the world's greatest basketball league." He pauses. "It's unbelievable."

Kostas had never wanted to emulate Giannis more than in that moment. "When he won MVP, it was like we all won MVP," Kostas says. "We're really grateful for what God has given us." As he watched Giannis on stage, Kostas thought of all the times Giannis sweat through his shirt, his shorts, during ball-handling drills. All the times he and Alex were there, getting Giannis's rebounds, tossing pass after pass to him, hoping each one was perfect, had enough *oomph*.

"You just feel like when your brother accomplishes his goal, it's your own goal too," Kostas says.

Giannis has always wanted to make it for his brothers. He has always wanted to be able to provide for *them*. He has always wanted to be a decent man for *them*.

*   *   *

Three days later, they were all back in Greece for the launch of Giannis's first signature shoe, the Nike Zoom Freak 1, set to debut the following month. Giannis became the first international player to have his own Nike signature shoe at just twenty-four.

It was unfathomable, having his own Nike signature shoe, something that didn't seem possible to Giannis growing up in Sepolia, when he was just grateful to be sharing one pair with Thanasis.

Even his rookie season in America, back in 2013, when the Bucks kept handing him shoes, he felt so uncomfortable receiving them—like one person should never be able to have that many when so many people don't have any.

Launching the Nike Zoom Freak in Greece was a way to honor his homeland and family. The Freak 1 titled "All Bros," a navy-and-orange version, had "I Am My Father's Legacy" etched on the sole. The names of Giannis's parents, Veronica and Charles, plus his brothers, Thanasis, Kostas, Alex, and Francis, were also inscribed. Giannis's logo—GA—plus number 34 and an image of the Greek flag were also displayed on the heel. Another version of the sneaker, "Roses," came in red, white, and gold, Charles's three favorite colors.

Giannis gushed to reporters that the shoe really wasn't just his shoe; it belonged to all his brothers. They helped him design it. He asked Veronica for her input, too, especially with choosing colors: her favorite color combination is black and white.

"This is *our* shoe," Giannis kept repeating to reporters, introducing the shoe.

Hundreds of locals came to see him, his family, the sneaker, as it was unveiled in the columned atrium of Athens's Zappeion. The prestigious Zappeion was the host of a fencing competition in the first modern Olympic Games in 1896.

Many of Giannis's former Greek national-team teammates came to support him, including Nikos Zisis. "It was amazing," Zisis says. Zisis and his own sons now wear Giannis's sneakers. "I'm really proud of him."

Every time Giannis was asked about winning MVP on the trip, he downplayed it. Reinforced that he was the same guy. "I'll always remember my roots. I remember where I'm from," he told reporters that day. "MVP is great, but I will not change."

He'd often get upset when Mariah or anyone else in his family told him how good he was, how he was one of the world's best. "No I'm not," he'd say, not wanting to relax. Not even for a second. He told reporters he felt he had reached only 60 percent of his potential and asked them not to call him MVP anymore.

Fans visited the Filathlitikos gym as part of the sneaker-release festivities. Behind one basket, a white Nike banner featured a picture of Giannis dunking, surrounded by the words "Fate can start you at the bottom. Dreams can take you to the top." Zografou's mayor, Vassilis Thodas, went to the front of the gym to announce that the gym name was being changed to AntetokounBros to honor Giannis and his brothers.

The little kids watching Giannis that day were in awe. That this person, this superstar, came from *here*. This gym. These walls. Back when it had leaky showers, cracked windows. Back when he had to take bus after bus just to make it on time. They saw the photos of him, now framed near the entrance: skinny Giannis in his red uniform, baby-faced and unsmiling, determined.

Kids started shooting around. One of the leaders of the event described to some kids how to Eurostep like Giannis, demonstrating the steps. Giannis came over, corrected him. "You're explaining it badly," Giannis said—jokingly but not so jokingly. This was his signature move; the kids needed to know how to do it right. "You're explaining the *regular* Eurostep," Giannis said, "but this is not how *I* do it." Giannis took the ball, ran to the three-point line, and then showed how he zoomed to the basket in two steps, starting with a high bounce of a ball and *then* the Eurostep.

Then some teenagers organized into groups of three-on-three for a tournament. Before the game, Giannis talked to them about being unique. About not being afraid to stand out. He was wearing his Nike "Freak" shirt, a nod to his Greek Freak nickname. "Guys, being a freak is *not* a bad thing," Giannis said. He spoke with an air of authority but also of sincerity, of someone who understood what it was like to be called *different*. Called *weird*. Glanced at strangely, bullied.

But the way he talked about being a freak, on this day, smiling in his warm, inviting way, made being unique sound . . . awesome.

"Being a freak makes you different," Giannis continued, "but different doesn't mean bad. Different is good."

*   *   *

Later that year, when the 2019–2020 season began, expectations rose even higher for the Bucks. After winning sixty games the previous season, the Bucks were expected to contend for the title. And with Kawhi Leonard joining the Clippers out west, the Eastern Conference seemed more open. The 76ers were formidable, but the Bucks were ready to compete.

There was also more pressure to win, given that, in about a year from that point, Giannis would be eligible to sign the supermax extension. With so much movement across the league, highlighted by James moving to the Lakers the year before, there was even more speculation about whether Giannis would leave Milwaukee for a bigger-market team or stay loyal to his home base.

Giannis didn't say much when asked about his future. He was just happy that the Bucks had signed Thanasis to a contract in July 2019. The two were finally on the same team again. It could be seen as a move to court Giannis to stay with the franchise, but, still, with Alex being a senior at Dominican, it was a dream come true to have them in the same city again.

"Giannis and Thanasis both play with so much intensity, so much energy," says Marvin Williams, a forward who joined the Bucks in 2020. Williams often noticed how Thanasis, despite not playing many minutes, pushed Giannis during practice, was always in his ear. "You can tell they genuinely don't take anything for granted. They prepare with a different attitude."

Giannis looked even bigger, even more chiseled, than he had the previous season. And he appeared even more dominant, dropping fifty points against the Jazz in late November. He averaged more than thirty points and thirteen rebounds in an impressive thirty minutes per game—his lowest minute total since 2013–2014, given Budenholzer's preference to rest him.

As incredible as he was playing, he still didn't want people to think they needed to do things for him just because he was an MVP. The Bucks video coordinators would bring a towel to wipe up the floor after Giannis's workouts because his sweat would drip everywhere, but Giannis would always grab the towel from them and insist that he wipe the floor himself. Giannis didn't think he was above doing that, any more than when he was back in Sepolia, mopping the Zografou court.

One afternoon, Giannis attended a Wisconsin Herd game, the Bucks minor-league affiliate, as Thanasis had been signed to a two-way contract with the Herd. As Giannis walked through the tunnel near the court, he saw a young man mopping the floor in the hallway.

"Good work in there—I see you out there," Giannis said to the young man, giving him a fist bump.

The young man, Gout Deng, was stunned. He was an intern for the Herd and didn't expect Giannis to be at the game, let alone say anything to him. He certainly didn't expect Giannis to say anything to him after that. But after the game was over, Giannis was about to walk out of the arena when he paused, turned around, and looked right at Deng. Something in him was pulled toward Deng, who was still hunched over, mopping the floor. Giannis walked over.

"What's your name?" Giannis said.

"Gout."

"How old are you?"

"Nineteen."

"Oh, really? Well, when I was around your age, sixteen, seventeen, I used to mop the floor too."

"No, you're lying—you're kidding." Gout laughed.

"No, no, I'm serious. I really used to do this when I was younger. Growing up, it was tough, and I had to make money in some way by doing some sort of work, and that's what I did. I was in your position. And when I saw you earlier, I told Thanasis that I saw myself in you, mopping that floor. Being that young kid."

Gout could barely speak. "I'm looking at myself like, 'What does he see in *me*?'" Deng says now. "It was insane. Just amazing." Then Giannis asked about his background.

Deng told him that he and his family were immigrants too. Deng was born in Cairo, Egypt; his parents were originally from Sudan. The family then immigrated to Oshkosh, Wisconsin, when Deng was two. He had grown up there. Deng then told Giannis that he too had four brothers. He was also close with his mother, as his dad was not around.

The similarities between them were striking. They both saw themselves in each other. Gout saw the superhero he wanted to be, Giannis the determined young kid he used to be. Giannis asked Deng what he wanted to do with his life.

"I'm a basketball player too," Deng told him. He had helped his high school to a state championship and wants to play college basketball and work in the NBA one day.

"I was where you are, and look where I am now," Giannis told him. "It is achievable. It is attainable. As long as you put in the hard work. You can do anything you set your mind to. I believe in you."

Deng had never had anybody tell him that before. That he was capable, that he could accomplish what he dreamed. When he asked Giannis if he could take a picture with him, he looked around to see if there was anybody who could take one. Giannis laughed. "No, no, I want you to take the pic! Like a selfie!"

The two smiled as Deng snapped the photo. It is a moment he thinks about often. The thought of Giannis pushes him. Makes him want to live up to those expectations. Deng has visions of one day working in the NBA, and seeing Giannis, and telling him that he did it. He achieved his dream.

* * *

It seemed like Giannis might be able to achieve his own dreams in 2020, given that the Bucks were looking like the best team in the NBA, on pace to win seventy games. Milwaukee went on an eighteen-game winning streak that stretched into December, ending on a loss to the Mavericks, though Giannis still scored forty-eight in that game.

But it was against Anthony Davis, LeBron James, and the Lakers that Giannis truly made a statement. LA came to Milwaukee in late December 2019 in one of the most anticipated showdowns of the season. Both teams stood atop the league.

One play, Davis sagged so far off Giannis that Giannis had no choice but to launch the three.

He made it.

As Giannis ran back on defense, he winked. The Lakers called a time-out, and Giannis did the unthinkable: he raised his hands over his head and made a circle with his fingers, placing an invisible sphere above his head. He was crowning himself king, living up to his Nigerian name, Ade.

"I wear the crown now," he seemed to say to the Bucks bench as he walked toward his teammates. It was an astonishing moment—and not just because James's nickname was King James. It was that Giannis finally understood his power, his worth. He was letting everyone know that *he* was the best player in the league.

"It finally felt like Milwaukee was truly at or past the level of a huge market juggernaut like the Lakers, which just hadn't been the case since Kareem left—my and plenty of other fans' whole lifetimes," says Ti Windisch, who covers the Bucks as cohost of the *Gyro Step* podcast. "It wasn't just audacious to be audacious; it really lifted up and emboldened Bucks fans to a place most of them had rarely, if ever, been—believing their team would be world champions."

After dominating with thirty-four points, including five threes, eleven rebounds, seven assists, a steal, and a block in just thirty-two minutes, to lead the Bucks to a win, Giannis almost seemed overwhelmed by the moment when talking to media afterward. He was taking in the magnitude of assuming a crown that was never meant for him. Never meant for somebody who comes from where he came from.

"I wasn't supposed to be here," Giannis said that night. "I wasn't the number-one pick. AD was. LeBron was. I wasn't supposed to be here."

Afterward, Giannis found Thanasis and Kostas, who was there now that he was a member of the Lakers' G League team. They all posed for a picture, feeling grateful to be there, three brothers in the NBA.

"It's hard," Giannis says, thinking about Alex coming up fourth, "when you see your brothers are doing good things, getting drafted. I know Alex is in a tough position seeing his three brothers getting drafted and thinking, *What is going to happen to me?* He wants it *so* bad."

Giannis reminds Alex that he can get there. He has the talent. And although Alex can't see it now, Giannis reminds Alex that he too couldn't see his own potential. Giannis had coaches point it out to him, put him in positions to succeed. "They saw the vision for me and helped me," Giannis would often tell Alex. "So I'm going to help you see the vision for you."

Oftentimes Giannis would think about how Alex must be processing the attention around him. How Alex might question himself, thinking, *If I'm not going to be as good as my brothers, should I just quit?* And then a reassuring thought pops into Giannis's head. That would never happen. "That's not Alex," Giannis says. "When something is in Alex's mind, he will do it. He is so determined. He is so stubborn. Our whole family is determined to keep going."

So Giannis would remind Alex, "In one year from now, you're going to be a completely different player. You're going to be way better."

"Yeah, but *how?*" Alex asked.

"Bro. Do you trust me?" Giannis said. "I've been there before. I've been in your shoes. I know what you feel. As long as you work hard, as long as you put the effort in, believe in yourself, you're gonna be better."

Alex wanted success *now*. But he couldn't speed up time. "Alex has this mentality of 'OK. My brothers have done it; I have to do it too,'" Kostas says. "But Alex is better than all of us at his age."

His brothers told him to keep faith, and now that Thanasis was in Milwaukee too, he was receiving in-game advice from both older brothers. Giannis and Thanasis would pull Alex aside at halftime of Alex's games, speak to him in Greek about what he needed to improve on. "When you're young, you don't know; you've never worked in your life," Giannis says. "I'm prepping Alex to be a pro, same thing I did with Kostas. Kostas didn't know what being a pro was until he went to the G League. It's making sure you have your fruit, your water, taking care of your body. I didn't know that my first year, my second year."

Like Giannis, Alex is known for his uncanny athleticism and versatility. He handles the ball like a guard and loves shooting the three, his skill set "so far ahead of everyone else as far as overall talent," says Jim Gosz, Alex's coach at Dominican High School, "[showing] signs of greatness at times."

When he wanted to. When he wasn't questioning himself. Or the plan. It was complicated. Alex wanted to be his own man. Alex wanted to be a combination of his brothers. The dream was his. The dream was theirs. "My end goal is not to be better than Giannis," Alex says. "My end goal is to be the best version of my own self. I just happen to think that the best version of my own self could possibly surpass what my brother's doing right now, which—I don't even think that's the best version of him."

So Alex stayed in the gym. Hardly took breaks. "I have to tell him, 'Alex, come home. Come and eat,'" Veronica says. But he didn't want to. He wanted to play with Giannis. When he wasn't with Giannis, Alex was in the family's basement. His spot. Where he went to think. To play video games. To stare at the handful of framed jerseys from his older brothers, wondering when he will earn a spot on the cream-colored walls.

There's Thanasis's Greek All-Star Game jersey and Kostas's Mavericks jersey. There's Giannis's NBA All-Star Game jerseys; the jersey he wore when torching the 76ers for fifty-two in March; and his first-ever Greek national team jersey, blue and white, which Giannis had all his brothers sign. Giannis might not own a more meaningful jersey, even though the adjacent wall showcases signed jerseys from some of his friends: Dirk Nowitzki, Dwyane Wade, and Vince Carter.

Alex didn't feel worthy of pinning his high school jersey on the wall; he was waiting for his NBA jersey. He points to a block of blank space. "That's the spot for me."

He felt certain he would be on that wall.

He felt uncertain he would be on that wall.

"I second-guess myself a lot," Alex says.

That is to say, he was a normal seventeen-year-old kid.

But he was not a normal seventeen-year-old kid.

Giannis would remind him he had a ways to go. That if Alex trusted him, believed in him, he'd be able to accomplish what Giannis had. Giannis was just always *there*. Thanasis and Kostas were always there too, but Alex and Giannis had a unique bond. Not just because the way they play was similar but because the way they *thought* was similar. Giannis was more outspoken, and Alex was shier, but when they stepped on the court, they believed they were the most dominant.

Giannis was often talked about as if he was genetically invincible. *A freak.* But people missed his *mind.* The fuel he finds late in fourth quarters has nothing to do with his vertical jump. His wingspan. That's why he was trying to teach Alex to not get in his own head. *Maybe this isn't for me,* Alex sometimes thought. He'd felt pressure, though he said he didn't believe in pressure.

"I couldn't imagine going through what he has to go through," says Magee, Alex's teammate and close friend. "With all the outside noise, he can't really be himself. Like, he is himself, but he can't be himself without somebody trying to compare him to Giannis.

"He's just a kid."

But he was no longer a kid. After the brothers lost their father, time kept speeding up, kept rewinding. Both Alex and Giannis kept repeating their father's sayings, as if to keep his memory alive. His legacy.

Alex didn't have time to fear not meeting expectations. Not reaching the heights Giannis has. So he kept pushing. He kept saying "When I get drafted" rather than "If I get drafted."

Sometimes, he was less sure. He spent so much time with Giannis, out at games, living an adult life, state to state, country to country, that he had less time to focus on school. His grades suffered. So low that he might not have qualified for a Division I scholarship, which is why he only had two college offers at the time.

Giannis always checked on Alex with Gosz, Dominican's coach, bringing up concerns: Alex has been late to school. We need to get Alex back on path. Alex has two big games—has he done his homework? The red carpet had been laid out for Alex in ways it hadn't for Giannis. Alex received a lot of attention on the road, as first, second, third graders, all wearing his and Giannis's jerseys, waited for his autograph. It was as if he had already made it. Already was where Giannis is. It seemed overseas might be the best choice, then aim for the NBA.

He struggled at a tournament in South Dakota. He felt like he'd played the three worst games of his career. "First thing I had to do was call my brother," Alex says.

"Yeah, I'm not playing too good. I don't know if this is for me," Alex said.

"Are you playing hard?" Giannis asked.

"Yeah."

"Are you giving it all you have?"

"Yeah. I'm just not playing good."

"How so? If you're playing hard, and you're doing everything you possibly think you can, then you're playing great. Your shots aren't always going to fall, but you can play hard and be a leader. That's all you can make sure you do every game. You can go one hundred percent every game."

Giannis hung up. The call had lasted a minute. Giannis was frugal with his words. He gave Alex just enough to chew on. Just enough to let him figure things out for himself. That's the only way Alex was going to grow up, into his own man: he had to decide if he was willing to give everything to make it.

* * *

Just as the Bucks were playing the best basketball of the season, they were stopped cold by grief. Kobe Bryant; his thirteen-year-old daughter, Gigi; and seven of Gigi's teammates and their family members and coaches had died in a helicopter crash on January 26, 2020, a tragedy of unspeakable magnitude.

Giannis had watched Kobe since he was a child. Worn his sneakers, emulated his dunks. His first NBA triple-double came against Kobe. His notebooks are filled with advice from Kobe. It was Kobe who challenged him to win MVP.

Giannis was so hurt, so broken by the news. He temporarily deleted his Instagram and Twitter accounts. He didn't know what to say when reporters asked how Kobe's death affected him. He held back tears. "Everybody deals with tragedy in their own way," he said. He wanted to keep his pain private, much like he had when his father died.

He thought about all the things he'd learned from Kobe: how to work hard, how to be fearless, how to not care what people say, how to do your job and have a smile on your face, how to sacrifice family time for this game.

He first thought that playing basketball that day, after Kobe's death, would help him feel better, much like it had when he went to the gym after Charles's death. But he was still crushed. He slowly opened up to reporters that day. "At the end of the day," Giannis said, "you think to yourself, *Is this worth it? Playing basketball for twenty years and then being gone. Is actually going through all this pressure, all this media, all this, is this actually worth it?*

"For me," he said, "it's definitely worth it."

But the thoughts lingered. It did with his brothers too, as they knew how much Kobe meant to Giannis. "I thought, *Kobe? Literally* Kobe?" Alex says. "*Nothing's going to happen to Kobe.*" It reminded Alex of one of Thanasis's sayings: "Nobody is untouchable."

Kobe's death reminded Kostas to be more appreciative. "You can't take life for granted," Kostas says. "Every time you come out here, you get an opportunity. You have to give it everything you've got."

Thanasis took that to heart as the season wore on. He was mostly coming in at cleanup time, after the Bucks had a big lead. But he hustled hard, as if they were the most important few minutes of his life. They were. He had worked hard to be respected in his own right, through disappointment after disappointment, going back overseas when Giannis was succeeding in America. And now that they could do it together? That was something nobody could take away from them.

"Everything I went through, I'm so happy," Thanasis says. "The thing is, it's not how much you work. It's not *work hard, work hard*. The key is actually patience. I been learning that. My dad made me like that: be patient, because you can grow into so much, persevering through these hardships."

Giannis and Thanasis started in the same game against the Nuggets in February 2020. It was special for both of them but reminded Thanasis of the first time Veronica and Charles had come to watch them play, back when they were kids. "Just seeing them cheer for us." Thanasis breaks into a giant smile, making sure to add, "And we won."

A few weeks later, Thanasis, Giannis, and Kostas all attended Alex's game at Dominican. It was senior night, and for the first time, all of them watched Alex play at the same time (Kostas had flown in from LA and surprised them).

Alex kept looking over to his brothers in the stands, all wearing black hooded sweatshirts with "Antetokounmpo 34" on the back in white letters. They carried green-and-white balloons, Dominican's colors. Veronica, in a black hat, was also there, in her customary spot: top left corner.

Alex wanted to put on a show for them. He showed a little bit of swagger in layup lines, but not too much, in the way younger brothers do when they are trying to impress their big brothers. "You could just see the glow in Alex," Gosz says. Before the game, Alex's brothers handed him flowers and balloons.

The game started, and Alex looked dominant. He rebounded the ball, went coast-to-coast, muscled his way to the basket for a quick layup. Giannis stood up, clapped. The brothers got even more vocal as the game went on, screaming in Greek, especially Thanasis: "Get back on D!" Giannis screamed out, "Screen, screen!" in Greek, warning Alex of the coming pick—as if he wanted to jump out of the stands and protect his baby brother from getting clocked.

When Alex made an and-one putback, screaming with the mean-mug face he'd seen Giannis do so many times, Giannis leaped out of his seat and was so impressed he walked down to the bottom, near the court, and screamed, "Let's gooooo!"

"My brothers all told me they were proud of me," Alex says. "They said I handled the pressure as good as anybody. That meant a lot coming from them."

When Alex reflects on that moment, he ranks it alongside other life moments that happened that year. "Giannis winning MVP, senior night, and my nephew being born—those are the best moments of my life."

Yes, his nephew—Giannis's first son—was born earlier that month. Giannis announced that Mariah gave birth to Liam Charles Antetokounmpo on February 10, 2020.

Giannis was so happy now that he was a father. He's always wanted a son. And that son came at the right time in his life. Still grieving his father, Giannis was ready to have a family of his own.

And his son is just like him. He already has sparks of personality. "He's got the best qualities from his mom and dad," Alex says. Then he laughs, thinking of how many adult mannerisms Liam already has. "He's like a grown person in a tiny-person body. He brings that same sparkle, that same energy, that a grown person would bring. That same positive energy."

The brothers wonder if Liam will play basketball. A lot of people ask them about it: Will they be upset if Liam doesn't like basketball? "Our love for each other was there way before basketball even came in the picture," Alex says. "We don't know what he wants to pursue. He might grow up and say, 'I want to do what my father and uncles do.' Or he might grow up and say, 'I have something different I'm interested in.' At the end of the day, whatever he chooses, we're going to support him fully."

DeVon Jackson, Dominican's assistant coach, remembers a conversation with Giannis about parenthood and basketball, as Jackson's son had just begun playing hoops. Giannis had asked Jackson how into basketball Jackson's son was, how he reacted when he first started going to practice.

"Whatever you do," Giannis told Jackson, "you give him a basketball, but don't do anything else after that. Don't try to coach him. That's what my dad did to me: he gave me a basketball, but he didn't try to teach me. He didn't put me in camps. I just started to love it on my own."

CHAPTER 15

HOME

A couple of hours before tip-off against the Thunder, a game in late February 2020, Giannis walked out to the court and began shooting close near the basket. He was the first out, as usual.

Kareem Abdul-Jabbar, in town for the game, later showed up courtside. Milwaukee fans greeted him with warm applause. He smiled, settling into his seat.

Looking at both men, here at Fiserv Forum, was eerie. In a matter of months, Giannis would be forced to decide whether to stay and sign the supermax extension or leave Milwaukee.

Leave like Abdul-Jabbar did.

The two men couldn't be more different, not just in terms of playing style but in terms of demeanor. Abdul-Jabbar kept his distance from fans. Wanted to be in a bigger city. Wanted the bright lights. Giannis was more gregarious and warm to fans and didn't seem to see the allure of living in a bigger city. He liked the quiet, the peace, of Milwaukee.

As different as they are, they represent something very similar to this city: hope. Some Bucks fans haven't allowed themselves to hope, to fully love their hero without fearing him leaving.

"We're still waiting for that championship after fifty years," says Dan Schnoll, a fifty-two-year-old Milwaukee native and lifelong fan whose family had season tickets in the 1970s and 1980s. "We've just never been able to get over that hump."

It is the Milwaukee mentality to have hopeful worry but to believe any-way, failed draft after failed draft. To love anyway, earning eighth seed after eighth seed. But to watch Giannis, at a time when the Bucks were once again on track for the NBA's best regular-season record, was to realize how far Milwaukee has come and to maybe even lean into the tantalizing possibility that history might not repeat itself. That the hero might stay.

*   *   *

Ashok Hermon, a Bucks guest-service attendant, hovered over a rail near the press section as the Thunder ran out onto the court. "Giannis means everything to us," Hermon said. "I'm hoping, keeping my fingers crossed, that he sticks around." It made him nervous, not knowing what would happen: "I can't control it. I can't do anything about it."

A couple of rows down and to the middle sat Kelvin and Sharonda Robinson. They've been watching the Bucks all their lives. "I kind of get the impression that he's not a person that would just leave us hanging," Kelvin said. Sharonda was a little more measured. She wasn't as sure. She chose to focus on gratitude. "I'm appreciative that he's here," she said, as if contemplating what could happen is too stressful to acknowledge. "I'm appreciative of his journey."

Matthew Smith, a fan standing with his kids near the far end of the court, opened up about his concerns. "I'm worried he's going to leave," Smith said. "Hopefully ownership has enough pieces around him to keep him here and pay him all the money he's worth. Because what he's worth is more than a financial impact. It's worth all these kids here having an idol to look up to."

Andy Carpenter, a longtime fan, steeled himself for the worst. "I want the best for Giannis, like a child, like, he might love someone else—but I just want him to be happy," Carpenter said. "He deserves everything and then some. I was prepared for, you know." He paused. "I would still root for the Bucks."

But for this night, Bucks fans could lose themselves in the joy. The fun. They watched Giannis zoom up and down the court, dunking with ease. They watched Thanasis come off the bench, score on a driving layup off a screen.

One section sang Biz Markie's "Just a Friend" at the top of their lungs, "Oh, baby, you, you got what I neeeed!" during a timeout when the game was well in hand, the Bucks up by thirty. They swayed side to side, smiling, laughing. Dreaming.

* * *

And then, suddenly, the dream was interrupted. Paused. The world shut down as the COVID-19 pandemic infected millions throughout the world. The NBA shut down the season about two weeks after that Thunder game, when Utah Jazz center Rudy Gobert tested positive on March 11.

Giannis gave $100,000 to Fiserv Forum staff to help workers stay afloat. He spent quarantine playing with baby Liam, taking up guitar. He found ways to shoot around and do home workouts, but it wasn't the same.

He felt lost without basketball. Without the momentum of the season. The Bucks had looked like a championship contender, but with the future of the season uncertain, none of it really mattered anymore.

Police killed George Floyd, a forty-six-year-old Black man, in May 2020, as well as Breonna Taylor, a twenty-six-year-old Black woman, who'd been sleeping in her home when she was murdered in March 2020. The killings sparked worldwide protests against police brutality and systemic racism.

Giannis and several Bucks teammates, including Thanasis, Sterling Brown, Donte DiVincenzo, Brook Lopez, and Frank Mason III, as well as Mariah and Liam, joined the protests in Milwaukee. They wore "I can't breathe" shirts, referencing Eric Garner, another Black man killed by police.

Giannis brought water and snacks for protesters, telling the crowd, "This is our city, man. We want change. We want justice."

"This is for unity," Giannis said. "I want my kid to grow up here in Milwaukee and not be scared to walk in the street. I want the city of Milwaukee to know I'm here."

And later, in early 2021, Giannis was even more explicit: "My kid is going to grow up here in America, and my kid is Black. I cannot imagine my kid going through what I see on TV."

"For a person like Giannis to just say, 'This is how close this is to *me*; what's happening with racial injustice in this country impacts me too,' it creates this sense of connection to so many other people who also have that experience and also have that fear," says Francesca Hong, representative of the Seventy-Sixth District of the Wisconsin State Assembly, who is a big Bucks fan. "He's taking what is a collective fear and helping to transform it into something good with the hope that he brings to this city.

"Those types of words resonate with more people than I think even he realizes," Hong says.

Former NBA player turned broadcaster Chris Webber and Clippers coach Doc Rivers poured their hearts out on camera, describing what it was like to be Black in America. To be constantly surveilled, mistreated, disenfranchised, killed by police. "We're the ones getting killed. We're the ones getting shot. We're the ones, that we're denied to live in certain communities," Rivers said. "It's amazing why we keep loving this country, and this country does not love us back. It's just, it's really so sad."

The Athletic's Marcus Thompson II wrote, "The very athletes we typically shroud with affection, with all their wealth and fame, can't shake the rage either. To not listen, to not watch, to turn away, is essentially affirming the very foundational ideology that produces the rage. It is all born of the frustration and anger of being human yet not being fully recognized for that."

Players debated whether or not they should continue the season, in order to focus their efforts toward protesting police brutality and advocating for racial justice full-time, especially given that they were performing for a largely white audience who didn't face the same violence at the hands of the state that they did.

"Why help the most comfortable Americans lull themselves more ardently to sleep?" wrote Vinson Cunningham of the *New Yorker*. "Why act like life was normal when it wasn't?"

Shortly after Giannis's comments at the protests, a mural of him back home, in Athens, was desecrated with swastikas. Greece had changed in some ways but hadn't much changed in others. Golden Dawn was found guilty of running a criminal organization in the ongoing trial that culminated in October 2020. It had lasted more than five years, with 69 defendants—and 120 witnesses for the prosecution. It was a historic result, but Neo-Nazism was still alive and well. New groups have formed, such as the Greek Solution.

About 16,500 asylum seekers were stuck on Greece's Aegean Islands, living in squalor, prompting Human Rights Watch to call it a "forgotten emergency." Migrants waited months, years, for papers, for salvation. To make matters worse, the European Union's border agency, Frontex, helped hide Greece's illegal practice of pushing back migrants to Turkey, helping to cover up the violations. Then, in November 2020, Moria, Europe's largest refugee camp, on the Greek island of Lesbos, was set on fire by an angry group of its inhabitants, leaving 12,600 people homeless. Stranded.

*   *   *

The NBA returned in late July, with teams stationed in a "bubble" near Orlando at Disney World. It was strange, not having fans in the stands, living so close to competitors. That was something Giannis wasn't used to. He said it would be the toughest championship one could ever win because of the difficult circumstances.

He did his best to work out, to stay in shape, but it was taxing not having the same routine. Still, he refused to complain about how small his living quarters were, remembering how his apartments growing up in Greece had been so much smaller.

But as playoffs began, the Bucks struggled against the Magic in the opening round, dropping game 1. They came back to win the next two games, taking a commanding 3–1 lead, but their attention soon shifted.

Police shot Jacob Blake, a Black man from Kenosha, Wisconsin, about forty miles from Milwaukee, in the back seven times in front of Blake's children. Led by veteran George Hill, the Bucks refused to emerge from the locker room to face the Magic in game 5.

Milwaukee's wildcat strike was a watershed moment in NBA players' protests against police brutality. It inspired other teams to contemplate their own forms of protest. The Houston Rockets and Oklahoma City Thunder, the Lakers and the Blazers, didn't play either. WNBA players, long at the forefront of the fight for racial justice, wore white T-shirts with Blake's name on the front and seven bullet holes on the back, the number

of times Blake had been shot. That led to protests in Major League Baseball and Major League Soccer and on the Women's Tennis Association
circuit, led by Naomi Osaka.

ESPN's Howard Bryant eloquently wrote that Black men and women
athletes "do not exist solely for the entertainment of the public, especially
a white public that often seems to thrive on diminishing Black pain. As a
job, yes, the players provide entertainment. As people, no.

"The accumulation of what is happening to Black people in this country is real, coming at a real cost," Bryant continued. "The pain is real. The
responsibility is real."

Eventually, Milwaukee decided to play, finishing off the Magic before
heading into round 2 against Miami. Jimmy Butler seemed unstoppable. The Heat defense swarmed Giannis, forcing him to become a jump
shooter, exposing his shaky form, his lack of confidence in his jumper, his
poor free throw percentages.

After losing the first two games, the Bucks took another fall, dropping
game 3 as Giannis tweaked his ankle after going up for a dunk. He kept
playing through the pain, but he played only thirty-five minutes. Reporters
were vocal about Budenholzer's substitutions, questioning why he wouldn't
play his star more. Giannis merely told reporters with a shrug after the
game, "Yeah, I could play more."

He missed most of game 4 with the ankle injury, scoring nineteen
before watching the rest from the locker room. His teammates kept the
season alive by winning in overtime, but Giannis didn't play in game 5, and
the Bucks were eliminated. It was brutally disappointing, especially for a
franchise that yet again played so well during the regular season, only to
crumble come playoffs.

Giannis, just twenty-five, won Defensive Player of the Year—and his sec-
ond consecutive MVP award, joining the distinguished roster of Stephen
Curry, LeBron James, Steve Nash, Tim Duncan, Michael Jordan, Magic
Johnson, Larry Bird, Moses Malone, Wilt Chamberlain, Bill Russell, and
Abdul-Jabbar as players who have repeated MVP in back-to-back seasons.

Tzikas, the Kivotos Café owner, called Giannis to congratulate him. "It
was such a special moment," Tzikas says. But Tzikas knew Giannis was still

in pain from losing, from the way the Bucks had wildly underperformed. The way his own weaknesses were on full display. And it thrust his super-max decision back to the center of national conversation. Giannis told reporters after the game that, as long as everyone was fighting for the same goal, to become a champion, he didn't see why he couldn't be in Milwaukee for the next fifteen years.

But his future was still uncertain. Rumors swirled about which teams would lure him, especially Miami and Golden State. And yet Giannis didn't talk about it. He downplayed his back-to-back MVPs, only reiterating that he wanted to win a championship.

"Don't call me MVP," he told reporters when he left for Greece in September 2020. "Don't call me two-time MVP until I'm a champion."

* * *

Not knowing when the NBA season might start during the ongoing pandemic, Giannis stayed in Athens with his family as long as he could. He and his brothers surprised Kostas at 6:00 a.m. at the airport, Kostas having flown in right after winning a ring with the Lakers, the 2019–2020 champions. Giannis and Thanasis brought him balloons, celebrating him, congratulating him.

This was also the first time Giannis brought nine-month-old Liam to Greece. Coming back as a father was different for Giannis. He watched little Liam peer out at the same streets, same sights, where he'd grown up.

Liam will grow up so differently. Liam will never have to Christmas carol around town for money. He will never have to dress up in his Sunday best to convince landlords that he and his family are capable of making rent. He will never know what it feels like to lie to teammates and coaches by telling them he has eaten when he hasn't.

Giannis was in awe of Liam. The cute gestures he made. The way he already looked like a grown person in such a tiny body. How he couldn't sit still. The first words Giannis wanted him to understand were "sit down," as Liam crawled everywhere, always on the move. Always curious.

Giannis brought some Bucks coaches to Greece, including Josh Oppenheimer, and trained at the arena that hosts Panathinaikos, the powerhouse that hadn't signed him just seven years back. One workout, Giannis shot free throws in between drills. If he missed a free throw, he had his *coaches* run. Giannis *hated* that—that they would have to suffer for *his* shortcomings.

Then he upped the stakes: if he missed, Mariah and Liam, who were in the gym watching, would also have to run. That gave him a different level of focus. A different level of accountability.

But mostly, he wanted to spend his time with those he loved. He went to Sweden to see his old friend and teammate Andrian Nkwònia, who was living there at the time, playing basketball, following his own dreams. Giannis helped Nkwònia renew his visa, staying two days to ensure his friend's application was submitted.

It was as if a day hadn't passed since the two were kids. Walking around Sepolia, trying to find some place of refuge, some excuse not to be at home. To Nkwònia, and all his childhood friends, Giannis was still Giannakis. Little Giannis. Even though so much had changed.

Giannis told Cosmote TV, a local Greek station, around that time, "I want to be Giannis who started from Filathlitikos, not the MVP of the NBA."

But he can't go back. Only forward. And as much as he wanted to focus purely on basketball, he couldn't escape supermax-contract questions. He told reporters it was one of the biggest decisions of his life but that he was just focusing on his game and allowing his agents to handle the contract.

Media obsessed over his decision. Sports TV and radio personalities kept glamorizing sexier potential big-market destinations for Giannis, assuring listeners, without any knowledge, that Giannis was a much better fit for a place like Golden State in particular. It was chaotic. Nonstop. Bucks fans were on edge, vacillating between nervousness, denial, and outright confidence.

Nobody *really* knew what was going on. The Bucks fumbled a trade for Kings star Bogdan Bogdanović, violating tampering rules. The team did manage to trade for talented point guard Jrue Holiday, a move that impressed Giannis and signified a commitment to improving the lackluster backcourt from the previous season.

The Bucks were optimistic that Giannis would stay, but the Bogdanović gaffe was embarrassing. Giannis had wanted Bogdanović on the Bucks.

Giannis and Thanasis were both in constant communication with him, as Giannis had respected the guard since playing against him in the world cup in Madrid.

The deadline to sign the extension was December 21, and Giannis had been in talks with Bucks management leading up to that date. He had a three-hour lunch with Lasry, the Bucks co-owner, after the playoffs, discussing players and coaches and free agents, with Giannis showing him texts from stars on rival teams pitching him.

Lasry and Edens, the other co-owner, met with Giannis again and reminded him they were just as committed to winning a championship as he was. The Bucks believed Giannis wanted to be a Buck, but the Bucks had to demonstrate they were as determined to win as he was.

Giannis's teammates gave him nineteen pens for his twenty-sixth birthday, right before the first preseason game of the 2020–2021 season, as a clever way to say, "Sign the extension. All nineteen of us want you here."

But no one had a clear indication of which way Giannis would turn. One day he seemed all in, the next more hesitant, asking new questions. And to many who were from Milwaukee, who knew the pain of what could happen, reality set in: maybe Giannis really would leave.

"It's a city that's holding on to hope," says Myron Medcalf of ESPN, "but there's a familiar sense of 'everybody leaves,' and if anyone is gonna leave, certainly it could be the most talented player in the league."

*   *   *

Budenholzer was pulling out of the parking lot of a garage when he saw that his sons had texted him the tweet. *The* tweet. Budenholzer hadn't known Giannis's decision until he read the tweet that afternoon, on December 15:

"This is my home, this is my city. I'm blessed to be able to be a part of the Milwaukee Bucks for the next 5 years. Let's make these years count. The show goes on, let's get it." Giannis followed that with a heart emoji, then a prayer-hands emoji, and two pictures of him side by side in a Bucks uniform: one smiling, one of him looking down at the basketball he was clutching.

Giannis signed a $228 million extension, the largest contract in NBA history. He could have held a press conference. He could have announced it on national TV. He could have done a live Instagram. But that wouldn't be *him*. So he dodged attention, even as he was the biggest story in the NBA—in all of sports—at that moment.

He wanted to raise Liam, and his future children, in Milwaukee.

And Veronica wanted to stay as well.

Home.

The city where he'd arrived as a skinny kid who couldn't speak much English, who didn't own a winter coat. Who shivered on Skype that year with his family.

Home.

The city where Bucks staff tried to make him feel at ease, giving every family member a key to the gym.

Home.

All his life he had been searching for it. A place to sleep at night. A place to feel safe, at ease, where he didn't fear Greek police knocking at his door, taking his parents from him. A place where he didn't have to fear making it in America on his own, trying to figure out how he could repay the Bucks for taking a chance on him and drafting him. For fighting like hell to get his parents visas to come to America. To call Milwaukee home.

When Milwaukeeans saw Giannis use that word—*home*—it meant something deep to them. They were so used to fans from other cities telling them to just be quiet, just be grateful that a talent like Giannis would even *consider* staying in a place like Milwaukee. "Nobody ever wants to play in Milwaukee" is what they heard before Giannis.

And then this sweet, fierce seven-footer from another country came along and talked about how awesome Milwaukee was. How he didn't mind the cold. He didn't mock their blue-collar jobs, their way of life.

"There's recognition, in Giannis's decision, that the little guy, so to speak, got one over on the big boys," says Kogutkiewicz, the longtime Bucks fan. "You can't take that away."

Giannis saw himself in this city, and in him, they saw themselves too. "This global superstar, this one-in-a-million-type player, he chose *us*," says

Alex Lanson, a twenty-three-year-old Milwaukee native and Bucks fan. "Before Giannis, we kept looking for a savior. Just looking for that person to bring Milwaukee back. Time after time, it was just disappointment, disappointment, disappointment. And finally, this is our guy."

Jamie and Joel Sarauer, longtime Bucks fans, cried when they read Giannis's tweet. They had met at the Bradley Center. Had their first date at the Bradley Center. Felt at *home* at the Bradley Center. *And* she had better seats than him? Keeper. They haven't missed a game.

Their dog died during the pandemic, and they say they're going to get a new one sometime soon. They're considering the name Bradley, in honor of the place that brought them together.

Giannis deciding to stay in Milwaukee, for them, is a gift. "It makes you really want to cry," Jamie says. "We deserve to have a generational type of player and human. Bucks fans, we always feel we get the short end of the stick. We're always ripped on. We're *still* ripped on.

"This isn't the prettiest state," Jamie says, "but I never want to leave Milwaukee. Ever."

* * *

After signing the supermax, Giannis's mind drifted to his father, as it often does. Giannis said his dad would be *dancing* if he could see him now. He'd be so proud of him and his brothers. What they've accomplished on the court, who they've become off the court. And he knew that even if his dad was not there to see him sign the document, he was there in spirit.

Now there is even more motivation for him to win. More pressure too. Milwaukee has five more years. They can't afford to squander Giannis's prime. They will likely have no better shot in the next few decades than with Giannis. Every second matters.

But there is another goal too: for all his brothers to make the NBA. "That would be something that, if my dad could see, he would probably just cry," Kostas says. "We really don't talk about it a lot, but it's a dream we have and think about a lot."

Alex is up next, as he's currently playing with Murcia, a competitive team in southern Spain that competes in EuroLeague. But Liam has replaced Alex as Giannis's workout buddy at the practice facility. At least during the season. Liam watches Giannis as he trains, as he pushes himself. He giggles on the side, intently watching his father sweat.

They are home.

ACKNOWLEDGMENTS

Thank you to the wonderful people at Hachette Books for publishing *Giannis*. This wouldn't have been possible without my editor, Brant Rumble, whose excitement and passion for this project motivated me from the beginning. Special thanks to Hachette publicity and marketing gurus Michael Giarratano and Julianne Lewis as well.

I'm grateful to Anthony Mattero of CAA, the best literary agent in the business. Thank you for seeing my vision from the start, for always keeping your door open. Thank you to Michael Klein of CAA, my other agent, for advocating for me and for supporting my aspirations.

So many people helped with *Giannis*. Thank you to Adam Fromal for your diligent fact-checking and incredible eye. Thank you to Ana Tosouni and Mary Christianakis for your immense help in translating Greek articles and interviews, for always being there when I messaged you: "Just one more question!" Thank you to Gabriel Rogers for your research on the ground in Sepolia. I am grateful for the help and kindness of all the Greek sports journalists I interviewed, especially Nikos Papadojannis, who was an invaluable source of information and perspective. A huge thank-you to Nicole Yang, Maggie Vanoni, Chris Lopez, and Lila Bromberg for help with early transcription. Special thanks to Chris Herring, Ti Windisch, Giannis Tzikas, Marcus Vanderberg, Anna Ilif, Harrison Faigen, Marcus Thompson, Myron Medcalf, Jean Wyatt, Noune Diarbekirian, Heidi Shaw, Brantley Watson, Chris Ballard, and Melissa Isaacson.

Thank you to my Ringer colleagues, who have embraced me with open arms: Matt Dollinger, Mallory Rubin, Sean Fennessey, Bill Simmons, Kevin O'Connor, Arjuna Ramgopal, and Rob Mahoney. I love working at a place that encourages me to pitch and pitch and follow the ideas that fascinate me.

I would not be here without my mentor and friend Jeff Pearlman. Thank you for always being there for me, for supporting me and challenging me and helping me become a better writer. Thank you to my other mentor Christina Tapper, whose love, friendship, and guidance helped me find my way in this industry. Thank you for encouraging me to be bold, courageous, and kind to myself. Thank you to my other Bleacher Report mag family: Ben Osborne, Jake Leonard, Elliott Pohnl, Matt Sullivan, Ian Blair, Mark Smoyer, Paige Kuhn, Paul Forrester, and Meredith Minkow. I love you all. Thank you for letting me write the stories that my heart craved. Thank you for allowing me to travel the world and live my dream. I feel lucky to have worked with people that I will be friends with for the rest of my life.

Thank you to my amazing family and friends for supporting me throughout this book, throughout everything. You know who you are. I love you.

Thank you to Toni Morrison and Wright Thompson for inspiring me to write. Thank you to the coffee shops of LA for letting me sit for hours, writing and struggling and sipping and rewriting. Thank you to the freeways of Orange County, where I spent day after day sitting in traffic, dreaming of writing a book while a cub reporter at the *Orange County Register*.

Most importantly, thank you, Mom, Dad, Lainna, Uncle Sidney, and Cookie. I love you more than words can describe. You are my world. Thank you for loving me, for believing in me, for teaching me to be resilient and to stand tall. I never gave up because you never gave up on me.

NOTES

Much of the information in this book is based on 221 interviews with family members, friends, coaches, and teammates both from Greece and America, as well as Bucks personnel, opponents, and others. There were a number of people who were interviewed off the record or on background. I include the names of the 221 primary source interviews in the coming notes, except those who spoke off the record or on background. Some interviews required a translator, and I note the translator's name in those instances. In instances where I describe scenes, I interviewed at least one person who was present or had firsthand knowledge of what took place. Where I've reconstructed dialogue, I interviewed at least one person who was present for the conversation. If the dialogue came from a secondary source article, I cite that article directly in the notes. When someone is said to have "thought" or "felt" something, I obtained that knowledge directly from the individual, from a source with direct knowledge of the individual's viewpoint, or from a secondary source article cited in the notes. I retained a Greek translator to translate secondary source articles written in Greek. I include both the Greek and English translated bibliographic information in the notes.

My reporting for this book was born out of a Bleacher Report feature I wrote on Giannis and his youngest brother, Alex, titled "The Rise of the Next Antetokounmpo," on July 18, 2019. I have used some scenes and dialogue and general reporting from that story and have cited those instances in the notes. During the course of the reporting for the Bleacher Report story, in June 2019, I visited Giannis's home, as well as the Bucks' practice facility, where I interviewed Giannis; his mother, Veronica; and his brothers Alex and Kostas. I originally intended to write the story solely on Alex. I hadn't known that Giannis was going to be there that day. But he was, and observing the chemistry and love between Giannis and Alex led me to the realization that the story had to focus on both of them. It also made me more curious about Giannis's own story. Giannis the person, not just the basketball player. Giannis the brother, the protector, the soon-to-be father. I realized I wanted to write a book about Giannis while also telling the story of his family. I developed a proposal for *Giannis* in early December 2019 and began officially working on the project in late February 2020. Shortly thereafter, I interviewed Alex and Kostas in person (separately) for a second time. I interviewed Giannis's other brother, Thanasis, in person on two occasions in March 2020. Many of the additional interviews with other subjects were completed over the phone or by video call over WhatsApp and Viber, due to the COVID-19 pandemic.

Prologue

Primary source interviews: Giannis Antetokounmpo, Veronica Antetokounmpo, Kostas Antetokounmpo, Alex Antetokounmpo, and Josh Oppenheimer.

Sometimes she'd leave the house at 11:00 p.m.: Steve Kroft, transcript of his *60 Minutes* interview with Giannis, 2018.

Nearly ten-thousand-square-foot: Kristine Hansen, "Milwaukee Bucks' Giannis Antetokounmpo Nets Wisconsin Home for $1.8M," Realtor.com, November 5, 2018, https://www.realtor.com/news/celebrity-real-estate/giannis-antetokounmpo-wisconsin-mansion/.

"You don't change": Mirin Fader, "The Rise of the Next Antetokounmpo," Bleacher Report, July 18, 2019, https://bleacherreport.com/articles/2845193-the-rise-of-the-next-antetokounmpo.

Rain settles: Ibid.

An elderly couple: Ibid.

Mariah opens the door: Ibid.

"Mila just wants to say hi": Ibid.
Inside there is a sign: Ibid.
Alex is downstairs in the basement: Ibid.
They've moved five times: Ibid.
Giannis preserves: Ibid.
"American Dream": Ibid.
"You see this in the seats": Ibid.
"It's a reminder": Ibid.
"God is here": Ibid.
His legs turn into scissors: Ibid.
He yearns to impress: Ibid.
"I get more nervous": Ibid.
The court is a cocoon: Ibid.
When Giannis speaks to Alex: Ibid.
"I definitely think Alex": Ibid.
"It's just me": Ibid.
"Lock that shit out": Ibid.
"Just trust me": Ibid.
The sharp parts: Ibid.
Share the same hearty: Ibid.
Sometimes Giannis looks at Alex and glows: Ibid.
He wants Alex to understand: Ibid.

1. Hunger

Primary source interviews: Giannis Antetokounmpo, Veronica Antetokounmpo, Alex Antetokounmpo, Kostas Antetokounmpo, Thanasis Antetokounmpo, Steve Kroft, Giannis Tzikas (via translator Maria Drimpa), Notis A. Mitarachi, Michael Carter-Williams, Father Evangelos Ganas, Spiros Velliniatis, Emmanuel Olayinka Afolayan, Harris Stavrou, Stefanos Dedas, Takis Zivas (via translator Lefteris Zarmakoupis), Giorgos Kordas, Grigoris Melas, Tselios Konstantinos, Giorgos Pantelakis, Christos Saloustros, Nikos Gkikas, Panos Prokos (via translator Ana Tosouni), Gabriel Rodgers, Rahman Rana, Niki Bakouli, and Katy Kostakis.

Giannis was six years old: Steve Kroft, transcript of his *60 Minutes* interview with Giannis, 2018.
Maybe one or two euros: Chris Mannix, "Out of Order?" *Sports Illustrated,* March 10, 2014.
21.5 million citizens of the European Union: Ian Kershaw, *The Global Age: Europe, 1950–2017* (New York: Penguin Books, 2020), 493.

Two-fifths of Greek youths were unemployed: Kershaw, *The Global Age*, 493.

Six coups and three presidential assassinations: James Brooke, "Nigeria Trying to Start Over amid Recession and Turmoil," *New York Times*, November 23, 1987.

Claimed the lives of an estimated one to three million people: Shayera Dark, "'I Looked for Death but I Couldn't Find It,' a Nigerian Town Relives the Brutal Civil War, 50 Years After It Ended," CNN, January 16, 2020, https://www.cnn.com/2020/01/15/africa/biafra-nigeria-civil-war/index.html.

Oil accounting for 95 percent: Brooke, "Nigeria."

$21 billion in foreign debt: Ibid.

"On the verge of external bankruptcy": Ibid.

Charles, from the Yoruba tribe: Elina Dimitriadi, "Η Βερόνικα Αντετοκούνμπο μιλάει αποκλειστικά στη Vogue Greece" ("Veronica Adetokunbo Speaks Exclusively to *Vogue Greece*"), *Vogue Greece*, September 27, 2020, https://vogue.gr/living/i-veronika-antetokoynmpo-milaei-apokleistika-sti-vogue-greece/.

Background singer for an album recorded in Nigeria: Ibid.

She loved Whitney Houston, Celine Dion, and reggae: Ibid.

Immortality: Nikos Papadojannis, "Αφρική, η άλλη πατρίδα" ("Africa, Giannis' Other Home"), *Hot Doc*, no. 119, February 2, 2017.

Veronica and Charles gave them Greek first: Joanna Kakissis, "NBA Rookie Wants to Bring Hope to Greece, and to Milwaukee," *NPR Morning Edition*, September 26, 2013.

"Crown that came from faraway seas": Dimitriadi, "Η Βερόνικα Αντετοκούνμπο" ("Veronica Adetokunbo Speaks Exclusively to *Vogue Greece*").

Ugo, means "the crown of God": Ibid.

An electrician: Papadojannis, "Αφρική, η άλλη πατρίδα" ("Africa, Giannis' Other Home").

"Don't worry about it. I'm not eating. I have to make sure my kids eat": Kroft, *60 Minutes* transcript.

"No, I'm coming with you": Nike, "Self-Made: I Am Giannis, Episode 1," July 1, 2019, https://www.youtube.com/watch?v=XyxLKFDwwU4.

He felt he was the best salesman in the family: Nike, "Self-Made: I Am Giannis, Episode 1."

"You want this glass": Kroft, *60 Minutes* transcript.

"Oh, they're really nice; they're going to help you do this": Ibid.

"But why?": Ibid.

Sometimes people would leave food items: Niki Bakouli, "Ο Γιάννης Αντετοκούνμπο πρέπει να χρησιμοποιήσει τη φωνή του" ("Giannis Antetokounmpo Must Use His Voice"), February 18, 2017, https://www.sport24

.gr/sthles/o-giannis-antetokoynmpo-prepei-na-chrisimopoiisei-ti-foni
-toy.8505535.html.

Seven days in a row, maybe two weeks: Kroft, *60 Minutes* transcript.

Drive for five hours, ten hours: Ibid.

Just like one of his idols, Thierry Henry: Adrian Wojnarowski, "The Giannis
Draft. Episode 1: Who Is Giannis?" *The Woj Pod*, November 16, 2020.

Avoid drugs and other negative influences: Mannix, "Out of Order?"

"Take care of your body": Nikos Papadojannis, "Θανάσης Ανττοκούνμπο: Οι
μετανάστες να ξέρουν ότι είμαστε δίπλα τους!" ("Let the Immigrants Know
That We Stand by Their Side"), *Documento*, October 13, 2019, https://
www.documentonews.gr/article/oanashs-antetokoynmpo-oi-metanastes
-na-xeroyn-oti-eimaste-dipla-toys.

He used juju medicine: Ibid.

"It's happened to me too": Ibid.

They'd run relay races at a nearby track: Malika Andrews, "Everything Is Fuel for
Giannis Antetokounmpo's Competitive Fire," ESPN, December 15, 2020,
https://www.espn.com/nba/insider/story/_/id/30521245/everything-fuel
-giannis-antetokounmpo-competitive-fire.

Filling in at goalie: Dimitriadi, "Η Βερόνικα Αντετοκούνμπο" ("Veronica Adetokunbo Speaks Exclusively to *Vogue Greece*").

Competitions to see which boy could clean up his room: Andrews, "Everything
Is Fuel."

"If you love your father, if you love your mother, you'll live long": Dimitriadi, "Η
Βερόνικα Αντετοκούνμπο" ("Veronica Adetokunbo Speaks Exclusively to
Vogue Greece").

Teaching him about Nelson Mandela: Sean Gregory, "Greek Freak Giannis
Antetokounmpo on Growing Up Undocumented, Taking On LeBron and
Gunning for MVP," *Time*, October 17, 2017.

He remembered Giannis's eyes: Marina Zioziou, "ΓΙΑΝΝΗΣ ΑΝΤΕΤΟ-
ΚΟΥΝΜΠΟ: Ο «ΤΣΟΛΙΑΣ» ΑΠΟ ΤΑ ΣΕΠΟΛΙΑ ΠΟΥ ΕΓΙΝΕ ΝΟ1 ΣΤΟΝ
ΚΟΣΜΟ" ("'Tsolias' from the Sepolia That Became No1 in the World"),
Ethnos.gr, June 25, 2019, https://www.ethnos.gr/athlitismos/46677_
giannis-antetokoynmpo-o-tsolias-apo-ta-sepolia-poy-egine-no1
-ston-kosmo.

His spirit just seemed buoyed: Ibid.

To stumbling on a young Mozart: Ken Maguire, "A Hunger for a Better
Life May Lead to the N.B.A.," *New York Times*, June 25, 2013, section B,
page 11.

He hated it: Nike, "Self-Made: I Am Giannis, Episode 1."

No hot water: Ben Cohen and Joshua Robinson, "The Greek Mythology of the NBA's Superstar," *Wall Street Journal*, April 2, 2019.

"They'd have to leave school": Mirin Fader, "The Rise of the Next Antetokounmpo," Bleacher Report, July 18, 2019, https://bleacherreport.com /articles /2845193-the-rise-of-the-next-antetokounmpo.

He shot bank shots with a soccer ball: Mannix, "Out of Order?"

He lasted for seven minutes: Jim Owczarski, "NBA Provides an Escape for Bucks Rookie Antetokounmpo," October 22, 2013, https://onmilwaukee .com/articles/giannisantetokounmpo.

One in three Greeks lived below the poverty line: Kershaw, *The Global Age*, 493.

Minimum wage was reduced by 22 percent: Ibid.

More than twenty thousand were homeless: Ibid.

"He loved us too much": Owczarski, "NBA Provides an Escape."

2. Dreaming

Primary source interviews: Giannis Antetokounmpo, Veronica Antetokounmpo, Alex Antetokounmpo, Kostas Antetokounmpo, Thanasis Antetokounmpo, Michalis Kamperidis, Nikos Papadojannis, Alexandros Trigas, Stefanos Dedas, Tselios Konstantinos, Takis Zivas (via translator Lefteris Zarmakoupis), Spiros Velliniatis, Nikos Gkikas, Christos Saloustros, Georgios Diamantakos, Grigoris Melas, Rahman Rana, Panos Prokos (via translator Ana Tosouni), Dimitrios Katifelis (via translator Gabriel Rogers), Giorgos Kordas, and Giannis Tzikas (via translator Maria Drimpa).

"What you are doing is not right": Nikos Papadojannis, "Θανάσης Αντετοκούνμπο" ("Let the Immigrants Know That We Stand by Their Side"), *Documento*, October 13, 2019, https://www.documentonews.gr /article/oanashs-antetokoynmpo-oi-metanastes-na-xeroyn-oti -eimaste-dipla-toys.

They'd challenge her to shoot three-pointers: Elina Dimitriadi, "Η Βερόνικα Αντετοκούνμπο" ("Veronica Adetokunbo Speaks Exclusively to *Vogue Greece*"), *Vogue Greece*, September 27, 2020, https://vogue.gr/living/i -veronika-antetokoynmpo-milaei-apokleistika-sti-vogue-greece/.

They made nearly $150: Steve Kroft, transcript of his *60 Minutes* interview with Giannis, 2017.

"Let's do something with our lives": Adrian Wojnarowski, "From Street Vendor to Surging NBA Player, Greek Freak Living the American Dream,"

Yahoo Sports, March 18, 2014, https://sports.yahoo.com/news/from-selling -sunglasses-on-street-to-nba-player-on-the-rise--greek-freak-living-the -american-dream-214309752.html.

"Always want more": Ben Golliver, "Giannis Antetokounmpo Wins NBA MVP Award, Completing Rise from Unknown to Superstar," *Washington Post*, June 24, 2019.

She always knew her sons would accomplish something: Dimitriadi, "Η Βερόνικα Αντετοκούνμπο" ("Veronica Adetokunbo Speaks Exclusively to *Vogue Greece*").

The boys thought Charles was the most successful man: Papadojannis, "Θανάσης Αντετοκούνμπο" ("Let the Immigrants Know That We Stand by Their Side").

Even his classmates at school wouldn't pick him: Aggeliki Katsini, "Giannis Antetokounmpo Is Hungry for His First Ring," Contra.gr, October 24, 2019, https://www.contra.gr/synentefxeis/giannis-antetokounmpo-is-hun gry-for-his-first-ring.7520012.html.

"He treats me like his own child": Sport24.gr, "Αντετοκούνμπο: Θα είμαι σίγουρα εκεί" ("Antetokounmpo: I Will Definitely Be There"), September 17, 2013, https://www.sport24.gr/basket/antetokoynmpo-tha-eimai-sigoy ra-kei.8114302.html.

He wouldn't eat his first meal of the day until 11:00 p.m.: Adrian Wojnarowski, "The Giannis Draft. Episode 1: Who Is Giannis?" *The Woj Pod*, November 16, 2020.

She would still wash her boys' socks: Dimitriadi, "Η Βερόνικα Αντετοκούνμπο" ("Veronica Adetokunbo Speaks Exclusively to *Vogue Greece*").

She wanted them to develop happy memories: Ibid.

A concert by the famous composer Mikis Theodorakis: Papadojannis, "Θανάσης Αντετοκούνμπο" ("Let the Immigrants Know That We Stand by Their Side").

The Brothers Karamazov: Ibid.

"Inch by Inch": "Amazing NBA Motivation Clip—Inch by Inch—[HD] By Din Basel," July 19, 2011, https://www.youtube.com/watch?v=wmYiiXwfaNU.

"Life's a game of inches": Ibid.

"When you want to succeed": "Don't Sleep Until You Succeed (NBA) [HD]," Bram dekkers, March 15, 2012, https://www.youtube.com/watch?v=-Sw3w QXC2EI&t=235s.

He knew he couldn't compete with him: Wojnarowski, "The Giannis Draft. Episode 1."

"How much money does Kobe make?": Kroft, *60 Minutes* transcript.

"Maybe around": Ibid.

I gotta make it to the NBA. I gotta try to make as much money as Kobe made: Ibid.

The boys would look at other kids funny: Mirin Fader, "The Rise of the Next Antetokounmpo," Bleacher Report, July 18, 2019, https://bleacherreport. com/articles /2845193-the-rise-of-the-next-antetokounmpo.

That ball could be the difference: Ibid.

He pushed Alex: Ibid.

Alex just looked at Giannis's body: Ibid.

Giannis told Alex that there were a lot more: Ibid.

"There's so much more": Ibid.

Blue mattress: Katsini, "Giannis Antetokounmpo Is Hungry."

3. Stateless

Primary source interviews: Giannis Antetokounmpo, Veronica Antetokounmpo, Alex Antetokounmpo, Kostas Antetokounmpo, Rahman Rana, Nikos Gkikas, Nikos Zisis, Konstantinos Georgousis, Gabriel Rodgers, Favor Ukpebor, Christos Saloustros, Kostas Missas, Kostas Kotsis, Yannis Psarakis, Nikos Papadojannis, Fotios Katsikaris, Nikos Deji Odubitan, Niki Bakouli, Grigoris Melas, Emmanuel Godwin, Emmanuel Olayinka Afolayan, Etinosa Erevbenagie, Takis Zivas (via translator Lefteris Zarmakoupis), Stefanos Dedas, Stefanos Triantafyllos, George Kouvaris, Alexandros Mistilioglou, Basileios Motsakos, Alexandros Trigas, Ioannis Papapetrou, and Michalis Kamperidis.

They'd gather with kids and parents: Elina Dimitriadi, "Η Βερόνικα Αντετοκούνμπο μιλάει αποκλειστικά στη *Vogue Greece*" ("Veronica Adetokunbo Speaks Exclusively to *Vogue Greece*"), *Vogue Greece*, September 27, 2020, https://vogue.gr/living/i-veronika-antetokoynmpo-milaei-apokleistika -sti-vogue-greece/.

Veronica remembered feeling that her family felt loved: Ibid.

They believed all immigrants should be deported: Rachel Donadio and Dimitris Bounias, "Hard Times Lift Greece's Anti-immigrant Fringe," *New York Times*, April 12, 2012.

"We will clean this square": Konstantinos Georgousis, director, *The Cleaners*, National Film and Television School, 37 minutes.

Sympathized with the military dictatorship: Donadio and Bounias, "Hard Times."

Getting just 0.3 percent: Nikos Konstandaras, "As Goes Greece, So Goes Europe?" *New York Times*, May 28, 2014.

Syriza, a leftist party, won 4.6 percent: Ibid.

"I think all history is written": Donadio and Bounias, "Hard Times."

They sold Mein Kampf: Max Fisher, "Are Greek Policemen Really Voting in Droves for Greece's Neo-Nazi Party?" *Atlantic,* June 22, 2012.

Eighteen seats: Helena Smith, "Neo-fascist Greek Party Takes Third Place in Wave of Voter Fury," *Guardian,* September 20, 2015, https://www.theguardian.com/world/2015/sep/21/neo-fascist-greek-party-election-golden-dawn-third-place.

Unemployment stood at 25 percent: Rachel Donadio, "Amid the Echoes of an Economic Crash, the Sounds of Greek Society Being Torn," *New York Times,* October 20, 2012.

Government allowed supermarkets to sell expired: Ibid.

Price of home heating oil had tripled: Ibid.

"The financial crisis will be solved": Georgousis, *The Cleaners.*

"We will make lamps": Ibid.

"Soon enough, the Greeks will become a minority": Matthaios Tsimitakis, "Greece's Fascists Are Gaining," *New York Times,* October 4, 2015.

"When immigrants hear Golden Dawn": Georgousis, *The Cleaners.*

"For a Greece that belongs to Greeks": Ibid.

"Next time it will be seventeen": Ibid.

Immigrants made up only about 10 percent: Jake Whitman, "Filmmaker Captures Unguarded Racist Hatred of Greece's Hostile Golden Dawn Party," *ABC News,* August 13, 2013.

Armed with heavy wooden poles: Liz Alderman, "Greek Far Right Hangs a Target on Immigrants," *New York Times,* July 10, 2012.

"You're the cause of Greece's problems": Ibid.

"Dark-skinned merchants": Liz Alderman, "Right-Wing Extremists' Popularity Rising Rapidly in Greece," *New York Times,* September 30, 2012.

"Alarming phenomenon": Human Rights Watch Report, July 10, 2012, https://www.hrw.org/report/2012/07/10/hate-streets/xenophobic-violence-greece.

Is this the day: Master Tesfatsion, "Giannis and Identity," *NBA on TNT: The Arena,* July 23, 2020, https://twitter.com/MasterTes/status/1286396995259817985.

Giannis wasn't worried about himself *getting deported:* Sean Gregory, "Greek Freak Giannis Antetokounmpo on Growing Up Undocumented, Taking on LeBron and Gunning for MVP," *Time,* October 17, 2017.

What to do in the aftermath: Tesfatsion, "Giannis and Identity."

Giannis felt God was with his family: Chris Mannix, "Out of Order?" *Sports Illustrated,* March 10, 2014.

"Why don't we have passports?": *EurohoopsTV*, "Giannis Antetokounmpo on Immigrants' Rights in Greece," June 28, 2019, https://www.youtube.com /watch?v=s4p4qgCVt3o&feature=emb_title.

A white traditional Akwa-Ocha dress: Dimitriadi, "Η Βερόνικα Αντετοκούνμπο" ("Veronica Adetokunbo Speaks Exclusively to *Vogue Greece*").

Zivas was focused on Giannis's development: Stefanos Triantafyllos, "Pick n Pop: Τι θα γίνει με τον Γιάννη" ("Pick n Pop: What Will Happen to Giannis?"), *Pick N Pop Podcast*, March 23, 2016, https://www.sport24.gr/sound/pod-casts/pick-n-pop-ti-tha-ginei-me-ton-gianni.8398888.html.

Claiming he didn't want to disrespect anyone: Bob Ryan, "United States Picked Apart by Greece," *Boston Globe*, September 1, 2006.

A black guy was part of that! We can do it!: Adrian Wojnarowski, "The Giannis Draft. Episode 1: Who Is Giannis?" *The Woj Pod*, November 16, 2020.

Sofo gave Giannis hope: Ibid.

Sofo dislikes working out alone: Vasilis Skountis, "Σοφοκλής Σχορτσανίτης | Η εξομολόγηση" ("Sofoklis Schortsanitis: The Confession"), Sport24.gr, December 23, 2020, https://www.youtube.com/watch?v=ZVEFzoDN4 ms&t=1437s.

Sofo was shocked when he first saw Giannis: Ibid.

"We don't think that Schortsanitis is Greek": Stav Dimitropoulos, "Golden Dawn Member Dismisses Top Bi-racial Athlete as 'Non Greek,'" Digital Journal, October 26, 2012, http://www.digitaljournal.com/article/335583.

"Believing that races are distinct": Ibid.

"For God's sake": Ibid.

"Greeks have never been Black": Richard Pine, "Beware of Greek Politicians Bearing Xenophobia," *Irish Times*, August 13, 2013.

"I bet you're not going to score": "Giannis Antetokounmpo: The One Guy Who Owned Him on the Court," Bally Sports Wisconsin, February 21, 2019, https://www.youtube.com/watch?v=0MfhSBO1nag.

"No, that's not happening": Ibid.

Remembered Giannis and his brothers as being modest: Marina Zioziou, "ΓΙΑΝΝΗΣ ΑΝΤΕΤΟΚΟΥΝΜΠΟ: Ο «ΤΣΟΛΙΑΣ» ΑΠΟ ΤΑ ΣΕΠΟΛΙΑ ΠΟΥ ΕΓΙΝΕ ΝΟ1 ΣΤΟΝ ΚΟΣΜΟ" ("'Tsolias' from the Sepolia That Became No1 in the World"), Ethnos.gr, June 25, 2019, https://www.eth nos.gr/athlitismos/46677_giannis-antetokoynmpo-o-tsolias-apo-ta-sepo lia-poy-egine-no1-ston-kosmo.

Remembered Giannis as being ambitious: Ibid.

"Charles, you gotta eat": Nike, "Angels: I Am Giannis, Episode 2," July 1, 2019, https://www.youtube.com/watch?v=aOFcC6nT3EY.

"No, let my kids eat first": Ibid.

"It's human nature": Mirin Fader, "The Rise of the Next Antetokounmpo," Bleacher Report, July 18, 2019, https://bleacherreport.com/articles /2845193-the-rise-of-the-next-antetokounmpo.

Dealt with some health issues: Wojnarowski, "The Giannis Draft. Episode 1."

Giannis hid in the bathroom: Ibid.

"I'm going to make it for you": Gregory, "Greek Freak Giannis Antetokounmpo on Growing Up."

Alex was terrified of heights: Fader, "The Rise of the Next Antetokounmpo."

A lot of heart: Ibid.

He'd pull from the corner: Ibid.

"Alex couldn't really hang": Ibid.

"Terrible": Ibid.

Because he didn't want to disappoint: Ibid.

They were already famous: Ibid.

He'd watch Giannis jab: Ibid.

Mesmerized by the way Kostas: Ibid.

4. Found

Primary source interviews: Alex Antetokounmpo; Kostas Antetokounmpo; Kornél Dávid; Willy Villar; Takis Zivas (via translator Lefteris Zarmakou-pis); Giannis Tzikas (via translator Maria Drimpa); John Hammond; Ross Geiger; Cody Ross; a former Bucks staffer now working for a different NBA team; Danny Ferry; Asterios Kalivas; Christos Saloustros; Michalis Kamper-idis; Kostas Kotsis; Nikos Gkikas; Georgios Diamantakos; Bob Donewald Jr.; Fotios Katsikaris; Eric Taylor; a former NBA assistant general manager who came to Greece to watch Giannis; Austin Ainge; Nikos Papadojannis; Nick Calathes; Kyle Hines; Josh Powell; Stefanos Dedas; Antonis Samaras; Kostas Missas; Panos Prokos (via translator Ana Tosouni); Giannis Palatos (via translator Gabriel Rogers); Stefanos Triantafyllos; Tasos Garas; Alex Lloyd, a former Hawks staffer present for Italy meeting; another former Hawks staffer; Brandon Knight; Tyler Herro; Bill Simmons; Josh Oppen-heimer; an executive in Hawks draft room; Tom Oates; Lori Nickel; and Draggan Mihailovich.

Red-and-white Nike Kobe 4s: Aaron Dodson, "The Story Behind Giannis Antetokounmpo's First Nike Signature Sneaker," Undefeated, July 12, 2019, https://theundefeated.com/features/the-story-behind-giannis-anteto kounmpos-first-nike-signature-sneaker/.

Thanasis said he wasn't going to share: Ibid.

Giannis would take them to practice: Ibid.

Thanasis was angry at him: Ibid.

"That's your younger brother": Ibid.

"Who is this kid?": NBA on TNT, "Finding Giannis," February 16, 2019, https://www.youtube.com/watch?v=HrCU305tzmM.

Around fall 2012 in a downtown Athens hotel: Adrian Wojnarowski, "How One NBA Scout Discovered Giannis Antetokounmpo," ESPN, November 16, 2020, https://www.espn.com/nba/insider/story/_/id/30325897/how-one-scout-discovered-giannis-antetokounmpo.

They ate burgers and fries: Ibid.

"You might be an NBA player next year": Ibid.

"The real NBA?": Ibid.

Explained to him that he would need to start eating: NBA on TNT, "Finding Giannis."

The doctor was stunned: Adrian Wojnarowski, "The Giannis Draft. Episode 1: Who Is Giannis?" The Woj Pod, November 16, 2020.

Giannis's liver was suffering: Ibid.

The doctor thought Panou had sent him a seventy-year-old: Ibid.

Nine minutes, forty-six seconds: Wojnarowski, "How One NBA Scout Discovered."

"I've got someone here": Ibid.

Sent the tape to a few college coaches: Chris Mannix, "Out of Order?" Sports Illustrated, March 10, 2014.

Panou and Dimitropoulos told Giannis that if he did end up: Wojnarowski, "The Giannis Draft. Episode 1."

"Excuse me?": Ibid.

"You're a young guy": Ibid.

Giannis started crying, tore up the contract. "I'm not going anywhere": Ibid.

Panou's Fiat: Ibid.

"Don't cry": Ibid.

"You think that now I've got money": Ibid.

Panou apologized: Ibid.

"What kind of basketball player are you?": Jonathan Givony, "Giannis Antetokounmpo Interview," DraftExpress, June 20, 2013, https://www.youtube.com/watch?v=ZZu9Y_4SCks.

"I'm an all-around": Ibid.

"What is your goal": Ibid.

"I want to be an NBA player": Ibid.

"What kind of player will you be": Ibid.

"I'll be": Ibid.

On a scooter smoking a cigarette: Lee Jenkins, "Giannis Antetokounmpo: The Most Intriguing Point Guard in NBA History," *Sports Illustrated,* January 3, 2017.

Giannis didn't believe his agents: Wojnarowski, "The Giannis Draft. Episode 1."

"I don't know what's going to happen": Jenkins, "Giannis Antetokounmpo: The Most Intriguing."

"Oh maaaan. He's gonna be good!": Nike, "Angels: I Am Giannis, Episode 2," July 1, 2019, https://www.youtube.com/watch?v=aOFcC6nT3EY.

"You look good!": Ibid.

Showed up on a motorcycle: Adrian Wojnarowski, "The Giannis Draft. Episode 2: Shut Him Down," *The Woj Pod,* November 16, 2020.

"I thought he was absolutely a worthwhile": Steve Bulpett, "In Different World, Celtics Could Have Giannis Antetokounmpo," *Boston Herald,* April 3, 2018.

Twenty NBA scouts showed up: Harris Stavrou, "Ο αγαπημένος μου αγώνας: Κηφισιά—Φιλαθλητικός, το τέλος της αθωότητας" ("My Favorite Match: Kifissia—Filathlitikos, the End of Innocence"), Sport24.gr, March 31, 2020, https://www.sport24.gr/sthles/o-agapimenos-moy-agonas-kifi-sia-filathlitikos-to-telos-tis-athootitas.8942168.html.

Adorned with ribbons: Ibid.

Twelve-, thirteen-year-olds watched: Ibid.

He participated in the preparation camp: Antonis Kalkavouras, "Αποκάλυψη: Νιγηριανός ο Αντετοκούμπο!"("Antetokounmpo Becomes a Nigerian"), Gazzetta.gr, April 11, 2013, https://www.gazzetta.gr/a2-andron/article/389373-apoklypsi-nigirianos-o-antetokoympo.

Giannis felt slighted: Antonis Kalkavouras, "Δεν ένιωσα ποτέ ρατσισμό στην Ελλάδα" ("I Have Never Felt Racism in Greece"), Gazzetta.gr, June 18, 2013, https://www.gazzetta.gr/basketball/article/516529/den-eniosa-pote-ratsismo-stin-ellada.

"It would mean that beyond any shadow of doubt": Stefanos Triantafyllos, "Το Sport24.gr παρουσιάζει τα αδέρφια Αντετοκούμπο" ("Sport24.gr Presents the Adetokunbo Brothers"), Sport24.gr, March 15, 2013, https://www.sport24.gr/opinions/stefanos-triantafyllos/to-sport24-gr-paroysiazei-ta-aderfia-antetokoympo.8096632.html.

Giannis had applied for a Nigerian passport: Kalkavouras, "Αποκάλυψη: Νιγηριανός ο Αντετοκούμπο!"("Antetokounmpo Becomes a Nigerian").

His preference still was for Greek citizenship: Kalkavouras, "Δεν ένιωσα ποτέ ρατσισμό στην Ελλάδα" ("I Have Never Felt Racism in Greece").

"I could become formally Greek": Kalkavouras, "Δεν ένιωσα ποτέ ρατσισμό στην Ελλάδα" ("I Have Never Felt Racism in Greece").

"If Giannis was an Einstein": Jim Owczarski, "NBA Provides an Escape for Bucks Rookie Antetokounmpo," October 22, 2013, https://onmilwaukee.com/articles/giannisantetokounmpo.

"You only got the Greek passport because": Nikos Papadojannis, "Θανάσης Αντετοκούνμπο: Οι μετανάστες να ξέρουν ότι είμαστε δίπλα τους!" ("Let the Immigrants Know That We Stand by Their Side"), *Documento*, October 13, 2019, https://www.documentonews.gr/article/oanashs-antetokoynmpo-oi-metanastes-na-xeroyn-oti-eimaste-dipla-toys.

"The passport is the least": Ibid.

"Why shouldn't a little girl who is capable": Ibid.

He pulled up clips from the Lakers: Wojnarowski, "The Giannis Draft. Episode 2."

"Pass the ball": Ibid.

Atkinson sensed that he liked to facilitate: Ibid.

Fifty of them: Wojnarowski, "The Giannis Draft. Episode 1."

"Poor man's Kevin Durant": Chares F. Gardner, "Bucks Pick Giannis Antetokounmpo of Greece in NBA Draft," *Milwaukee Journal Sentinel*, June 27, 2013.

"He's a mysterious prospect": Ken Maguire, "A Hunger for a Better Life," *New York Times*, June 26, 2013, section B, page 11.

"He's a true international man": Aran Smith, "What Insiders Say," NBADraft.net, 2013, http://archive.nba.com/draft/2013/prospects/giannis-antetokounmpo.

"Absurd length, gigantic hands": Jonathan Wasserman, "Why Giannis Antetokounmpo Could Be Biggest Surprise of 2013–14 NBA Rookie Class," BleacherReport.com, October 16, 2013, https://bleacherreport.com/articles/1813666-why-giannis-antetokounmpo-could-be-biggest-surprise-of-2013-14-nba-rookie-class.

"Antetokounmpo's physical profile": NBADraft.net, "Prospect Profile: Giannis Antetokounmpo," 2013, http://archive.nba.com/draft/2013/prospects/giannis-antetokounmpo.

"He is a high risk": Giovanni Conte, "What Insiders Say," NBADraft.net, 2013, http://archive.nba.com/draft/2013/prospects/giannis-antetokounmpo.

Cooling system was so antiquated: Amos Barshad, "In Giannis We Trust," *Grantland*, March 6, 2014, https://grantland.com/features/milwaukee-bucks-giannis-antetokounmpo.

Adam Silver said: Rich Kirchen, "Incoming NBA Commissioner Silver Says Bradley Center Unfit for League," *Milwaukee Business Journal*, September 18, 2013, https://www.bizjournals.com/milwaukee/blog/2013/09/milwau kee-needs-a-new-arena-nbas.html.

Refused to get on the plane: Wojnarowski, "The Giannis Draft. Episode 2."

"My whole family has to come": Ibid.

Charles suggested he take Thanasis: Ibid.

Giannis was shaking: Ibid.

The doctor told the staff that his growth plates: Ibid.

Chicken wings and Sprite: Ibid.

This is what NBA money gets you?: Ibid.

Flip-flops, shoes, socks: Ibid.

They really care about me: Ibid.

He has kept the shoes: Ibid.

He bought an I Love New York hat: Adrian Wojnarowski, "The Giannis Draft. Episode 3: And with the 15th Pick," *The Woj Pod*, November 16, 2020.

Show up in shorts and a T-shirt: Ibid.

Amazed at all the things that go into a suit: Ibid.

An extravagant purple: Jake Fischer, "Thanasis Antetokounmpo: A Different Greek Freak," *SLAM*, May 31, 2014, https://www.slamonline.com/nba /thanasis-antetokounmpo-nba-draft/.

Please just let me get drafted: Nike, "Coming to America: I Am Giannis, Episode 3," July 1, 2019, https://www.youtube.com/watch?v=qE13bfZvOO I&list=LLyHc2gH5K1r0ho37zEXpF8w&index=568.

An hour before the draft: Mannix, "Out of Order?"

"He's the most mysterious": Balling and Talking, "Giannis Antetokounmpo 2013 NBA Draft Analysis," July 3, 2020, https://www.youtube.com /watch?v=5X14kIzy2ns.

"What's going to happen now?": Wojnarowski, "The Giannis Draft. Episode 3."

"Don't worry": Ibid.

Choosing between guard Dennis: Ibid.

Didn't want to go: Ibid.

Standing with a European teenager and practicing: Wojnarowski, "The Giannis Draft. Episode 1."

"Look over here": Wojnarowski, "The Giannis Draft. Episode 3."

Smiling when Giannis smiled: Fischer, "Thanasis Antetoounmpo: A Different Greek Freak."

Threw a large plant: Chris Vivlamore, "Anatomy of 2013 Draft: Antetokounmpo Was So Close to Being a Hawk," *Atlanta Journal-Constitution*, June 17, 2018.

"It's a wonderful feeling": Joanna Kakissis, "NBA Rookie Wants to Bring Hope to Greece, and to Milwaukee," *NPR Morning Edition*, September 26, 2013.

"I know I'm not ready": Charles F. Gardner, "Going out on a Limb: Bucks Take Chance on 'Long Arms, Big Hands,' of Greece's Antetokounmpo," *Milwaukee Journal Sentinel*, June 28, 2013.

"People say I play like Kevin Durant": Craig Sager, "Draft Interview with Giannis Antetokounmpo," June 28, 2013, https://www.youtube.com/watch?v=8I906fd_6ww&feature=youtu.be.

"You have your choice": Ibid.

"Right away in the NBA": Ibid.

"Mystery Man Worth Shot": Tom Oates, "International Man of Mystery Worth a Shot by Bucks," *Wisconsin State Journal*, June 28, 2013.

"Playing it safe": Charles F. Gardner, "Bucks Select Giannis Antetokounmpo with Their First Pick in NBA Draft," *Milwaukee Journal Sentinel*, June 27, 2013.

"No team swung for the fences": Adi Joseph, "2013 NBA Draft Grades: Eastern Conference Teams," *USA Today*, June 28, 2013.

"Give the Bucks credit": Chad Ford, "Draft Grades: 30 Team Evaluations," ESPN, June 28, 2013, https://www.espn.com/nba/draft2013/story/_/id/9427270/2013-nba-draft-grades-every-team.

"It will be a little bit difficult": Charles F. Gardner, "Foreign History: Bucks Hope Antetokounmpo Follows Ilyasova's Path," *Milwaukee Journal Sentinel*, July 1, 2013.

5. America

Primary source interviews: Alex Antetokounmpo, Rahman Rana, Michalis Kamperidis, Antonis Samaras, Josh Oppenheimer, Kostas Missas, Petros Melissaratos, Larry Drew, John Hammond, Stefanos Triantafyllos, Ross Geiger, Nikos Papadojannis, John Henson, Caron Butler, Stephen Graham, Nate Wolters, Lori Nickel, Chris Wright, Mike Sergo, Jim Cleamons, Ersan Ilyasova, Sam Reinke, Luke Ridnour, Larry Sanders, Dave Weber, Robert Hackett, Brandon Knight, Zaza Pachulia, Jeff Adrien, Telly Hughes, Cody Ross, Skip Robinson, Kurt Leitinger, Melissa Mangan, Michael Clutterbuck, Theodore Loehrke, Carmelo Anthony, Nick Metallinos, Mike Grahl, Eddie Doucette, Takis Zivas (via translator Lefteris Zarmakoupis), Jane Gallop, Ti Windisch, and Bob Bender.

"Now that I am in the NBA": Chris Mannix, "Out of Order?" *Sports Illustrated*, March 10, 2014.

"If you give a chimpanzee in the zoo": Dave Zirin, "Powerful Beyond Measure," *SLAM,* February 10, 2017.

"Fanatical Jew and Zionist": Annie-Rose Strasser, "Meet the NBA Player Being Targeted by Greece's Nazi Party," Think Progress, November 13, 2013, https://thinkprogress.org/meet-the-nba-player-being-targeted-by -greeces-nazi-party-2eefcefbaa28/.

Giannis said he wasn't angry: Lori Nickel, "Bucks Rookie Giannis Antetokounmpo Learning on the Job," *Milwaukee Journal Sentinel,* March 25, 2014.

"I can't click a button": Mannix, "Out of Order?"

"How many years before you get an MVP?": Sport24.gr, "Αντετοκούνμπο: "Θα είμαι σίγουρα εκεί" ("Antetokounmpo: I Will Definitely Be There"), September 17, 2013, https://www.sport24.gr/basket/antetokoynmpo-tha-ei mai-sigoyra-ekei.8114302.html.

"Haha, too soon": Ibid.

"We are expecting so much": Ibid.

"My goal is to become one of the best": Ibid.

"I don't feel pressure": Jim Owczarski, "NBA Provides an Escape for Bucks Rookie Antetokounmpo," October 22, 2013, https://onmilwaukee.com/ articles/giannisantetokounmpo.

"Anything they say, even if it was in the past": Ibid.

"Who's O. J.?": Nike, "Coming to America: I Am Giannis, Episode 3," July 1, 2019, https://www.youtube.com/watch?v=qE13bfZvOI&list=LLy Hc2gH5K1r0ho37zEXpF8w&idex=568.

Giannis texted Drew and told him he noticed an error: Nickel, "Bucks Rookie Giannis Antetokounmpo Learning."

"Sexual chocolate!": Sean Gregory, "Greek Freak Giannis Antetokounmpo on Growing Up Undocumented, Taking on LeBron and Gunning for MVP," *Time,* October 17, 2017.

Insist on splitting the bill: Lee Jenkins, "Giannis Antetokounmpo: The Most Intriguing Point Guard in NBA History," *Sports Illustrated,* January 3, 2017.

"I just taste for the first time": Giannis Antetokounmpo (@Giannis_An34), Twitter, January 20, 2014, https://twitter.co/Giannis_An34/status/425376 868334727168.

David Morway's wife's homemade peanut butter: Adrian Wojnarowski, "From Street Vendor to Surging NBA Player, Greek Freak Living the American Dream," Yahoo Sports, March 18, 2014, https://sports.yahoo.com/news /from-selling-sunglasses-on-street-to-nba-player-on-the-rise--greek-freak -living-the-american-dream-214309752.html.

"Get whatever you want": Vice Sports, "The Greek Freak Is Back for Round Two: The Cusp," October 23, 2014, https://www.youtube.com/watch?v =QGIrZJ0VnHY.

"What are you doing?": Ibid.

"It's a buffet": Ibid.

Carrying a couple of frozen pizzas at Target: Wojnarowski, "From Street Vendor."

"Let me see—I think I am very handsome!": *Fox 6 Now Milwaukee*, "Giannis Antetokounmpo Meets Other Greeks on Basketball Court," January 21, 2014, https://www.fox6now.com/sports/giannis-antetokounmpo-meets -other-greeks-on-basketball-court.

"His naiveté and willingness to be forthcoming": Scoop Jackson, "Freakishly Happy," ESPN, February 5, 2014.

"Five-syllable surname": Mannix, "Out of Order?"

"You still struggle to consistently pronounce": Matt Velazquez, "NBA Ambition Runs in Family: Bucks Thanasis Antetokounmpo at Combine with Eye on Draft," *Milwaukee Journal Sentinel*, May 17, 2014.

"Man, this is going to be rough": Dan Devine, "Bucks Rookie Giannis Anteto-kounmpo's Name Is Hard to Say, and We Have Proof (Video)," Yahoo, August 9, 2013, https://sports.yahoo.com/bucks-rookie-giannis-antetok ounmpo-name-hard-proof-video-200828432.html?.tsrc=amxaros&a20=1.

"Gee-ah-nay-us Ant-te-toe-kenopio": Milwaukee Bucks, "Say My Name," August 9, 2013, https://www.youtube.com/watch?v=Qcg3joGpNvQ.

"Oh, that is . . . hydroplaning!": Wojnarowski, "From Street Vendor."

"Bald tires are bad!": Ibid.

"I want to take the test right now!": Ibid.

6. Lonely

Primary source interviews: Alex Antetokounmpo, Ross Geiger, John Ham-mond, Giannis Tzikas (via translator Maria Drimpa), Bob Bender, Steve Kroft, Skip Robinson, Mike Sergo, Brandon Knight, Caron Butler, Luke Ridnour, Larry Sanders, Scott Williams, D. J. Stephens, Jim Cleamons, Zaza Pachulia, Larry Drew, Robert Hackett, Cody Ross, Josh Oppenheimer, Sal Sendik, Jay Namoc, and Charles F. Gardner.

"Take me back": Steve Kroft, transcript of his *60 Minutes* interview with Giannis, 2017.

Given that Greek law prohibits: NBA on TNT, "Finding Giannis," February 16, 2019, https://www.youtube.com/watch?v=HrCU305tzmM.

"Being scared to walk": Kroft, *60 Minutes* transcript.

Survived a near-fatal motorcycle accident: Vahe Gregorian, "NBA Executive's Career Takes Improbable Turns," *St. Louis Post Dispatch*, June 29, 2010.

Scott Burgess, who died of a brain injury: Ibid.

Cover the length of the floor in six strides: Lee Jenkins, "The Larry Sanders Show," *Sports Illustrated*, April 15, 2013.

Dropped below zero twenty-four times: Jesse Garza, "Return of Polar Vortex Expected to Drop Temperatures Below Zero," *Milwaukee Journal Sentinel*, February 24, 2014.

"Life threatening": Brendan O'Brien and Kim Palmer, "'Life-Threatening' Cold Bites U.S. Midwest," Reuters, January 4, 2014.

Bringing cupcakes for the team: Charles F. Gardner, "Friday Game Report: Bucks at Wizards," *Milwaukee Journal Sentinel*, December 6, 2013.

He felt like he was making at least *twenty mistakes:* Lori Nickel, "Bucks Rookie Giannis Antetokounmpo Learning on the Job," *Milwaukee Journal Sentinel*, March 25, 2014.

Welp *shrug:* Amos Barshad, "In Giannis We Trust," *Grantland*, March 6, 2014, https://grantland.com/features/milwaukee-bucks-giannis-antetokounmpo.

"Get whatever you want to eat": Adrian Wojnarowski, "From Street Vendor to Surging NBA Player, Greek Freak Living the American Dream," Yahoo Sports, March 18, 2014, https://sports.yahoo.com/news/from-selling -sunglasses-on-street-to-nba-player-on-the-rise--greek-freak-living-the -american-dream-214309752.html.

"Whatever you want": Ibid.

Thanasis ordered a salad: Ibid.

What if we all went to sleep: Mirin Fader, "The Rise of the Next Anteto-kounmpo," Bleacher Report, July 18, 2019, https://bleacherreport.com /articles /2845193-the-rise-of-the-next-antetokounmpo.

Giannis was terrified: Vice Sports, "The Greek Freak Is Back."

I'm guarding Kevin Durant: Ibid.

"He's just sneaky athletic": Charles F. Gardner, "Antetokounmpo Is Foreign, for Now: Bright Future Awaits the Bucks' Greek-Born Rookie," *Milwaukee Journal Sentinel*, January 13, 2014.

7. Hope

Primary source interviews: Mike Sergo; Rick Stoffel; Jerry Brittain; Ralph Gross; Ross Geiger; John Hammond; Scott Williams; Luke Ridnour; Nate Wolters; Jon McGlocklin; Eddie Doucette; Doug Russell; a former Bucks employee; Theodore Loehrke; Dan Bilsky; Melissa Mangan; a Bucks longtime staffer; Caron Butler; Myron Medcalf; Kurt Leitinger; Paul Henning; Charles F. Gardner; Tom Oates; Mickey Davis; Andy Gorzalski; Sharonda Robinson; Kelvin Robinson; Andy Carpenter; Matthew Smith; Jim Kogutkiewicz; George Karl; Coby Karl; Raj Shukla; Dan Shafer; Carmelo Anthony; Josh Oppenheimer; Larry Drew; Bob Bender; Frank Madden; Jenny Fischer; and Terry Driscoll.

Lone publicity department: Bill Glauber, "Steinmiller Has Seen It All in 50 Seasons with Bucks," *Milwaukee Journal Sentinel*, October 7, 2019.

Only ten full-timer staffers: Ibid.

Every ticket had to be dealt with: Ibid.

Suits off the rack and his reading glasses: John Steinbreder, "The Owners," *Sports Illustrated*, September 13, 1993.

A modest, early 2000s Buick sedan: Doug Russell, "Endangered Species," *Milwaukee Magazine*, September 30, 2013.

He sometimes bagged groceries: Ibid.

"Oh man. Milwaukee. Damn": Alex Boeder, "Day and the Night," NBA.com, July 1, 2014, https://www.nba.com/bucks/features/boeder-day-and-tonight.

"We have to find a way": Eric Nehm, *100 Things Bucks Fans Should Know and Do Before They Die* (Chicago: Triumph Books, 2018), 38.

Long lines of snake dancers: Peter Carry, "Milwaukee Is Falling in Love Quietly This Time," *Sports Illustrated*, April 27, 1970.

"Carpetbaggers": Tracy Dodds, "Arena Roulette: Milwaukee Style," *Los Angeles Times*, April 15, 1985.

"Black eye": Marvin L. Fishman with Tracy Dodds, *Bucking the Odds: The Birth of the Milwaukee Bucks* (Milwaukee: Raintree, 1978), 56.

"A terrible, terrible trauma": Dodds, "Arena Roulette."

"He is as close to a meld of Wilt Chamberlain": Tex Maule, "A Coming-Out Party for Lew and Connie," *Sports Illustrated*, October 6, 1969.

"Milwaukee had spent a year sucking": Fishman with Dodds, *Bucking*, 17.

Four-dollar one-way Greyhound: Ibid., 26.

"I was delighted!": Ibid., 44.

"Do you really think you can cut it": Ibid., 55.

A 1964 Kennedy half-dollar: Rick Schabowski, *From Coin Toss to Championship: 1971—the Year of the Milwaukee Bucks* (Milwaukee: HenschelHAUS, 2019), 7.

"A monumental, once-in-a-lifetime": Nehm, *100 Things*, 9.

Seventh Street and Wisconsin Avenue: Schabowski, *From Coin Toss*, 5.

Erickson, who couldn't sit still: Fishman with Dodds, *Bucking*, 108.

Pavalon, who was chain-smoking cigarettes: Ibid.

Winston Churchill silver dollar: Ibid.

They were all praying: Ibid.

Pavalon jumped up and accidentally jammed his cigarette: Tex Maule, "Lew Turns Small Change to Big Bucks," *Sports Illustrated*, March 9, 1970.

"I didn't care, once we had Lew": Ibid.

Five to seven dollars: Maule, "Lew Turns Small Change."

"Goodbye, Lewie": Nehm, *100 Things,* 1.

"We'll be back": Ibid.

Drinking a Coke and chewing gum: Peter Carry, "Hey, Look, Ma! Only One Hand," *Sports Illustrated,* May 10, 1971.

"People expect us to win": Ibid.

"I don't know about dynasties": Schabowski, *From Coin Toss,* 311.

Legally changed his name to Abdul-Jabbar in fall 1971: Kareem Abdul-Jabbar, *Giant Steps: The Autobiography of Kareem Abdul-Jabbar* (New York: Bantam Books, 1985), 235.

"This is the first champagne": Ibid., 309.

Ten thousand fans: Ibid., 311.

Beef wellington, red wine: Thomas Bonk, "June 16, 1975: A Banner Day for Lakers; Kareem Takes His Post; 4 Players Got in Trade Gone, but He's Still on Job," *Los Angeles Times,* December 25, 1987.

"I'm not criticizing": Steve Cady, "Abdul-Jabbar Traded by Bucks for Four Lakers," *New York Times,* June 17, 1975.

A window in his home that faced north: Don Greenberg, "Kareem Recalls His Biker Days; Bucks Give Their Former Center a New Motorcycle as a Farewell Gift," *Orange County Register,* December 12, 1988.

"Live in Milwaukee?": Rick Gano, "Abdul-Jabbar Says Goodbye to His First NBA Home," Associated Press, December 9, 1988.

"Where I work": Bonk, "June 16, 1975: A Banner."

"Everybody in Milwaukee was mad": Ibid.

Disco music: Anthony Cotton, "There's No Stopping the Bucks," *Sports Illustrated,* February 22, 1982.

"This is the first time I've ever lost": Bob Wolfley, "SportsDay with Bob Wolfley: In '83 Playoffs, Bucks' Fitzgerald Encountered Smoking Hot Red," *Milwaukee Journal Sentinel,* June 6, 2012.

$27,500: Sarah Kessler, "How Milwaukee's Forgotten Iconic Basketball Court Reemerged as Art," *Fast Company,* August 23, 2013.

"Something akin to the ceiling": Ibid.

Nelson said at first he thought he had to wear sunglasses: Ibid.

"We just knew if we jumped": Jack Maloney, "Bucks Legend Marques Johnson Discusses Milwaukee's 'Return to the MECCA' Game," CBS Sports, October 25, 2017, https://www.cbssports.com/nba/news/bucks-legend-marques-johnson-discusses-milwaukees-return-to-the-mecca-game/.

"This team couldn't be kept": JR Radcliffe, "Pettit Saved Bucks with Donation for New Arena; Bradley Center Was Needed to Keep Team," *Milwaukee Journal Sentinel*, April 23, 2020.

Fitzgerald was adamant: Associated Press, "Bucks for Sale as TV Venture Fails," printed in *New York Times*, February 6, 1985.

"We feel this is where they belong": Ibid.

"It's not the end of the earth": Bob Logan, "Milwaukee's Biggest Heroes? Lloyd and Jane Pettit," *Chicago Tribune*, October 27, 1985.

"Miracle": Dodds, "Arena Roulette."

"Hysteria": Ibid.

"We couldn't afford to lose them": Nehm, *100 Things*, 13.

"It doesn't cure the city's financial": Dodds, "Arena Roulette."

"Lots of expectations and no results": Jackie MacMullan, "Who's Responsible for Milwaukee's Disappointing Season? Mourning, Kukoc and Now Mason: The Latest in Foot Injuries," *Sports Illustrated*, March 31, 1997.

Dived on the floor too many times: Frank Deford, "Love & Basketball; Basketball for Milwaukee Bucks Coach George Karl, Romance—and an NBA Career—Are Clearly Better the Second Time Around," *Sports Illustrated*, November 12, 2001.

One hundred stitches: Ibid.

"You went to see George Karl play": Ibid.

"The reason was Carmelo": Matt Velazquez, "Bucks Blog: Giannis Antetokounmpo Impressive in First Start, Battle with Carmelo Anthony," *Milwaukee Journal Sentinel*, December 19, 2013.

"Of course he is going to get in my head": Ibid.

A warning: Charles F. Gardner, "Drew Says Freak Start Is the New Normal for Antetokounmpo: Bucks Rookie Impressed Staff, Teammates vs. Knicks," *Milwaukee Journal Sentinel*, December 20, 2013.

"I don't care who you are": Velazquez, "Bucks Blog: Giannis Antetokounmpo Impressive in First Start."

"Just wait out the clock": Barshad, "In Giannis We Trust."

8. Reunited

Primary source interviews: Alex Antetokounmpo; Kostas Antetokounmpo; Nate Wolters; a person familiar with the family's immigration situation; John Hammond; a former Bucks employee; Ross Geiger; Zaza Pachulia; Skip Robinson; Nate McMillan; Josh Oppenheimer; Antonio Gil; Luke Ridnour; Larry Drew; European agent with clients in Greece; Chris Wright; Nick Calathes;

Nikos Zisis; Fotios Katsikaris; Asterios Kalivas; and Giannis Tzikas (via translator Maria Drimpa).

P-1 Visa: Charles F. Gardner, "Giannis Antetokounmpo's Family Reunites in Milwaukee," *Milwaukee Journal Sentinel*, February 4, 2014.

Support personnel to Charles: Ibid.

"My parents were here": Matt Velazquez, "Knight's Heroics Provide Dagger: Bucks 101, Knicks 98. Late Three-Pointer Secures Victory," *Milwaukee Journal Sentinel*, February 4, 2014.

"You're either going to work extra": Mirin Fader, "The Rise of the Next Antetokounmpo," Bleacher Report, July 18, 2019, https://bleacherreport.com /articles /2845193-the-rise-of-the-next-antetokounmpo.

McDonald's: Ibid.

"It's tough for them to have friends": Sean Gregory, "Greek Freak Giannis Antetokounmpo on Growing Up Undocumented, Taking on LeBron and Gunning for MVP," *Time*, October 17, 2017.

Ask Giannis to give her the names and numbers: Ibid.

"It was crazy": Fader, "The Rise of the Next Antetokounmpo."

"You've been smiling": Jim Paschke, "Giannis Reacts to Being Named to Rising Stars," Bucks.comTV, January 29, 2014, https://www.nba.com/bucks /video/2014/01/29/giannisrisingstarwebmov-3128277.

"It's very fun": Ibid.

"I'm ready to go": Ibid.

"I got my license": Amos Barshad, "In Giannis We Trust," *Grantland*, March 6, 2014, https://grantland.com/features/milwaukee-bucks-giannis-anteto kounmpo.

"277 games to injuries": "Bucks History. Season Recaps. 2013–14 Season," Bucks.com, accessed April 15, 2021, https://www.nba.com/bucks/history /season-recaps.

"I wasn't going to live forever": Richard Sandomir, "Former Senator Is Selling the Bucks After Three Decades," *New York Times*, April 16, 2014.

"Somebody could have offered me": Eric Nehm, *100 Things Bucks Fans Should Know and Do Before They Die* (Chicago: Triumph Books, 2018), 80.

"Milwaukee fans deserve": Genaro C. Armas, "Bucks Owner Herb Kohl Reaches Deal to Sell Team," Associated Press, April 17, 2014.

"New York hedge-fund billionaires": Nehm, *100 Things*, 37.

Drew had sensed he was stressed: Charles F. Gardner, "Antetokounmpo Set to Team with Parker for First Time," *Milwaukee Journal Sentinel*, July 4, 2014.

"I know he's capable": Charles F. Gardner, "Bucks Could Find Room on the Roster for Another Antetokounmpo," *Milwaukee Journal Sentinel*, June 3, 2014.

"I think I'm happier today": Charles F. Gardner, "Older Brother Gets Shot," *Milwaukee Journal Sentinel*, June 27, 2014.

"D-minus": Charles F. Gardner and Matt Velazquez, "Bucks' Antetokounmpo Hopes to Build on Early Success," *Milwaukee Journal Sentinel*, April 17, 2014.

"I am happy with myself": Ibid.

"I love Milwaukee": Ibid.

"It makes my heart feel great": *Fox 6 Now Milwaukee*, "Celebrating Their Greek Heritage: Giannis Antetokounmpo & Family Take In a Greek Festival," June 17, 2014, https://www.fox6now.com/sports/celebrating -their-greek-heritage-giannis-antetokounmpo-family-take-in-a -greek-festival.

9. Mean

Primary source interviews: Jabari Parker; Sean Sweeney; Greg Foster; Joe Prunty; Brandon Knight; Skip Robinson; Caron Butler; Josh Oppenheimer; Kerry Kittles; Robert Hackett; a former player of Jason Kidd; a former teammate of Jason Kidd; a former Bucks staffer; Chris Copeland; another ex-player of Jason Kidd; Johnny O'Bryant III; Nicholas Turner; Jason Terry; Nixon Dorvilien; Thon Maker; two more ex-players; Charles F. Gardner; Matthew Dellavedova; Zaza Pachulia; Shawn Zell; Josh Broghamer; Zach Randolph; Jared Dudley; John Hammond; Michael Carter-Williams; Kostas Antetokounmpo; Alex Antetokounmpo; Mike Sergo; Greg Signorelli; Jay Namoc; Michael Clutterbuck; another ex-staffer; Larry Sanders; Bill Simmons; Alvin Gentry; Tyler Ennis; Doug McDermott; Aaron Brooks; and Jim Kogutkiewicz.

"A human wormhole": Jason Concepcion, "NBA Shootaround: Our Favorite Players So Far," *Grantland*, December 18, 2014, https://grantland.com/the -triangle/nba-shootaround-our-favorite-players-so-far/.

"The Giannis Antetokounmpo experiment": Charles F. Gardner, "Antetokounmpo Gets Run of Offense: He Will Start at Point Against Cavs," *Milwaukee Journal Sentinel*, October 14, 2014.

Olajuwon told Giannis: Charles F. Gardner, "Golden Chance to Shine on World Stage: Young Players Focused on Winning at O2; Bucks Build

International Audience with Trip," *Milwaukee Journal Sentinel*, January 15, 2015.

"It doesn't look like me": Charles F. Gardner, "Antetokounmpo Impresses McHale: Bucks vs. Rockets. Late Improvement Shows Potential, Coach Says," *Milwaukee Journal Sentinel*, November 30, 2014.

Ever since his rookie year, when he saw the Bucks hand out Larry Sanders: Ibid.

When is it going to be my turn?: Ibid.

"I didn't think I was going to have one": Ibid.

"Try not to be stressed": Giannis Antetokounmpo, "Giannis Antetokounmpo: A Day in My Life," January 29, 2015, https://www.youtube.com/watch?v =iwiFDgTx_Tc.

"Bravo, Alex! Bravo!": Ibid.

He didn't wear headphones and didn't listen to music: Lori Nickel, "Surrounded by Those Who Want to Deny Him, Giannis Adapts to Uncomfortable Life in a Bubble," *Milwaukee Journal Sentinel*, July 15, 2020.

Two hours and forty-five minutes: Aggeliki Katsini, "Giannis Antetokounmpo Is Hungry for His First Ring," Contra.gr, October 24, 2019, https:// www.contra.gr/synentefxeis/giannis-antetokounmpo-is-hungry-for-his-first -ring.7520012.html.

"I can be like Kareem": Vice Sports, "The Greek Freak Is Back for Round Two: The Cusp," October 23, 2014, https://www.youtube.com/watch?v= QGIrZ J0VnHY.

"Seeing the Greek Freak in person": Bill Simmons, "2015 NBA Trade Value, Part 2: The Temple of Doom," *Grantland*, February 25, 2015, https://grant land.com/features/2015-nba-trade-value-part-2-the-temple-of-doom/.

"On any given possession the Greek Freak": Zach Lowe, "The 2015 Marc Gasol All-Stars: Your Guide to the Most Watchable Players in the NBA," *Grantland*, March 17, 2015, https://grantland.com/the-triangle /the-2015-marc-gasol-all-stars-your-guide-to-the-most-watchable -players-in-the-nba/.

"He's learning on the job": Ibid.

Giannis told reporters he had played "angry": Charles F. Gardner, "Hoping for Plenty of Face Time: Antetokounmpo Snarling at Foes," *Milwaukee Journal Sentinel*, April 13, 2015.

"His ugly face": Ibid.

"I try to be angry when I play": Tony Manfred, "Jason Kidd Benched the 'Greek Freak' 5 Games Before the Playoffs with No Explanation, and It Seems Like It Worked," *Business Insider*, April 14, 2015.

10. Star

Primary source interviews: Giannis Antetokounmpo, Thanasis Antetokounmpo, Alex Antetokounmpo, Kostas Antetokounmpo, Chris Copeland, Bo Ryan, Shawn Zell, Malcolm Brogdon, Josh Oppenheimer, Tyler Ennis, Coby Karl, Yannis Psarakis, Jabari Parker, Greivis Vásquez, Sean Sweeney, Nixon Dorvilien, Jared Dudley, Michael Carter-Williams, Thon Maker, Eddie Doucette, Doug Russell, Telly Hughes, Jim Gosz, Jason Terry, Carmelo Anthony, Sterling Brown, Jim Kogutkiewicz, DeVon Jackson, Draggan Mihailovich, and Laura Dodd.

"I can do this every night": *NBA on TNT*, "Finding Giannis," February 16, 2019, https://www.youtube.com/watch?v=HrCU305tzmM.

"I was kind of forced": Steve Kroft, transcript of his *60 Minutes* interview with Giannis, 2017.

The first playoff game Giannis had ever watched: Charles F. Gardner, "Garnett's Voice Still Carries; Players Enjoy His Visit to Practice," *Milwaukee Journal Sentinel*, December 7, 2016.

Oh shit: Jake Fischer, "To the Point: Giannis Antetokounmpo Blossoming with the Ball," *Sports Illustrated*, March 8, 2016.

Kobe told him to work on: Charles F. Gardner, "Greek Feast a Triple Portion: Antetokounmpo Stars in Bryant's Last Game Here," *Milwaukee Journal Sentinel*, February 23, 2016.

Giannis vowed to shoot: Ibid.

"Be serious": Ibid.

The importance of recovery: Ibid.

Kobe felt he had the physical tools: Fischer, "To the Point."

Postponing the signing by four hours: Lee Jenkins, "Giannis Antetokounmpo: The Most Intriguing Point Guard in NBA History," *Sports Illustrated*, January 3, 2017.

He accepted a slightly lower: Matt Bonesteel, "Giannis Antetokounmpo Gives Bucks Flexibility by Re-signing for Less Than the Max," *Washington Post*, September 19, 2016.

"I just wanted to say thank you": Jenkins, "Giannis Antetokounmpo: The Most Intriguing."

Capital Grille: Ibid.

Steak: Ibid.

"I don't know who's paying": Ibid.

Just because your bank account changes: Mirin Fader, "The Rise of the Next Antetokounmpo," Bleacher Report, July 18, 2019, https://bleacherreport.com/articles/2845193-the-rise-of-the-next-antetokounmpo.

First time he ever flew first-class: Adrian Wojnarowski, "Giannis Anteto-kounmpo on Money, Motivation, the MVP and More," ESPN, March 28, 2019, https://www.youtube.com/watch?v=4EmY0uxetWQ.

"We can't be sitting": Ibid.

Giannis wouldn't pay if an airline charged: Ibid.

Giannis had transformed from a lanky: Fader, "The Rise of the Next Antetokounmpo."

"It was like he went from 'Oh, you might'": Ibid.

He has still never purchased: Aaron Dodson, "The Story Behind Giannis Antetokounmpo's First Nike Signature Sneaker," Undefeated, July 12, 2019, https://theundefeated.com/features/the-story-behind-giannis-antetok ounmpos-first-nike-signature-sneaker/.

"I don't like all these flashy cities": Marc Stein, "The Unspeakable Greatness of Giannis Antetokounmpo," *New York Times*, November 3, 2017.

"Knock knock": Genaro C. Armas, "Antetokounmpo Poised to Handle Ball, Bigger Load, for Bucks," Associated Press, October 20, 2016.

"Obama": Ibid.

"Ohhhhhhh-baaaaaa-myyyyseeeelf": Ibid.

"Have you guys seen the new movie": Milwaukee Journal Sentinel, "Bucks Giannis Tells a Bad Joke," September 26, 2017, https://www.youtube.com /watch?v=iVtSHwA6RvY.

"Constipation. That's because": Ibid.

Dinka tribe: Howard Beck, "Thon Maker Is the Bucks' Secret Unicorn," Bleacher Report, February 8, 2017, https://mag.bleacherreport.com/thon -maker-bucks-unicorn/.

He was the first one in: Fader, "The Rise of theNext Antetokounmpo."

He was more upset than anyone: Ibid.

"Remember this feeling": Ibid.

Brogdon compared him to Kobe: Charles F. Gardner, "Thunderous Stat Stuffing," *Milwaukee Journal Sentinel*, January 2, 2017.

"Really, me?": Ibid.

"I'm not going to lie": Ibid.

1,059 new messages: Nikos Papadojannis, "Γιάννης Αντετοκούνμπο: «Για τους δικούς μου ανθρώπους είμαι ακόμη ο Γιαννάκης»—Αποκλειστική συνέντευξη στο Documento" ("Giannis Antetokounmpo: 'For My Own People, I Am Still Giannakis'"), *Documento*, February 19, 2017, https:// www.documentonews.gr/article/giannhs-antetokoynmpo-gia-toys-dikoys -moy-anthrwpoys-eimai-akomh-o-giannakhs-apokleistikh-synenteyxh-sto -documento.

Stayed off his phone: Ibid.

He didn't believe he'd be named: Charles F. Gardner, "Very Pleasant Surprise," *Milwaukee Journal Sentinel*, January 21, 2017.

When he saw James: Ibid.

Veronica and Mariah showed up: Ibid.

Called to congratulate him: Ibid.

Asked him if he: Charles F. Gardner, "Ascent No Accident; Antetokounmpo Has Worked Tirelessly to Get to This Moment," *Milwaukee Journal Sentinel*, February 19, 2017.

"If I get the first layup": Ibid.

"You're too big to be nervous": Ibid.

"Let me take a picture first": Charles F. Gardner, "Durant Gives Giannis All-Star Praise; He Expects Him Back Each Year," *Milwaukee Journal Sentinel*, February 18, 2017.

"I expect him": Ibid.

Durant admitted he couldn't have predicted: Ibid.

The first thing Giannis does: Elina Dimitriadi, "Η Βερόνικα Αντετοκούνμπο μιλάει αποκλειστικά στη *Vogue Greece*" ("Veronica Adetokunbo Speaks Exclusively to *Vogue Greece*"), *Vogue Greece*, September 27, 2020, https:// vogue.gr/living/i-veronika-antetokoynmpo-milaei-apokleistika -sti-vogue-greece/.

"I'm proud of you": Ibid.

"He has the agility": Scott Cacciola, "Al Horford Brings Giannis Anteto-kounmpo Down to Earth in Celtics' Win," *New York Times*, April 28, 2019.

He's always nervous: Charles F. Gardner, "Too Much Excitement; Giannis with Late Technical," *Milwaukee Journal Sentinel*, April 16, 2017.

"See now, this is how it feels": Matt Velazquez, "Woes from Free Throw Line Costly; Giannis Tires Late in the Game," *Milwaukee Journal Sentinel*, April 28, 2017.

"Still waiting for my challenge": Giannis Antetokounmpo(@Giannis_An34), Twitter, August 24, 2017, https://twitter.com/Giannis_An34/status/9007 67397556232192.

Still saw himself as Giannakis: Papadojannis, "Γιάννης Αντετοκούνμπο: «Για τους δικούς μου ανθρώπους είμαι ακόμη ο Γιαννάκης" ("Giannis Anteto-kounmpo: 'For My Own People, I Am Still Giannakis'").

"He looked like a baby deer": Fader, "The Rise of the Next Antetokounmpo."

Top left, behind the team's bench: Ibid.

"I [didn't] want Alex to get nervous": Ibid.

"Alex would [play] five times better": Ibid.